DATE DUE

53589

REF
920
FRI

Friedman, Ian C.

Latino athletes

CONNELL MIDDLE SCHOOL LIBRARY
400 HOT WELLS BLVD. 78223

774446 04500   23758D   0004

LATINO ATHLETES

Ian C. Friedman

Facts On File

An imprint of Infobase Publishing

For my brothers
Al, Jeff, and Keith Friedman
whose excitement upon hearing Al Kaline get his 3,000th hit
sparked a lifetime love of sports in me

Latino Athletes

Copyright © 2007 by Ian C. Friedman

Facts On File, Inc.
An imprint of Infobase Publishing
132 West 31st Street
New York NY 10001

Library of Congress Cataloging-in-Publication Data
Friedman, Ian C.
   Latino athletes / Ian C. Friedman.
      p. cm.—(A to Z of Latino Americans)
   Includes bibliographical references and index.
   ISBN-13: 978-0-8160-6384-0 (alk. paper)
   1. Hispanic American athletes—Biography—Dictionaries. I. Title. II. Series.
   GV697.A1F696 2007
   796.092'368073—dc22
   [B]   2006016901

Facts On File books are available at special discounts when purchased in bulk quantities for businesses, associations, institutions, or sales promotions. Please call our Special Sales Department in New York at (212) 967-8800 or (800) 322-8755.

You can find Facts On File on the World Wide Web at http://www.factsonfile.com

Text design by Annie O'Donnell
Cover design by Salvatore Luongo

Printed in the United States of America

VB CGI 10 9 8 7 6 5 4 3 2

This book is printed on acid-free paper.

CONTENTS

List of Entries   iv

Acknowledgments   vi

Author's Note   vii

Introduction   viii

A-to-Z Entries   1

Bibliography   253

Entries by Sport   255

Entries by Year of Birth   257

Entries by Ethnicity or Country of Origin   259

Index   261

LIST OF ENTRIES

Alomar, Roberto
Alou, Felipe
Aparicio, Luis
Archuleta, Adam
Arenas, Gilbert
Argüello, Alexis
Arroyo, Carlos
Ballesteros, Seve
Barbosa, Leandro
Benitez, Wilfred
Blackman, Rolando
Bonilla, Bobby
Brown, Panama Al
Bruschi, Tedy
Bueno, Maria
Cabrera, Miguel
Camacho, Héctor
Campos, Jorge
Canseco, Jose
Canto, Miguel
Capilla, Joaquín
Carew, Rod
Carlos, John
Casals, Rosie
Casillas, Tony
Castilla, Vinny
Castroneves, Hélio
Cepeda, Orlando
Cervantes, Antonio
Chacon, Bobby
Chávez, Julio César
Chilavert, José Luis

Clemente, Roberto
Concepción, Davey
Cordero, Angel, Jr.
Cuevas, Pipino
De La Hoya, Oscar
Dihigo, Martín
Dimas, Trent
Di Stefano, Alfredo
Domínguez, Maribel
Durán, Roberto
Escobar, Sixto
Fears, Tom
Fernández, Gigi
Fernandez, Lisa
Fernández, Mary Joe
Fernández, Tony
Fittipaldi, Christian
Fittipaldi, Emerson
Flores, Tom
Franco, Julio
Furtado, Juli
Galarraga, Andrés
Galíndez, Víctor
Galindo, Rudy
García, Francisco
Garcia, Jeff
Garciaparra, Nomar
Garrincha
Gasol, Pau
Ginobili, Manu
Gomez, Lefty
Gomez, Scott

Gómez, Wilfredo
Gonzales, Pancho
González, Juan
González, Kid Gavilan
Gonzalez, Tony
Gramática, Martín
Guerin, Bill
Guerrero, Vladimir
Guevara, Ana
Guillén, Ozzie
Hernandez, Keith
Hernández, Willie
Kuerten, Gustavo
Laguna, Ismael
Leônidas
Lima, Vanderlei de
Lobo, Rebecca
Lopez, Al
Lopez, Nancy
Lopez, Steven
Luque, Dolf
Maradona, Diego
Marichal, Juan
Marta
Martínez, Dennis
Martinez, Edgar
Martínez, Pedro
Méndez, José
Mendoza, Saúl
Miñoso, Minnie
Miranda, Patricia
Montoya, Alvaro

iv

Montoya, Juan Pablo
Monzón, Carlos
Morales, Pablo
Mulanovich, Sofía
Muñoz, Anthony
Nadal, Rafael
Nájera, Eduardo
Nalbandian, David
Nápoles, José
Negron, Esmeralda
Nenê
Nocioni, Andrés
Ochoa, Lorena
Oliva, Tony
Olivares, Rubén
Olmedo, Alex
Ortiz, Carlos
Osuna, Rafael
Palmeiro, Rafael
Palomino, Carlos
Parra, Derek
Pascual, Camilo
Pedroza, Eusebio
Pelé
Pérez, Tony
Perez, Yuliana
Pérez del Solar, Gaby

Pincay, Laffit, Jr.
Pineda-Boutte, Leticia
Piquet, Nelson
Plunkett, Jim
Poll, Claudia
Pujols, Albert
Ramírez, Manny
Ramos, Sugar
Rentería, Edgar
Reyna, Claudio
Ríos, Marcelo
Rivelino, Roberto
Rivera, Marco
Rivera, Mariano
Rivera, Ron
Rodriguez, Alex
Rodríguez, Chi Chi
Rodríguez, Iván
Rodriguez, Jennifer
Ronaldinho
Ronaldo
Rosales-St. John, Mia
Ruiz, John
Sabatini, Gabriela
Salas, Marcelo
Salazar, Alberto
Saldívar, Vicente

Sanchez, Felix
Sánchez, Salvador
Santana, Johan
Sardinas, Kid Chocolate
Schmidt, Oscar
Segura, Pancho
Senna, Ayrton
Sócrates
Sosa, Sammy
Stevenson, Teófilo
Taurasi, Diana
Tejada, Miguel
Tiant, Luis
Torres, Dara
Torres, José
Torres, Regla
Trevino, Lee
Trinidad, Félix, Jr.
Valenzuela, Fernando
Vilas, Guillermo
Villa, Brenda
Villanueva, Charlie
Vizquel, Omar
Williams, Bernie
Zárate, Carlos
Zico

ACKNOWLEDGMENTS

Thank you to my editor at Facts On File, Nicole Bowen, for offering me this fascinating and enjoyable project and for providing guidance and support throughout the course of my work on it. Thanks also to editorial assistants Laura Shauger and Liza Trinkle of Facts On File for their invaluable assistance.

I also greatly appreciate the help of many others whose research, consultation, and time helped me write this book: Marcia Friedman, Leon Friedman, Keith Friedman, Arturo Vargas, Nancy Vargas, Neil Johnson, Rebecca Tull, Jeff Bell, Leticia Pineda-Boutte, Manny Fernandez, Josh Sekine, Michael Pehanich, Cindy Slater, Liz Parsons, Michael Gorman, Don Bowden, Marcia Schiff, Pat Kelly, Barbara Moore, and Frank O'Brien.

My deepest gratitude is given to my family—my wife Darlene, sons Evan and Mason, and daughter Lily—for their kindness, love, and unending inspiration.

AUTHOR'S NOTE

There are 176 athletes profiled in this book. Collectively, they trace their Latino heritage to 17 different nations; they represent 26 separate sports; and they were born in 11 distinct decades. Many of their surnames are Spanish, though some have last names of English, Italian, German, or other origin.

The rich diversity of these athletes reflects that of Latino Americans in other fields of endeavor, but these men and women are featured on the following pages because they have excelled on the fields, tracks, streets, rings, rinks, courts, pools, waters, courses and mats of competition. They are not only the best Latino Americans in the history of their sports. They are also among the greatest of any national or ethnic background who have ever participated in athletics.

INTRODUCTION

The lives of Latino-American athletes provide more than simply compelling accounts of accomplishment. They also tell stories steeped in themes of national/ethnic identity definition, athletic evolution, and transcendent greatness that reflect and guide the history and culture of Latin America.

It is certainly not unique to Latin Americans to be intensely proud of those from their nations who excel in any field. But the admiration in their respective lands of, for example, Brazilian soccer players, Mexican boxers, and Dominican baseball players matches or exceeds the extent to which any nation defines itself and has been defined by sports. Among the nations justifiably proud of its athletes is a uniquely conflicted one—Cuba, which has seen some of its greatest competitors flee the island during the almost five-decades-long dictatorship of Fidel Castro.

Ethnic Latino identity has been significantly shaped by athletes, such as Mexican Americans PANCHO GONZALES in tennis and NANCY LOPEZ and LEE TREVINO in golf, who successfully challenged the rules—both written and unwritten—that had precluded so many from sports that often restricted participation based on class, race, or ethnicity.

The Latino-American contribution to the evolution of sports and its subsequent impact on society is seen in the efforts and examples of many athletes. It is found in the life of ROD CAREW, who was born in a "coloreds only" section of a train traveling in the Panama Canal Zone and later batted common perceptions of Latino baseball players as undisciplined and inarticulate with the same skilled, elegant precision that led him to become regarded as one of the greatest hitting tacticians in the history of baseball. It is seen in the skillful artistry of MANU GINOBILI, whose leading roles on Argentina's Olympics gold medal–winning squad and two National Basketball Association (NBA) championship teams have profoundly redefined the game of basketball as a truly global sport.

Latinos have also been at the forefront of the battle for greater opportunities for women and girls in sports. Among the pioneers in this area are LISA FERNANDEZ, the American of Cuban and Puerto Rican descent who dominated the world of softball in the 1990s, and Mexican sprinter ANA GUEVARA, the 2004 Olympic silver medalist who has inspired male and female fans throughout her country in a way few would have thought possible just a generation earlier.

Greatness in competition is at the foundation of legendary Latino athletes, bridging Cuban Negro League baseball player JOSE MENDEZ to the burgeoning brilliance of Dominican slugger ALBERT PUJOLS and Brazil's first soccer icon, LEONIDAS, to its most current one, RONALDINHO. But transcendent greatness has also been a crucial theme in the history of Latino athletes. Such meaning that extends beyond the fields of competition is best personified by Brazilian soccer player PELÉ and Puerto Rican baseball star ROBERTO CLEMENTE.

Pelé, long the most popular player in the most popular game in the world, once brought about a cease-fire in an African civil war simply because he was traveling there for a game. Clemente, whose all-around excellence on the diamond earned him the admiration of fans and a place in the Baseball Hall of Fame, was especially adored by Latinos for his outspoken dignity and strength during his playing days, which ended when a plane he was traveling in crashed on its way to bring aid to earthquake victims in Nicaragua. Clemente's elite place in baseball history remains secure, as is his status around the world as sport's most respected humanitarian.

Understanding the legacy of these athletes provides invaluable insight into the Latino-American experience over the past 100 years. It also allows for an exhilarating glimpse into the future of Latino Americans in sports, reflected in the words of Ginobili, who said of the NBA in 2005, "If you want the best league in the world, you need the best players in the world." By extension, if you want to know about the best athletes in the history of the world, you need to know about the enormous and increasing contributions of Latino-American athletes.

Alomar, Roberto
(1968–   ) *baseball player*

One of the best all-around second basemen in baseball history, Roberto Alomar won 10 Gold Glove awards and was named to the All-Star teams in 12 consecutive seasons, yet his legacy is tarnished by an ugly confrontation with an umpire. He was born on February 5, 1968, in Ponce, Puerto Rico. The youngest of three children in his family, he was raised by his mother, María, in Puerto Rico and in some of the six cities in which his father, a speedy infielder named Sandy Alomar, Sr., played during his 15-year major league career. Alomar's older brother, Sandy, Jr., also excelled at baseball, signing a contract with the San Diego Padres in 1983. Two years later, the Padres again came to the Alomar home in Ponce, signing Roberto to a professional contract.

Displaying a dynamic combination of speed, keen eyes, and sure hands, the switch-hitting Alomar quickly moved up the Padres farm system. On April 22, 1988, only two months after his 20th birthday, Alomar made his professional debut with the Padres. He remained the Padres' starting second baseman the rest of the year, hitting for a respectable .266 batting average and stealing 24 bases. Over the next two years, Alomar established himself as one of the elite young players in baseball. In 1989, he ranked second in the National League in stolen bases, with 42, while boosting his batting average to .295, and in 1990, he hit .287,

leading to the first of a remarkable 12 consecutive All-Star Game appearances.

Despite Alomar's youth and his early success in the majors, San Diego traded him and outfielder Joe Carter to the Toronto Blue Jays for shortstop TONY FERNÁNDEZ and first baseman Fred McGriff on December 5, 1990. This blockbuster trade helped solidify an already potent Blue Jays team into a championship contender. Alomar batted .295 and won the first of his 10 Gold Glove awards in 1991, helping the Blue Jays win the American League (AL) East Division. In 1992, he began a streak of six consecutive seasons with a batting average over .300, stole 53 bases, was named the Most Valuable Player (MVP) of the AL championship series, and played a critical role in leading Toronto's six-game victory over the Atlanta Braves, giving the Blue Jays their first World Series championship in franchise history.

The next year, the 25-year-old Alomar ranked third in the AL in hitting, with a .326 average, and ranked second in the league in stolen bases, with 55, helping the Blue Jays to another AL pennant. In the World Series against the Philadelphia Phillies, Alomar reached base an astounding 14 times in 27 played appearances, as Toronto repeated as champions. In 1994, despite being hobbled by a preseason leg injury, Alomar set an AL record for consecutive games by a second baseman (104) without an error, eclipsing the previous mark by 15 games, and set an AL record for consecutive errorless chances, with 482. However, in 1995, Alomar again missed many games due to injury, and there were rumblings that he wanted to leave Toronto. On December 21, 1995, Alomar did leave the Blue Jays, signing as a free agent with the Baltimore Orioles for a contract worth $17 million over three years.

During Alomar's three years in Baltimore, he continued to rack up impressive offensive statistics, All-Star appearances, and Gold Glove awards. In 1996, he hit .328, with 22 home runs and 94 runs batted in (RBI). But Alomar's 1996 season is best remembered for a few volatile moments in Toronto on the evening of September 27. After Alomar was called out on strikes in the first inning of a critical late season game by home plate umpire John Hirschbeck, he argued the call and was returning to the dugout when Hirschbeck ejected him from the game, prompting Alomar to quickly turn and angrily confront Hirschbeck. During their argument, Alomar spit in the umpire's face, before finally leaving the field.

Following the game, Alomar added to the controversy by saying of Hirschbeck, whose eight-year-old son had recently died from a rare brain disease, "I used to respect him a lot. He had problems with his family when his son died. I know that's something real tough in life. But after that he just changed personality-wise. He just got real bitter." Alomar was quickly slapped with a five-game suspension by Major League Baseball, for the spitting incident. He appealed the suspension, which allowed him to serve it at the beginning of the following season rather than during the playoffs, where the Orioles went after Alomar's game winning a three-run home run the night after his confrontation with Hirschbeck clinched a postseason appearance for Baltimore.

Though Alomar and Hirschbeck publicly made up, Alomar was frequently booed during his injury-plagued 1997 season. In 1998, Alomar's otherwise disappointing season was highlighted by his All-Star Game MVP award, just a year after his brother Sandy had won the same award. Alomar

left Baltimore after the 1998 season for a five-year $38 million contract with the Cleveland Indians, where he joined his brother Sandy and teamed with shortstop OMAR VIZQUEL to form one of the greatest double-play combinations in baseball history. Alomar played in all but 12 games during three seasons in Cleveland, batted over .300 each year, and averaged more than 20 home runs, 100 RBIs, and 35 stolen bases, leading the Indians to the AL Central Division titles in 1999 and 2001.

After the 2001 season, Alomar was traded with two minor leaguers to the New York Mets for five prospects. He played for three teams over the next three seasons, never coming close to replicating his earlier success. After struggling in the 2005 spring training camp of the Tampa Bay Devil Rays, Alomar retired from baseball on March 19, saying, "My back, legs, and eyes aren't the same. I just can't go anymore."

Further Reading

Hermoso, Rafael. "Finding Alomar Where He Lives." *New York Times,* 11 April 2003, p. S5.

"Hot Pursuit: Baseball Player Robbie Alomar May Hit .400 in 1996." *Sporting News,* 10 June 1996, p. 9.

"Roberto Alomar." Baseball Library Web site. Available online. URL: http://baseballlibrary.com/baseballlibrary/ballplayers/A/Alomar_Roberto.stm. Downloaded on July 1, 2005.

Alou, Felipe
(1935–   ) *baseball player*

The oldest and most powerful of three baseball-playing Alou brothers of the 1960s and 1970s, Felipe Alou later became one of the most respected and successful major league managers. He was born on May 12, 1935, in Haina, Dominican Republic. Alou grew up poor and had aspirations of becoming a doctor. An outstanding track and field athlete as a teen, Alou also excelled at baseball, earning, while in college, a spot on the Dominican team that won a gold medal at the 1955 Pan-American Games in Mexico. He returned to college but soon signed a contract with the New York Giants for $200 to help alleviate his family's poverty.

Alou moved quickly up the Giants' farm system and made his major league debut on June 8, 1958, during the team's first year in San Francisco. A thin and solidly built right-handed hitter, Alou spent his first three seasons as a part-time outfielder. In 1959, he was joined on the Giants by his younger brothers Jesus and Matty to form an "All Alou" outfield, becoming the only set of three brothers to play on the same major league team simultaneously. In 1961, Alou began demonstrating the offensive consistency he would become known for throughout the 1960s, batting .289 with 18 home runs and 52 runs batted in (RBIs).

In 1962, Alou was the Giants' full-time right fielder, and he usually held the critical third spot in the batting order, typically occupied by a team's best all-around hitter. That season, he joined teammate and future Hall of Fame pitcher JUAN MARICHAL on the National League (NL) All-Star team, becoming the first Dominicans to earn that honor. Alou batted .316, hit 25 home runs, drove in 98 RBIs, and scored the winning run in the Giants' one-game playoff victory over their archrival, the Los Angeles Dodgers, for the NL pennant. In the 1962 World Series, Alou tied for the Giants' lead in hits (seven), but San Francisco lost to the New York Yankees in seven games.

Following another productive season in 1963, Alou was traded to the Milwaukee Braves. He played six years for the Braves, the first two in Milwaukee, before the franchise moved to Atlanta. He enjoyed his finest statistical year in 1966, batting .327, belting 33 home runs, and leading the NL with 218 hits and 122 runs. During his tenure with the Braves, Alou exhibited rare versatility, playing in many positions, rarely striking out, and hitting throughout the batting order. Alou also earned a reputation as a "five-tool player" (speed, power, hitting, fielding, and throwing) who was

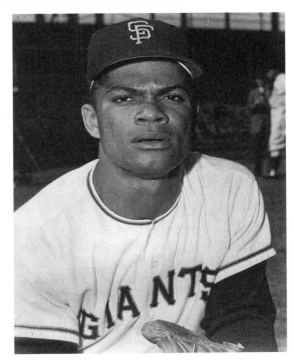

Felipe Alou, seen here early in his playing career, later became the winningest Latino manager in Major League Baseball history. *(National Baseball Hall of Fame Library)*

a serious student of the game and a consummate teammate.

A solemn, respected presence among teammates, fans, and media, Alou often spoke out against the stereotypes of Latino baseball players as undisciplined hotdogs, and he was one of the first prominent born-again Christians in the sport. After an injury-plagued season in 1969, the Braves traded Alou to the Oakland A's. He played for just over a year in Oakland before he was traded to the New York Yankees, where he played until 1973, when he was released and claimed by the Montreal Expos. Alou's final year playing in the major leagues was in 1974, when he batted only three times, striking out twice, for the Milwaukee Brewers.

Although Alou retired from baseball with 2,101 hits, 206 home runs, 107 stolen bases, and a career .286 batting average, his greatest contributions to the game still lay ahead. When his playing days concluded, Alou found work as a batting coach and minor league manager in the Montreal Expos organization. In May 1992, Alou became Major League Baseball's first manager from the Dominican Republic when he replaced Expos manager Tom Runnells following a disappointing 17-20 start to the season. Under Alou's guidance, the Expos won 70 of 125 games, placing them in second place in the NL East.

In 1993, Alou's Expos again finished in second place, this time with a 94-68 record, the second-best mark in franchise history. In 1994, Montreal raced out the best record in the majors, 74-40, when a players' strike halted play, eventually canceling the rest of the season, including the World Series. The Expos would never recover. Focused on ridding themselves of highly paid players, the team traded or allowed to leave via free agency young stars, including PEDRO MARTÍNEZ, Larry Walker, and Alou's son, Moises. From 1995 to 2000, the Expos' only winning season came when they recorded an 88-74 record in 1996. During this time, Alou received interest from other teams, including an offer to manage the Los Angeles Dodgers, yet he refused, citing his connection to Montreal and loyalty to the organization. However, the losing took its toll on the team and Alou, and after another poor start in 2001, the Expos fired Alou. With 691 victories, he was the winningest manager in franchise history.

Alou was the bench coach for the Detroit Tigers in 2002 before becoming the manager of the San Francisco Giants in 2003. Upon accepting the job, Alou called himself a "soldier of the game" and reflected on his history in baseball, saying, "I'm going back home to where I started and hopefully I'm going to end it right there." In his first season as San Francisco manager, the Giants won 100 games and the 2003 NL West before losing in the playoffs to the eventual World Series champion, the Florida Marlins. In 2004, the Giants tallied 91 wins and missed the playoffs by only two games, though the team struggled with injuries and a losing record in 2005. Alou began the 2006 season at age 70, making him the oldest manager in Major League Baseball.

Following a 76-85 record in 2006, the Giants did not renew Alou's contract as manager. San Francisco general manager Brian Sabean described the decision to release Alou as "especially painful," adding, "Felipe is a man of unquestioned integrity who has put his heart and soul into the Giants."

Further Reading

Albee, Dave. "More Is Good, Too: New Giants Manager Felipe Alou Made 'Less Is More' Work for Years in Montreal, So It's Only Natural He Is Winning More with San Francisco—Even if Offseason Losses Had Many Expecting Less." *Sporting News,* 23 April 2003, p. 10.

"Felipe Alou." Baseball Library Web site. Available online. URL: http://baseballlibrary.com/baseball library/ballplayers/A/Alou_Felipe.stm. Downloaded on July 1, 2005.

Regalado, Samuel O. *Viva Baseball! Latin Major Leaguers and Their Special Hunger.* Champaign: University of Illinois Press, 1999.

Aparicio, Luis
(Luis Aparicio, Jr., Little Looie)
(1934–) *baseball player*

A graceful fielder and speedy base runner, Luis Aparicio played every inning of his 18-year career at shortstop, setting all-time records in games played and assists and putouts at that position, while earning nine Gold Glove awards, 10 All-Star game appearances, and induction into the Baseball Hall of Fame. He was born on April 29, 1934, in Maracaibo, a populous city on Venezuela's northwest coast, into a baseball family. Aparicio's father, Luis, Sr., was a shortstop in Venezuela who later owned a Venezuelan winter league team with his brother Ernesto.

Aparicio decided that he wanted to play professional baseball while still in grammar school and soon attracted interest from American scouts. He replaced his father as shortstop for the Maracaibo Gavilanes (Sparrow Hawks) in 1953 and signed a contract with the Chicago White Sox early in 1954.

Aparicio excelled during the two years he played in the White Sox minor league system. Prior to the 1956 season, the White Sox traded four-time All-Star shortstop and Venezuelan Chico Carrasquel to Cleveland in order to clear a starting position for 21-year-old Aparicio. In his rookie year of 1956, the 5'7", 160-pound "Little Looie" won the American League (AL) Rookie of the Year award by batting .263, driving in 56 runs, and flashing his trademark speed to lead the AL in stolen bases with 21. In 1958, Aparicio made the first of seven consecutive All-Star game appearances (he would later earn three more) and won the first of his nine Gold Glove awards.

In 1959, Aparicio, along with the White Sox's second baseman and future Hall of Famer Nellie Fox, personified the scrappy "Go Go Sox" that won the team its first pennant in 40 years. Although the White Sox lost the World Series to the Los Angeles Dodgers in six games, Aparicio had established himself as a steady hitter, prolific base stealer (winning AL stolen base titles in each of his first nine seasons), and acrobatic and sure-handed fielder. White Sox owner Bill Veeck, who purchased the team in 1959, echoed the thoughts of many who had observed Aparicio, saying, "He's the best (infielder) I've ever seen. He makes plays which I know can't possibly be made, yet he makes them almost everyday."

Following a subpar year in 1962 and the hiring of a new general manager, the White Sox traded Aparicio to the Baltimore Orioles on January 14, 1963. He bounced back with the Orioles, enjoying his best season with them in 1966, batting .276, stealing 25 bases, and finishing ninth in Most Valuable Player award voting. That season culminated in Aparicio's second World Series, this time resulting in Baltimore's four-game sweep of the Los Angeles Dodgers. In the series, the Dodgers scored only two runs, suffering shutouts in the final three games due to dominant Baltimore pitching and the spectacular defensive play of Aparicio and his partner on the left side of the infield, future Hall of Famer Brooks Robinson.

White Sox fans were excited when Chicago reacquired Aparicio in a trade with Baltimore prior to the 1968 season. The durable Aparicio was the everyday shortstop for the White Sox for the next three seasons, and though the speed of his earlier years was diminished, he enjoyed two of his best hitting seasons, including a career high .313 batting average in 1970. Aparicio finished the decade of the 1960s ranked second in hits in the AL, with 1,548, behind only Brooks Robinson and ahead of such legendary players as Al Kaline and Carl Yastrzemski. He was traded by the White Sox to the Boston Red Sox in December 1970. His last three years in baseball were spent in Boston, where his playing time and productivity declined. He retired weeks prior to the beginning of the 1974 season.

In August 1984, Aparicio was inducted in the Baseball Hall of Fame. When the announcement was made at a winter league game in January in Caracas, Venezuela, that he had been elected to the Hall of Fame, the more than 10,000 fans in attendance erupted into a standing ovation. Soon, pockets of fans spontaneously began singing the Venezuelan national anthem before play was stopped, allowing the players on the field to join the crowd in honoring Aparicio.

In 2006, the White Sox unveiled a statue of Aparicio at the team's Cellular One Park prior to a game. Attending the ceremony were Aparicio and his wife of 52 years, Sonia. At the conclusion of the tribute, Aparicio addressed the crowd, saying, "This is my greatest moment in baseball."

Further Reading

Isle, Stan. "Venezuelans Sing Out for Native Hero Aparicio." *Sporting News,* 6 February 1984, p. 9.

"Luis Aparicio." Baseball Library Web site. Available online. URL: http://www.baseballlibrary.com/

baseballlibrary/ballplayers/A/Aparicio_Luis.stm. Downloaded on July 1, 2005.

Vanderburg, Bob. "Modest Start to Hall of Fame Story: Luis Aparicio Opened His Career 50 Years Ago on a Cold Day at Comiskey Park." *Chicago Tribune,* 17 April 2006, p. 6.

Archuleta, Adam
(1977–) *football player*

A high school all-star football player who enrolled at Arizona State University without an athletic scholarship, Adam Archuleta became the Pacific 10 (Pac 10) Defensive Player of the Year before being selected in the first round of the 2001 National Football League (NFL) draft by the St. Louis Rams. He was born on November 27, 1977, in Rock Springs, Wyoming. His family moved to Arizona, and he attended Chandler High School, where he earned All-State Honorable Mention as a defensive back and running back in both his junior and senior seasons and earned the Most Valuable Player award on the Arizona All-Hispanic team.

Despite his impressive accomplishments on the football field during high school, Archuleta was offered few athletic scholarships to colleges. He decided to pursue his football career by enrolling at Arizona State University and trying out for the team as a walk-on player. He was chosen to join the team, and by his sophomore year, he became one of the team's starting linebackers.

Archuleta was soon awarded a full athletic scholarship to the university. He held his position as a starting linebacker throughout his junior and senior seasons. By the end of his college career, Archuleta had recorded 330 tackles, 14 quarterback sacks, six fumble recoveries, and five forced fumbles. He ranks fourth in school history with 54 tackles behind the line of scrimmage.

In his senior season at Arizona State, Archuleta was named to the All-Pac 10 Conference First Team, earned All-American Second Team honors from the Walter Camp Foundation, and was selected as one of three finalists for the Dick Butkus Award, given annually to the top linebacker in college football. He was also named the Pac 10's Defensive Player of the Year.

Archuleta's talent gained the attention of professional football scouts. Prior to the 2001 NFL draft, ESPN commentator Mel Kiper described the energetic Archuleta as a "relentless warrior" and as a "tackling machine." In April, Archuleta was the 21st pick of the first round in the NFL draft by the St. Louis Rams. As a rookie, Archuleta changed his position to safety, and he started in 12 of the Rams' 16 regular season games and all three of the team's playoff contests, including Super Bowl XXXV, which the Rams lost to the New England Patriots. Archuleta finished his rookie season sixth on the team in tackles and second in tackles behind the line of scrimmage. He was named to the NFL All-Rookie team by *Pro Football Weekly* magazine.

In his second pro season, Archuleta started all 16 games and led the Rams in tackles. In 2003, he led the NFL in quarterback sacks by a defensive back despite missing three games with an ankle injury. In 2004, despite playing most of the year with a herniated disc in his back, Archuleta ranked second on the Rams in tackles and helped lead the team into the playoffs for the third time in his first four seasons, solidifying his reputation as one of football's top young defensive backs.

Following another productive season with the Rams in 2005, Archuleta signed a six-year, $30 million free-agent contract with the Washington Redskins. However, both Archuleta and the Redskins struggled through a very disappointing season in 2006, in which they lost eleven games and only managed to win five games, placing them last in their division. After this Archuleta blasted the team's coaches for lying to him about the role he was expected to play.

Further Reading
"Archuleta Played '05 with Herniated Disc." ESPN Web site. Available online. URL: http://sports.

espn.go.com/nfl/news/story?id-2062457. Downloaded on July 1, 2005.

La Canfora, Jason. "For Redskins' Archuleta, an Imposing Body of Work." *Washington Post,* 18 June 2006, p. E1.

Wagoner, Nick. "Fear: Adam Archuleta May Not Possess It, but His Opponents Do." St. Louis Rams Web site. Available online. URL: http://www.stlouisrams.com/article/46872. Downloaded on July 1, 2005.

Arenas, Gilbert
(1982–) *basketball player*

A high-scoring guard for the University of Arizona's National Collegiate Athletic Association (NCAA) finalist basketball team in 2001, Gilbert Arenas was named the National Basketball Association's (NBA) Most Improved Player in 2003 and vaulted onto the top 10 scoring list in 2005 while leading the Washington Wizards to their first playoff series victory in 23 years. He was born on January 6, 1982, in Los Angeles. Arenas's father, Gilbert, Sr., was granted full custody of him before his third birthday after Arenas's mother, who struggled with substance abuse, left the family. Arenas lived in Tampa, Florida, until his father moved them to the Los Angeles area, where the elder Arenas worked the night shift at a parcel company while pursuing acting jobs in commercials and soap operas.

Arenas developed a reputation as a fun-loving youth who spent most of his free time playing basketball at available courts and gyms. He was a three-year starter at Grant High School in the San Fernando Valley city of Van Nuys, overcoming frequent double and triple teams from opposing defenders to shatter the school record book and become, in the opinions of many, the best high school basketball player in this populous region north of Los Angeles. Reflecting on Arenas's dynamic skills on the court, his high school coach, Howard Levine, stated, "Gilbert had the best

instincts I had ever seen. He knew more about the game than I did."

Following his high school graduation in 1999, Arenas enrolled at the University of Arizona after receiving an athletic scholarship to play basketball. Despite his accomplishments in high school, many observers believed that Arenas would struggle in big time college basketball because he was too slow to be a great point guard and, at 6'2", not tall enough to be a top shooting guard. Arenas chose to wear the number 0 on his uniform to remember these critics, who told him that was the number of minutes he would play at Arizona.

In his freshman year, Arenas made an immediate impact, posting 20 points, five steals, and four rebounds in Arizona's preseason National Invitational Tournament (NIT) championship win over Kentucky. He was named the Most Valuable Player (MVP) of the NIT and, following the season, was named to the All Pacific 10 (Pac 10) freshman team and was honorably mentioned in the All Pac 10.

Arenas's all-around skills were evidenced in his sophomore season, in which he averaged 16 points, four rebounds, two assists, and two steals while leading Arizona to the NCAA championship game, which they lost to Duke. By the season's end, Arenas had been named First Team All Pac 10, the NCAA tournament's Midwest Regional Most Outstanding Player, First Team All America by the *Sporting News,* and co-MVP of the Arizona team.

Following the successful season, Arenas ignored the advice of many by entering himself in the NBA draft. He was not selected until early in the second round because of familiar concerns that he was a "tweener" (between two positions), when the Golden State Warriors chose him with the 31st pick in the draft. Though disappointed with his low selection and lack of playing minutes early in the season, Arenas dedicated himself to improvement by working on his outside shot. Arenas started the final 30 games of the season, averaging an impressive 14 points and five assists,

In the 2004–05 season, Gilbert Arenas (wearing a throwback Washington Bullets jersey) led the Washington Wizards to their first playoff series victory in 23 years. *(Kirby Lee/WireImage.com)*

bringing his rookie season averages to 11 points, three rebounds, and four assists with an average playing time of less than 25 minutes a game.

In his second season, 2002–03, Arenas started all 82 games for Golden State and raised his averages to more than 18 points a game, six assists, and five rebounds, earning the NBA's Most Improved Player award. Following this outstanding season, Arenas signed a lucrative free-agent contract with the Washington Wizards. Although Arenas continued to develop as one of the league's top scorers in his first season in Washington, he struggled with injuries and turnovers as the Wizards suffered their sixth consecutive losing season.

The 2004–05 season was a stellar one for both Arenas and the Wizards. Arenas finished among the top 10 in the NBA in points per game (26; seventh), minutes per game (41; third), and three-point field goals made (205; fifth). The Wizards enjoyed a 20-game improvement from the previous year, finishing with a 45-37 record and their first playoff appearance in eight years. In game five of their first-round series versus Chicago, Arenas provided one of the most exciting plays of the season by making a buzzer beater jump shot with two defenders lunging at him to give the Wizards a thrilling 112-110 win that helped them earn their way to the Eastern Conference semifinals, where they lost to the Miami Heat.

During the 2004–05 season, Wizards director of player personnel Ernie Grunfeld praised Arenas, who would later that year be named Third Team All NBA, saying, "I don't know too many players who come in at two, three in the morning or put up 500 jump shots every day to try and improve their game . . . He wants to prove something to people." Following his playoff heroics against Chicago, Arenas echoed Grunfeld's thoughts and offered evidence that his dedication and talent may lead to more such moments: "I knew I was going to make it. I shoot those shots every day."

Arenas continued his stellar play in the 2005–06 season. He repeated as an All Star and solidified his place as one of the NBA's most dynamic players, finishing first in the league in minutes played (3,384) and second in points per game (29.3), steals (161), and three-point baskets made (199). Arenas again led the Wizards to the playoffs, where they lost in the first round to the Cleveland Cavaliers four games to two.

Further Reading

Ballard, Chris. "The Incredible Lightness of Being Gilbert: His Routines Are Eccentric, His Workouts Defy Logic and His Jokes Inspire Teammates to Choke Him. So How Is It That Gilbert Arenas Is the Driving Force of the Resurgent Wizards?" *Sports Illustrated,* 21 March 2005, p. 72.

"Gilbert Arenas." NBA Web site. Available online. URL: http://www.nba.com/playerfile/gilbert_arenas/bio.html. Downloaded on January 13, 2006.

Hruby, Patrick. "Two of a Kind." *Washington Times* Web site. Available online. URL: http://washingtontimes.com/sports/20050218-124035-4425r.htm. Downloaded on January 13, 2006.

"Wizards One Win Away from Second Round: Arenas' Buzzer-beater Foils Comeback Attempt by Bulls." MSNBC Web site. Available online. URL: http://msnbc.msn.com/id/7740205/. Downloaded on January 13, 2006.

Argüello, Alexis
(1952–   ) *boxer*

The first Latino to win boxing championships in three different weight categories, Alexis Argüello used his graceful quickness and rangy precision to become the most renowned fighter in the history of Nicaragua before becoming embroiled in that nation's political turmoil. He was born on April 19, 1952, in Managua, Nicaragua. Amid the deep poverty of the capital, Argüello became a street fighter before being taught how to box by his brother-in-law. He left school at the age of 14 to train exclusively for a career in the ring. In 1968, the 16-year-old Argüello became a professional boxer.

His first pro fight was a first-round technical knockout loss. Eight months later, after his first two victories, Argüello lost again, though he followed that fight with 20 consecutive victories. After a loss in June 1972, Argüello began another impressive winning streak, emerging victorious in 13 consecutive bouts, 12 of them by knockout.

On February 16, 1974, Argüello had his first fight outside Nicaragua, battling Ernest Marcel for the World Boxing Association (WBA) featherweight title in Panama City. Argüello lost in a 15-round decision, but he gained the WBA featherweight title in Los Angeles less than a year later when, behind on points on all the judges' scorecards, he knocked out RUBÉN OLIVARES in the 13th round.

Argüello defended his title with an undefeated record throughout 1975–77. On January 28, 1978, he won the World Boxing Council (WBC) junior lightweight title by knocking out Alfredo Escalera in Puerto Rico.

At the peak of Argüello's boxing career, political strife in his homeland of Nicaragua exploded. In 1979, a civil war led to the overthrow of the dictatorship of the Somoza family and the beginning of the 11-year control of Nicaraguan government by the socialist regime known as the Sandinistas. Though Argüello was now living in Miami and initially supported the revolution, he turned against the Sandinistas in 1980 after they seized his bank account and personal property and killed one of his brothers. Argüello postponed his boxing career to return to Nicaragua to join the contras, the anti-Sandinista armed resistance. After a few months of jungle warfare, however, he returned to the United States and resumed boxing.

After eight straight successful junior lightweight title defenses, Argüello moved up to become a lightweight and won that division's WBC championship when he defeated Jim Watt in a 15-round decision. With this title, Argüello became the first Latino to win championships in three different weight categories. After four title defenses, Argüello sought another challenge—becoming boxing's first four-division champion by again stepping up in weight to square off against Aaron Pryor for the WBA welterweight title.

Argüello and Pryor met before almost 24,000 fans in Miami's Orange Bowl on November 12, 1982, in a bout dubbed "The Battle of Champions." At 5'10", Argüello usually enjoyed an advantage in being able to reach over opponents in lower weight classes. But against Pryor, Argüello relied on his tactical skill and explosive power. After round 12 of this classic fight, Pryor appeared dazed and in danger of losing, but he rallied to defeat Argüello with a flurry of punches in the 14th round. The HBO television network, which broadcasted the fight, later recognized it as the best of the 1980s.

A rematch between Argüello and Pryor on September 9, 1983, was again won by Pryor, this time in a 10th-round knockout. Years later, Argüello recalled why he did not rise after being knocked down a third time, saying, "I didn't want to risk my life. I thought of how good Pryor is and I said, 'Jesus, I will stay here.'" Argüello retired after this loss, though he would later return several times for brief periods, never again winning a championship. He finished his boxing career in 1995 with a record of 80 victories—64 by knockout—and eight losses. He was inducted into the International Boxing Hall of Fame in 1992.

Argüello had difficulty adjusting to life outside the boxing ring. He battled depression and drug addiction for almost five years before apparently overcoming his problems and opening a boxing gym in one of Managua's toughest neighborhoods. In 2004, he was elected vice mayor of Managua, running as a member of the Sandinista Party that he had once fought against.

Further Reading

"Alexis Arguello." International Boxing Hall of Fame Web site. Available online. URL: http://www.ibhof.com/alexis.htm. Downloaded on June 22, 2006.

Guevara, Edgar. "Alexis Arguello: 'El Flaco Explosivo.'" Eastsideboxing.com. Available online. URL: http://eastsideboxing.com/news.php?p=1226&more=1. Downloaded on July 1, 2005.

Myler, Patrick. *A Century of Boxing Greats: Inside the Ring with the Hundred Best Boxers.* London: Robson Books, 2000.

Arroyo, Carlos
(1979–) *basketball player*

A quick and dynamic point guard whose skillful ball handling and pinpoint passing have earned him greater prominence than any other Puerto Rican in the history of the National Basketball Association (NBA), Carlos Arroyo was the star performer in Puerto Rico's stunning blowout victory over the United States in the 2004 Olympics. He was born on July 30, 1979, in Fajardo, Puerto Rico. Arroyo was raised by his parents, Alberto, Sr., and Gloria, and honed his talents in Fajardo by playing with his twin brother, Alberto, Jr., who is a professional basketball player in Puerto Rico, during the 1980s and 1990s, when basketball began to supplant baseball as the island's second most popular sport, behind only boxing.

In 1997, Arroyo began a stellar college basketball career at Florida International University. He was a four-year letterman at Florida International, where he set school records in career assists (459) and steals (177), becoming only the second player in school history to score more than 1,600 points.

Arroyo was not selected in the 2001 NBA draft due to concerns among professional scouts about his diminutive size and perceived low level of college competition. Prior to the season, however, he signed a free-agent contract with the NBA's Toronto Raptors. He became only the fifth Puerto Rican ever to play in the NBA, appearing in 12 games with the Raptors before being released. He finished the season with a brief stint on the Denver Nuggets.

In September 2002, the Utah Jazz signed Arroyo with the hope of having him learn as an understudy to legendary point guard John Stockton. Arroyo appeared in just over half of the Jazz's games that season, averaging less than three points a game. But when Stockton retired at the end of the season, Jazz coach Jerry Sloan elevated Arroyo to a starting role for the 2003–04 season. Arroyo immediately responded in the first month of the season with impressive performances, including a 30-point game against Minnesota and a 13-assist game versus Portland. He finished the season with averages of almost 13 points and five assists a game.

Though the Jazz failed to make the playoffs, optimism over the team's future under the leadership of Arroyo was high. Those high hopes grew following Arroyo's stellar play in the 2004 Olympics in Athens. In Puerto Rico's stunning 92–73 win over the heavily favored U.S. team, Arroyo blistered the Americans by leading all players in points (24) and assists (seven). Before exiting the game with a few minutes remaining, Arroyo proudly displayed his jersey for the cheering crowd, holding up the uniform's "Puerto Rico" script for all to see.

Although the Puerto Rican team failed to win any medals, the Olympics elevated Arroyo's status in the eyes of basketball fans around the world. Puerto Rico's Olympics coach, Carlos Morales, praised Arroyo's emotional and physical maturity, and Philadelphia 76ers and U.S. Olympics star guard Allen Iverson noted how, under Arroyo's direction, the Puerto Rican team "play the game the way it is supposed to be played." The Jazz seemingly agreed with these assessments, signing Arroyo to a four-year contract worth $4 million a year.

However, the highs of the summer of 2004 quickly unraveled once the NBA season began in the fall. Injuries and lack of playing time early in the season strained the relationship between Arroyo and Jazz coach Sloan, leading to Arroyo's trade to the reigning NBA champion, the Detroit Pistons, on January 21, 2005. With Detroit, Arroyo played for a new coach, Larry Brown, who had been the head coach of the 2004 U.S. Olympic team, against whom Arroyo enjoyed his greatest glory. Playing a key role as a spark plug off Detroit's bench, Arroyo helped the Pistons reach the 2005 NBA Finals, where they lost four games to three to the San Antonio Spurs.

Arroyo was traded by the Pistons to the Orlando Magic in February 2006. In his role as backup point guard, Arroyo helped lift the Magic from the bottom of the NBA into playoff contenders and boosted interest in basketball among Florida's large Latino population.

Further Reading

Carlos Arroyo Web site. Available online. URL: http:// carlosarroyo.com. Downloaded on July 1, 2005.

McNeal, Stan. "Q & A: Carlos Arroyo, PG, Pistons." *Sporting News,* 18 March 2005, p. 70.

Paese, Gabrielle. "Carlos Arroyo, Puerto Rico Show Team USA How It's Done." *Puerto Rico Herald,* 20 August 2005.

B

Ballesteros, Seve
(Severiano Ballesteros)
(1957–) *golfer*

A charismatic golfer whose skill, passion, and success raised European golfing to new heights, Seve Ballesteros is a three-time winner of the British Open (1979, 1984, 1988), and he is the first Spaniard ever to win the prestigious Masters Tournament (1980 and 1983.) He was born on April 9, 1957, in Pedrena, Spain. Ballesteros grew up in Pedrena, a small village in the north of Spain, in a golfing family. His uncle Ramón Sota was one of the best golfers in Europe during the 1960s, who finished sixth at the 1965 Masters. Ballesteros began golfing at the age of seven, and by the time he was 10, he followed his three older brothers, Baldomero, Manuel, and Vicente (all of whom later became professional golfers) as a caddy at the Royal Pedrena Golf Club. By his early teens, Ballesteros was demonstrating impressive enthusiasm and talent for golf, and he frequently won junior tournaments, leading him to turn professional in 1974.

Ballesteros won the Spanish Professionals Tournament in 1974 just weeks before his 17th birthday. In 1976, he won five times on the European Tour, claimed the European Tour Order of Merit (awarded to that tour's top money winner), and made a remarkable run at the British Open championship before finishing second to Johnny Miller. Ballesteros attracted admiration not only because of his precocious success but also because of his aggressive and creative style of play, which was infused with powerful drives and calculated risks that thrilled golf fans.

In 1978, Ballesteros enjoyed one of the most amazing runs of any golfer in his generation when he won eight tournaments on four different continents (Europe, North America, Asia, and Africa). In 1979, Ballesteros claimed the first of his five major tournament victories when he won the British Open, becoming at age 22 the youngest player in the 20th century to win that event and the first golfer from continental Europe (Europe excluding Great Britain and Ireland) to win the event since Frenchman Arnaud Massy won in 1907. His next appearance in a major tournament was the 1980 Masters, where Ballesteros cruised past the field to lead by 10 shots with only nine holes left to play on his way to the championship. Following this victory, Ballesteros wore the traditional green jacket awarded to the winner at the Masters Augusta National Golf Course, becoming the first European ever to earn that honor.

Controversy soon followed Ballesteros for various reasons. In 1980, he was disqualified from the U.S. Open when he arrived a few minutes late for a tee time. In 1981, he was voted off the European Ryder Cup Team (consisting of players who compete against a team of American players) because he played so many tournaments in the United States. He then clashed with the U.S. Professional Golfers Association (PGA) over the governing body's insistence of exclusivity, with Ballesteros choosing to play full time in Europe when the PGA rejected his request to play part time in both Europe and the United States. As a result of Ballesteros's stance, the rules were soon eased to allow more flexibility in playing commitments for professional golfers.

The apex of Ballesteros's career came in 1983, when he won his second green jacket at the Masters, leaving runner-up Tom Kite to say, "When he gets going, it's almost as if Seve is driving a Ferrari and the rest of us are in Chevrolets." Legendary golfer LEE TREVINO noted of Ballesteros, "On a golf course he's got everything—I mean everything: touch, power, know-how, courage, and charisma." Added Ben Crenshaw, another top player of the 1980s, "Seve plays shots I don't even see in my dreams."

Ballesteros continued to enjoy enormous success throughout the 1980s and early 1990s. His highlights during this period were his wins at the British Open in 1984 and 1988 and his nine appearances on the European Ryder Cup team, including playing a key role in victories over U.S. teams in 1985, 1987, 1989 (tied, with the championship remaining with the Europeans), 1995, and 1997 (serving as a nonplaying captain at the tournament held in his native Spain). Ballesteros's commitment to world golf then led him to create the Seve Trophy, awarded to the winner of competition between teams from continental Europe and Great Britain/Ireland, held in alternate years from the Ryder Cup.

Back injuries slowed Ballesteros's ability to either participate or make the cut in most major tournaments in the late 1990s and early years of the 21st century. He was inducted into the World Golf Hall of Fame in 1997. Ballesteros lives in Spain, with his wife and three children, where he enjoys success as the owner of a golf course design business.

Further Reading

St. John, Lauren. *Seve: Ryder Cup Hero.* Nashville, Tenn.: Ruthledge Hill Press, 1997.

"Severiano Ballesteros." Severiano Ballesteros Web site. Available online. URL: http://www.seveballesteros.com/ing/bbiografia/htm. Downloaded on June 18, 2006.

Tait, Alistair. *Seve: A Biography of Severiano Ballesteros.* London: Virgin Books, 2005.

Barbosa, Leandro
(Leandrohino)
(1982–   ) *basketball player*

The first Brazilian guard ever drafted by a National Basketball Association (NBA) team, Leandro Barbosa quickly became one of the top players in the distinguished rookie class of 2003–04. He was born on November 28, 1982, in São Paulo, Brazil. Barbosa grew up in Brazil's largest city, attending school, selling fruits and vegetables in a farmer's market, and developing his skills as a soccer and basketball player.

Barbosa's length, quickness, and soft shooting touch helped him earn a spot on Brazil's national under-21 team at the age of 15. He soon acquired the nickname "Leandrohino," meaning little Leandro, following the one-word monikers popular among Brazil's soccer heroes. At the age of 16, he was playing professionally in a minor league in Brazil. In 2001–02, Barbosa was named the Brazilian League Rookie of the Year after totaling averages of 16 points, six assists, and two rebounds a game. Later that year at the age of 19, he became the youngest player to earn a roster spot on the Brazilian National Team that competed at the 2002 World Championships in Indianapolis.

In 2003, Barbosa entered his name for eligibility for the NBA draft. Before the draft, he described his style of play by saying, "I try to model my game after great players such as Allen Iverson and Gary Payton. I like Iverson because he always plays at such high speed, and he is really aggressive attacking the basket. I love to lead the fast break. Like Payton, I try my best to use my height [6'3"] against smaller point guards."

The Phoenix Suns made a trade to acquire the 28th pick in the 2003 NBA draft and used it to select Barbosa. He played sparingly in the first half of the season, but his opportunity to contribute increased after the Suns traded their starting point guard, Stephon Marbury, to the New York Knicks. After the trade, Barbosa started the remaining 46 games. In his first start on January 5, 2004, Barbosa scored a Suns rookie record 27 points. He also set a Suns rookie record by scoring three-point shots in 10 consecutive games. By the end of the season, Barbosa ranked among the top 10 rookies in scoring, assists, field goal percentage, and steals, placing him among the impressive field of that season's rookies including LeBron James, Carmelo Anthony, and Dwyane Wade.

Barbosa lost his starting position before the 2004–05 season when the Suns signed point guard Steve Nash to a lucrative free-agent contract. But Barbosa proved to be an important force off the bench, averaging seven points, two assists, and two rebounds a game, as the high-scoring Suns more than doubled their previous year's victory total, led the NBA in wins, and reached the Western Conference finals.

In the 2005–06 season, Barbosa assumed a more significant role with the Suns, playing almost 28 minutes a game and averaging 13.1 points, 2.4 assists, and 2.1 rebounds a contest in the regular season. He shined even brighter in the playoffs as the Suns reached the Western Conference finals, where they fell to the Dallas Mavericks in six games. Following Barbosa's 24-point performance in game five of that series, Phoenix guard James Jones said of his speedy and rapidly improving teammate, "We play fast as it is. But he gives us a level nobody else can reach."

Further Reading

"Leandro Barbosa." NBA Web site. Available online. URL: http://www.nba.com/playerfile/leandro_barbosa/bio.html. Downloaded on July 1, 2005.

Maurer, Matthew. "Leandrinho Barbosa Interview." NBADraft.net. Available online. URL://nbadraft.net/barbosainterview.htm. Downloaded on July 1, 2005.

Tulumello, Mike. "Barbosa's Speed Can Kill Opponents." *East Valley Tribune,* 1 June 2006.

Benitez, Wilfred
(the Radar, the Bible of Boxing)
(1958–   ) *boxer*

A boxing prodigy who combined poetic style, explosive power, and technical superiority in the ring, Wilfred Benitez is the youngest fighter ever to win a world title in boxing. He was born on September 12, 1958, in New York City. His parents, Clara and Gregorio, soon moved the family to their native Puerto Rico, where Benitez began receiving boxing lessons from his father at the age of eight. Demonstrating remarkable skill and command of boxing fundamentals, he joined his two older brothers, Frankie and Gregory, in the world of professional boxing when he was only 15.

Benitez won his first professional bout in a first-round knockout over Hiram Santiago in San Juan, Puerto Rico, on November 22, 1973. Over the next few years, Benitez fought in Puerto Rico, the Virgin Islands, and New York City, winning 24 consecutive fights with a stunning combination of speed, power, and instinct that earned him the nickname "the Radar." His preferred name for himself, "the Bible of Boxing," reflected his admired technical superiority in the ring.

On March 6, 1976, the undefeated Benitez earned his first opportunity to gain the World Boxing Association's (WBA) light welterweight title in a fight against ANTONIO "Kid Pambele" CERVANTES. Benitez won this fight in a 15th-round split decision (disagreement among the three judges regarding who won the fight) and became, at the age of 17 years and six months, the youngest boxer ever to win a world title.

He defended his light welterweight championship three times before the lure of a high-priced fight against emerging star and soon-to-be Olympic champion Sugar Ray Leonard enticed Benitez to rise in weight to the welterweight division. On January 14, 1979, Benitez won his second world title by defeating Carlos Palomino in a 15th-round split decision in San Juan to become the World Boxing Council's (WBC) welterweight champion.

The much-anticipated fight between Benitez and Leonard took place at Caesars Palace in Las Vegas on November 30, 1979. Both men fought brilliantly, displaying their scientific precision and athletic prowess. Benitez was knocked down briefly in the third round and suffered a cut on his forehead in the sixth round. With Leonard on the verge of a knockout victory, the referee stopped the fight with only six seconds remaining, giving Benitez his first loss as a professional boxer.

After that fight, Benitez again moved up in weight to light middleweight, and within a year and a half he became the youngest three-time world champion in boxing history following his May 23, 1981, pummeling of Maurice Hope in Las Vegas. His next fight, a unanimous decision over Carlos Santos, was the first-ever title bout between two Puerto Rican fighters. Benitez then won a unanimous decision over ROBERTO DURÁN, setting up a battle with Thomas "Hitman" Hearns, on December 3, 1982, in the Superdome in New Orleans. Hearns used his long arms for a reach advantage that penetrated the defensive wizardry of Benitez, knocking him down in the fifth round and staggering him in the sixth round. Benitez managed to last until the end of the fight but lost to Hearns in a majority decision.

Following only his second loss, the 24-year-old Benitez began a downward spiral in his career and personal life. Between 1983 and 1986, Benitez won only seven of 11 fights, none of which were for a title belt. Following a November 28, 1986, loss in Argentina to Carlos Herrera, Benitez lost his money (much of which had already been squandered by his extravagant lifestyle and his father's longtime gambling) and passport, leaving him stranded for more than a year until he was finally allowed to return to Puerto Rico. He attempted a comeback in 1990, though he won only half of his four bouts that year against lightly regarded competition.

In late 1990, Benitez, who had not communicated with his family and friends for months, was found homeless and acting erratically in Argentina. His mother retrieved him and brought him to Puerto Rico, where he was diagnosed with dementia pugilistica, a neurological condition caused by repeated blows to the head. He never fought again, finishing his career with a 53-8-1 record, with 31 knockouts.

Newly crowned junior welterweight Wilfred Benitez waves to celebrating fans at a parade in his hometown of Carolina, Puerto Rico. *(Associated Press)*

Benitez was inducted into the International Boxing Hall of Fame in 1996. He lives outside San Juan at a small facility serving patients with mental disabilities. Almost all of his expenses are paid by the Puerto Rican government in recognition for his being "the most important boxer Puerto Rico has ever had," as stated by the commonwealth's recreation and sports secretary.

Further Reading

Torres, Jose. "Wilfred Benitez: One More Victim." Boxing Ranks Web site. Available online. URL: http://www.boxingranks.com/Articles/Article71.htm. Downloaded on July 1, 2005.

"Wilfred Benitez." International Boxing Hall of Fame Web site. Available online. URL: http://www.ibhof.com/benitez.htm. Downloaded on June 22, 2006.

Wilfred Benitez Web site. Available online. URL: http://www.wilfredbenitez.com. Downloaded on July 1, 2005.

Blackman, Rolando
(Mr. Silk)
(1959–   ) *basketball player*

The first Latino to be named to a National Basketball Association (NBA) All-Star team and have his number retired by an NBA franchise, Rolando Blackman played for 13 seasons, becoming the Dallas Mavericks' career scoring leader. He was born on February 26, 1959, in Panama City, Panama. Blackman spent his boyhood playing soccer in that nation's largest city before his family moved to New York City. He lived in the Flatbush section of Brooklyn and became one of the city's best basketball players at William Grady High School. Blackman left the playgrounds of Brooklyn for the fields of Manhattan, Kansas, choosing to accept a basketball scholarship at Kansas State University.

As a member of the Kansas State Wildcats, Blackman became one of the best all-around players in the history of the Big Eight Conference. A prolific scorer, Blackman was the Wildcats starting shooting guard for all four years in college, finishing his career with 1,844 points, ranking second in Kansas State history. Blackman's smooth style earned him the nickname "Mr. Silk," and his unselfish play led his coach, Jack Hartman, to call him "the consummate player."

A three-time unanimous All-Big Eight selection and three-time Big Eight Defensive Player of the Year, Blackman was the Conference Player of the Year as a junior. After that season, Blackman earned All-American honors and was named a starter for the 1980 U.S. Olympic basketball team. That team, along with the rest of the American delegation, never competed in the 1980 Olympics in Moscow because the United States boycotted the games to protest the Soviet Union's invasion of Afghanistan. In Blackman's senior season at Kansas State, he led the Wildcats to a stunning victory in the National Collegiate Athletic Association (NCAA) tournament over number-one ranked Oregon State, making a game-winning jump shot with just two seconds remaining.

In 1981, the Dallas Mavericks selected Blackman as the ninth selection of the first round in the NBA draft. After a solid rookie season in which he averaged 13 points a game, Blackman's scoring average jumped to almost 18 points a game in his second season and then to more than 22 points a game in his third year. In the 1984–85 season, Blackman began a span of six years in which he averaged more than 18 points, three assists, and three rebounds per game, gaining All-Star recognition four times.

In 1988, Blackman helped lead the Mavericks to the Western Conference finals against superstar player Magic Johnson and the NBA champion Los Angeles Lakers. The Mavericks pushed the Lakers to the final minutes of the decisive seventh game before losing. Following that series, Johnson called Blackman, "one of the best shooters of all time and one of the most difficult players to guard."

Blackman continued to provide Dallas with consistent scoring punch and steady defense in the 1990–91 and 1991–92 seasons. He returned to New York City when the Mavericks traded him to the New York Knicks for a first-round draft pick. Though Blackman reached his first NBA finals in 1994 when the Knicks lost to the Houston Rockets, his production and role diminished in two seasons in New York. He retired from the NBA following the 1993–94 season before playing a season in Greece. The next year Blackman played in Italy, leading his team to the Italian championship.

Since his playing days ended, Blackman graduated from Kansas State with a bachelor's degree in social science, and he served as the Mavericks director of player development and a television analyst before becoming an assistant coach for the team, which won the NBA's Western Conference in 2005–06 before losing in The Finals to the Miami Heat in six games.

Further Reading

Kirkpatrick, Curry. "Hey, You'd Be Hog Wild, Too." *Sports Illustrated*, 23 March 1981.

"Mavs History." Dallas Mavericks Web site. Available online. URL: http://www.nba.com/mavericks/history/00400544.html. Downloaded on July 1, 2005.

"Rolando Blackman." Basketball Reference Web site. Available online. URL: http://www.basketballreference.com/players/playerpage.htm?ilkid=BLACKRO01. Downloaded on July 1, 2005.

Bonilla, Bobby
(Roberto Martin Antonio Bonilla)
(1963–   ) *baseball player*

One of the most productive hitters of his era, Bobby Bonilla played for eight teams during a 16-year career marked by his high salaries, strained relationships with fans and media, and eventually a world championship. He was born Roberto Martin Antonio Bonilla on February 23, 1963, in the Bronx, New York. His father, Roberto, and mother, Regina, separated when he was eight, and though he lived primarily with his mother in the Bronx, he remained extremely close to his father, an electrician living in the Flushing, Queens, section of New York City.

Bonilla attended Lehman High School not far from Shea Stadium, where he would later play for the New York Mets. In his senior year, he was chosen to play on an all-star baseball team touring Scandinavia. On this trip, he met a teammate's father, Syd Thrift, who was an executive in the Pittsburgh Pirates organization.

Soon after graduating from high school in 1981, Bonilla signed a contract with the Pirates. Over the next five years, Bonilla compiled mediocre statistics in the minor leagues. When Bonilla finally showed that he might be ready to be called up to the majors, he broke his ankle, putting him on the disabled list for four months. In December 1985, Bonilla was selected by the Chicago White Sox in a draft of unprotected minor league players.

Bonilla made his major league debut and appeared in 75 games for the White Sox in 1986. But the Pirates remained interested in their former switch-hitting farmhand whose size and stroke had attracted them earlier. On July 26, 1986, Pittsburgh traded for Bonilla. He would hit only one home run in almost 200 at-bats for the Pirates in 1986.

In the 1987 season, Bonilla began to redeem the faith placed in him by the Pirates, hitting .300 with 15 home runs and 77 runs batted in (RBI). Bonilla was named to the National League (NL) All-Star team as a third baseman in 1988 and 1989, serving with teammate Barry Bonds as half of Pittsburgh's young and potent "BB Gunners." In 1990, Bonilla, now playing in the outfield, earned another All-Star appearance and second place in Most Valuable Player (MVP) voting during a breakout season in which he hit

.280 with 32 home runs and 120 RBIs, helping lead the Pirates to their first NL East division title since 1979. In the Pirates six-game loss in the NL Championship Series to the Cincinnati Reds, Bonilla mustered just four hits in 21 at-bats with only one RBI.

Bonilla's excellence continued in 1991, when his .302 batting average and 100 RBIs led to another All-Star Game appearance, third place in MVP voting, and another NL East division championship for the Pirates. However, Bonilla again was able to drive in only one run during the heartbreaking seven-game Pirates loss in the NL Championship Series to the Atlanta Braves.

Bonilla became a free agent after the 1991 season. A bidding war among many teams including the Pirates was eventually won by the New York Mets, who made Bonilla the highest-paid player in baseball with a five-year $29 million contract. At his official Mets introduction, Bonilla established the sour relationship he would have during his tenure in his hometown, telling assembled reporters, "I know you are all gonna try, but you're not gonna be able to wipe the smile off my face. I grew up in New York. I know what it's all about."

With the exception of his first game, in which he hit two home runs, including a game winner, Bonilla's stint as a Met was a miserable one. In 1992, his offensive numbers plummeted, and he briefly wore ear plugs to drown out the boos of Mets fans. Television cameras even caught him calling the press box during a game to complain about an error charged to him. In 1993, Bonilla's performance improved, allowing him to earn another All-Star Game appearance, but his season is best remembered for his threats to New York writer Bob Klapish, whose exposé of the Mets titled *The Worst Team Money Could Buy* angered Bonilla.

In 1995, Bonilla was enjoying his best season as a Met, including an appearance in his sixth and final All-Star Game, when he was traded to the Baltimore Orioles. In 1996, Bonilla drove in 116 runs, helping lead the Orioles to the playoffs. Again, however, Bonilla's postseason struggles emerged when he managed just one hit in 20 at-bats during Baltimore's American League Championship Series loss to the New York Yankees.

Prior to the 1997 season, Bonilla signed as a free agent with the Florida Marlins. In just their fifth year of existence, the Marlins won the NL pennant, largely because of Bonilla's .297 batting average, 17 home runs, and 96 RBIs. With the Marlins trailing the Cleveland Indians 2-0 in the deciding seventh game of the World Series, Bonilla hit a seventh-inning home run. With the score tied in the 11th inning, Bonilla led off with a single, igniting a rally that culminated in the World Series championship for the Marlins.

Bonilla played for five teams over his final four seasons, including another brief disastrous stint with the Mets featuring clashes with his manager, Bobby Valentine, a career low .160 batting average, and strike outs in his only two at-bats in the Mets 1999 World Series loss to the New York Yankees. He retired following the 2001 season with 2,010 hits, 1,173 RBIs, and 287 home runs, fifth highest among all switch-hitters in baseball history. Bonilla now works for the Major League Baseball Players Association and lives in Connecticut.

Further Reading

"Bobby Bonilla." Baseball Library Web site. Available online. URL: http://www.baseballlibrary.com/ baseballlibrary/ballplayers/B/Bonilla_Bobby.stm. Downloaded on July 8, 2005.

Klapisch, Bob. *The Worst Team Money Could Buy: The Collapse of the New York Mets.* New York: Random House, 1993.

O'Neill, Dan. "The Bucs' Bobby Bonilla: His Best Is Yet to Come!" *Baseball Digest.* August 1990, p. 25.

Shouler, Kenneth. "Swinging for the Fences with a World Series Championship under His Belt, Bobby Bonilla Sets His Sights on His Place in Baseball History." *Cigar Aficionado,* July/August 1998.

Brown, Panama Al
(Alfonso Teófilo Brown, the Elongated
Panamanian)
(1902–1951) *boxer*

A tall, thin, muscular bantamweight boxer with explosive punching power and an expansive reach, Panama Al Brown was the first Latino to win a world boxing championship. He was born Alfonso Teófilo Brown in Colón, Panama, on July 5, 1902. Brown worked as a clerk with the United States Shipping Board in the Panama Canal Zone as a young man, where he was introduced to boxing by watching bouts between U.S. military personnel stationed there. Brown was encouraged by his boss to give boxing a try, and he soon enjoyed great success as a teenage amateur fighter.

Brown stood about 5'11" and weighed between 112 and 126 pounds throughout his professional boxing career, which began when he was 19 or 20 (boxing records were often not well preserved in the early part of the 20th century). His 76-inch reach earned him the nickname "the Elongated Panamanian" and was his most unique and dangerous weapon. Most historians list his first fight as a win over José Moreno in Colón on March 19, 1922. In his seventh fight, he won the Isthmus (Panamanian) flyweight title on December 12, 1922, in a decision over Sailor Pritchett.

His first fight outside Panama, on August 22, 1923, was a draw versus Johnny Breslin in New York. He remained undefeated over the course of a year and half and 18 fights until suffering his first loss at the hands of Jimmy Russo in New York on January 3, 1925. He avenged that defeat later that year and continued to fight about once or twice a month (all in the United States) before traveling to Paris, where he knocked out Antoine Merlo on November 20, 1926.

Brown enjoyed Paris so much that he decided to spend much of the rest of his life there. The city in turn embraced Brown, making him one of France's most popular athletes. All 10 of Brown's fights in 1927 were held in Paris, as were many more later in his career.

On June 18, 1929, Brown finally gained an opportunity to win the world bantamweight title in a Long Island City, New York, fight with Vidal Gregorio. Before a crowd of 15,000, Brown handily disposed of his opponent in a 15-round decision, becoming the first Latino to win a world boxing championship. Brown successfully defended his title 10 times over the next six years in a truly global set of venues including New York, Paris, Montreal, Marseilles, Toronto, Milan, London, and Tunis. He finally relinquished the title when he lost the decision to Baltazar Sangchili in Valencia, Spain, on June 1, 1935.

Brown continued to fight over the next seven years, mostly in Paris and New York, and after two brief retirements in Panama. His last fight, a victory over Kid Fortune on December 4, 1942, gave him a record of 123-18-10 with 55 knockouts. Brown was never knocked out in any of his losses.

Sadly, Brown's postboxing life lasted only a few years. He fronted an orchestra on the French Riviera for a short time and was later arrested in New York City for using cocaine, leading to a brief deportation from the United States. Brown eventually returned, and despite the great wealth he had accumulated during his boxing career, he died poor of tuberculosis in New York City on April 11, 1951, at the age of 49. Brown, still widely considered among the greatest bantamweights of all time, was enshrined in the International Boxing Hall of Fame in 1992. The sports arena in his birthplace of Colón is named in his honor.

Further Reading
"Boxing: The Top Fighters of the Century." *London Independent,* 15 December 1999.
"Panama Al Brown." International Boxing Hall of Fame Web site. Available online. URL: http://www.ibhof.com/brown.htm. Downloaded on July 8, 2005.
"Panama Al Brown—'The Elongated Panamanian.'" Cyber Boxing Zone Web site. Available online.

Bruschi, Tedy
(Tedy Lecap Bruschi)
(1973–   ) *football player*

The captain of the 2004 Super Bowl champion New England Patriots defense, Tedy Bruschi displayed intensity and intelligence that earned him the reputation as the heart and soul of the National Football League's (NFL) first dynasty of the 21st century. He was born Tedy Lecap Bruschi on June 9, 1973, in San Francisco. His mother, Juanita, a

New England Patriots linebacker Tedy Bruschi prepares for a play in his second game after returning from a stroke in 2005. *(Steven Murphy/WireImage.com)*

Mexican-American real estate agent, divorced his father, Tony, a high school football coach, when Tedy was in elementary school. He lived with his mother in downtown San Francisco, playing football in the city's streets and parks until his mother and stepfather moved the family to the Sacramento, California, suburb of Roseville.

Bruschi excelled in high school sports, competing in wrestling, shot put, and discus and earning all-conference and all–Northern California honors as a captain and defensive tackle on the Roseville High football team. Despite sterling credentials, which would later earn him distinction as the best all-time Sacramento area high school football player by the *Sacramento Bee* newspaper, Bruschi was not overwhelmed with college scholarship offers. Many college recruiters believed that Bruschi was too short (6') to be an effective defensive lineman and not fast enough to play well at linebacker. Impressed by the college atmosphere of Tucson and the commitment of head coach Dick Tomey, Bruschi chose to play for the University of Arizona Wildcats.

His collegiate career began in 1991 with a broken thumb that caused him to miss almost the entire season. The next year, Bruschi played linebacker before moving to defensive line in 1993, when he set a school record for quarterback sacks (19), was named to the All Pacific 10 team, and was honored as the team's Most Valuable Player.

Prior to the 1994 season, Bruschi was pictured with teammates from Arizona's vaunted "Desert Swarm" defense on the cover of *Sports Illustrated*'s College Football Preview issue. The Wildcats did not live up to the number-one ranking predicted by the magazine, but Bruschi had another very productive season. Though consistently double- and triple-teamed by opponents, Bruschi managed 10 sacks, earning consensus All-American honors, and he was one of the four finalists for the Lombardi Award, given to the nation's top college defensive lineman. After another All-American performance during his senior season, Bruschi finished his college career tied for the National Collegiate Athletic Association (NCAA) division 1-A record with 52 sacks and 74 tackles for a loss, sixth highest in division 1-A history.

As was the case when he was leaving high school for college, many experts believed that Bruschi was too small to be a star as he prepared to enter the 1996 NFL draft. The New England Patriots selected Bruschi in the third round of the draft with the 86th overall pick. As a rookie, he appeared in every game, contributing mainly as a special teams player. His interception late in the fourth quarter in the American Football Conference (AFC) championship game versus Jacksonville helped lead the Patriots to their first Super Bowl in 11 years. He closed out his rookie season with two sacks in the Patriots' loss to the Green Bay Packers in Super Bowl XXXI.

Bruschi played in every game during the next two years, becoming a starting linebacker by the middle of his third season. Bruschi's improvement continued in 1999, when he ranked second on the Patriots in tackles (106) despite missing two games due to an injury. During the 2000 season, Bruschi again tallied more than 100 tackles, and in 2001, he led the Patriots back from a 5-11 record the previous season to a victory in Super Bowl XXXVI.

During the 2002 and 2003 seasons, Bruschi was chosen by his teammates as the defensive captain of the Patriots. In each of those seasons, he returned two interceptions for touchdowns, becoming the first linebacker in Patriots history to accomplish that feat. In 2003, Bruschi notched a career high 131 tackles, spearheading a defense that became the first in 65 years not to allow a touchdown in four consecutive home games in one season. Bruschi capped that season with four tackles in New England's Super Bowl XXXVIII win over the Carolina Panthers.

The 2004 season brought more glory to Bruschi and the Patriots. He started every game and collected 122 tackles, as the Patriots went 14-2 through the regular season. Patriots linebacker Mike Vrabel foreshadowed Bruschi's postseason value, saying, "Everybody needs a Tedy Bruschi, but good luck finding one. When he walks into a meeting or a huddle, he brings instant credibility." In the

playoffs, Bruschi recovered two fumbles in a victory over Indianapolis and he intercepted two passes, including one in the final minute, of New England's Super Bowl XXXIX victory over Philadelphia.

On February 16, 2005, just a few days after playing in his first Pro Bowl, Bruschi's career and life were shockingly threatened by what was later termed a "mild stroke." In March, Bruschi reportedly underwent a procedure to repair a hole in his heart. Though doctors did not categorically rule out a return to football for Bruschi, his status heading into the 2005 season was very unclear.

Bruschi received doctors' permission and returned to the team midway through the 2005 season. He solidified New England's injury-plagued defense and helped the Patriots repeat as AFC East division champions. Following the season, Bruschi was named co-Comeback Player of the Year in the NFL. In 2006, Bruschi played in all but one of New England's regular season games and led the team with 112 tackles as the Patriots again won the AFC East championship.

Further Reading
Boston Globe. Driven: The Patriots' Ride to a Third Title. Boston: *Boston Globe,* 2005.
"Patriots Linebacker to Go Home Friday." ESPN Web site. Available online. URL: http://sports.espn.go.com/nfl/news/story?id=1993188&CMP=OTC-DT9705204233. Downloaded on July 8, 2005.
Spander, Art. "Wildcat Bruschi Stands Tall." *San Francisco Examiner,* 18 October 1992.
"Tedy Bruschi." National Football League Players Association Web site. Available online. URL: http://www.nflplayers.com/players/player.aspx?id=23979. Downloaded on July 8, 2005.

Bueno, Maria
("São Paulo Swallow")
(1939–) *tennis player*

A tennis player admired for her athletic grace and flare for fashion, Maria Bueno became the first

South American to win a Wimbledon singles title, contributing enormously to the international popularity of women's tennis. She was born on October 11, 1939, in São Paulo, Brazil. She never took a formal tennis lesson as a youth but learned by playing against boys and men starting when she was six years old. Bueno won her first tournament in São Paulo at the age of 12 and the women's championship of Brazil at 15.

Bueno's elegance on the tennis court earned her the nickname the "São Paulo Swallow." She was tall (5'7"), slim, and quick, blending power and touch that led to 10 top-10 rankings between 1958 and 1968, including the rating of top woman tennis player in the world in 1959, 1960, 1964, and 1966.

She won her first grand slam title in 1958, with the doubles championship at Wimbledon with partner Althea Gibson. In 1959, Bueno won the Wimbledon singles championship at the age of 19 and the U.S. National Championship (later renamed the U.S. Open). In 1960, Bueno repeated her Wimbledon singles title and teamed with Darlene Hard to win the Wimbledon and U.S. National Championship doubles titles.

Bueno was stricken with hepatitis in 1961 and took that year off before returning to the court in 1962, again winning the U.S. doubles title with Hard. She went on to win singles titles at Wimbledon (1964) and the U.S. National Championship (1963, 1964, 1966), as well as doubles titles at Wimbledon (1963, 1965, 1966) and the U.S. National Championship (1962, 1966, 1968).

As impressive as her titles was the style in which she won them. A hard server who liked to come to the net and volley, Bueno said, "To me tennis was more of an art than a sport." She was renowned for displaying attractive and unconventional tennis dresses designed by Ted Tinling. Among these dresses was a 1964 outfit that wowed Wimbledon spectators with a bright pink lining that showed whenever she served or made one of her many acrobatic shots. Bueno's style of play was often linked to French star Suzanne Lenglen, who preceded her, and Australian Evonne Goolagong, who followed her, for their distinctive fluidity and artistry on the court.

By the time the open era of tennis began, when professionals were permitted to enter tournaments for prize money, Bueno was beset by a variety of arm and leg injuries. After a long retirement, she joined the pro tour and won her only professional title, the Japan Open, in 1974.

Bueno returned to Wimbledon in 1976 after a hiatus of seven years. She showed glimpses of her former brilliance, advancing to the fourth round before losing to Billie Jean King. Her inability to rise to the top of the rankings did not seem to bother her, however. "I have always loved tennis," she said following her Wimbledon loss to King, "I've had my glory." Bueno was enshrined in the International Tennis Hall of Fame in 1978.

Further Reading

Collins, Bud. *Bud Collins' Tennis Encyclopedia.* Canton, Mich.: Visible Ink Press, 1997.

"La Bueno." Beckenham Tennis Club Web site. Available online. URL: http://www.beckenhamtennisclub.co.uk/Maria_bueno_biog.php. Downloaded on June 19, 2006.

"Maria Bueno." International Tennis Hall of Fame Web site. Available online. URL: http://www.tennisfame.org/enshrinees/maria_bueno.html. Downloaded on July 8, 2005.

Cabrera, Miguel
(José Miguel Cabrera)
(1983–) *baseball player*

One of the youngest players in Major League Baseball's 2003 season, Miguel Cabrera burst onto the scene to help power the resurgent Florida Marlins to an improbable World Series victory over the New York Yankees. He was born José Miguel Cabrera in Maracay, Venezuela, on April 18, 1983. Cabrera's mother, Gregoria, played for 12 years on the Venezuelan National Softball Team and met Cabrera's father, José Miguel, on a baseball field. Three of Cabrera's uncles played professional baseball in the United States. One of them, José Torres, said of young Miguel, "When kids are born in Venezuela parents put a bat and a ball in the crib. But we also put a glove under his arm."

Cabrera began playing organized baseball before he started kindergarten. He practiced on a baseball field next to his house in the hardscrabble La Padrera barrio of Maracay, a city of 600,000 located at the foot of Venezuela's coastal mountain range. By age 14, he had developed into Venezuela's most highly sought-after prospect. At the age of 16, Cabrera signed a contract with the Florida Marlins that included a $1.8 million bonus, the largest ever paid to a Venezuelan player.

Once in the minor leagues, Cabrera played most games at shortstop, though he demonstrated his versatility by excelling at third base and in the outfield. He also showed an amazing array of offensive skills—speed, power to all fields, and a keen hitting eye—that prompted the struggling Marlins to call him up to the majors only two months after his 20th birthday. On June 20, 2003, Cabrera made his major league debut, hitting a game-winning home run to defeat the Tampa Bay Devil Rays. That win lifted the Marlins record to 37-39. With Cabrera playing almost every day, they proceeded to win almost 63 percent of their remaining games, bringing the Marlins to a 91-71 record and a wild card berth in the National League playoffs.

Cabrera was even more spectacular in the playoffs. In the National League (NL) Championship Series, Cabrera played a critical role in the Marlins' comeback from trailing 3-1 to winning the series 4-3 over the Chicago Cubs. Cabrera, who moved from third base to right field in that series, hit .333 with three home runs, including a three-run shot in the first inning of the decisive game seven.

In the 2003 World Series, Cabrera continued his heroics, following a pitch from Yankees superstar pitcher Roger Clemens that almost hit him, with a two-run home run in the Marlins' game four victory over the New York Yankees. The Marlins eventually won the World Series 4-2.

Expectations were high for Cabrera entering the 2004 season, and he did not disappoint. Cabrera made the NL All-Star team and finished the season with 33 home runs, 112 runs batted in (RBIs), and 101 runs scored, becoming only the eighth player in baseball history to record a

30-100-100 season before the age of 22, joining a group that includes Jimmie Foxx, Ted Williams, and ALEX RODRIGUEZ.

Cabrera continued his brilliance in the 2005 season, repeating as a National League All-Star while playing in all but four of Florida's games and ranking in the top 10 in the NL in hits (198; second), batting (.323; third), home runs (33; ninth), RBIs (116; fourth), and batting (.323; ninth). Cabrera further burnished his reputation as one of Major League Baseball's greatest young players in 2006, finishing second in the National League in batting (.339) and ninth in RBIs (114), while helping the surprisingly young Marlins to compete for a playoff spot late into the season.

Further Reading

Baxter, Kevin. "Natural Talent from the Start." *Miami Herald,* 15 January 2005, p. 15C.
"Miguel Cabrera." Florida Marlins Web site. Available online. URL: http://florida.marlins.mlb.com/NASApp/mlb/team/player_career.jsp?player_id=408234. Downloaded on July 8, 2005.
Schmuck, Peter. "Florida's Miguel Cabrera: A Star in the Making: At 21, Marlins Right-handed Hitting Slugger Has Fun Making the Game Look Easy and Promises to Make a Big Impact in the Majors." *Baseball Digest,* August 2004.

Camacho, Héctor
(Héctor Luis Camacho, Macho Camacho)
(1962–) *boxer*

A lightning-quick boxer who was a three-time world champion, Héctor "Macho" Camacho had a boisterous and flamboyant style in and out of the ring that drew intense reactions from admirers and critics. He was born Héctor Luis Camacho on May 24, 1962, in Bayamón, Puerto Rico. As a child, he moved with his family to the eastern Manhattan section of New York City known as Spanish Harlem. Of his hardscrabble childhood neighborhood, Camacho later said, "When you grow up in the ghetto, you've got to be tough or fast. Luckily for me I was both."

He spent much of his time as an adolescent at the Boys Club, where he emulated martial arts movie star Bruce Lee and eventually earned a second-degree black belt in American Go-Ju karate. Camacho also developed his quickness and power to become one of the city's most promising teenage boxers. In 1978, Camacho won the local Golden Gloves competition, the oldest and most prestigious national amateur boxing tournament. That year, he also fathered the first of his four sons, Héctor, Jr., and served three and a half months in jail for an auto theft conviction.

Camacho won the first professional fight of his career in New York's Felt Forum on September 12, 1980. He proceeded to win his next 21 fights (13 by knockout) before gaining his first chance to win the World Boxing Council's (WBC) junior lightweight title in a bout with Rafael "Bazooka" Limón in San Juan, Puerto Rico, on August 7, 1983. Camacho knocked down Limón in the first and third rounds before the referee stopped the fight in the fifth and awarded the victory to Camacho.

Camacho remained undefeated throughout the entire decade of the 1980s, picking up the WBC lightweight title along the way in an August 10, 1985, victory over José Luis Ramírez in Las Vegas. During this time he became almost exclusively known by the nickname "Macho" and became almost as famous for his flashy robes with matching sequined shoes and trunks as he was for his devastating combination of power and speed in the ring. Camacho added a third boxing title when he won a unanimous decision over Vinnie Pazienza in Atlantic City, New Jersey, on February 3, 1990, for the World Boxing Organization (WBO) light welterweight championship.

Just over a year later, however, Camacho suffered his first defeat in 40 pro fights, when he lost to Greg Haugen in Las Vegas in a split decision (two of the three judges scoring in favor of Haugen). Camacho regained that title from Haugen less than three months later in Reno, Nevada, setting up a battle with legendary Mexican champion Julio César Chávez on September 12, 1992, in Las Vegas. Camacho, who entered the ring for this much-anticipated fight dressed in a complete Captain America themed ensemble, lost a unanimous decision that night, charting a 10-year course of losses in marquee fights and wins only in second-tier bouts.

On January 29, 1994, Camacho lost a unanimous decision to young welterweight champion Félix Trinidad in Las Vegas. He defeated boxing legends Roberto Durán in 1996 and Sugar Ray Leonard in 1997, both long after those fighters' primes. Camacho's last grasp at big time boxing glory was a unanimous decision loss to Oscar De La Hoya on September 13, 1997, in Las Vegas.

Camacho continued to fight and win over the next seven years, though he was more often in the sports pages for arrests for drug possession, domestic violence, and drunken driving. By late 2004, Camacho was still fighting, though he had been increasingly focusing on training his oldest son, boxer Héctor "Machito" Camacho, Jr.

In January 2005, Camacho was sought by police in Biloxi, Mississippi, for the burglary of a computer store. When Camacho was arrested, he was found in a $35-a-night hotel with a stash of Ecstasy pills, an illicit synthetic drug known for its mood-altering and hallucinogenic properties. He was soon released on bail, though his legacy as one of the greatest fighters of his time, as evidenced by his 78-5-2 record, had been tarnished.

Further Reading

Fitzgerald, Robin. "Camacho Denies Drug Ties." *Biloxi Sun Herald,* 12 January 2005, p. A1.

"Hector 'Macho' Camacho." Latino Legends in Sports Web site. Available online. URL: http://www.latinosportslegends.com/stats/boxing/Camacho_Hector_career_boxing_record.htm. Downloaded on July 8, 2005.

Smith, Geroge Diaz. "Boxing: Once Upon a Macho Time." Ringside Report Web site. Available online. URL: http://www.ringsidereport.com/Smith11420052.htm. Downloaded on July 8, 2005.

Campos, Jorge
(1966–   ) *soccer player*

The top Mexican soccer goalie in the 1990s, Jorge Campos is renowned not only for his skill defending the net but also for his flashy jerseys and unique ability to contribute on offense. He was born on October 15, 1966, in Acapulco, Mexico. Campos grew up in the picturesque tourist destination on Mexico's southern Pacific coast, taking part in the most popular sports in that region—surfing and soccer.

When Campos was 14 years old, he played goalie for a team coached by his father. Although he excelled as a goalie, he repeatedly urged his father, Álvaro, to let him play forward. Eventually his father complied, and Campos demonstrated offensive skills, which he would flash during his illustrious career. Campos would later explain, "A forward has more chance to express his joy at scoring than a goal keeper does at saving."

However, saving is what would make Campos one of Mexico's greatest soccer players of his generation. At 5'9" and about 150 pounds, Campos was not the typical physically imposing net minder. He used extraordinary quickness, athleticism, and savvy to earn an invitation to join the UNAM (Universidad Nacional Autónoma de México) club team in 1989 as a goalie, though he managed to leave the team with 14 goals as a forward. He remained with UNAM for four more years, playing primarily in goal but still scored at least six goals each season.

In 1994, Campos was named to the Mexican national team. He had a 9-2-1 record in World Cup qualifying games, including seven shutouts. His improvisational and aggressive style that often found him straying from the net aided the Mexican offensive attack but also led to criticism. Late in the 1994 qualifying game in which Mexico had a 1-0 lead late in the contest, Campos carelessly played a ball near the net, leading to a goal and a 1-1 tie. The next morning's headline in a Mexican sports daily announced, "One goal for Mexico, one blunder for Campos." Responding to such criticism, Mexican coach Miguel Mejía Barón reflected the feelings of most Mexican fans, saying, "We accept the risks he takes since he's so fast and supple."

Campos shined in the 1994 World Cup held in the United States. Mexico emerged from the first round with a 1-1-1 record following games in which Campos allowed only three total goals (1-0 loss to Norway, 2-1 win over Ireland, and 1-1 tie with Italy). Mexico failed to reach the quarterfinals after losing a shootout following a 1-1 tie with Bulgaria.

Along with the adulation that accompanied being Mexico's top goalie, Campos was famous for his specially made uniforms featuring fluorescent neon colors and spectacular designs. During much of the 1990s, replicas of Campos's brightly hued jerseys were as popular with Mexican children as Michael Jordan's were in the United States. Critics of Campos ridiculed these jerseys, charging that he looked like a jockey or a clown and suggesting that they gave him an unfair advantage because of the way they helped him blend into the bright colors of stadium crowds. Campos explained that the jerseys allowed him to express his passion for the game and his background, noting, "People tell me 'you act like a kid!' That's because I still feel like a kid . . . I like bright colors because they remind me of my homeland in Acapulco."

In 1996, Campos joined the Los Angeles Galaxy in the fledgling Major League Soccer (MLS) in the United States. Campos helped lead the Galaxy to a 19-13 record and first place in the Western Conference. He also made headlines by playing two entire games in one day—one for the Mexican national team in the daytime and the other for the Galaxy at night. With Campos in goal, the Galaxy led 2-0 in the second half of the MLS Cup game, before DC United rallied for two goals and later won the game in overtime. Two years later, Campos was traded to the expansion Chicago Fire, where he helped the team to the MLS Cup, though

he did not play in the Fire's 2-0 championship victory over DC United.

In 1998, Campos was again Mexico's goalie in the World Cup played in France. He helped lead Mexico to the second round with a 1-0-2 record (a 3-1 win over South Korea and 2-2 ties with Belgium and Holland) when the team was eliminated by eventual runner-up Germany (2-1). He returned to the World Cup in 2002 held in Japan and South Korea, though as a backup. He did not see action as Mexico was again knocked out in the second round—this time in a huge upset to the United States.

In 1999, Campos's wealth and fame made his family a target of Mexican kidnappers, who abducted his father. After a frightening few weeks of uncertainty, the kidnappers released Álvaro when an undisclosed ransom was reportedly paid to them.

Campos remains very active in soccer. He was the assistant coach for the Mexican national team in 2004. Also in 2004, he starred in the MLS Celebration Game, leading a comeback for the world legends to a 2-2 tie with the U.S. legends by making several incredible saves and assisting on the game-tying goal. He currently works as a commentator for soccer broadcasts for ESPN Deportes, the Spanish-language outlet of the popular sports network.

Further Reading

Halpin, Jason. "Campos Helps World Team Draw USA Former Galaxy, Fire Goalkeeper Saves PK, Assists on Game-tying Goal." Major League Soccer Web site. Available online. URL: http://www.mlsnet.com/MLS/news/mls_events_news.jsp?ymd=20040731&content_i d=10178&vkey=allstar2004&fext=.jsp. Downloaded on July 8, 2005.

"Mexican Gang Frees Soccer Star's Father." *New York Times,* 24 February 1999, p. A8.

"23 Campos, Jorge." FIFA World Cup 2002 Web site. Available online. URL: http://2002.fifaworldcup.yahoo.com/02/en/t/t/pl/47245/. Downloaded on July 8, 2005.

Canseco, Jose
(José Canseco)
(1964–) *baseball player*

A muscular and fleet hitter who was the first player in Major League Baseball history to bash 40 home runs and steal 40 bases in the same season, Jose Canseco powered the winning Oakland A's of the late 1980s and early 1990s but later rocked baseball with a book detailing the rampant steroid use by himself and others. He was born on July 2, 1964, in Havana, Cuba. Canseco's father, José, Sr., a former oil company executive who lost his job after the Cuban Revolution, moved with his wife, Bárbara, and their children to Miami before young José was one year old.

A tall, skinny youth, Canseco did not play on the Coral Park High School varsity baseball team until his senior year, when he impressed scouts enough that the Oakland A's selected him in the 13th round of the 1982 Major League Baseball amateur draft. Canseco surprised A's officials with how quickly he rose through the minors by displaying a combination of speed and power that helped him earn recognition as the Minor League Player of the Year in 1985 after batting .333 and blasting 36 home runs with 127 runs batted in (RBIs) in only 118 games.

Canseco made his major league debut on September 2, 1985, and enjoyed a solid final month of the season before returning in 1986 as one of the most highly touted rookie prospects in baseball. Although he struggled with his batting average (.240), Canseco showed his prodigious power in his first full season in the majors, hitting 33 home runs, driving in 117 runs, and winning the 1986 American League (AL) Rookie of the Year award. He also displayed a penchant for the limelight, enjoying the crowds of fans, reporters, and even players who had assembled just to watch the 6'4", 200-plus-pound outfielder launch home runs in batting practice. Commented Lou Piniella, the New York Yankees manager in 1986, "I think the next time we play them, I might tell my pitchers they shouldn't watch him in BP [batting practice]. It can be a little intimidating."

Jose Canseco displays the stroke that made him one of the most feared hitters of the 1980s and 1990s. *(National Baseball Hall of Fame Library)*

In 1987, Canseco again produced impressive power statistics, hitting 31 home runs and finishing sixth in the AL with 113 RBIs, though his batting average finished at a mediocre .257 and his heavy, undisciplined swing led to 157 strikeouts. Canseco put it all together offensively in 1988 and, with the help of teammate and fellow "Bash Brother" Mark McGwire, led Oakland to 100 wins and the AL West championship. That season, Canseco batted .307, led the AL with 42 home runs and 124 RBIs, stole 40 bases (becoming the first player in major league history to have 40 home runs and 40 steals in the same season), and was the runaway winner of the AL Most Valuable Player (MVP) award.

Canseco followed this dream season with three home runs and a four-game American League Championship Series (ALCS) win over the Boston

Red Sox. In the 1988 World Series pitting Oakland against the Los Angeles Dodgers, Canseco drilled a second-inning grand slam in a game one A's loss, best remembered for the dramatic game-winning home run hit by the Dodgers' Kirk Gibson. Canseco failed to get another hit, finishing the series with a .053 batting average in Oakland's five-game defeat to Los Angeles.

Canseco missed most of the 1989 season after suffering a broken wrist but did return to play in 65 games, hitting 17 home runs and driving in 57 runs to help the A's repeat as AL West champions. In the ALCS versus the Toronto Blue Jays, Canseco became the first player to hit a home run into the fifth deck of Toronto's SkyDome with a blast estimated at 500 feet. Canseco then batted .357 and drove in three runs as Oakland swept the San Francisco Giants in four games to win the 1989 World Series.

Over the next two seasons, Canseco continued to display his hitting prowess, averaging more than 40 home runs and 110 RBIs and helping lead the A's to a third consecutive AL pennant before losing to the Cincinnati Reds in the 1990 World Series. He also topped the AL in home runs in 1991 with 44. However, Canseco was increasingly becoming a distraction off the field as a result of whispered accusations of steroid use and charges of domestic abuse by his wife, Esther. His brash statements were often perceived as self-promotion, which rankled some opponents and teammates. Despite being only 28 and having been a Rookie of the Year, MVP, and three-time pennant winner, Canseco was traded by the A's to the Texas Rangers on August 31, 1992, for three players.

In his two seasons with the Rangers, Canseco played in just over half of the team's games. In 1993, he asked to pitch during a lopsided loss. He gave up three runs in one inning and tore ligaments in his right arm. Canseco was traded to Boston before the 1995 season and was a productive power hitter in part-time duty before being traded back to Oakland, where he spent the 1997 season. After signing free agent contracts with the

Toronto Blue Jays and Tampa Bay Devil Rays, respectively, in 1998 and 1999, Canseco enjoyed a brief resurgence, averaging 40 home runs and more than 100 RBIs a season. After brief, injury-plagued stints with the New York Yankees in 2000 (where he won a World Series ring in occasional duty) and the Chicago White Sox in 2001, Canseco's career was finished. His career total of 462 home runs places him 24th in major league history.

Although Canseco's playing days were over in 2001, he had an enormously significant impact on the game in 2005, when his book *Juiced: Wild Times, Rampant 'Roids, Smash Hits, and How Baseball Got Big* was published. In the book, Canseco contended that steroid use was pervasive in baseball and that he had used them to help create his famously muscular physique. Canseco also named players he claimed to have personally given steroid shots to or seen using steroids, including former teammates and stars McGwire, JUAN GONZÁLEZ, IVÁN RODRÍGUEZ, and RAFAEL PALMEIRO.

In March 2005, with his book climbing the *New York Times* best-seller list, Canseco appeared with McGwire and Palmeiro before a congressional committee investigating steroid use in professional sports. McGwire's conspicuously noncommittal answers to questions about his suspected use and Palmeiro's bold denials (contradicted months later by a positive steroid test and suspension) helped darken the reputations of the two players and jeopardized their chances for induction into the Baseball Hall of Fame.

Feeling redeemed, Canseco maintained a high profile as the book continued to sell briskly. Meanwhile, the issues of steroid use and more stringent testing for performance enhancement substances in professional sports remained prominent on the minds of baseball players, fans, and media.

Further Reading

Canseco, Jose. *Juiced: Wild Times, Rampant 'Roids, Smash Hits, and How Baseball Got Big.* New York: Regan Books, 2005.

"Jose Canseco." Baseball Reference Web site. Available online. URL: http://www.baseball-reference. com/c/cansejo01.shtml. Downloaded on January 15, 2006.

Price, S. L. "The Liars Club: The Congressional Hearings on Steroids in Baseball, the Bigger-than-Sports Story of the Year, Turned into a Three-ring Circus. And Only the Clown, Jose Canseco, May Have Told the Truth." *Sports Illustrated,* 26 December 2005, p. 25.

Reilly, Rick. "Whaddya Say, Jose? A's Slugger Jose Canseco Has Been Burned by the Spotlight, but He's Way Too Big to Hide from It." *Sports Illustrated,* 20 August 1990, p. 42.

Canto, Miguel
(1948–) *boxer*

An exciting fighter who overwhelmed his opponents with his attacking proficiency, Miguel Canto is considered by many experts the greatest flyweight champion in boxing history. He was born on January 30, 1948, in Mérida, Mexico, the capital and largest city on the northwest coast of the state of Yucatán. His professional career began at the age of 20 when he lost in a technical knockout to Raúl Hernández in Mérida. In 1970, however, Canto would become the Yucatán state flyweight champion when he won a decision over Vicente Pool.

Canto lost his first chance to gain the World Boxing Council's (WBC) flyweight title in a 15-round decision to Betulio González. He won the title on January 8, 1975, when he defeated Shoji Oguma in Sendai, Japan.

For four years, Canto went unbeaten in fights that took him from Mexico to Japan, Venezuela, Chile, and the United States. The 5'1" boxer, who never fought at more than 115 pounds, did not possess devastating power but used a high punch rate and savvy, steady style to set a flyweight division record of 14 consecutive successful title defenses. During that span, Canto avenged his

earlier defeat to González and beat Oguma two more times.

On March 18, 1979, the 30-year-old Canto's reign finally came to an end when he lost a 15-round decision to Chan Hee Park in Pusay, South Korea. Coming into the contest, Canto had more title defenses (14) than Park had fights (11). They met again six months later in Seoul, South Korea, in a bout that ended in a draw. Canto had eight more fights and lost half of them, including four of his last five.

Canto finished his career with a record of 61-9-4. He was enshrined in the International Boxing Hall of Fame in 1978.

Further Reading

"Miguel Canto." About.com. Available online. URL: http://boxing.about.com/gi/dynamic/offsite. htm?site=http://boxrec.com/boxer%5Fdisplay.php %3Fboxer%5Fid=009002. Downloaded on July 8, 2005.

"Miguel Canto." International Boxing Hall of Fame Web site. Available online. URL: http://www.ibhof. com/canto.htm. Downloaded on July 8, 2005.

Capilla, Joaquín
(1927–) *diver*

The only Latino ever to win an Olympic gold medal in diving, Joaquín Capilla won a total of four medals for Mexico covering three Olympic games between 1948 and 1956 and remains the most decorated of Mexican Olympians. He was born on December 23, 1927, in Mexico City. He grew up in the Mexican capital and demonstrated an early athletic aptitude, joining his brothers at a local pool where his father offered money to the boys for jumping from increasingly higher points. While practicing his diving at Mexico City's Chapultepec Park, Capilla was noticed by renowned diving trainer Mario Tovar, who soon became his instructor.

Under Tovar's guidance, Capilla practiced diving several hours a day. Capilla began competing in tournaments around the world by 1946. In 1948, Capilla was selected to represent Mexico at the Olympics in London, where he finished fourth in the springboard event but won the bronze medal in the high board (or platform), becoming the first Latino to win an Olympic medal in diving.

Capilla returned to the Olympics in 1952 in Helsinki, Finland, and competed despite suffering from an injured hand. Although he was injured and prohibited from wearing a protective glove, Capilla managed again to finish fourth in the springboard and win a medal, this time a silver, in the high board.

The 1956 Olympics in Melbourne, Australia, were the site of Capilla's greatest success, though it was marked by controversy. After recovering from a backward fall in competition—what he called a "childish mistake"—Capilla won a bronze medal in the springboard and a gold medal in the high board.

Capilla's victory came by three-hundredths of a point over silver medalist Gary Tobian of the United States, when Tobian received curiously low scores from the Russian and Hungarian judges. Though Tobian may have suffered from the intensity of athletic rivalry between the United States and the Soviet bloc nations during the cold war, Capilla reveled in his historic victory and was welcomed by thousands of elated Mexicans during a celebration at Mexico City's Revolution Monument upon his return.

Following the 1956 Olympics, Capilla retired from competition, married, and had a daughter. However, he struggled with alcoholism and eventually was divorced. Capilla later received treatment for his alcoholism and married a psychologist, whom he described as the only person who has "loved him for who he is and not what he did."

Further Reading

Aburto, Ivis. "Joaquin Capilla: Recuperar el piso." *Reforma,* 15 February 2003.

"The 1956 Olympics." Hickok Sports Web site. Available online. URL: http://www.hickoksports.com/history/ol1956.shtml. Downloaded on January 13, 2006.

Carew, Rod
(Rodney Cline Carew)
(1945–) *baseball player*

The 16th player in Major League Baseball history to accumulate more than 3,000 hits, Rod Carew combined artistic flair and scientific precision to earn seven hitting titles, a Rookie of the Year award, a Most Valuable Player (MVP) award, 18 consecutive All-Star Game appearances, and first ballot election to the Baseball Hall of Fame, solidifying his place as one of the greatest hitters in the history of baseball. He was born Rodney Cline Carew on October 1, 1945, on a train traveling through the Panama Canal Zone town of Gatun. His name was given to honor the man who delivered him, Dr. Rodney Cline, who exited the "whites only" section of the train to assist Carew's mother when she went into labor. Carew spent his childhood in Panama, later recalling, "There is a special sensation in getting good wood on the ball and driving it for a double down the left field line as the crowd in the ballpark rises to its feet and cheers. But I also remember how much fun I had as a skinny barefoot kid batting a tennis ball with a broomstick on a quiet, dusty street in Panama." Carew left Panama at the age of 16, when his mother moved the family to live with his godmother in an impoverished part of the Bronx in New York City.

Carew attended Washington High School in the Bronx. Reportedly, when a scout for the Minnesota Twins first saw Carew, he was playing baseball at a park across the street from Yankee Stadium. After a five-minute tryout, the scout turned to a colleague and said of the young, thin left-handed hitter, "Let's get him out of here and sign him before the Yankees see him."

Carew signed with the Twins one day after graduating from high school in 1964. He played three seasons in the Twins minor league system before making his major league debut on April 11, 1967, collecting his first hit off Baltimore Orioles star pitcher Dave McNally. He was named American League (AL) Rookie of the Year in a season highlighted by a five-hit game, a 15-game hitting streak, and the first of his 18 consecutive All-Star Game appearances.

Carew batted .273 in 1968 but followed with 15 consecutive seasons with a batting average above .300, an achievement exceeded in major league history only by Hall of Famers Ty Cobb, Stan Musial, and Honus Wagner. In 1969, Carew won the first of his seven batting titles with a .332 average, despite missing two weeks and several weekends for military commitments. That season he also tied the single season record with seven steals of home.

Rod Carew shows the unique batting precision that helped him earn seven American League batting titles. (National Baseball Hall of Fame Library)

Carew continued his torrid hitting in 1970, racing out to a .366 batting average after 51 games, when he was sidelined for the remainder of the season with torn ligaments in his right knee.

The Twins, who had won AL West titles in 1969 and 1970, struggled over the next two seasons, but its starting second baseman did not. In 1972, Carew employed his relaxed, crouched batting stance to win the first of four consecutive AL batting titles, joining Cobb as the only player ever to achieve that feat. His batting championship in 1972 remains the only one earned by a player without a home run. A uniquely skilled bunter, Carew collected hits on 27 of his 35 bunt attempts that season.

By the age of 28, Carew was regularly recognized as among the greatest hitters of his generation. Journeyman Chicago White Sox infielder Allen Bannister joked about Carew, "He's the only guy I know who can go four for three," and Oakland A's pitching star Ken Holtzman observed of Carew, "He has an uncanny ability to move the ball around as if the bat were some kind of magic wand."

Carew led the AL in hits in 1973 and in 1974, exceeding the gold standard of 200 each year, and he buried his closest competition for the AL batting crowns by hitting .350 and .364, respectively. In 1975, Carew changed positions, becoming a first baseman in an effort to prolong his career and improve the team's overall defense. He hit .359 to win another batting title and the next year had his string of batting crowns halted when George Brett of the Kansas City Royals edged him on the final day of the season.

Carew's best individual season was 1977, when he won the AL MVP award with a single season résumé rarely matched in excellence. He led the league in hitting, with a career high .388 average—52 points higher than the runner-up and the highest marks since Ted Williams hit .406 in 1941, the league leader in hits (239)—the most in the AL in 49 years. He was also league leader in runs (128) and triples (16) and enjoyed a career high 100 runs batted in (RBI).

Despite his personal excellence, Carew was frustrated by the Twins' mediocrity as well as by the notoriously cheapskate approach and racial attitudes of owner Calvin Griffith. Like many other black players, Carew had experienced racial bigotry in baseball, and he endured death threats following his marriage to his wife, Marilyn, a white Jewish woman with whom he had three daughters. Griffith, who once told a Minneapolis audience that he moved the team from Washington, D.C., because Minneapolis had "only 15,000 black people" and had "good hardworking white people," was widely disliked by Twins players including Carew, who openly feuded with him. Concerned that the Twins would never be champions while under Griffith's control, Carew threatened to leave when his contract expired. Worried that the team would get nothing in return for Carew, the Twins traded him to the California Angels for four young players on February 3, 1979.

In his first season with the Angels, Carew hit .318, helping lead the team to its first AL West title. In the AL Championship Series that the Angels lost to the Baltimore Orioles 3-1, Carew set a record for most hits in a four-game series with seven. In 1982, Carew hit .319 as the Angels again won the AL West title and met the Milwaukee Brewers in the American League Championship Series. Carew struggled in the series, in which the Angels became the first team to lose a championship series by losing three consecutive games after winning the first two.

His last great season came in 1983, when he got off to one of the best hitting starts in baseball history, batting .500 five weeks into the season. After battling through a variety of injuries, the 38-year-old Carew finished the season with an Angels' record .339 batting average, ranking second in the AL. On August 4, 1985, Carew singled off Minnesota's Frank Viola for his 3,000th hit. He retired following the 1985 season with 3,053 hits (the most by any player who never appeared in a World Series) and a career .328 batting average.

His number 29 was officially retired by both the Twins and Angels.

Carew's postplaying years included stints as the batting coach for the Angels and the Milwaukee Brewers, and he was also active in registering bone marrow donors in an effort to help fight leukemia, which claimed the life of the youngest of his three daughters, 17-year-old Michelle, in 1996. He was elected to the Baseball Hall of Fame in 1991 in his first year of eligibility. Undoubtedly destined to be forever remembered as among the greatest hitting tacticians in baseball history, Los Angeles sports writer Jim Murray captured the essence of Carew's legacy to baseball: "Rod Carew doesn't make hits," wrote Murray, "he composes them."

Further Reading

Berkow, Ira, and Rod Carew. *Carew*. New York: Simon & Schuster, 1979.

Carew, Rod. *Rod Carew's Art and Science of Hitting*. New York: Viking, 1986.

"Rod Carew." Baseball Reference Web site. Available online. URL: http://www.baseball-reference.com/c/carewro01.shtml. Downloaded on June 19, 2006.

"Rod Carew." National Baseball Hall of Fame Web site. Available online. URL: http://www.baseballhalloffame.org/hofers_and_honorees/hofer_bios/carew_rod.htm. Downloaded on July 8, 2005.

Strege, John. "Carew Saving Best for Last?" *Sporting News,* 9 May 1983, p. 24.

Carlos, John
(1945–) *sprinter*

The bronze medal winner in track's 200-meter event at the 1968 Olympics, John Carlos is best remembered for holding his left fist in the air at his medal ceremony in a display of support for civil rights in the United States. He was born on June 5, 1945, in New York City. His father, who was of Puerto Rican descent, owned a shop in the heart of Harlem, where Carlos grew up. In Harlem, he learned firsthand how even the famous black athletes, such as shop customers and Brooklyn Dodgers stars Jackie Robinson and Roy Campanella, often suffered from racist attitudes against blacks. Carlos excelled in the classroom and on the field, accepting a full track and field scholarship to attend East Texas State University (ETSU).

In his freshman year at ETSU, Carlos played a key role in helping the school win its first conference championship in track. Following that year, Carlos transferred to San Jose State University to train with renowned coach Lloyd "Bud" Winter. At San Jose State, Carlos befriended fellow sprinter and teammate Tommie Smith and campus activist Harry Edwards. In 1967, Carlos became a founding member of the Olympic Project for Human Rights (OPHR), a group organized by Edwards. The OPHR hoped to inspire a boycott of the 1968 Olympics in Mexico City to highlight the struggle of blacks in the United States and the injustices forced on black athletes. When one of their demands (that the apartheid nations of South Africa and Rhodesia be barred from the Olympics) was supported by the International Olympic Committee, momentum for the boycott diminished.

However, Carlos and Smith still sought to publicize the OPHR's mission. Carlos, who won the gold medal in the 200 meters at the 1967 Pan-American Games in Winnipeg, Canada, also won the 200 meters at the 1968 Olympic trials, further establishing himself as among the best sprinters in the world. On October 17, in the 200 meters final at the 1968 Olympics, Carlos placed third, behind gold medal winner Smith and Australian Peter Norman.

Following the race, Carlos took his place on the medal stand. As the U.S. flag was raised and the "Star Spangled Banner" began to honor the gold medal-winning American Smith, Carlos and Smith each silently thrust a fist into the air, stunning the crowd and the millions around the world watching on television. Norman, informed by his fellow medal winners of their intentions, also joined in the protest by wearing an OPHR patch.

American track star John Carlos (right) joins teammate Tommie Smith in making a Black Power salute on the medal stand at the 1968 Olympics in Mexico City. *(Library of Congress)*

The controversial demonstration was rife with symbolism. Carlos raised his left fist to combine with Smith's right fist in a formation of unity and power. They both wore only socks on their feet to represent the poverty of blacks around the world. Carlos wore his shirt open to honor the working-class blacks in the United States, and he carried beads, as he would later explain, ". . . (to honor) those individuals who were lynched or killed that no one said a prayer for . . . that were thrown off the side of boats in the middle passage."

The reaction to Carlos's gesture was intense. Though many supported his courage and message, most Americans sharply rejected it. Within two days, Carlos and Smith were suspended by their team and expelled from the Olympic Village by the International Olympic Committee. *Time* magazine ran a picture of the Olympic logo but replaced the Olympic motto—"Faster, Higher, Stronger"—with a reference to Carlos and Smith: "Angrier, Nastier, Uglier."

Carlos returned to the United States and, despite often being the object of scorn and threats, led San Jose State to the 1969 National Collegiate Athletic Association (NCAA) track and field championship with wins in the 100-yard dash, 220-yard dash, and as a member of the 4 × 110-yard relay team. After graduating from San Jose State, he tried professional football, playing one year for the Philadelphia Eagles before suffering a knee injury. He played two seasons in the Canadian Football League before retiring from athletic competition and beginning a career in education. He is now a counselor at Palm Springs High School in California. Carlos was inducted into the National Track and Field Hall of Fame in 2003.

In December 2003, Carlos reflected on his powerful, memorable, and controversial action on the medal stand in Mexico City more than 35 years earlier, saying "All athletes black, red, brown, yellow, and white need to do some research on their history: their own personal family . . . they need to find out how hard their ancestors had to work . . . and then they need to speak up. You got to step up to society when it's letting all its people down."

Further Reading

Jackson, C. D. *Why: The Biography of John Carlos.* Los Angeles: Milligan Books, 2000.

"John Carlos." USA Track and Field Web site. Available online. URL: http://www.usatf.org/HallOfFame/TF/showBio.asp?HOFIDs=195. Downloaded on July 8, 2005.

"Mexico City 1968: The World Is Watching." Canadian Broadcasting Corporation Web site. Available online. URL: http://archives.cbc.ca/IDC-1-41-1289-7330/sports/olympics_cbc/clip4TEST. Downloaded on July 8, 2005.

Zirin, Dave. "The Living Legacy of Mexico City: An Interview with John Carlos." Counterpunch Web site. Available online. URL: http://www.counterpunch.org/zirin11012003.html. Downloaded on July 8, 2005.

Casals, Rosie
(Rosemary Casals)
(1948–) *tennis player*

An undersized player whose aggressive style and dynamic personality helped lift women's tennis to new heights of popularity in the late 1960s and early 1970s, Rosie Casals ranked in the top 10 in 12 consecutive years between 1966 and 1977. She was born Rosemary Casals on September 16, 1948, in San Francisco, California. Casals, a distant relative of world-famous cello virtuoso Pablo Casals, received early instruction in tennis from her father, who had been a member of the El Salvador national soccer team. The rebellious nature that would later mark her public persona was evident in her teenage years, when Casals would often skip school to play tennis at Golden Gate Park and other public courts in San Francisco. She managed to graduate from high school only after receiving special permission from the school's principal, who allowed Casals to obtain her diploma a month early so she could play at Wimbledon.

From the mid-1960s to the early 1980s, Casals was one of the most exciting and influential players in women's tennis. She was ranked in the top 10 in the world every year from 1966 to 1977, including a high rank of number three in 1970. Although her speed, agility, and arsenal of effective strokes led her to U.S. Open finals in 1970 and 1971, Casals achieved her greatest success in doubles. Paired primarily with her good friend tennis legend Billie Jean King, Casals won five Wimbledon doubles titles (1967, 1968, 1970, 1971, and 1973) and four U.S. Open doubles championships (1967, 1971,

1974, and 1982). She also reached the doubles finals in grand slam tournaments 12 other times.

Casals was a fan favorite throughout her career. Author Grace Lichtenstein described Casals as "a pugnacious outcast . . . Like Pancho Gonzales years before her, she brought color and charisma, fire and fury to a sport that ladies and gentlemen were in the habit of applauding politely. You didn't applaud a Rosie Casals, you cheered her until your throat got hoarse . . . because [she] brought a gut-clutching excitement to the women's game, an excitement that was the natural extension of her personality."

Her dynamic play was often accented with outfits that upset the tennis establishment and delighted legions of fans. In addition to her brightly colored bandanas displayed at countless competitions, Casals wore a spangled, sequined, multicolored dress during competition at Wimbledon in 1972 that led the referee to order Casals to change. She complied, though later commented regarding the incident, "I loved to get their goat and enjoyed the whole scene."

Casals also made waves with her involvement in the creation of the Virginia Slims women's tennis circuit that began in the fall of 1970. With King and six others, Casals helped create this tour to increase the opportunities and pay for women in tennis. In 1971, the Slims tour (named for the sponsoring cigarette brand) played matches in 19 cities with a total purse of more than $300,000. By contrast, Casals made only $31,750 when she lost in the U.S. Open finals the year before. The original Virginia Slims tour has had many different sponsors since its inception, but it remains in existence and is often credited with providing a critical catalyst in boosting the enormous growth in popularity and prize money in women's tennis over the past 40 years.

Casals retired in 1988 with a total of 11 professional singles titles and 112 doubles championships, second in history only to Martina Navratilova's 162 doubles titles. Casals was inducted into the International Tennis Hall of Fame in 1996 and remains active in tennis as the president of her own sports promotion company, Sportswoman, Inc., and as

a regular competitor at the Senior Invitational at Wimbledon and the U.S. Open.

Further Reading
Lichtenstien, Grace. *A Long Way Baby.* New York: Morrow, 1974.
"Rosie Casals." International Tennis Hall of Fame Web site. Available online. URL: http://www.tennisfame.org/enshrinees/rosie_casals.html. Downloaded on July 8, 2005.
"Rosie Casals." Women's Tennis Association Web site. Available online. http://www.sonyericssonwtatour.com/players/playerprofiles/PlayerBio.asp?ID=&Ent ityID=1&CustomerID=0&OrderID=0& ReturnURL=/&Play erID=30070. Downloaded on June 19, 2006.

Casillas, Tony
(1963–   ) *football player*

A dominant college defensive lineman for the 1985 National Collegiate Athletic Association (NCAA) champion Oklahoma Sooners, Tony Casillas was later a key contributor on two Super Bowl–winning Dallas Cowboys teams. He was born on October 26, 1963, in Tulsa, Oklahoma. The Mexican-American Casillas grew up in Tulsa, becoming a standout on the football field for East Central High School. He attracted football scholarships from colleges around the nation but elected to stay in state and play for the University of Oklahoma.

Casillas's head coach at Oklahoma, Barry Switzer, described him as "born to play nose tackle." At 6'3" and more than 260 pounds, Casillas loomed in the middle of the defensive line with a combination of strength and quickness that punished the opposition. In his junior year, Casillas was named a consensus first team All-Big Eight and All-America selection. As a senior, Casillas led Oklahoma to the NCAA Championship, racking up first team All-Big Eight, All-American, and Academic All-Big Eight honors, as well as receiving the Lombardi Award, given to the nation's top lineman. Casillas, who graduated from Oklahoma with a bachelor's degree in public relations, finished his college football career with 18 career sacks and 213 total tackles.

In the 1986 National Football League (NFL) draft, the Atlanta Falcons selected Casillas with the second pick of the first round. He enjoyed a stellar rookie season, starting every game at nose tackle and compiling more than 100 tackles. Casillas's style of play, described by sports writer Paul Attner as "absorbing blocks and plugging holes like a human sacrificial lamb," allowed teammates better opportunities to make tackles.

Though injuries limited his second season contribution to just over half of the Falcons' games, Casillas continued his dominance in 1988 and 1989, starting every game and averaging more than 130 tackles a season. However, Casillas's relationship with his head coach, Jerry Glanville, was strained, and his attitude became questioned by teammates, media, and fans.

Following a severe drop-off in production during the 1990 season, Casillas was becoming increasingly known for his squabbles over his contract, holding out of training camp, being suspended for missing a team flight, and bickering with Glanville. Just prior to training camp in 1991, Casillas announced that he would retire, though he privately told Falcons management that he would play if traded. A few days later, Atlanta sent him to the Dallas Cowboys for second- and eighth-round draft picks.

In Dallas, Casillas was reborn, starting 45 of the 46 games in which he played, seamlessly adjusting to his new position of defensive tackle. The Cowboys were ranked 18th (of 28 teams) in rushing defense the year before Casillas arrived, and they ranked first in the league just two years later. Cowboys defensive coordinator Dave Wannstedt reflected on Casillas's value by saying, "When people are preparing their run offense against us, the first guy they look at is Tony. They realize they have to stop him first, and you can't do it with one blocker."

Casillas's best game for Dallas may have been his three-sack performance in the Cowboys' 1993

National Football Conference championship win over the San Francisco 49ers, propelling Dallas to Super Bowl XXVII, where they defeated the Buffalo Bills. Casillas followed that season with another solid effort in the 1993 season, which again ended with a Dallas Super Bowl victory over Buffalo.

Casillas left Dallas as a free agent before the 1994 season to sign with the New York Jets. He struggled through two lackluster campaigns in New York before signing a lucrative free-agent contract with the Kansas City Chiefs. However, Casillas never reported to the Chiefs, citing "personal reasons." In fact, Casillas decided that he wanted to return to Dallas, which had recently hired his college coach, Barry Switzer, as its head coach. With Kansas City's approval, the NFL voided the contract, and Casillas returned to Dallas, where he played two more seasons. Casillas retired prior to the 1998 season, and he was inducted into the College Football Hall of Fame in 2004.

Further Reading

Bayless, Skip. *Hell-Bent: The Crazy Truth About the "Win or Else" Dallas Cowboys.* New York: HarperCollins, 1996.

"Casillas Receives On-Campus Salute." National Football Foundation and College Hall of Fame Web site. Available online. URL: http://www.footballfoundation.com/news.php?id=457. Downloaded on June 22, 2006.

O'Donnell, Chuck. "Tony Casillas—The Game I'll Never Forget." *Football Digest,* September 2003.

Castilla, Vinny
(Vinicio Soria Castilla)
(1967–   ) *baseball player*

A powerful third baseman who became a fan favorite of the expansion Colorado Rockies in the mid-1990s, Vinny Castilla has hit more home runs and driven in more runs than any other Mexican-born player in Major League Baseball history. He was born Vinicio Soria Castilla on July 4, 1967, in Oaxaca, Mexico. Castilla grew up in Oaxaca, excelling at baseball, becoming the most valuable player of his high school team and starring for the Benito Juárez University team. He played professionally for the Saraperos de Saltillo before signing with the Atlanta Braves organization in 1990. A year later, he appeared in just 12 games for the Braves, managing just one hit in five at-bats.

Castilla played sparingly in 1992 as well, leading the Braves to leave him unprotected in Major League Baseball's 1992 expansion draft. He was selected by the Colorado Rockies, and by midseason of the team's first campaign in 1993, he became the team's starting shortstop. Castilla's promising start in 1994 was impeded by injuries and frequent position changes.

Castilla's career took off after he became the Rockies starting third baseman in 1995, a season in which he hit .309 with 32 home runs and 90 runs batted in (RBIs), helping lead the Rockies to the playoffs in only their third year. From 1996 to 1999, Castilla was one of the top third basemen in the majors, missing only nine games while hitting 159 home runs and ranking in the top 10 in RBIs three times. During this time, Castilla also became the face of the Rockies team and a favorite among the team's fans, who consistently ranked among the league leaders in attendance.

Early in the 1999 season, the Rockies played a regular season series against the San Diego Padres in Monterrey, Mexico. A Mexican newspaper, *El Imparcial,* reflected Castilla's popularity in his native country with a headline hailing him as *"el Jordan mexicano"* (the Michael Jordan of Mexico). He received standing ovations from the fans when his name was announced in the lineup and even more cheers following a performance in which he had three singles and a double in a Rockies win.

Although Castilla had a strong season in 1999, his high salary combined with the Rockies' poor performance prompted the team to trade him to the Tampa Bay Devil Rays on December 13, 1999. Castilla had a miserable tenure in Tampa, hitting only .221 with six home runs in an injury-plagued 2000 season. When Castilla began 2001 poorly,

the Devil Rays released him. He was signed a few days later by the Houston Astros.

Back in the National League, Castilla reverted to his previous form, helping power the Astros to the 2001 playoffs. In December 2001, Castilla returned to the team that first signed him, the Atlanta Braves. Over the next two seasons, he was the starting third baseman for the Braves division champion teams, though his offensive statistics were well below his career averages.

Following his second stint with the Braves, the 36-year-old Castilla again joined the Colorado Rockies, signing a free agent contract before the 2004 season. Playing for the team with which he enjoyed his greatest success, Castilla had a remarkable season, hitting 31 home runs and leading the National League with 131 RBIs.

In 2005, Castilla was a member of the Washington Nationals inaugural team (the franchise had relocated from Montreal after the 2004 season) and batted .319 with 12 home runs and 66 RBIs. Following that season, Castilla signed as a free agent with the San Diego Padres. He struggled with the Padres before being released. Castilla then finished his career with the Colorado Rockies, for whom he became a special assistant after his retirement as a player.

Further Reading

Knisley, Michael. "Mexican Treasure—Baseball Player Vinny Castilla." *Sporting News,* 12 April 1999.
"Vinny Castilla." Baseball Library Web site. Available online. URL: http://www.baseballlibrary.com/baseballlibrary/ballplayers/C/Castilla_Vinny.stm. Downloaded on July 8, 2005.

Castroneves, Hélio
(Spiderman)
(1975–) *auto racer*

The 2001 and 2002 winner of the Indianapolis 500, Hélio Castroneves is the first driver ever to win that prestigious auto race in his first two starts. He was born on May 10, 1975, in São Paulo,

Brazil. At the age of 12, Castroneves began racing go-carts, winning the Brazilian Karting Championships just two years later. He quickly progressed in the world of auto racing, becoming one of the top drivers on the Formula Three circuit (featuring single-seat vehicles smaller than the more renowned Formula One cars).

At the age of 23, Castroneves finished second in CART (Championship Auto Racing Teams) Rookie of the Year standings, driving for Bettenhausen Motorsports. His steady climb in the CART standings continued as he jumped from a 15th place overall ranking in 1999, to seventh in 2000, and to fourth in 2001. The highlight of this period for Castroneves came on June 18, 2000, when he won his first career CART victory in Detroit. Castroneves marked that win by hopping out of his car, climbing the fence separating the cheering fans from the racetrack, and pumping his fist. This celebration has been repeated by Castroneves after other victories and has earned him the nickname "Spiderman."

Castroneves joined the Indy Car Series racing circuit in 2001 and made an immediate impact on May 2 by winning the Indianapolis 500, becoming only the eighth rookie to win that race. On May 26, 2002, Castroneves won the Indianapolis 500 again, becoming only the fifth person to win the race in consecutive years and the first since racing legend Al Unser, Sr., accomplished the feat in 1971.

The astonishing success Castroneves enjoyed in competition brought exposure to racing and publicity to Castroneves. The *New York Times* echoed the thoughts of many racing fans, noting, "Helio Castroneves is the perfect defending Indy [Indianapolis 500] champion. He is charismatic. He is handsome. He loves the limelight." He was featured in *People* magazine's popular "Sexiest Man Alive" issue, as well as in the pages of many other top sports, fashion, and women's magazines.

In 2003, Castroneves came within three-tenths of a second of becoming the first racer ever to win the Indianapolis 500 three consecutive years. His second-place finish that season was accompanied by 10 other top-10 finishes. In 2004, Castroneves went without a victory until winning the Texas 500, the final race of the Indy Car Series season. Following that win, Castroneves pleased fans by performing his signature fence climb, reflecting the skill and colorful personality that have placed him among the best and most popular drivers in the world.

Castroneves followed that victory with a successful 2005 season, finishing in the top five in eight of the 17 races in which he participated, including one victory. He enjoyed even greater success in 2006, winning four of the 14 Indy Car Series races and finishing first among all racers in total points.

Further Reading

Cavin, Curt. "Castroneves Avoids Fence, Then Climbs It." *Indianapolis Star,* 26 June 2005.

Helio Castroneves Web site. Available online. URL: http://www.heliocastroneves.com.br. Downloaded on July 8, 2005.

O'Malley, J. J. "Casting His Web: This Summer's Other 'Spider-Man', Helio Castroneves, Is Swinging into the Hearts of American Race Fans." *Auto Racing Digest,* October–November 2002, p.

Cepeda, Orlando
(Baby Bull, Cha Cha)
(1937–   ) *baseball player*

The unanimous selection for 1958 National League (NL) Rookie of the Year and the 1967 NL Most Valuable Player (MVP), Orlando Cepeda helped lead three teams to the World Series during the 1960s, and in 1999, he became only the second Puerto Rican ever inducted into the Baseball Hall of Fame.

He was born on September 17, 1937, in Ponce, Puerto Rico. His father was Pedro "Perucho" Cepeda, a legendary Puerto Rican League slugger sometimes referred to as "the Babe Ruth of the Caribbean."

As a child, Cepeda initially resisted playing baseball because of the pressure that the inevitable comparisons to his father would bring. With the encouragement of his father and mother, Carmen, Cepeda did play baseball, however, and he excelled, signing a professional contract with the New York Giants prior to the 1955 season.

The 6', 200-plus-pound Cepeda moved up the Giants' farm system rapidly, impressing team officials so much that he was named the starting first baseman prior to the 1958 season, the team's first in its new home of San Francisco. In his major league debut on April 15, Cepeda became the first player to hit a regular season home run on the West Coast when he connected off Los Angeles Dodgers pitching ace Don Drysdale for the first of his 379 career home runs.

This auspicious start to his rookie season was followed by more success as Cepeda, commonly called "Baby Bull" for his sturdy intensity and strength, finished the year with a .312 batting average, 25 home runs, 96 runs batted in (RBIs), and an NL-leading 38 doubles. Late in the season, Giants manager Bill Rigney noted of Cepeda, "He's the best young right handed power hitter I've ever seen."

In fact, Rigney's praise of Cepeda's early power stands up to statistical analysis. Following Cepeda's first five seasons in the majors (1958–62), he had more RBIs (553) than Willie Mays (514), Ernie Banks (512), and Hank Aaron (494) after their first five seasons. Cepeda enjoyed playing alongside fellow Giants standouts Mays, FELIPE ALOU, JUAN MARICHAL, and Willie McCovey and earned All-Star Game appearances in each of these seasons, including a prolific 1961 campaign in which he hit .311 and led the NL with 46 home runs and 142 RBIs. He followed that with a .306 batting average, 35 home runs, and 114 RBIs in the Giants' pennant-winning 1962 season.

After the Giants fell to the New York Yankees four games to three in the 1962 World Series, Cepeda returned to Puerto Rico, as he usually did, to play winter league baseball in order to stay in shape and earn extra money. During a workout late in 1962, Cepeda injured his knee. He missed only 26 games over the next two seasons and continued to record elite-level statistics, but the pain was becoming increasingly difficult to bear. This challenge compounded Cepeda's already tense relationship with Giants manager Alvin Dark, who Cepeda believed was bigoted toward Latino and black players.

In 1965, Cepeda played in only 33 games due to his knee injury, which had earned him a reputation among some as a malingerer. On May 8, 1966, Cepeda was traded by the Giants to the St. Louis Cardinals for starting pitcher Ray Sadecki. Cepeda, now sometimes referred to as "Cha Cha" because of his love of salsa music, which he played in the clubhouse before and after games, was rejuvenated in St. Louis. In 1967, he won the NL MVP Award after hitting .325, with 25 home runs and 111 RBIs, helping power the Cardinals to a World Series victory over the Boston Red Sox. Cepeda's offensive numbers dropped in 1968, but he still played a critical role in helping the Cardinals reach another World Series, where they fell to the Detroit Tigers.

Cepeda was traded to the Atlanta Braves for Joe Torre prior to the 1969 season. He had a strong 1970 season before knee injuries again cut into his production, leading to a trade to the Oakland Athletics, for whom he appeared in only three games. Cepeda signed a free-agent contract with the Boston Red Sox before the 1973 season, in which he batted .289, with 20 home runs and 86 RBIs. He briefly played for the Kansas City Royals in 1974 before being released.

In 1975, the newly retired Cepeda was arrested at the airport in San Juan, Puerto Rico, for claiming two packages containing 165 pounds of marijuana. He admitted his guilt and spent 10 months in a federal prison in Florida. His marriage broke up, he suffered financially, and he was shunned by many former friends in Puerto Rico and in baseball. Cepeda's prospects for election into the Baseball Hall of Fame also were severely diminished by the arrest and incarceration.

In the 1980s, Cepeda sought to rehabilitate himself and his public image. He began practicing Buddhism and returned to the San Francisco area, where he eventually became a community relations representative for the Giants.

In 1999, Cepeda's number 30 jersey was retired by the Giants, and he was elected by the veterans committee to the Hall of Fame. Upon his enshrinement in the Hall of Fame, Cepeda joined ROBERTO CLEMENTE as the only members of baseball's most prestigious institution to come from Puerto Rico.

Further Reading

Cepeda, Orlando. *Baby Bull: From Hardball to Hard Time and Back.* Lanham, Md.: Rowman & Littlefield, 1998.

"Induction Speeches: Orlando Cepeda." National Baseball Hall of Fame Web site. Available online. URL: http://www.baseballhalloffame.org/hof_weekend/1999/speeches/cepeda_orlando.htm. Downloaded on July 8, 2005.

Markusen, Bruce. *The Orlando Cepeda Story.* Houston, Tex.: Pinata Books, 2001.

Further Viewing

Viva Cepeda. Brooklyn, N.Y.: Cinemar Productions, 2000.

Cervantes, Antonio
(Kid Pambele)
(1945–) *boxer*

The greatest boxing champion ever to come from Colombia, Antonio Cervantes used a powerful punching style to become a two-time world junior welterweight champion. He was born on December 23, 1945, in San Basilio de Palenque, Colombia. Cervantes, who is black (blacks are a minority in Colombia), grew up in the slums of San Basilio de Palenque, the site of the first slave revolt in Latin America (1603), selling contraband cigarettes and shining shoes in order to stave off hunger. He also

began developing his impressive natural athletic skills after meeting boxing trainer Carmelo Prada. With Prada helping shape his style, Cervantes won two of his first three amateur bouts.

Cervantes entered the ring as a professional for the first time at the age of 18 on January 31, 1964. He won that fight and 26 of his next 31. All of those fights took place in Colombia. Recognizing that Cervantes needed more publicity and tougher challengers, Prada moved with Cervantes to Venezuela at the end of 1968, where the fighter, nicknamed "Kid Pambele," knocked out his first opponent and won another bout just three days later.

In 1969, Cervantes fought in Colombia and Venezuela, winning five and losing two, before moving to Los Angeles in 1970. In the United States, Cervantes used his lean, muscular body and gritty fighting approach to rise in the junior welterweight rankings. On December 11, 1970, he stepped into the ring to seize the World Boxing Association (WBA) junior welterweight championship against Argentinian Nicolino Loche in Buenos Aires. Though he lost the 15-round decision to the champion, Cervantes gained the attention and respect of boxing fans around the world.

On October 28, 1972, Cervantes won the junior welterweight championship by defeating Alfonzo "Peppermint" Frazer in Panama City in a 10th-round knockout. Cervantes's already-high popularity in Colombia skyrocketed after this victory, his success a source of enormous pride for Colombians during the three-plus years of his reign, in which he defended his title nine times, including wins over Loche and Frazer.

Cervantes lost his title on May 6, 1976, in San Juan, Puerto Rico, when he was defeated by Puerto Rican boxing prodigy WILFRED BENITEZ, who at age 17 became the youngest world champion in boxing history. Benitez soon left the junior welterweight title vacant to move up in weight class, and Cervantes regained the championship on June 25, 1977, in a fifth-round knockout of Carlos María Giménez in Venezuela. He defended the title five times, winning fights in Thailand, South Korea, and Botswana before he was beaten by American Aaron Pryor on August 2, 1980. He continued to box until 1983 but never again in a title bout.

Since his retirement, Cervantes has worked as a boxing trainer in Colombia. He was inducted into the International Boxing Hall of Fame in 1998, and in 2000 he was declared by the Colombian Boxing Federation as Colombia's "Fighter of the Century."

Further Reading

"Antonio Cervantes." International Boxing Hall of Fame Web site. Available online. URL: http://www.ibhof.com/cervant.htm. Downloaded on July 8, 2005.

Smith, George Diaz. "They Called Him 'Kid Pambele' Cervantes . . . One Under Appreciated Over Achiever." Ringside Report Web site. Available online. URL: http://www.ringsidereport.com/george_diaz_101304.htm. Downloaded on July 8, 2005.

Chacon, Bobby
(Schoolboy)
(1951–   ) boxer

An electrifying fighter whose brawling style made him enormously popular in his native California, Bobby Chacon won featherweight and junior lightweight boxing championships inside the ring but has suffered deep tragedy outside it. He was born on November 28, 1951, in Sylmar, California. Chacon grew up among the housing projects and street gangs in the east San Fernando Valley town of Pacoima. Despite standing 5'5" and weighing less than 130 pounds, Chacon distinguished himself as a tough street fighter, earning the nickname "Schoolboy" because he was still a high school student when he began boxing as an amateur.

Chacon's first professional fight took place on April 17, 1972, when he knocked out Jose Antonio Rosa in Los Angeles. Over the next year, he won all of his 18 fights, setting up a North American Boxing Federation (NABF) title bout with RUBÉN OLIVARES. Chacon suffered his first pro loss in this fight, but he rebounded to post five consecutive victories, all by knockout or technical knockout, before knocking out Alfredo Marcano in the ninth round for the World Boxing Council (WBC) featherweight title on September 7, 1974, in Los Angeles. His hold on the title would prove short lived, as he lost his second defense of the belt, again to Olivares, on June 20, 1975, in Inglewood, California.

Following a victory, Chacon lost a decision to Rafael "Bazooka" Limón in the first of what would become a four-fight rivalry that many boxing historians consider among the most exciting in the sport's history. Over the course of the next four years, Chacon won 16 of his 18 fights, his only blemishes being another loss and a draw with Limón. He also became entangled with heavy drinking, legal troubles, and extravagant spending. His image as a fearless fighter and high-living partier enhanced his popularity and invigorated the burgeoning boxing scene in Los Angeles during the late 1970s.

On November 16, 1979, Chacon was defeated in his attempt to gain the WBC super-featherweight title by ALEXIS ARGÜELLO, but he rebounded four months later by finally beating his archrival, Limón, in a split decision. Chacon again failed to grasp the WBC super-featherweight title when he lost to Uganda's Cornelius Boza-Edwards on May 30, 1981. He remained a top contender by winning his next five fights, including a technical knockout of Salvador Ugalde on March 16, 1982. Following that victory, a crying Chacon dedicated the win to his late wife, Valorie, who had committed suicide a day earlier.

On December 12, 1982, Chacon won the WBC super-featherweight title by overcoming two early knockdowns to defeat Limón in a unanimous decision. Ring Magazine named that clash the "1982 Fight of the Year." Chacon's next fight, a victory over Edwards, was named Ring's "1983

Fight of the Year." Chacon moved up in weight class but lost to Ray "Boom-Boom" Mancini in a World Boxing Association (WBA) lightweight title fight on January 14, 1984.

Chacon won his next fight and then announced his retirement. During this brief time away from boxing, Chacon fell deeper into trouble with substance abuse and the law. He returned to the ring in 1985, winning his final six fights but never gaining the chance to fight for a title.

He retired for good in 1989 with a record of 59-7-1 with 47 knockouts. Later, tragedy returned to Chacon when his son Bobby, Jr., was murdered in a drive-by shooting. By the end of the 1990s, he was destitute and suffering from pugilistic dementia, a chronic brain damage condition caused by frequent blows to the head. With the help of friends, Chacon moved into a transient hotel in Los Angeles, where local nonprofit organizations pay rent for the homeless. He works as a boxing instructor at a nearby gym, though he is too mentally incapacitated to manage his own affairs.

In 2005, Chacon was inducted into the International Boxing Hall of Fame. Supporting the selection, boxing writer Scott Yaniga noted, "Chacon was an all-action, heavy-fisted, face-first crowd exciter who made up for his lack of polish with a surfeit of testosterone."

Further Reading

Alvord, Valerie. "Chacon in Fight to Get His Life Back in Order: Ex-boxer Tries to Help Save Kids." *USA Today,* 25 May 2000, p. C7.
"Bobby Chacon." International Boxing Hall of Fame Web site. Available online. URL: http://www.ibhof. com/chacon.html. Downloaded on July 8, 2005.

Chávez, Julio César
(1962–   ) *boxer*

A boxing champion in four different weight classes who holds records for most undefeated title fights (27) and total championship fights (36), Julio César Chávez won more than 100 bouts during a legendary career that earned him the distinction among most boxing experts as the greatest Mexican boxer. He was born on July 12, 1962, in Ciudad Obregón, Mexico. The fourth of 10 children in his family, Chávez grew up in Culiacán, a western coastal city amid the mountains of the Sierra Madre, notorious for its active drug trade and gang violence.

Chávez followed his older brothers into boxing by the age of 11 and dropped out of school at 16 to dedicate himself to training. Chávez drove out to local ranches on weekends to earn $5 per bout on the way to forging a reputation as one of Mexico's toughest and best amateur boxers. Of this early display of toughness that would come to mark his style and career, Chávez later explained, "The most important thing is to want, because to want is to be able. That is what has always separated me from other fighters, much more than talent."

Chávez began his professional career at age 17 on February 5, 1980, with a sixth-round knockout of Andrés Félix in Culiacán. He won nine more fights in 1980 and his first in 1981 before earning a knockout victory over Michael Ruiz when his disqualification for hitting Ruiz while he was on the floor was overturned. Chávez relentlessly pursued success in the ring by maintaining a far more rigorous bout schedule than most other boxers. By 1984, he had a perfect record of 42-0 and was ranked among the top contenders for the super-featherweight title.

On September 13, 1984, Chávez had his first opportunity to fight for a championship, meeting Mario Martínez for the vacant World Boxing Council (WBC) super-featherweight title in the Olympic Auditorium in Los Angeles. Chávez won that match with an eighth-round technical knockout. Chávez continued to dominate the super-featherweight division over the next three years. Fighting in Mexico, the United States, and France, he defeated highly touted challengers including Roger Mayweather, Juan Laporte, and Rocky Lockridge.

Julio César Chávez celebrates after defeating Roger Mayweather for the light welterweight title in 1989. *(Associated Press)*

With his record still a pristine 56-0, Chávez stepped up in weight to 135 pounds and the lightweight division. Employing the same iron will and equally durable chin, Chávez claimed the World Boxing Association (WBA) lightweight crown in the November 21, 1987, 11th-round technical knockout of Edwin Rosario in Las Vegas. Chávez won all five of his 1988 bouts as a lightweight before again moving up in weight to box as a light welterweight.

Chávez continued his undefeated streak in his new division, defeating former super-featherweight foe Mayweather on May 13, 1989, to win the WBC light welterweight title at The Forum in Inglewood, California. He won his next five bouts before meeting Meldrick Taylor on March 17, 1990, in Las Vegas. In what most boxing fans remember as his greatest fight, Chávez found himself exhausted after being battered by Taylor before attacking in the final round and stunning Taylor with an overhand right punch with less than 30 seconds remaining in the bout. Another short, powerful right buckled Taylor, leading the referee to stop the fight with only two seconds remaining.

Over the next three years, Chávez remained undefeated, his greatest highlight being his September 12, 1992, unanimous decision over once beaten HÉCTOR CAMACHO in Las Vegas. On February 20, 1993, Chávez fought before 127,000 highly partisan supporters in Mexico City's famed Azteca Stadium against American Greg Haugen. Prior to the fight, Haugen added to the fervor of Chávez's fans by saying that Chávez built his spotless record by beating up on "Tijuana taxi drivers" and arriving to the ring to the sound of Bruce Springsteen's "Born in the U.S.A." After losing in five brutal rounds at the hands of Chávez, Haugen conceded that Chávez's previous opponents "must have been tough taxicab drivers."

Despite his heroic, even mythical, status in Mexico, Chávez was largely ignored by advertisers and casual boxing fans in the United States. He did not speak English or seem to crave fame, and his fighting style, though devastating, was remarkable mostly for its steadiness.

Chávez raised his record to 87-0 when he met Pernell "Sweet Pea" Whitaker on September 10, 1993, in San Antonio's Alamo Dome. He emerged from that fight with a draw, a result that served as his record's first blemish and was considered undeserved by many observers who believed Whitaker should have won. A few months later on January 29, 1994, in Las Vegas, Chávez suffered his first loss in a split decision to Frankie Randall. Chávez regained the lightweight crown from Randall in a controversial technical decision on May 7, 1994, in Las Vegas, when a cut to Chávez caused by a head butt from Randall forced an end to the fight, with Chávez surprisingly ahead on judges' scorecards.

In his 100th professional bout, Chávez met young American star OSCAR DE LA HOYA in a much-anticipated fight for the WBC light welterweight title. Chávez, who had sustained a cut in sparring while preparing for the fight, was bloodied early and suffered a fourth-round technical knockout. In the rematch, Chávez battled valiantly but was clearly outclassed by the younger, quicker, and more effective De La Hoya, whose domination forced Chávez to remain on his stool after the eighth round.

Against the advice of many of his friends, family, and advisers, Chávez continued to fight, going 7-3 through 2005 against lower-tier competition. His career record after his last bout stood at 108-6-2, a mark unlikely to be matched ever again in wins or total fights. Reflecting on Chávez's historic legacy for determination, Angelo Dundee, who spent decades as a boxing trainer, including several years training Muhammad Ali, said, "[He's] the toughest fighter I've ever seen, bar none."

Further Reading

Harrison, Simon. "Julio Cesar Chavez." Saddo Boxing Web site. Available online. URL: http://www.saddoboxing.com/44-julio-cesar-chavez.html. Downloaded on January 13, 2006.

"Julio Cesar Chavez." Boxing Records Web site. Available online. URL: http://www.boxrec.com/boxer_display.php?boxer_id=008119. Downloaded on January 13, 2006.

McKinley, James C., Jr. "Old Chavez Approved for Risky Title Shot." *New York Times,* 8 June 2000, p. D1.

Smith, Gary. "Bearing the Burden." *Sports Illustrated,* 22 Februrary 1993, p. 50.

Further Viewing

Champions Forever—The Latin Legends (DVD). New Champions, Inc./Panorama Entertainment, 2000.

Chilavert, José Luis
(1965–   ) *soccer player*

The most celebrated soccer player ever to come from Paraguay, José Luis Chilavert made headlines during the 1990s with his standout performance in goal, his unusual offensive expertise, and his penchant for outspokenness and controversy. He was born on July 27, 1965, in Luque, Paraguay. As a youth he stood out on the soccer field by demonstrating a formidable combination of size (eventually growing to be 6'2" and more than 200 pounds), speed, and intense competitiveness. Chilavert made his professional debut as a goalie at the age of only 15 with Sportivo Luqueño before heading to Argentina to play for the San Lorenzo Club.

Chilavert continued his career in Spain with Real Zaragoza, where he spent two years as a starter before being relegated to the bench. He returned to Argentina in 1991 to play for Velez Sarsfield and led the team to the Argentine League title in 1993, 1996, and 1998 and the Copa Libertadores (South American Club championship) in 1994. Chilavert's excellence in goal was recognized by the International Federation of Football History and Statistics when they honored him with its World's Goalkeeper of the Year award in 1995, 1997, and 1998.

Although Chilavert experienced glory as a professional, he made his most significant impact in international play anchoring the Paraguayan national team. He first joined Paraguay's national squad in 1989. In 1998, he allowed only two goals in four games (386 minutes) of the World Cup, leading Paraguay to the second round, where they fell to France in overtime. His pretournament boast—"I am the best in the world"—was affirmed when he was named the 1998 World Cup's top goalie.

Chilavert's penchant for controversy, which has found him tussling with journalists, opponents, and even teammates, was prominent in two high-profile incidents. In 1999, he infuriated Paraguayan government officials by boycotting the Copa América tournament, insisting that authorities should spend more money on education for Paraguay's people. In 2002, Chilavert was suspended for three games (including one World Cup contest) for spitting in the face of Brazil's Roberto Carlos. After losing the game missed by Chilavert, Paraguay earned a tie and a win before falling to eventual runner-up Germany.

Among the most unusual aspects of this unique goalie was his ability to score. Chilavert scored more than 60 goals, including eight for the Paraguayan team, with curling free kicks crafted from hours of practice.

Following the 2002 World Cup, Chilavert returned to professional competition, finishing his career with Strasbourg in France. In 2003, he quit the Paraguayan national team after being left off the roster for a series of games. Now retired, Chilavert has expressed interest in pursuing the presidency of Paraguay, where, despite his episodes of impulsive behavior, he remains a beloved folk hero.

Further Reading

"Jose Luis Chilavert: Paraguay." Canadian Broadcasting Corporation Web site. Available online. URL: http://www.cbc.ca/sports/soccer/playerprofile_chilavert.html. Downloaded on January 15, 2006.

"Paraguay: Chilavert." ESPN Soccer net Web site. Available online. URL: http://worldcup.espnsoccernet.com/player?id=20142&lang=en. Downloaded on January 15, 2006.

Clemente, Roberto
(1934–1972) *baseball player*

The greatest Puerto Rican player in the history of baseball, Roberto Clemente was a rifle-armed right fielder with an unorthodox batting stance who resurrected a moribund Pittsburgh Pirates franchise, collecting 12 All-Star Game appearances, 12 Gold Glove awards, a 1966 National League (NL) Most Valuable Player (MVP) award, the 1971 World Series MVP award, four batting titles, and 3,000 hits. The legendary achievements he earned on the baseball diamond were only exceeded by the global

admiration he attracted for his humanitarianism, exemplified by his mission to bring aid to earthquake victims in Nicaragua that led to a plane crash, ending his life at the age of 38.

He was born on August 18, 1934, in Carolina, Puerto Rico. Clemente grew up in Carolina, a small town of about 15,000 people located near Puerto Rico's capital of San Juan, the fifth and last child of his parents, Melchor and Luisa. As a child he attended school, helped his father (who worked as a sugar plantation foreman) load and unload trucks, and took advantage of the year-round warm weather to play baseball. Clemente's graceful athleticism and relentless passion for the game made him a top teenage player in Puerto Rico. While still in high school, he signed a $60 a month contract (also receiving a $5,000 bonus and a new glove) with Santurce, a professional team in the Puerto Rican League.

Clemente batted .352 with Santurce late in 1952 and quickly attracted the attention of major league scouts, among them Al Campanas of the Brooklyn Dodgers, who offered the talented Clemente a contract with a $10,000 bonus. By Major League Baseball rule, Clemente was prohibited from signing a major league contract until he graduated from high school. Although he subsequently received far more lucrative offers from other teams, Clemente kept his word and signed with the Dodgers in 1952.

He played briefly with the talent rich Brooklyn minor league team in Montreal before he was selected by the Pittsburgh Pirates just after the conclusion of the 1954 season in baseball's Rule V draft. Clemente was eligible for this draft because he had received a bonus of $4,000 or more but was not on a major league roster within one year.

The 20-year-old Clemente made his major league debut for a hapless Pittsburgh Pirates team on April 17, 1955. He was a steady but unspectacular hitter from 1955 through 1959, missing many games due to a variety of physical ailments including complications from a back injury suffered in 1954 that would bother him throughout

Roberto Clemente spent his entire 18-year career with the Pittsburgh Pirates, distinguishing himself as among the greatest all-around talents ever to play baseball. *(National Baseball Hall of Fame Library)*

who said of Clemente, "He could feel the ball in New York and throw out a guy in Pennsylvania." Although a solid power hitter, averaging 18 home runs a year during this span, Clemente took pride in his skills as a complete hitter and understood its importance, explaining, "I am more valuable to my team hitting .330 than swinging for home runs."

In Clemente's breakout season of 1960, he batted .314 with 15 home runs and 94 runs batted in (RBIs), helping lead Pittsburgh to the NL pennant. In the World Series, Clemente played in all seven games and batted .310 in the Pirates' victory over the New York Yankees. He enjoyed his greatest offensive production in 1966 with 29 home runs and 119 RBIs. Despite his prolific skills and performance, Clemente was often overshadowed early in his career by other stars of the 1960s, including Willie Mays, Mickey Mantle, and Hank Aaron. However, Clemente's 1966 NL MVP award clearly announced to the baseball world that his name belonged among the very best players of his time.

But Clemente was far more than one of the greatest baseball players. He was also an outspoken hero to players and others throughout the Latin American world. A Latino of African descent, Clemente openly challenged the common stereotypes of his era held about Latino baseball players, stating, "Latin American Negro ballplayers are treated today much like all Negroes were treated in baseball in the early days of the broken color barrier. They are subjected to prejudices and stamped with generalizations. Because they speak Spanish among themselves, they are set off as a minority within a minority, and they bear the brunt of the sport's remaining racial prejudices. 'They're all lazy, look for the easy way, the short cut' is one charge. 'They have no guts' is another. There are more."

Clemente was renowned for supporting fellow Latinos as they acclimated to their new surroundings and for providing a model of pride in Latino heritage, bristling, for instance, when others referred to him by the Anglicized names of "Bob" or "Bobby." Explained Venezuelan OZZIE GUILLÉN, a three-time All-Star shortstop who in

his career. Indications of his future greatness were evident, however, including his ranking third in the NL and batting in 1956 (with a .311 average), consistently placing among the leaders in triples, and ranking up an astounding 22 assists from right field to lead the major league in 1958.

From 1960 through 1967, Clemente was a perennial all-star, overcoming injuries to play in 144 games and bat .314 or better in each season. He ranked in the top eight in batting in every one of those seasons, using his neck rolling, back stretching batting stance to win NL batting titles in 1961 (.351 average), 1964 (.339), 1965 (.329), and 1967 (.357). Clemente's stellar defense earned him the first seven of his 12 straight Gold Gloves and led to amazed admiration, reflected in the words of Los Angeles Dodgers broadcaster Vince Scully,

2005 became the first Latino to manage a World Series championship team, "For me, he [Clemente] is the Jackie Robinson of Latin baseball. He lived racism. He was a man happy to be not only Puerto Rican, but Latin American. He let people know that. And that is something that is very important for all of us."

Though revered by Latinos and admired by fans of baseball brilliance, Clemente remained somewhat of an enigmatic figure. Well liked and respected by teammates, Clemente spent much of his time on the road in his hotel room. When he made public appearances in working-class Pittsburgh, he usually appeared in a coat and tie, his handsome face portraying an expression easily interpreted as dignified or aloof. In an era when players rarely spoke about their physical problems, Clemente, a notorious insomniac, was considered a hypochondriac and an eccentric, one who embraced alternative therapies including chiropractic and various homemade potions.

The last stage of Clemente's career, from 1968 through 1972, was marked by continued excellence and nagging injuries that limited the Pirates star to about 80 percent of the team's games. In 1969, the 34-year-old Clemente batted .345 with 19 home runs and 91 RBIs. In 1970, he batted .352 and helped Pittsburgh win the first of three consecutive NL East Division titles.

In 1971, Clemente batted .341 and drove in four runs in Pittsburgh's National League Championship Series (NLCS) victory over the San Francisco Giants. He also shined in the Pirates' World Series triumph over the Baltimore Orioles, batting .414, with two home runs and four RBIs, and demonstrated the defensive prowess that reinforced the opinions of many baseball experts who called him the greatest right fielder in the history of baseball. Clemente hit the decisive game seven's only home run in Pittsburgh's 2-1 victory and was named the World Series MVP. Reflecting on Clemente's outstanding World Series performance, sports writer Roger Angell wrote, "There was . . . Clemente playing a kind of baseball none of us had ever seen before—throwing and running and hitting at something close to the level of perfection."

In 1972, Clemente played in a career low 102 games but still was a major contributor to another successful Pirates squad by batting .312 and driving in 60 runs. He became only the 11th player in major league history to compile 3,000 career hits when he lined a double off Jon Matlack of the New York Mets at Pittsburgh's Three Rivers Stadium. Though Clemente would get four more hits in Pittsburgh's NLCS loss to the Cincinnati Reds, Major League Baseball does not count postseason statistics in career records, making that 3,000th hit Clemente's last.

Clemente returned to Puerto Rico following the 1972 season. On December 23, a massive earthquake ripped through the Nicaraguan capital of Managua, eventually killing about 6,000 people and leaving tens of thousands homeless. Reports soon surfaced that relief was not reaching those who needed it, so Clemente organized a relief mission. Clemente collected eight tons of emergency goods and left with four others on a propeller-driven DC-7 on the evening of December 31. The plane, which later was found to have been carrying too much weight, took off but soon exploded and crashed into the Atlantic Ocean. There were no survivors, and Clemente's body was never found.

In 1973, the standard five-year waiting period for consideration for the Baseball Hall of Fame was waived for Clemente, and he became the first Latino ever inducted after receiving more than 93 percent of the votes. Clemente's legacy lives on in other meaningful ways as well. His widow and two sons have realized Clemente's vision of supporting underprivileged children in Puerto Rico and Pittsburgh through several ongoing charitable projects. Scores of schools, parks, and even hospitals throughout the United States, Puerto Rico, and Latin America are named to honor his memory and contribution. Major League Baseball renamed the Commissioner's Award the Roberto Clemente Award to recognize the player who best exemplifies sportsmanship, community involvement, and contribution to his team.

Clemente continues to hold a sturdy place in baseball history, not only for his legendary achievements, but also for his influence in redefining the image of Latino players and for his example as a human being, reflected in his own words: "Any time you have an opportunity to make a difference in this world and you don't, then you are wasting your time on Earth."

Further Reading

Markusen, Bruce. *Roberto Clemente: The Great One.* Champaign, Ill.: Sagamore Publishing, 1998.

Posnanski, Joe. "Remembering Roberto Clemente." *Kansas City Star,* 4 April 2003, p. .

"Roberto Clemente." Baseball Reference Web site. Available online. URL: http://www.baseball-reference.com/c/clemero01.shtml. Downloaded on January 13, 2006.

Schwartz, Larry. "Clemente Quietly Grew in Stature." ESPN Classic Web site. Available online. URL: http://espn.go.com/classic/biography/s/Clemente_Roberto.html. Downloaded on January 13, 2006.

Coimbra, Arthur Antunes   *See* ZICO

Concepción, Davey
(David Concepción)
(1948–   ) *baseball player*

The slick-fielding and steady-hitting shortstop for the Big Red Machine dynasty of Cincinnati Red teams of the 1970s, Davey Concepción was a member of nine National League (NL) All-Star teams and a five-time Gold Glove Award winner for his defensive excellence. He was born David Concepción on June 17, 1948, in Ocumare de la Costa, Venezuela. He grew up in Maracay, a nearby industrial city close to the northern Venezuelan coast.

Concepción was a thin athletic child who emerged from poverty to become one of the top baseball prospects in Venezuela. At the age of 17,

Concepción began playing for the local professional team, the Aragua Tigres (Tigers), and within two years, he signed a contract with a $3,500 bonus with Major League Baseball's Cincinnati Reds.

Concepción moved up the Reds' minor league system quickly and made his major league debut with the Reds on opening day on April 6, 1970. He appeared in 101 games for the Reds that season, playing mostly at shortstop. Concepción demonstrated rangy skill in the field, and he batted a respectable .260, helping the Reds reach the World Series, where they lost to the Baltimore Orioles four games to one.

Over the course of the next two seasons, Concepción remained Cincinnati's primary shortstop, and his already-solid fielding continued to improve. But he struggled offensively, batting a paltry .205 in 1971 and .209 in 1972, when the Reds again won the NL pennant, losing to the Oakland A's in the World Series in seven games.

From 1973 through 1976, Cincinnati, renowned as the Big Red Machine, was the best team in Major League Baseball, winning the NL West division in 1973 and consecutive World Series championships in 1975 (over the Boston Red Sox in seven games) and 1976 (defeating the New York Yankees in four games). Though largely overshadowed by his superstar teammates Pete Rose, Joe Morgan, Johnny Bench, and TONY PÉREZ, Concepción played a critical role in the team's success. During those four seasons, Concepción's batting average ranged between .274 and .287, and he averaged almost 30 stolen bases per season. Despite his lanky frame (6'1", 180 pounds), the right-handed batting Concepción also managed to be a consistent run producer, which helped him earn a place on the NL All-Star team in 1973, 1975, and 1976.

Concepción continued to be a stalwart of Cincinnati teams from 1977 to 1985, playing in more than 90 percent of games. During this period, Concepción made five All-Star teams (1978–82) and twice ranked among the top 10 in the NL in voting for Most Valuable Player (ninth in 1979 and fourth in 1981). Though he was a very consistent and productive hitter, Concepción was still most admired for his defense. Explained Sparky Anderson, the manager of the Big Red Machine teams of the 1970s, "He's one of the few shortstops that when the ball is hit to him with two out, I've seen pitchers heading for the dugout without looking back."

The illustrious 18-year career of Concepción came to an end following the 1988 season, capping a three-year span in which he served mainly as a backup infielder. Concepción's final career statistics are highlighted by his 2,488 games played, 2,326 total hits, and a stellar fielding percentage of .972. Concepción is also admired by later generations of shortstops, particularly Venezuelans such as OZZIE GUILLÉN and OMAR VIZQUEL, who each chose the uniform number 13 to match that of their childhood hero Concepción. Concepción lives on a large estate in Maracay, where he enjoys fishing and following Venezuelan League baseball, while continuing to hope that he will one day be elected into the Baseball Hall of Fame.

Further Reading

"Dave Concepcion." Baseball Reference Web site. Available online. URL: http://www.baseball-reference.com/c/conceda01.shtml. Downloaded on June 16, 2006.

Sanchez, Jesse. "Concepcion Keeping Busy at Home: Former Reds Great Enjoying Comfortable Lifestyle in Venezuela." Major League Baseball Web site. Available online. URL: http://mlb.mlb.com/NASApp/mlb/news/article.jsp?ymd=20060203&content_id=1305669&vkey=news_mlb&fext=.jsp&c_id=mlb. Downloaded on June 18, 2006.

Cordero, Angel, Jr.
(1942–   ) jockey

The winning jockey in six Triple Crown races, Angel Cordero, Jr., ranks fourth in horse racing's all-time career wins list (7,057) and is the only Puerto Rican enshrined in the National Museum of Racing's Hall of Fame. He was born on November 8, 1942, in Santurce, Puerto Rico. Cordero

was attracted to horse racing at an early age, regularly accompanying his father, Angel Cordero, Sr., a famous rider and trainer, to the track beginning when he was only five years old. Soon Cordero started working at horse tracks and learning about racing. When he was 17, Cordero began racing in Puerto Rico. He won his first race in 1960. In 1962, Cordero traveled to New York to begin his career as a professional jockey.

Cordero established a reputation as a talented jockey and fierce competitor throughout the 1960s and rose to be among the elite in the horse racing world in 1968, when he led all jockeys in wins. Cordero continued to rack up mounts and victories during the 1970s, reaching the pinnacle of horse racing by winning two Kentucky Derbys, aboard Cannonade in 1974 and Bold Forbes in 1976. Cordero also took Bold Forbes, known as the "Puerto Rican wonder horse," to victory in the 1976 Belmont Stakes.

Though Cordero enjoyed success in races across the United States, he was considered the king at the Saratoga Race Track in upstate New York, where he won 13 titles, including 11 consecutive ones from 1976 to 1986. Cordero's supreme confidence, reflected in his quote, "If a horse has four legs and I'm riding it, I think I can win," was viewed as abrasive cockiness by some of his many opponents, as was his habit of celebrating wins by standing in the saddle while twirling his whip. However, fans saw Cordero as a proud and self-assured champion jockey who backed up his boasts.

Cordero, described by the Triple Crown winning jockey Steve Cauthen as "the elite stylist in the last 50 years," continued his excellence into the 1980s. Cordero won the Preakness Stakes with Codex in 1980 and on Gate Dancer in 1984. In 1982 and 1983, Cordero was the leading money-winning jockey and the recipient of the Eclipse Award given to thoroughbred racing's top jockey. Cordero won his third Kentucky Derby in 1985 aboard Spend a Buck.

Injuries and age began to take a toll on Cordero's intense racing schedule in the late 1980s. In 1987, Cordero lacerated his liver in a fall from a horse, and he had his spleen removed in 1990. He retired in 1991 but returned briefly against doctors' orders in 1995 before finally retiring from racing permanently. Cordero remained closely involved with horse racing as a trainer and agent for respected jockey and fellow Puerto Rican John Velazquez.

Cordero's role as a trainer was interrupted in 2001 following the tragic hit-and-run death of his wife, Marjorie Clayton Cordero, a former jockey and the mother of his three children. Cordero lives in upstate New York and remains the third-winningest jockey in thoroughbred racing history with 7,057 victories.

Further Reading

"Angel Tomas Cordero, Jr." Latino Legends in Sports Web site. Available online. URL: http://www.latinosportslegends.com/bios/Cordero_Angel-bio.htm. Downloaded on January 13, 2006.

"Angel Cordero, Jr." National Museum of Racing and Hall of Fame Web site. Available online. URL: http://www.racingmuseum.org/hall/jockey.asp?ID=177. Downloaded on January 13, 2006.

Cuevas, Pipino
(José Cuevas)
(1957–   ) *boxer*

A Mexican boxer best known for an explosive left hook, Pipino Cuevas was the World Boxing Association (WBA) welterweight champion during the second half of the 1970s. He was born José Cuevas in Mexico City on December 27, 1957. He grew up in the poor neighborhoods of Mexico's largest city, becoming known as a boxing prodigy early in his adolescence. Regularly referred to by his nickname, "Pipino," he began his professional career on November 11, 1971, more than a month before his 14th birthday, losing in a second-round knockout.

He had 11 more fights before he turned 16 years old, losing four decided as a result of points and winning seven decided by knockout. At the age of 17, Cuevas won the Mexican welterweight title by knocking out José Palacios in Mexico City. Cuevas's training habits declined as he soaked in the accolades and indulged in the lifestyle available to a sports hero. This lack of discipline soon cost Cuevas when he was defeated by Andy Price in Los Angeles on June 2, 1976.

Cuevas recovered from this embarrassing loss the following month. WBA welterweight champion Angel Espada, mistakenly believing that Cuevas would make for an easy defense, met him on July 17, 1976, in San Juan, Puerto Rico. Displaying his rugged offensive style of digging to his opponent's body and firing powerful left hooks, Cuevas knocked out Espadas in the second round. At 18 years old, Cuevas was one of the youngest ever boxing champions. For more than four years, Cuevas successfully defended his crown 11 times, winning all but one of these fights by knockout.

Cuevas's reign came to an end in a flurry of jolting knockout punches from the undefeated Thomas Hearns in Detroit, on August 2, 1980. Cuevas's descent from the top was swift. Over the next seven years, Cuevas never had another title bout and lost seven of his 13 fights.

Following a brief retirement, Cuevas returned in 1989 for three more bouts versus low-level competition. After his loss to Lupe Aquino on September 25, 1989, Cuevas ended his boxing career at the relatively young age of 31, with a record of 35-15 with 31 knockouts.

Cuevas was inducted into the International Boxing Hall of Fame in 2002. He lives in Mexico City, where he is the owner of a restaurant and security company.

Further Reading

"Pipino Cuevas." International Boxing Hall of Fame Web site. Available online. URL: http://www.ibhof.com/cuevas.htm. Downloaded on July 8, 2005.

Way, John. "Remembering the Career of Pipino Cuevas." Eastsideboxing.com. Available online. URL: http://www.eastsideboxing.com/news.php?=5709&more=1. Downloaded on June 19, 2006.

D

De La Hoya, Oscar
(Golden Boy)
(1973–) *boxer*

The most successful American boxer during the 1990s, nicknamed "Golden Boy" because of his handsome charm and gold medal at the 1992 Olympics, Oscar De La Hoya won his first 31 fights (29 by knockout) and eventually claimed titles in six weight classes, becoming the first fighter in history to accomplish that feat. He was born on February 4, 1973, in Montebello, California. De La Hoya's grandfather Vicente had been an amateur boxer in Mexico, and his father, Joel, Sr., was briefly a professional boxer in Mexico and the United States before stopping to support his family by working as a clerk at a warehouse.

As a child, De La Hoya was extremely close to his mother, Cecilia, a former professional singer who worked as a seamstress, and, according to his brother Joel, Jr., "hated physical confrontations (and) never had a street fight. He preferred to play with skateboards near the house and baseball in the park. Nothing violent." But when De La Hoya was six years old, his father took him to a local boxing gym near the family's East Los Angeles home so the young boy could learn how to defend himself. He trained at that gym almost every day through his teens, sharpening his prolific skills to become one of the top amateur boxers in the United States.

De La Hoya accumulated an amateur record of 223-5 with 163 knockouts. A tall, thin, broad-shouldered boxer with generous amounts of speed, strength, and versatility, the 17-year-old De La Hoya won the lightweight gold medal as the youngest boxer at the 1990 Goodwill Games and followed that triumph with a victory over German Marco Rudolph to win the lightweight gold medal at the 1992 Olympics in Barcelona.

Despite his success, De La Hoya's amateur years were difficult. His trainer, Roberto Alcazar, explained in 2000 that De La Hoya's intense focus on training meant that, "He didn't grow up like a normal kid; he don't know what it is to pick up the phone and call his friend to go to the movies . . . Why? Because it was from school to boxing, and from boxing to bed." De La Hoya also struggled at the age of 17 when his 35-year-old mother died of breast cancer.

De La Hoya embarked on his professional boxing career on November 23, 1992, with a first-round knockout of Lamar Williams at the Forum in Inglewood, California. He won his next 10 fights, nine by knockout, before competing in his first title bout on March 5, 1994, with Jimmi Bredahl, for the World Boxing Organization's (WBO) super-featherweight championship. De La Hoya won that fight and successfully defended his crown before moving up in weight class to face Jorge Perez for the vacant WBO lightweight title. After gaining that championship in a second-round knockout, De La Hoya continued to dominate the

Oscar De La Hoya exults after defeating Julio César Chávez for the super-lightweight championship in 1996. *(Associated Press)*

lightweight division, using his superior reach, athleticism, and powerful left hand in six victorious title defenses.

In 1996, De La Hoya rose to the light welterweight class, fighting at a solid 5'10" and 140 pounds. In a highly anticipated clash of style, the young, glamorous American golden boy De La Hoya bloodied the aging, hard-nosed Mexican legend JULIO CÉSAR CHÁVEZ on June 7, 1996, in Las Vegas to win the World Boxing Council's (WBC) light welterweight championship. De La Hoya again quickly jumped weight classes and won the WBC welterweight title in his first bout in his new division in a unanimous decision over Pernell "Sweet Pea" Whitaker on April 12, 1997.

While defending his welterweight title seven times over the next two and a half years, including a unanimous decision over HÉCTOR CAMACHO and an eighth-round technical knockout of Chávez, De La Hoya became recognized as one of the best pound for pound boxers in the world. His popularity was enhanced by his movie-star looks and smooth public persona, which led to lucrative endorsement deals in addition to the record-setting purses he attracted in the ring.

However, De La Hoya was criticized, particularly by some in the Mexican-American community, for being a "sell out"—a characterization captured by *Esquire* magazine writer Mark Kriegel, who noted in 1996 that De La Hoya was "barrio by birth, country club by inclination." De La

Hoya was also criticized as being a "pretty boy" who, despite the greatness of his record, did not have the heart or spirit of a true champion. Others decried the image of the Golden Boy who became embattled in a palimony suit with the mother of one of his children.

De La Hoya's detractors finally had cause for rejoicing when he suffered his first loss in a majority decision to FÉLIX TRINIDAD on September 18, 1999, in Las Vegas. After a seventh-round knockout win five months later, De La Hoya lost again in a WBC welterweight title fight to Shane Mosley on June 17, 2000. Following these losses, De La Hoya took a brief respite from boxing to begin a singing career, releasing his first album of bilingual ballads entitled *Ven a mi* (Run to me), which was later nominated for a Grammy award.

Rejuvenated upon his return to the ring, De La Hoya defeated Arturo Gatti before winning the WBC light middleweight title with a unanimous decision over Javier Castillejo on June 23, 2001, in Las Vegas. His first defense of the light middleweight crown was an exciting 11th-round technical knockout of Fernando Vargas on September 14, 2002, in Las Vegas, in which De La Hoya silenced his critics with an impressive display of determination and courage in addition to his usual speed, power, and durability.

De La Hoya's reign as light middleweight champion ended with a unanimous decision loss to Mosley on September 13, 2003, in Las Vegas. De La Hoya then became the first boxer in history to win a championship in six different weight divisions when he defeated Felix Sturm for the WBO middleweight title. In his attempt to unify the title with three other world middleweight championships, De La Hoya lost to Bernard Hopkins, suffering his first knockout on September 18, 2004.

Not wanting his discouraging loss to Hopkins to be his last fight, De La Hoya took off 20 months before returning to the ring on May 6, 2006, in Las Vegas in a bout with WBC super-welterweight champion Ricardo Mayorga. De La Hoya pounded Mayorga, knocking him down in the first round before winning the fight and his 10th world title with a sixth-round technical knockout. The next month, De La Hoya announced that he would not fight again in 2006 but soon he announced that he would fight welterweight champion Floyd Mayweather, Jr.—the estranged son of De La Hoya's trainer, Floyd Mayweather, Sr.—on the Mexican holiday of Cinco de Mayo (May 5) 2007.

Further Reading

Kawakami, Tim. *Golden Boy: The Fame, Money, and Mystery of Oscar De La Hoya.* Kansas City, Mo.: Andrews McMeel Publishing, 1999.

Kreigel, Mark. "The Great (Almost) White Hope: Boxer Oscar De La Hoya." *Esquire,* November 1996.

"Oscar De La Hoya." Boxing Records Web site. Available online. URL: http://www.boxrec.com/boxer_display.php?boxer_id=008253. Downloaded on January 13, 2006.

Price, S. L. "He Says He's a Gladiator, but Oscar De La Hoya Has Yet to Give a Definitive Ring Performance That Proves He Has the Heart of a Great Champion." *Sports Illustrated,* 19 June 2000, p. 80.

Puma, Mike. "Oscar's Stage Is the Ring." ESPN Classic Web site. Available online. URL: http://espn.go.com/classic/biography/s/DeLaHoya_Oscar.html. Downloaded on January 13, 2006.

de Lima, Vanderlei   *See* LIMA, VANDERLEI DE

Dihigo, Martín
(El Maestro)
(1905–1971) *baseball player*

A Negro League baseball star whose unique versatility allowed him to play all nine positions skillfully, Martín Dihigo is the only baseball player enshrined in the Cuban, Mexican, and American Baseball Halls of Fame. He was born on May 24, 1905, in Matanzas, Cuba. By the time Dihigo was 17, he was already large (eventually growing to 6'3" and more than 200 pounds) and extremely athletic, earning his place on a professional team in Cuba.

In 1923, Dihigo began his American playing career. However, this was more than two decades before Jackie Robinson broke the color barrier, and because Dihigo was black, he was not allowed to play in Major League Baseball, instead playing first base and second base for the Negro League traveling team, the Cuban Stars.

Dihigo played in the United States until 1936 with the Cuban Stars, the Homestead Grays, the Philadelphia Hilldales, and the Baltimore Black Sox. He played mainly in Cuba from 1937 through 1944 before returning to the United States in 1945 as the player/manager of the New York Cubans.

Statistics documenting Dihigo's American career exist for 12 of those 15 years. In seasons that typically included approximately 40 games, the right-handed Dihigo batted more than .300 six times, including a .325 average in 1926 with a league-leading 11 home runs. In 1935, he batted .333 and topped the Negro League with nine home runs.

During the late fall, winter, and early spring, Dihigo played professionally in Latin America, where he was primarily a pitcher admired for his blazing fastball. In 10 seasons in the Mexican League, where he was called "El Maestro" (the Master), Dihigo totaled a .317 batting average, including a league-leading .387 mark in 1938. Also in 1938, Dihigo went 18-2 as a pitcher with the remarkably low earned run average of 0.90. The highlight of that season was a legendary pitching matchup between Dihigo and American pitching great Satchel Paige that ended when Dihigo broke a 1-1 tie with a game-winning ninth-inning home run off Paige's replacement. Dihigo also threw the first no-hitter in Mexican League history and duplicated this same rare pitching accomplishment in Venezuela and Puerto Rico.

Dihigo played 24 seasons in his native Cuba, where his skill and masterful versatility sometimes allowed him to play all nine positions in the same game. Although the statistics from these seasons are

fragmentary, he was documented as batting above .300 nine times and won 93 games as a pitcher. In Dihigo's one year of play in the Dominican Republic (1937), he batted .351.

In addition to his excellence on the field, Dihigo was beloved for his warm, fun-loving personality. An example of this was reflected during a game in which he was standing on third base when he suddenly began shouting, "You balked! You balked!" to the pitcher. While the pitcher and others on the field stared at one another in confused disbelief, Dihigo slowly strutted home to score a run, to the delight of cheering and amused fans.

After Dihigo left the United States following the 1945 season, he played and managed in Cuba and Mexico until the early 1950s. Dihigo then served as Cuba's minister of sports until his death in 1971 at the age of 65. According to the National Baseball Hall of Fame, which inducted Dihigo posthumously in 1977, he earned more than 260 victories as a pitcher. Negro League star Buck Leonard captured the thoughts of many who played with and witnessed Dihigo on the baseball diamond, saying, "He was the greatest all-around player I know. I say he was the best player of all time. Black or white. He could do it all."

Further Reading

"Martin Dihigo." National Baseball Hall of Fame Web site. Available online. URL: http://www.base
ballhalloffame.org/hofers_and_honorees/hofer_
bios/dihigo_martin.htm. Downloaded on January 13, 2006.

"Martin Dihigo." Negro League Baseball Players Association Web site. Available online. URL: http://
www.nlbpa.com/dihigo_martin.html. Downloaded on January 13, 2006.

Dimas, Trent
(1970–   ) *gymnast*

A gold medalist at the 1992 Olympics in Barcelona, Trent Dimas was the first American gymnast

Trent Dimas won a gold medal in gymnastics at the 1992 Olympics in Barcelona. *(U.S. Olympic Committee)*

to win a gold medal in nonboycotted Olympics competition and the first to win a gold away from American soil. He was born on November 10, 1970, in Albuquerque, New Mexico. Dimas followed his older brother Ted into gymnastics at the age of five. The son of evangelical Christian parents, Ted and Bonnie, Dimas was homeschooled through his elementary education. Though Dimas also competed in karate and soccer, both he and Ted chose to pursue gymnastics exclusively because, as Dimas later explained, "We were both huge cartoon fans. Gymnastics was the closest thing to being a superhero." Dimas's intense dedication to gymnastics increased once he began attending public middle school. On a typical day, he would train beginning at 6:00 A.M. for two hours and then for a few hours after school. He excelled as a

private club competitor and earned spots on U.S. junior national teams, though he failed to make the 1988 U.S. Olympic team. When he graduated from high school in 1989, Dimas rejected offers from all other major universities with gymnastics programs to accept an athletic scholarship at the University of Nebraska. Together with his brother Ted, Dimas led the gymnastics powerhouse to the 1990 National Collegiate Athletic Association (NCAA) Championship in his freshman year.

Following this championship season, Dimas left Nebraska to give his full effort to making the 1992 U.S. Olympic team. Unlike his unsuccessful attempt four years earlier, this time Dimas was selected to participate on the U.S. team in Barcelona.

Although Dimas was highly regarded by many world gymnastics experts, few expected him to win a medal and were even more dubious of his chances to win a gold. The 1992 men's gymnastics competition was dominated by the Unified Team, made up of most of the nations that had been part of the recently dissolved Soviet Union. Belarussian Vitaly Scherbo swept six individual events, the all-around, and a team gold medal for the Unified Team, but he failed to qualify in Dimas's strongest event, the high bars. Dimas's gold medal–winning routine on the high bars was executed with near flawless precision, a necessity because, as Dimas later explained, "The difference between making a perfect routine and falling off that bar is a quarter of an inch."

In 1996, Dimas again tried out for a place on the U.S. men's gymnastics team competing at the Olympics in Atlanta. Though he failed to make the squad, his legacy as one of the greatest American gymnasts remains solid with three top-10 individual finishes at the World Championships and Pan-American and Goodwill Games medals complementing his Olympic gold.

Following his retirement from competitive gymnastics, Dimas has been active in promoting the sport as a coach and goodwill ambassador and through charitable activities. He is a graduate of Columbia University's School of General Studies and was inducted into the U.S.A. Gymnastics Hall of Fame in 2002.

Further Reading

Beshkin, Abigail. "Life after the Gold: Olympic Gymnast Finds New Routines to Perfect at GS." Columbia University News Web site. Available online. URL: http://www.columbia.edu/cu/pr/00/01/trent Dimas.html. Downloaded on January 13, 2006.

"Trent Dimas." USA Gymnastics Web site. Available online. URL: http://www.usa-gymnastics.org/hof/2002/tdimas.html. Downloaded on January 13, 2006.

Di Stefano, Alfredo
(La Saeta Rubia, the Blond Arrow)
(1926–   ) *soccer player*

A midfielder noted for his exceptional intelligence, skill, and stamina, Alfredo Di Stefano is widely regarded as one of the best soccer players of all time. He was born on July 4, 1926, in Barrancas, Argentina. The oldest son in the family, Di Stefano worked on a farm owned by his Italian immigrant parents near the Argentine capital of Buenos Aires. The work was rigorous, which Di Stefano would later credit for helping develop his admired endurance on the soccer field.

At the age of 12, Di Stefano joined a youth team called Los Cardales and soon won an amateur championship with them. By the remarkably young age of 16, he earned a place with his country's famed River Plate squad. Because he was playing behind two well-established stars, River Plate loaned Di Stefano to Huracán so he could strengthen his impressive talent. In his first match against his former team, Di Stefano scored a goal 15 seconds into the game in a 1-0 victory for Huracán.

In 1947, Di Stefano was recalled by River Plate and quickly proved himself to be one of the most fearsome offensive players in South America. That year, he was the league's top goal scorer, with 27 goals in 37 games, helping lead River Plate to the championship. Later in 1947, Di Stefano, whose speed and power earned him the nickname "La Saeta Rubia" (the Blond Arrow), led the Argentine national team in scoring, helping them retain the South American championship (Copa América).

After a soccer player strike began in Argentina in 1949, Di Stefano joined many other top players by playing in a high-paying Colombian league. When he arrived in Bogotá to begin his career with the Millonarios, Di Stefano was greeted by hundreds of admiring fans. The famed young Argentine star did not disappoint, scoring 267 goals in 292 games for the Millonarios, who became known as the Blue Ballet (Ballet Azul) because of their precision, artistry, and beauty, leading the team to the league championship in 1949, 1951, 1952, and 1953.

At the age of 27, Di Stefano was established as the greatest player in South America. He moved to Europe to play with the Spanish team Real Madrid. In his first season with the team, Di Stefano helped transform Real Madrid from a perennially mediocre club to the Spanish championship. During his 11-year career with Real Madrid, Di Stefano led the league in scoring in four straight seasons (1956–59) and helped lead the team to eight championships from 1954 through 1964, five European Champion Cups (1956–60), and the inaugural Intercontinental Cup in 1960, played annually between the European and South American champions.

By the early 1960s, the only major soccer accomplishment not attained by Di Stefano was playing in a World Cup final. The Argentine national teams that Di Stefano played for had not qualified in 1950, 1954, and 1958. After becoming a Spanish citizen, Di Stefano's last chance to realize this dream came in 1962, when he was named to be a member of the Spanish national team. However, he suffered an injury prior to the tournament and was unable to play. Spain subsequently was eliminated in the first round.

in 1991. In 2000, he was honored by countless publications and organizations as one of the greatest soccer players of the 20th century, and he was named honorary president of Real Madrid.

Di Stefano continues to work as a soccer commentator, though he was slowed by quadruple heart bypass surgery at the age 79 in 2006. He is still remembered by fans for his leadership, tactical brilliance, and versatility, reflected in the words of his Real Madrid coach, Miguel Muñoz: "The greatness of Di Stefano was that, with him on your side, you had two players in every position."

Further Reading

"Alfredo Di Stefano." International Football Hall of Fame Web site. Available online. URL: http://www.ifhof.com/hof/alfredodistefano.asp. Downloaded on July 8, 2005.

Ball, Phil. *White Storm: 101 Years of Real Madrid.* Edinburgh, Scotland: Mainstream Publishing, 2004.

MacDonald, Tom. *The World Encyclopedia of Soccer: A Complete Guide to the Beautiful Game.* London: Lorenz Books, 2001.

Argentine soccer legend Alfredo Di Stefano follows through on a kick in a 1963 game between England and a team of players from the rest of the world. *(EMPICS)*

The final years of Di Stefano's playing career provided few echoes of his former glory. Now in his late 30s, Di Stefano's trademark speed, versatility, and determination were waning. He left Real Madrid in 1964 and played his final two seasons for Española of Barcelona, scoring 19 goals. In 1966, a back injury finally forced Di Stefano into retirement.

Following his illustrious playing career, Di Stefano became a coach, leading the Boca Juniors to the Argentine championship in 1970, the Spanish club Valencia to their first championship in 24 years in 1971, and returning to coach his first professional team, River Plate, to the Argentine championship in 1981. He retired from coaching

Domínguez, Maribel
(Mari-gol)
(1978–) *soccer player*

The all-time leading scorer in Mexican women's national soccer team history, Maribel Domínguez made headlines by attempting to play in a men's professional league before being rejected by soccer's world governing body. She was born on November 18, 1978, in Mexico City. The youngest of nine children, Domínguez fell in love with soccer while watching her two older brothers play it. When she was 10, they got her onto a boy's team. Her unique quickness and her crafty and aggressive play earned the respect of her male teammates, who jokingly called her "Mario."

Domínguez passionately pursued the life of a *futbolista* (female soccer player), though her father disapproved. Domínguez credits her mother for hiding her soccer cleats from her father and taking her to practice in the fields of Mexico City when he was away from home. By the age of 14, Domínguez was playing on an all-women's team.

In her late teens, Domínguez continued to improve as a soccer player and at the age of 21, she earned a starting spot on the Mexican national team that competed at the 1999 Women's World Cup. Though that team only scored one goal and lost all three games it played in the tournament, it helped women's soccer gain acceptance and popularity in Mexico. Domínguez then continued her production in the United States, winning the Most Valuable Player award of a semi-pro league before signing with the Women's United Soccer Association's (WUSA) Atlanta Beat.

After arriving in Atlanta, Domínguez earned a new nickname—"Mari-gol"—because of her ability to score. Playing striker in only her second game with Atlanta, she scored three goals and one assist, tying a league mark for most points in a game. Injuries and commitments to Mexico's national team soon limited her contribution to the Beat, however, and the WUSA folded due to lack of attendance and financial support in fall 2003.

The year 2004 was a monumental one for Domínguez. In March, she scored both goals in Mexico's 2-1 upset win over Canada, propelling the Mexican team into the Olympic games for the first time. In the 2004 Olympics in Athens, Domínguez led the Mexican women to a quarterfinals finish. In December, she signed a two-year contract with the Mexican second division men's team, Celaya, creating a storm of controversy in Mexico and among soccer fans around the world. The thin 5'4" Dominguez dismissed claims that the unprecedented signing was a publicity stunt, saying, "This is a dream I have had. The hard thing is going to be equaling the physical force of the men, but the technique, the desire, the willpower, those are things I already have."

The Fédération Internationale de Football Association (FIFA), soccer's governing body, ruled against the contract and a proposal that would have allowed Domínguez to play in an exhibition with men. Though her plan to play in a men's league was rejected, Domínguez is credited with attracting more support from the Mexican Soccer Federation and helped establish plans to form a Mexican women's league in 2006.

In June 2005, Domínguez became the first Mexican woman to play in a European women's league, signing with F.C. Barcelona. In her first game, she scored two goals in a 5-0 victory.

Further Reading

"Maribel: 'I'm Dying to Be in Barcelona.'" FC Barcelona Web site. Available online. URL: http://www.fcbarcelona.com/eng/noticias/noticias/n05012424.shtml. Downloaded on July 8, 2005.
"Publicity Stunt or Not? Mexican 2nd Division Team Signs Female Player." Colorado Rapids Web site. Available online. URL: http://www.coloradorapids.com/News/newsdetails_global.asp?ID=863. Downloaded on July 8, 2005.

Durán, Roberto
(Manos de Piedra, Hands of Stone)
(1951–   ) boxer

A boxer whose hard-hitting style earned him the nickname "Manos de Piedra," or "Hands of Stone," Roberto Durán won more than 100 bouts in championships in four different weight classes, becoming the only boxer to compete in five different decades, though he remains tethered to the words *No más* (No more) that he uttered in one of the most notorious episodes of quitting in sports history. He was born on June 16, 1951, in Guarava, Panama. Durán was the second of nine children born to his Mexican father, Osvaldo, and Panamanian mother, Clara.

He grew up in poverty, earning meager income as a boy by fishing, shoe shining, and street hustling. Durán dropped out of school at age 14 and began spending much of his time training in a boxing gym with his older brother. Durán emulated Panamanian boxing legend ISMAEL LAGUNA and quickly demonstrated the talent, toughness, and tenacity that would mark his career. After a brief stint as an amateur, during which he won 13 of 16 fights, Durán became a professional boxer.

Durán's first professional bout took place on February 23, 1968. Fighting at 119 pounds, the 16-year-old Durán defeated Carlos Mendoza in a unanimous decision and then won his next 10 contests by knockout. Durán's aggressive, hard-punching style kept him undefeated, leading to the biggest fight of his young career and his first in the United States, when he met Benny Huertas at New York City's Madison Square Garden on September 13, 1971. His first-round knockout of the more experienced Huertas helped make Durán one of the lightweight division's most respected challengers.

After defeating former junior lightweight champion Hiroshi Kobayashi, Durán earned his first opportunity to fight for a world title in a June 26, 1972, bout with Ken Buchanan of Scotland in Madison Square Garden. Durán knocked down Buchanan in the first round and continued to dominate the fight with a steady flurry of heavy right crosses and left hooks to the champion, until the referees stopped the fight, raising Durán's arm in victory in the 13th round.

Now the World Boxing Association (WBA) lightweight champion, Durán followed up with several nontitle matches. He lost his first fight in one of these matches on November 11, 1972, to Esteban de Jesús. However, Durán defended his title 12 times over five and a half years, including a 1974 pounding of de Jesús in Panama City. Only one of Durán's title defenses went the 15-round distance. Durán's last fight as a lightweight, a January 21, 1978, bout against de Jesús in Las Vegas, resulted in a 12th-round knockout victory for Durán and represented his professional

apex. Durán's balance of intense attacking, sound defense, fluid footwork, impressive command of a full repertoire of punches, and legendary powerful punch flung from his solid 5'7", 135-pound body made Durán a uniquely complete boxer. His personal reputation was captured by former heavyweight champion Joe Frazier, who, when asked whether Durán's style reminded him of his own, responded, "No. He reminds me of [serial murderer] Charles Manson."

Within a year, Durán had gained 15 pounds in his quest to pursue the world welterweight boxing crown. Durán's spotless record in his new weight class earned him an opportunity for the championship in a bout with popular champion Sugar Ray Leonard in Montreal, where Leonard had won the gold medal for the United States in the 1976 Olympics. Though Durán sported an impressive record of 72-1 coming into this fight, the charismatic and undefeated Leonard was the favorite of most betters, fans, and media, a fact that genuinely bothered Durán. The much-anticipated June 20, 1980, fight did not disappoint, as Durán and Leonard battled for the full 15 rounds, with Durán's aggressiveness and experience providing him with a unanimous decision in the World Boxing Council's (WBC) welterweight championship.

Now one of the richest and most famous boxers in the world, Durán indulged in his new heights of glory. He devoured food and spent lavishly on himself, family, and friends, gaining more than 40 pounds while eschewing his previously disciplined training habits. His fight with Leonard ranked among the most lucrative nonheavyweight bouts in history, and a rematch was scheduled for November 25, 1980, at the Superdome in New Orleans. Durán managed to make the weight but failed to provide much of a challenge for the energized, revenge-minded, and peak-of-his-talents Leonard, who mocked the champion with a lightning fast attack. In the eighth round, the lethargic Durán shockingly surrendered to Leonard by softly waving his glove and reportedly uttering, *"No más"*—the Spanish words for "No more." Durán later claimed that he had stomach cramps and that he actually said, *"No peleo,"* meaning "I won't fight."

The shame of *"No más"* had a devastating effect on Durán's reputation, who had been renowned for his warrior ethic in the ring. Mocked throughout the boxing world and even in Panama, where he had been the nation's most revered citizen, Durán stumbled in his attempt to regain his prominence, losing to Wilfred Benitez and Kirkland Laing in consecutive fights in 1982, the latter of which was named the upset of the year by *Ring Magazine.* Durán persevered by winning his next two fights, including a fourth-round technical knockout of Pipino Cuevas to earn a shot at the WBA light middleweight title in a match with Davey Moore. On his 32nd birthday—June 16, 1983—Durán pummeled the previously undefeated but relatively inexperienced Moore with speed, power, and tech-

nical precision to win a world title in a third weight class.

Durán then pursued a fourth title by stepping up in weight class to take on Marvelous Marvin Hagler for the WBC middleweight crown on November 12, 1983, at Caesar's Palace in Las Vegas. The underdog Durán performed admirably but cautiously and lost the unanimous decision to Hagler. Durán's next fight took place seven months later against former welterweight champion Thomas Hearns, who used his height advantage in a flurry of powerful punches to do something no other boxer had ever done—knock out Roberto Durán.

After the loss to Hearns, Durán took off a few years before returning to the ring as a middleweight. He won seven of his first eight fights to earn a match for the WBC middleweight cham-

Roberto Durán (left) pounds Carlos Palomino in a 1979 bout in New York City. *(Associated Press)*

pionship against Iran Barkley on February 24, 1989. In a bout featuring furious action, which later earned it *Ring Magazine*'s distinction as 1989 Fight of the Year, Durán outlasted the larger and heavily favored Barkley in a split decision. Almost 17 years after first winning a world title, Durán was again a champion.

The rest of Durán's career, however, was filled with many lackluster affairs in which the greatest attraction was not Durán's now dwindling abilities, but rather his still admired name. He lost a unanimous decision to Leonard on December 7, 1989, and never defeated a legitimate contender for the rest of his career, which stretched over 26 more fights. In his final fight on July 14, 2001, at the age of 50, Durán lost a unanimous decision to HÉCTOR CAMACHO.

On October 3, 2002, any thoughts Durán might have had about a comeback ended when he was involved in a near-fatal car accident in Buenos Aires. He ended his career with the remarkable record of 103-16, with 70 knockouts. Since leaving the ring, Durán has been involved in music and boxing promotion and travels the world with his wife of 33 years, Felicidad, and their eight children.

Further Reading

Boy, Yuri. "Remembering Roberto." Boxing Fanatics Web site. Available online. URL: http://www.boxingfanatics.com/yoriboy102703.html. Downloaded on January 13, 2006.

Hoffer, Richard. "Lost in Translation: A Quarter Century after He Famously Quit Against Sugar Ray Leonard, the Former Champ Still Doesn't Understand Why He Was Held in Such Disdain." *Sports Illustrated,* 11 July 2005, p. 126.

"Roberto Duran." Boxing Records Web site. Available online. URL: http://www.boxrec.com/boxer_display.php?boxer_id=000080. Downloaded on January 13, 2006.

Further Viewing

Champions Forever—The Latin Legends (DVD). New Champions, Inc./Panorama Entertainment, 2000.

E

Escobar, Sixto
(El Gallito)
(1913–1979) *boxer*

A rugged bantamweight fighter who was never knocked down during a bout, Sixto Escobar was the first boxing champion from Puerto Rico. He was born on March 23, 1913, in Barceloneta, Puerto Rico. Following a successful amateur career, during which he became known as "El Gallito" (The Rooster), Escobar had his first professional fight at the age of 17 on September 1, 1930, defeating Luis Pérez in San Juan, Puerto Rico. He won his next four fights, including two more over Pérez, before suffering his first defeat on May 1, 1931.

Escobar's next 17 fights all took place in Caracas, Venezuela. His 10-6-1 record in those fights did not portend a future as a boxing champion, but following three consecutive wins in Puerto Rico, Escobar took advantage of an unlikely opportunity. Stepping in on one week's notice as a substitute for another fighter, Escobar, in his first fight in the continental United States, surprised the boxing world by beating bantamweight title contender Bobby Leitham by technical knockout on May 7, 1934, in Holyoke, Massachusetts.

After another win in Holyoke just two weeks later, Escobar met Leitham again on June 6, 1934, in the fabled Montreal Forum. Escobar won in a fifth-round knockout, ending Leitham's career. The *Montreal Gazette* noted, "A crowd of about 4,500 saw Escobar unleash the lightning in his right hand early in the fourth round, and knock Leitham to the canvas three times. At the beginning of the fifth, another right punch to the jaw sent Leitham flat on his back and his second [manager] climbed into the ring to stop the fight."

Escobar's first chance to gain the world bantamweight title followed less than three weeks later, on June 26, 1934, when he met Rodolfo "Baby" Casanova in Montreal. Escobar knocked out Casanova in the ninth round and two months later successfully defended his title again in Montreal before returning to Puerto Rico, where he was received as a national hero.

His hold on the title did not last long, however, ending when he lost a 15-round decision to Lou Salica in New York's Madison Square Garden on August 26, 1935. Escobar quickly regained the title from Salica three months later, then lost the title to Harry Jeffra in 1937 before regaining it from Jeffra in 1938.

Though Escobar closed his career with a 3-9-1 record in his final 13 bouts, finishing with a career record of 45-22-3, his popularity in the Puerto Rican community did not diminish. After his retirement from boxing, Escobar served in the U.S. Army during World War II, then was honored in 1946 with the dedication of Sixto Escobar Stadium in San Juan.

After he retired from boxing in 1940, Escobar moved his family to New York City, where he worked as a spokesman for liquor and beer companies. In the 1970s, he returned to Puerto Rico, living his final days there before succumbing to diabetes on November 17, 1979, at the age of 66. Escobar was posthumously inducted into the International Boxing Hall of Fame in 2002.

Further Reading

"Sixto Escobar." About.com Web site. Available online. URL: http://boxing.about.com/gi/dynamic/off site.htm?site=http://boxrec.com/boxer%5Fdisplay. php %3Fboxer%5Fid=009002. Downloaded on July 8, 2005.

"Sixto Escobar." International Boxing Hall of Fame Web site. Available online. URL: http://www.ibhof.com/ escobar.htm. Downloaded on July 8, 2005.

F

Fears, Tom
(Thomas Jesse Fears)
(1922–2000) *football player*

The first professional football receiver to catch 400 passes, Tom Fears became the National Football League's (NFL) first Latino all-pro head coach and Hall of Fame inductee. He was born Thomas Jesse Fears on December 23, 1922, in Guadalajara, Mexico. His American father and Mexican mother soon moved to Los Angeles, where Fears starred in football at Manual Arts High School. Fears began his college football career at Santa Clara University before leaving for three years to serve in the U.S. Air Force during World War II. When Fears returned from military service, he enjoyed continued success on the gridiron after enrolling at the University of California–Los Angeles (UCLA).

Fears was selected by the Los Angeles Rams in the 11th round of the 1945 NFL draft. The team held Fears's professional rights as he completed his eligibility at UCLA, and they were quickly rewarded for their patience. Originally selected to play defensive back, Fears intercepted two passes, returning one for a touchdown, in the first game of his 1948 rookie season. Rams coaches then switched his position to wide receiver, where Fears was able to use his precise route running and strong dependable hands to lead the league with 51 receptions.

In 1949, Fears again led the NFL in receptions, setting a new league record of 77 catches in a season. That season, Fears also led the league with nine touchdown receptions and 1,013 receiving yards. He smashed his single-season receptions record in his third year of 1950, catching 84 passes for 1,116 yards. Among his stellar performances that year was an 18-catch game versus the Green Bay Packers, which was the NFL's single-game reception record for 50 years. He also scored all three Rams touchdowns on catches of 43, 68, and 27 yards in Los Angeles' 24-14 win over the Chicago Bears, clinching the NFL Western Division title.

The 1951 season witnessed more heroics by the 6'2", 216-pound Fears. That year's NFL championship game between the Rams and the Cleveland Browns was tied at 17 in the fourth quarter when Fears snagged a short pass from quarterback Norm Van Brockline and raced to the end zone for the touchdown that gave Los Angeles a 24-17 victory and the city its first NFL championship. This play helped cement Fears's reputation as one of the best clutch receivers in the history of the NFL.

Injuries significantly reduced Fears's productivity during the second half of his career. Teammate Elroy "Crazy Legs" Hirsh described him as "the best third down receiver in the league." By the time Fears finished his playing days following the 1956 season, he had totaled 400 receptions, 5,397 yards, and 38 touchdowns. He soon became an NFL assistant coach, including five years with the Green Bay Packers under legendary head coach Vince Lombardi. In 1967, he was hired to be the first head coach of the expansion New Orleans Saints. He was replaced as Saints coach in 1970 after compiling a 13-34-2 record. That year, Fears was also elected to the NFL Hall of Fame.

Fears never coached again but remained active in football, working as a scout and director of player personnel for the Los Angeles Express of the fledgling United States Football League of the 1980s, where he signed future Hall of Fame quarterback Steve Young. Fears died of complications from Alzheimer's disease in Palm Desert, California, in 2000 at the age of 77.

Further Reading

"Tom Fears." Official Site of Tom Fears. Available online. URL: http://www.cmgworldwide.com/football/fears/image2.html. Downloaded on July 8, 2005.

"Tom Fears." Pro Football Hall of Fame Web site. Available online. URL: http://www.profootball hof.com/hof/member.jsp?player_id=66. Downloaded on July 8, 2005.

"Tom Fears—Head Coach." Football Reference Web site. Available online. URL: http://www.pro-foot ball-reference.com/coaches/FearTo0.htm. Downloaded on July 8, 2005.

Fernández, Gigi
(Beatriz Fernández)
(1964–) *tennis player*

The first female professional tennis player from Puerto Rico, Gigi Fernández won 17 grand slam titles and two Olympic gold medals in doubles. She was born Beatriz Fernández on February 22, 1964, in San Juan, Puerto Rico. Her father, Tuto, was a wealthy physician and her mother, Beatriz, a renowned socialite. *Sports Illustrated* writer Sally Jenkins noted that during Fernández's childhood, "[she] had an unlimited supply of attention, rackets, and lessons, and seldom heard the word 'no.'" By the age of nine, Fernández was receiving attention from the Puerto Rican press for her talent on

the tennis court, and she was also developing what would become a career-long reputation for having an explosive temper during competition.

Fernández played one season at Clemson University in 1982–83. In that season, she was named an All-American in both singles and doubles, and she advanced to the National Collegiate Athletic Association (NCAA) singles final.

Six months later, Fernández began her professional career. As a singles player, Fernández advanced to the Wimbledon semifinals in 1994 and the U.S. Open quarterfinals twice. But many tennis experts and fans, believing that Fernández had top-10 level talent, were disappointed that she never advanced higher than the number 17 ranking in singles, blaming her emotional outbursts that occasionally led to broken rackets and fines.

A self-described "insecure perfectionist," Fernández carved a legendary legacy in doubles. In 1988, with partner Robin White, she won her first grand slam doubles title at the U.S. Open. In 1990, she teamed with Martina Navratilova to win the U.S. Open doubles title. In the next year, with partner Jana Novotna, Fernández won the doubles title at the French Open.

From 1992 to 1996, Fernández won 12 more grand slam doubles championships, all of them with partner Natasha Zvereva. Fernández also won gold medals in doubles in both Olympics in which she participated, the 1992 games in Barcelona and the 1996 Olympics in Atlanta, with partner MARY JOE FERNÁNDEZ (no relation). In 1997, Fernández and Zvereva, employing their skillful finesse and tactical brilliance, won the Wimbledon and French Open doubles titles without losing a single set throughout either of the entire tournaments. She retired from tennis following a loss in the U.S. Open doubles finals in 1997.

Since retiring, Fernández has remained active in tennis. She earned a bachelor's degree in psychology from the University of South Florida before being named that school's women's tennis head coach in 2002. In 2004, she coached the Puerto Rican women's tennis team at the Olympics in Athens. Fernández also continues to manage the Gigi Fernandez Charitable Foundation, which has contributed more than $500,000 to various Latino and Puerto Rican organizations.

Further Reading

Bricker, Charles. "Tennis Lessons from a Pro: Gigi Fernandez." *South Florida Sun Sentinel,* 22 February 2003, p. 9C.

Duerin, Jessica. "Gigi the Great." University of South Florida Oracle Web site. Available online. URL: http://www.usforacle.com/vnews/display.v/ART/2005/01/26/41f7a6d425de6. Downloaded on July 8, 2005.

Jenkins, Sally. "Terrible Two Gigi Fernandez Favors Armani; Natasha Zvereva Digs Army Surplus. But on the Tennis Court They Join to Form a Perfectly Matched Set." *Sports Illustrated,* 20 February 1995, p. 156.

Fernandez, Lisa
(1971–　) *softball player*

A four-time All-American pitcher at the University of California–Los Angeles (UCLA), where she led the Bruins to two National Collegiate Athletic Association (NCAA) softball championships, Lisa Fernandez solidified her status as the greatest all-around softball player in history by starting for the United States in consecutive gold medal performances at the 1996, 2000, and 2004 Olympics. She was born on February 22, 1971, in Long Beach, California. The younger of two girls in her family, Fernandez followed her sister onto softball diamonds at an early age. By the age of four, she was practicing playing catch with her sister, mother, and father, a former political prisoner in Cuba, in her backyard in Lakewood, California, and by six she was able to efficiently backhand a ground ball.

Fernandez was a batgirl for her parents' recreational softball team and began playing competitively at the age of eight, with her mother as her coach. By the age of 11, Fernandez's strength, skill, and dedication were helping her become a dominant pitcher and hitter for the Gordon Panthers, a youth team that won the national championship in their age division for the next five years.

Fernandez's school career at St. Joseph's High School in Lakewood was remarkable from the beginning. In her first year, she threw a 29-inning shutout, played over two days, scoring the winning run in a 1-0 victory. In four years at St. Joseph's, Fernandez compiled an astonishing record of accomplishments: 12 perfect games (including three consecutive as a senior), 37 no-hitters, 69

Most experts consider Lisa Fernandez the greatest player in the history of women's softball. *(U.S. Olympic Committee)*

shutouts, a 0.07 earned run average (ERA), 80 victories, and 1,503 strikeouts.

With athletic scholarship offers from scores of universities, Fernandez chose to attend UCLA following her high school graduation in 1989. Fernandez was the Bruins's top pitcher and a star hitter for two NCAA championship teams (1990 and 1992) and was named to the All-American Team for all four years in college. Fernández's 93-7 pitching record set an all-time mark (since eclipsed) for winning percentage. Her 29-0 record in 1992 is one of only three perfect seasons in NCAA history (minimum 25 decisions), and her 0.14 ERA that season ranks in the top 10 in NCAA history. She went 33-3 as a junior with 28 shutouts, helping her to achieve an astounding 42 consecutive victories in 97 straight scoreless innings.

Fernandez demonstrated that her talent was not limited to her powerful and precise underhanded pitching motion by winning the NCAA batting crown with a .510 average during her senior year. She finished college with a .382 career batting average, 11 no-hitters, three Honda Cup awards (given to the best collegiate softball player), and the Honda Broderick Award in 1993 (given to the outstanding female collegiate athlete in the United States).

Following her stellar college playing career, Fernandez began working as an assistant softball coach at UCLA. In 1996, she was one of five Bruins to play for the U.S. softball team at the 1996 Olympics in Atlanta. She earned a save and recorded the final three outs of the U.S. gold medal victory over China. In the 2000 Olympics in Sydney, Fernandez again led the U.S. team during a 1-0, one-hit victory in the semifinal game against Australia and the gold medal win over Japan.

In the 2004 Olympics, Fernandez again pitched the U.S. to gold, defeating Australia 5-1, completing a tournament in which the American team, considered by many the best softball team ever assembled, set 18 Olympic records, including most runs, most hits, most home runs, highest batting average, and lowest ERA while outscoring

opponents by a cumulative tally of 47-1. Fernandez's dominance was reflected by comments made by an Australian player who noted of the American star, "[Scoring a run off Fernandez] was our mini-goal."

Fernandez earned a bachelor's degree in psychology from UCLA in 1995 and married Michael Lujan in 2002. Fernandez and Lujan welcomed their first child, son Antonio, in December 2005. Now a mother and in her mid-thirties—many years beyond the age of most softball Olympians—Fernandez is strongly considering competing in the Olympics again. As she explained in early 2006, "I still plan to play in the 2008 Games in Beijing. I think I've recovered nicely from the pregnancy . . . I think I'll be able to regain my former skills. At least I hope so . . . Can I still be the same athlete? Will I have the same burning desire? I think I will, but becoming a mother has changed everything for me."

Further Reading
Diaz, George. "U.S. Softball Player Does Family Proud." *Orlando Sentinel,* 27 May 2004.
Krikorian, Doug. "Fernandez Adds to Lineup." *Long Beach Press Telegram,* January 10, 2006, p. D1.
"Lisa Fernandez." UCLA Bruins Web site. Available online. URL: http://uclabruins.collegesports.com/sports/w-softbl/mtt/fernandez_lisa00.html. Downloaded on January 13, 2006.
"Triple Play: U.S. Wins 3rd Straight Softball Gold: Fernandez Shuts Down Aussies Despite Losing Shutout Streak." MSNBC Web site. Available online. URL: http://www.msnbc.msn.com/id/5794478/. Downloaded on January 13, 2006.

Fernández, Mary Joe
(María José Fernández)
(1971–   ) *tennis player*

The youngest tennis player to win a U.S. Open match, Mary Joe Fernández battled injuries and illness to rank as high as fourth in both singles and doubles. She was born María José Fernández on August 19, 1971, in Santo Domingo, Dominican Republic. By the time she was six months old, her family had settled in Miami, Florida, where as a toddler she often followed her real estate investor father, José, and older sister to local tennis courts and soon displayed early signs of interest and skill. She began taking tennis lessons at five and playing in tournaments by the age of six.

Before Fernández reached her teen years, she was identified as one of the top junior players in the United States. A tall, thin athlete with grace and savvy, Fernández began playing professionally in 1985, but unlike most other teenage tennis prodigies, she refused to participate in events that interfered with her high school education. Just eight days after her 14th birthday, Fernández defeated Sara Gomer to become the youngest player of either gender to win a match at the U.S. Open.

Fernández continued to climb in the women's tennis rankings during her late teens, reaching the French Open quarterfinals in 1986 and the fourth round at Wimbledon from 1987 to 1989. In 1989, she missed her high school graduation in Florida because she was in Paris competing her way to the French Open semifinals.

When Fernández began playing tennis professionally full time, she was already ranked among the top 10 players in the world. She continued to impress, advancing to the finals of the 1990 Australian Open, losing to Steffi Graf. That year she also advanced to the quarterfinals of the French Open and the semifinals in the U.S. Open. Fernández finished 1990 with a career high ranking of fourth in the world. In 1991, Fernández, now 20 and familiar for her long lean frame, long single braid, consistent ground strokes, and patient approach, reached the quarterfinals of the French Open and the semifinals of the Australian Open and Wimbledon.

In 1992, Fernández again reached the finals of the Australian Open before losing to Monica Seles. That year, playing for the United States, she won the gold medal in doubles with partner Gigi Fernández and earned the bronze medal in singles at the Olympics in Barcelona. Following those achievements, Fernández remarked, "I'm an American. I could play for Spain, where my father was born, or the Dominican Republic, where I was born. But it would be very difficult to play for another country. I am very patriotic."

The remaining years of Fernández's career were marked by a continuous string of injuries and illnesses that prevented her from reaching another grand slam final. In 1993, Fernández struggled with a persistent pain in her side that was eventually diagnosed as endometriosis. Following surgery and rehabilitation, Fernández found that the medication prescribed to treat her condition made her more susceptible to illnesses, including pneumonia and asthma. As a result, the thin Fernández sometimes appeared frail and struggled with stamina.

Still, between 1995 and 1997, she was able to reach the quarterfinals of Wimbledon twice and the quarterfinals at the French and U.S. Opens once. Fernández won another doubles gold medal with Gigi Fernández at the 1996 Olympics in Atlanta and remained among the top 15 players on the women's tour.

In 1998, a wrist injury kept Fernández out of three of the grand slam tournaments. She soon retired but has remained involved in tennis as a commentator for ESPN's coverage of tennis tournaments and as a member of the World Tennis Association board of directors.

Further Reading

Danzinger, Lucy. "Tennis Someone—America's Mary Joe Fernandez." *Interview,* June 1994.
"Mary Joe Fernandez." ESPN Web site. Available online. URL: http://espn.go.com/tennis/wta/profiles/fernandez.html. Downloaded on July 8, 2005.
Mewshaw, Michael. *Ladies of the Court: Grace and Disgrace on the Women's Tennis Tour.* Kingston, R.I.: Olmstead Press, 2001.

Fernández, Tony
(Octavio Antonio Fernández)
(1962–) *baseball player*

The Toronto Blue Jays' career leader in games, hits, doubles, and triples, Tony Fernández played 18 seasons in the major leagues, earning five Gold Glove awards, four All-Star selections, and one World Series championship. He was born Octavio Antonio Fernández on June 30, 1962, in San Pedro de Macorís, Dominican Republic. Fernández, like many other future baseball stars, including SAMMY SOSA and PEDRO MARTÍNEZ, practiced and lived baseball year-round among the dusty streets and sugarcane fields located in San Pedro de Marcoris, a largely poverty-stricken town on the island's southern coast. The Toronto Blue Jays, one of the first teams to widely scout the talent-rich island nation of the Dominican Republic, signed Fernández to a minor league contract two months before his 17th birthday.

Fernández spent four years in Toronto's minor league system before being called up to the majors on September 2, 1983. Midway through his first full season of 1984, Fernández replaced fellow Dominican Alfredo Griffin as the Blue Jays' full-time shortstop, and he was later named the team's Rookie of the Year.

In 1985, Fernández hit .284 and missed only one game as the Blue Jays won their first American League East championship. The next year, the lanky, switch-hitting Fernández made the American League All-Star team and became the first Blue Jay in the team's 11-year history to have a 200-hit season, collecting 212 of his 213 total hits as a shortstop, setting a single-season major league record at the time for most hits by a player at that position.

From 1987 to 1989, Fernández was named to two All-Star teams and won three more Gold Gloves, challenging two greats of his era, Cal Ripken of Baltimore and Detroit's Alan Trammell, as the best shortstop in the American League. During this time, Fernández also showed tremendous toughness. In 1987, Fernández suffered an elbow injury when he was upended by a sliding Bill Madlock in a decisive late-season series against Detroit. In April 1989, Fernández hit the first grand slam of his career before being hit in the face by a pitch in his next at-bat by Texas Rangers pitcher Cecilio Guante. Fernández required reconstructive facial surgery but missed only three weeks of action, hitting a career-high 11 home runs that season.

On December 5, 1990, Fernández was a key component of one of the biggest trades of the decade, when he was sent to the San Diego Padres with Fred McGriff in exchange for Joe Carter and ROBERTO ALOMAR. He spent two years in San Diego before being traded to the New York Mets following his All-Star season of 1992.

Fernández struggled with kidney stones and unhappiness in New York, hitting only .220 when he was traded back to Toronto on June 11, 1993. Rejuvenated with his old team, Fernández had five hits in his first two games with Toronto and later batted more than .300 in both the 1993 American League Championship Series and World Series as the Blue Jays repeated as major league champions with a thrilling six-game victory over the Philadelphia Phillies.

Fernández played with the Cincinnati Reds in 1994 and the New York Yankees in 1995 before sitting out the 1996 season with an elbow injury. He then returned as a free-agent signee of the Cleveland Indians in 1997 and helped them reach the World Series for the first time in 43 years. Though Fernández had eight hits and 17 at-bats in this World Series, he committed an error at second base in the 11th inning of game seven that set up the Florida Marlins' eventual game-winning run.

Fernández returned to Toronto for the 1998 and 1999 seasons, again experiencing a career revival. Now primarily a third baseman, Fernández enjoyed two very productive seasons with the Blue Jays, including an All-Star year in 1999, during which he shocked the baseball world by hitting more than .400 more than three months into the season. In 2000, he played in Japan, ranking fourth in batting average, and then he returned to the majors in 2001 with the Milwaukee Brewers and, for the fourth time, the Toronto Blue Jays.

Following his retirement after the 2001 season, Fernández became only the fourth player enshrined in the Toronto Blue Jays' Level of Excellence, a section of the team's home stadium honoring their top players in franchise history. He lives in southern Florida where he has been an ordained Pentecostal minister since 2003.

Further Reading

Klein, Alan. *Sugarball: The American Game, the Dominican Dream.* New Haven, Conn.: Yale University Press, 1993.

Sexton, Joe. "From Poverty to Pushcart to Pros: For Tony Fernandez, the Days of Swallowing Pride Are Over." *New York Times,* 6 December 1992, p. S6.

"Tony Fernandez." Baseball Library Web site. Available online. URL: http://www.baseballlibrary.com/baseballlibrary/ballplayers/F/Fernandez_Tony.stm. Downloaded on July 5, 2005.

Fittipaldi, Christian
(1971–) *auto racer*

The first driver from outside the United States to race in National Association of Stock Car Auto Racing (NASCAR) competition on a regular basis, Christian Fittipaldi has enjoyed success as a Formula One and Indy Car racer. He was born on January 18, 1971, in São Paulo, Brazil. He was exposed to racing early in his life by his father, Wilson, and uncle EMERSON FITTIPALDI, both Formula One champions. Fittipaldi competed in his first go-cart race when he was 10 years old. Over the next six years, he competed in 51 races, winning 29 of them.

Though not yet 18, Fittipaldi received special clearance to make his debut in auto racing, finishing as the runner-up in the 1988 Brazilian Formula Ford 2000 Championship. Over the next three years, Fittipaldi excelled in races throughout South

America. In 1991, he competed in Europe, winning the Formula 3000 Intercontinental Championship in his first attempt. By 1992, Fittipaldi had become the youngest person ever to receive an FIA (Fédération Internationale de Automobile) Formula One Super License, which is required for competition in Formula One races. He ranked 17th after his first year and finished 13th in each of the next two years.

Despite this auspicious beginning, Fittipaldi stunned racing fans in 1995 by leaving Formula One competition to race on the Indy Car circuit. At 24, he was the first young, rising driving star to make such a move, but he quickly realized success. Brazilian fans, media, and sponsors were attracted to Fittipaldi's pedigree, measured but aggressive racing style, and performance on the track. In his first year in Indy Car racing, Fittipaldi was named the Indianapolis 500 Rookie of the Year after his second-place finish, and he was second in the Championship Auto Racing Teams (CART) Rookie of the Year standings.

A broken leg suffered during a race in Australia sidelined Fittipaldi for much of 1997, but he returned from the injury sooner than expected to finish 16th in the CART rankings, including two fourth-place finishes. He won his first CART race in 1999, winning another in 2000 as well as racking up eight top 10 finishes. Fittipaldi remained one of the top competitors on the CART circuit over the next few years, including a successful 2002 in which he earned five top-three finishes.

In 2005, Fittipaldi joined the booming NASCAR circuit. Though Fittipaldi was the first racer from outside the United States to compete in NASCAR full time, he was unable to translate that distinction in history to distinction on the track, where he failed to finish higher than 24th in the 16 races he started.

In early 2005, with NASCAR sponsorship deals unavailable to him, Fittipaldi decided to return to Brazil to race stock cars, explaining, "For various reasons, I didn't have the success I was hoping for. But I'm glad I got the opportunity in Brazil where everybody knows stock car racing is growing rapidly."

Further Reading
Dolack, Chris. "Today Brazil, Tomorrow the World; Once Considered a Purely Regional Sport, NASCAR Could Be on the Verge of Global Dominance with the Signing of Christian Fittipaldi." *Auto Racing Digest,* December 2002.

"History." Christian Fittipaldi Web site. Available online. URL: http://www.fittipaldionline.com/current_season/mainpage_1.shtml. Downloaded on July 5, 2005.

Fittipaldi, Emerson
(1946–   ) *auto racer*

The youngest world champion in the history of Formula One racing whose success is often credited for igniting the influx of Brazilian drivers into the sport, Emerson Fittipaldi suffered through a deep five-year slump before resurrecting his career as an Indy Car driver, winning the Indianapolis 500 twice. He was born on December 12, 1946, in São Paulo, Brazil. Fittipaldi gained insight into the world of competitive racing early in his life through his father, Wilson, Sr., who was a renowned motor sports journalist in Brazil.

With his older brother Wilson, Jr., Fittipaldi began racing before he was old enough to have a driver's license, beginning with motor bikes and then moving on to go-carts. At the age of 19, Fittipaldi and his brother designed and built their own go-carts, which were then used in winning races. The money Fittipaldi earned in these races financed his move to Europe and his quest to ultimately race on the prestigious Formula One circuit.

In 1969, Fittipaldi drove a Lotus Formula Three car to the Lombank Formula Three Championship in Europe, displaying the smooth and controlled style for which he would become well known. The next year, Fittipaldi progressed to Formula Two racing when he was signed to compete as part of the English Lotus Formula One racing team. He finished in eighth place in his first race, fourth place in his second race, and later that year, won the United States Grand Prix.

Fittipaldi was only 25 years old in 1972 when he became the youngest person ever to win the World Driving Championship. The next year, Fittipaldi appeared poised to repeat his championship after winning both the Argentine and Brazilian Grand Prix before a late season loss dropped him to second place for the year. In 1974, Fittipaldi accepted a lucrative offer to race for Team McLaren and responded by finishing in the top three in six races, including victories in Brazil, Belgium, and Canada, finishing the year with his second world championship.

Fittipaldi raced in 1975 for Team McLaren before shocking racing enthusiasts by bolting for a fledgling racing team sponsored by Brazil's state-run sugar marketing cartel and managed by him and his brother Wilson. He was reportedly one of the highest-paid athletes in the world, with an income of close to $2 million a year. But Fittipaldi was unable to win another Grand Prix race or championship, finishing 16th in Formula One points in 1976, 12th in 1977, ninth in 1978, and 21st in 1980.

Fittipaldi retired from Formula One racing following the 1980 season and returned to Brazil deeply in debt and unclear of his future path. Of his failed attempt to run a team with his brother, Fittipaldi said, "So much money. So much effort. So much prestige—everything gone."

After returning to Brazil, Fittipaldi, whose successes helped pave the way for other Brazilian Formula One greats such as NELSON PIQUET and AYRTON SENNA, spent most of his time tending to his orange orchard. Soon, he began racing supercarts and won nine of 11 races. In 1984, Fittipaldi received an offer to drive on the Indy Car circuit, and he accepted. In 1985, Fittipaldi finished fifth in his first race, won the Michigan 500, and ranked second among Indy Car racing rookies.

Fittipaldi enjoyed increasing degrees of success, winning a total of six races in his first four years as an Indy Car racer, becoming more familiar with the oval tracks of that circuit. His greatest accomplishments as an Indy Car driver came in 1989 and 1993, when he was the Indianapolis 500 champion.

In 1996, Fittipaldi was injured in the Michigan 500, and he later suffered back injuries sustained from a crash of a small plane, forcing his retirement. He remains involved in motor sports and is still beloved and admired for his skill and sportsmanship in South America, North America, and Europe.

Fittipaldi's 22 Indy Car victories place him in the top 20 all-time, and his 14 Grand Prix wins place him in the top 15 all-time. Explaining the philosophy that led to such success, Fittipaldi said, "To be a good racing driver, you have to balance the brave and the afraid."

Further Reading

"Emerson Fittipaldi." Motorsport Publishing Group Web site. Available online. URL: http://www.ddavid.com/formula1/fitti_bio.htm. Downloaded on January 13, 2006.

Moses, Sam. "Designs on Indy: Defending Champion Emerson Fittipaldi Will Have a Lot More Going for Him at the 500 Than His Give-no-quarter Driving Style." *Sports Illustrated,* 29 May 1990, p. 44.

Flores, Tom
(Thomas Flores)
(1937–   ) *football player*

The first starting quarterback for the Oakland Raiders and the first Latino to start professionally at that position, Tom Flores played for seven seasons in the American Football League (AFL) before making history as the first Latino head coach to win a major sports championship by leading the Raiders to two Super Bowl victories. He was born Thomas Flores on March 21, 1937, in Fresno, California. He grew up in California's fertile Central Valley and attended Sanger High School near Fresno, where he was a standout quarterback. Following high school, Flores played quarterback for two years at Fresno City College and then was the signal caller for two more years at the University of the Pacific in Stockton, California, where he graduated in 1958.

With American professional football teams uninterested in him, Flores hoped to prove himself by playing in the Canadian Football League (CFL). He was cut by the Calgary Stampeders of the CFL in 1958 and by the National Football League's (NFL) Washington Redskins in 1959. In 1960, a fledgling competitor to the NFL—known as the AFL—began play, and Flores became the first starting quarterback for the new league's Oakland Raiders. In the 14-game schedule of the AFL, Flores completed 54 percent of his passes and threw for 1,738 yards and 12 touchdowns as a rookie. In 1961, he passed for 2,176 yards and 15 touchdowns, ranking second in the league in completions with 190.

Flores missed all of 1962 with an injury but returned to play in 1963, helping the Raiders improve from a 1-13 record the previous year to finish 10-4. Flores's steady leadership and occasional long bottom completions to wide receiver Art Powell helped the Raiders achieve winning records in two of the next three seasons, highlighted by his All-Star season of 1966, in which Flores passed for 2,638 yards and 24 touchdowns, ranking second in the AFL.

Flores was traded to the Buffalo Bills prior to the 1967 season, where he served primarily as a backup for three seasons. He concluded his playing career in 1969, the last season of the AFL before it merged with the NFL, as a backup with the Kansas City Chiefs, connecting on a touchdown in the only pass he attempted. The Chiefs proceeded to beat the Minnesota Vikings 23-7 in Super Bowl IV.

Although Flores had an impressive career as a player, his greatest impact on the sport came during his career as a football coach. He was an assistant in Buffalo, New York, before joining the coaching staff of John Madden in Oakland in the 1970s. In 1976, the Raiders won Super Bowl XI 32-14 over the Minnesota Vikings, and after Madden retired from coaching in 1979, Flores was hired by Raiders owner Al Davis, one of his head coaches from his Raider playing days, to become Oakland's head coach.

In Flores's first season in charge, the Raiders finished 9-7. The next year, 1980, Oakland went 11-5 and marched through the playoffs before defeating the favored Philadelphia Eagles in Super Bowl XV 27-10 to become the first wild card team (playoff qualifier that does not win its division) to win an NFL championship. Flores's cool demeanor, sharp strategy, and ability to derive excellent play from the Raiders' quarterback, former Heisman Trophy winner and NFL disappointment Jim Plunkett, were often credited for the Raiders' success.

After a surprisingly poor 7-9 season in 1981 and an 8-1 record in a strike-abbreviated 1982 season, Flores led the Los Angeles Raiders to Super Bowl XVIII following a 12-4 1983 campaign. The Raiders pummeled the Washington Redskins 38-9, making Flores only the fifth NFL head coach at the time to win two or more Super Bowls, joining a list that included coaching legends Don Schula, Vince Lombardi, Tom Landry, and Chuck Noll.

Flores coached two more seasons with the Raiders before moving into the team's front office. He returned as coach and president of the Seattle Seahawks in 1992, where he struggled with a 14-34 record over three seasons.

After being fired from Seattle, Flores eventually returned to the Raiders, again playing in Oakland, where he works as the team's radio broadcast analyst. He remains (with Mike Ditka) one of only two men to win Super Bowl rings as a player, an assistant coach, and a head coach.

Further Reading

Flores, Tom, and Matt Fulks. *Tom Flores' Tales from the Oakland Raiders.* Champaign, Ill.: Sports Publishing, 2003.

"Flores, Tom (Thomas R.)." Hickok Sports Web site. Available online. URL: http://www.hickoksports.com/biograph/florestom.shtml. Downloaded on January 13, 2006.

"Tom Flores." Pro Football Reference Web site. Available online. URL: http://www.pro-football-reference.com/players/FlorTo00.htm. Downloaded on January 13, 2006.

Franco, Julio
(1958–) *baseball player*

The oldest baseball player ever to appear in more than 100 games in a season, Julio Franco was the 1990 All-Star Game Most Valuable Player and is the all-time Dominican hits leader in Major League Baseball. He was born on August 23, 1958, in San Pedro de Macorís, Dominican Republic. Franco grew up there, becoming one of the first of many major league stars who would make the town of only about 200,000 people famous around the world for its baseball excellence. He graduated from Divine Providence High School in 1978 and then signed a contract to play in the Philadelphia Phillies organization. Despite consistent problems with his fielding, Franco's quick bat helped him swiftly move up in Philadelphia's farm system.

Franco debuted with the Phillies on April 23, 1982. He played in only 16 major league games that year and was traded along with four other prospects to the Cleveland Indians for outfielder Von Hayes before the 1983 season. For the next six seasons, Franco was a staple in the Cleveland lineup. Though the Indians had only one winning season during that time, Franco became one of the most feared hitters in the American League (AL) and a consistent base-stealing threat. Employing a distinctive close-kneed batting stance and holding his bat high behind his right ear, Franco was a dynamic offensive force, increasing his batting average from .273 in 1983 to .319 in 1987.

Franco's weak defense led him to rank among the league leaders in errors at shortstop. However, his defensive statistics improved after he was moved to second base in 1988, when he again hit more than .300. But after that season the Indians traded Franco to the Texas Rangers for three players.

Franco flourished in the heat of suburban Dallas, making the AL All-Star team in each of his first three seasons as a Ranger. In the 1999 All-Star Game at Chicago's Wrigley Field, Franco knocked a pinch-hit, two-run double that led to the AL's 2-0 victory. His greatest season was 1991, when he led the AL in hitting with a .341 average, also contributing 15 home runs, 17 runs batted in (RBIs), and 36 stolen bases. Amazed by how the 165-pound Franco was able to be so productive, Texas manager Bobby Valentine commented, "I watch it every night and can't believe it. He hits the ball as hard as anyone. If I were to teach a young kid to hit, I'd tell him to watch Julio. Amazing hands. He keeps them high then right to the ball."

In 1992, Franco injured his right knee, limiting him to only 35 games. More important, the injury forever damaged his speed. He returned in 1993 with another productive season, playing most of the games as Texas's designated hitter. He left Texas before the 1994 season as a free-agent signee of the Chicago White Sox. His .319 batting average, 20 home runs (a career high), and 98 RBIs were the main reasons the White Sox were leading the AL Central Division in mid-August, when a players' strike ended the season.

The next 10 years took Franco on an unparalleled baseball journey around the world. He played in Japan with the Chiba Lotte Marines in 1995, Cleveland again in 1996 and part of 1997, before ending the season with the Milwaukee Brewers. In 1998, he returned to Japan to play with Chiba and then returned to the majors in 1999 for one at-bat (a strikeout) with the Tampa Bay Devil Rays.

Franco played in South Korea in 2000, Mexico in 2001, and then signed a contract at the age of 43 with the Atlanta Braves on August 31, 2001. From 2001 to 2004, Franco's batting average as a pinch hitter and part-time starter at first base has been at or above .300, helping the Braves make the playoffs each year. In 2004, at the age of 46, Franco also contributed in the field, making only one error in 465 chances. On June 27, 2005, Franco became the oldest player to hit a grand slam and the oldest player to hit a pinch-hit home run when he broke an eighth-inning tie to lead Atlanta to a victory over the Florida Marlins.

In 2006, the 47-year-old Franco signed with the New York Mets and began the season as the team's primary pinch hitter. Franco turned 48 during the season, in which he appeared in 95 games, batted .273, and helped the Mets reach the National League Championship Series, where they fell to the eventual World Series champion St. Louis Cardinals four games to three.

Franco has repeatedly expressed his desire to play until he is 50 years old, citing a seemingly undiminished bat speed and desire to compete. His former Braves teammate Chipper Jones echoed the thoughts of many who believe Franco can achieve this goal, noting, "Just look at him. He's in better shape than anyone on this team."

Further Reading

"Julio Franco." Baseball Reference Web site. Available online. URL: http://www.baseball-reference.com/f/francju01.shtml. Downloaded on July 5, 2005.

Kurkjian, Tim. "The Ageless Wonder." ESPN Web site. Available online. URL: http://sports.espn.go.com/mlb/columns/story?columnist=kurkjian_tim&id=1782868. Downloaded on July 5, 2005.

O'Brien, David. "Franco Smacks a Grand Slam." *Atlanta Journal-Constitution,* 28 June 2005, p. D1.

Furtado, Juli
(Juliana Furtado)
(1967–   ) *mountain biker*

A member of the U.S. women's ski team from 1982 to 1987, Juli Furtado later became the world's winningest mountain bike racer before retiring due to illness. She was born Juliana Furtado in New York City on April 4, 1967. Her father, Tommy, was a successful lounge singer in Manhattan, and her mother, Nina, abandoned her career as a ballet dancer to raise Furtado and her two siblings. Furtado's parents divorced when she was six, and she moved with her mother to New Jersey and later Vermont, where she developed a passion for skiing. By the age of 13, Furtado was among the top young female skiers in the United States, winning several Junior Olympic racing titles.

In 1982, at the age of 15, Furtado became the youngest member of the U.S. ski team. She remained on the team until 1987, though she was slowed by five surgeries on her knees. Furtado retired from competitive skiing and enrolled at the University of Colorado to study business.

While a student in 1989, she added bike riding to her physical therapy and quickly discovered the love and skill for that activity that she had felt for skiing. Later that year, Furtado started riding touring bikes and remarkably won the 1989 National Cycling Championship.

The next year, she switched to mountain bike racing. John Parker, whose cycle company was Furtado's first mountain bike racing sponsor, said of her, "She was brazen, unsophisticated, and faster than everyone else from the beginning." Despite having participated in only a handful of races, Furtado won the first-ever Cross Country World Championship in 1990. Described by her coach, David Farmer, as "the best climber and descender, not to mention the most intense woman in the world," Furtado dominated women's mountain bike racing for the next five years, winning four U.S. national championships, two Cross Country World Cup titles, and earning two World Cup second-place finishes. In 1993, Furtado won every race she entered, becoming the first woman to be named Cyclist of the Year by the prestigious cycling magazine *VeloNews.*

Furtado was on the U.S. Olympic mountain biking team when the sport debuted at the 1996 Olympics in Atlanta. She was the clear gold medal favorite but finished a shocking and disappointing 10th place.

After a string of other lower-than-expected finishes, Furtado revealed that she had been recently diagnosed with Lyme disease, a serious illness that results in muscle stiffness, fatigue, and headaches. Furtado took medication to combat Lyme disease, but her condition did not improve. In 1997, additional medical tests determined that Furtado was actually suffering from lupus, an autoimmune disease that causes inflammation of the skin, joints, blood, and kidneys. Though lupus is usually controlled with proper treatment, Furtado announced her retirement from racing in November 1997, explaining, "After countless days of pedaling my bike and going nowhere, I finally realized my body couldn't compete at world class level while fighting this disease."

Since retiring, Furtado has retained much of her enormous popularity in the bike racing community by producing a line of bicycles for women, serving as a member of the USA Cycling Olympic Selection Committee, and teaching mountain bike racing courses near her home in Colorado.

Further Reading

Corbett, Sara. "The Marvelous, Manic Drive of Juli Furtado." *Outside Magazine,* August 1995.

Hughes, Morgan. *Juli Furtado: Rugged Racer.* Minneapolis, Minn.: Lerner Publishing, 1998.

"#88: Juli Furtado." *Sports Illustrated for Women* Web site. Available online. URL: http://sportsillustrated.cnn.com/siforwomen/top_100/88/. Downloaded on July 5, 2005.

G

Galarraga, Andrés
(Big Cat)
(1961–) *baseball player*

The all-time Venezuelan career leader in home runs and runs batted in (RBIs) and the first Venezuelan ever to win a batting title, Andrés Galarraga was one of the most productive hitters in the 1990s, later providing inspiration to baseball fans around the world by making a triumphant return to baseball after missing a season due to cancer. Galarraga was born on June 18, 1961, in Caracas, Venezuela. By the time he graduated from the capital's Enrique Fermi High School, he had already signed a professional contract with the Montreal Expos organization. Though only 17, Galarraga stood 6'3" tall and weighed more than 230 pounds, and he possessed quick hands and nimble feet that earned him the nickname "Big Cat."

The right-handed hitting Galarraga gradually worked his way up in the Expos farm system, developing a reputation as a power prodigy. He made his major league debut on August 23, 1985, and was inserted as a platoon starter at first base against left-handed pitchers at the beginning of the 1986 season. During this year, he showed flashes of his offensive prowess but was slowed by injuries.

In 1987, Galarraga became the full-time first baseman for Montreal, batting an impressive .305, with 13 home runs and 90 RBIs. Galarraga's performance during the 1988 season (.302 batting average, 29 home runs, and 92 RBIs) earned

him a spot on the National League (NL) All-Star Team and firmly established him as one of the best first basemen in the major leagues. The next two years, Galarraga's batting average dipped into the mediocre .250 range, though his power numbers remained high, and his outstanding defense earned him two Gold Glove Awards.

Following an injury-plagued, subpar 1991 season, the Expos, concerned about Galarraga's high strikeout rate and growing salary, traded him to the St. Louis Cardinals. He played poorly in St. Louis in 1992 before signing a free-agent contract with the expansion Colorado Rockies. Playing half his games in the thin Denver air, Galarraga revived his career by piling up staggering offensive numbers. In 1993, Galarraga became the first Venezuelan to win a batting title, leading the NL in hitting with a .370 average, the highest mark by a right-handed hitter in Major League Baseball since Joe DiMaggio hit .381 in 1939. He won the NL home run (46) and RBI (150) crowns in 1996 and repeated as the league's RBI champion in 1997 with 140. Among the highlights of Galarraga's 1997 season was his mammoth grand slam off Florida Marlins pitcher Kevin Brown that was estimated to have traveled about 550 feet.

Hoping to add a World Series title to his list of career accomplishments, Galarraga signed a free-agent contract with the National League East champion Atlanta Braves in November 1997. His first season in Atlanta, 1998, was among his best, as he finished with a .305 batting average, 44 home runs, and 121 RBIs.

Before the 1999 season, however, Galarraga was stunned to learn that the back pain he was experiencing was caused by non-Hodgkin's lymphoma, a form of cancer. He missed the entire 1999 season to undergo chemotherapy before working his way back into playing shape. Galarraga returned to action in 2000, hitting a home run in his first game back and following that performance with another outstanding season, hitting .302, with 28 home runs and 100 RBIs. He was voted by fans as the NL starting first baseman for the 2000 All-Star Game in Atlanta and received a prolonged standing ovation from the Atlanta fans when he was introduced before the game.

The Braves passed on bringing the 39-year-old Galarraga back in 2001, so he signed with the Texas Rangers, who soon traded him to the San Francisco Giants. Now a part-time starter and pinch hitter, Galarraga returned to Montreal in 2002 and San Francisco in 2003. After that season, the cancer returned, and Galarraga underwent a stem-cell transplant to fight it. He again amazed many by returning to baseball in 2004, playing with the AAA Minor League affiliate of the Anaheim Angels. He was called up to the Angels in September and hit a home run, the 399th of his career, in their division-clinching victory.

In 2005, Galarraga attended spring training with the New York Mets with hopes to extend his career for one more season. He retired late in spring training, explaining "This is a sad day for me, but I honestly felt it was the right time to step away. I just wasn't playing up to the expectations that I have set for myself throughout my entire career, and I wanted to walk away on my own terms."

Further Reading

"Andres Galarraga." Baseball Reference Web site. Available online. URL: http://www.baseball-reference.com/g/galaran01.shtml. Downloaded on July 5, 2005.

Borzi, Pat. "Galarraga Decides to Retire to Spare Mets Some Angst." New York Times, 30 March 2005, p. D5.

Downey, Charles. "Andres Galarraga's Cancer: Going . . . Going . . . Gone!" Swedish Medical Center Web site. Available online. URL: http://www.swedish.org/17193.cfm. Downloaded on July 5, 2005.

Galíndez, Víctor
(Víctor Emilio Galíndez, El Leopardo de Morón)
(1948–1980) boxer

The first Argentine to win the light heavyweight boxing crown, Víctor Galíndez realized his dream of becoming a Formula One driver before tragically losing his life during his first race. Víctor Emilio Galíndez was born on November 2, 1948, in Vedia, Argentina. As a young boy growing up in Morón, outside Buenos Aires, he worked on his uncle's farm with aspirations of becoming a famous boxer or racecar driver. The path to glory in boxing was far clearer for Galíndez, who demonstrated talent in the ring by his mid-teens. By the age of 16, Galíndez was fighting in unlicensed bouts wearing a flamboyant leopard skin–patterned robe and trunks that would later earn him the nickname "El Leopardo de Morón" (the Leopard from Morón).

At the age of 19, Galíndez, hiding his past professional fights, was on the Argentine boxing team that competed in the 1968 Olympics in Mexico City, where he lost in a preliminary round contest. Following the Olympics, Galíndez officially began his professional boxing career on May 10, 1969, with a fourth-round knockout of Ramón Ruiz in Buenos Aires. His career sputtered, as he failed to win more than two fights in a row until October 30, 1971, when he defeated Jorge Ahumada for the second time in three months after splitting two earlier fights with him.

Galíndez then asserted his dominance over the light heavyweight field with a bull-like style that led to a 43-0-1 streak. Included in this run of success was Galíndez's victory over Juan Aguilar for the Argentine light heavyweight title on July 22, 1972, his victory over Avenemar Peralta on October 7, 1972, for the South American light heavyweight crown, and his December 7, 1974, 13th-round technical knockout of Len Hutchins for the World Boxing Association (WBA) light heavyweight championship.

Once he held the title, Galíndez, who had never fought outside Argentina, defended his crown around the world, including victories in South Africa; Las Vegas, Nevada; Madison Square Garden in New York City (where he again defeated Ahumada); Norway; and Denmark. In 1977, he successfully defended his title with three consecutive 15-round decisions in Italy. Galíndez lost the title belt he had held for more than four years to American Mike Rossman in a 13th-round technical knockout in New Orleans on September 15, 1978.

Galíndez backed out of a rematch with Rossman scheduled for early 1979, claiming that the judges chosen for the fight would favor his opponent. On April 14, 1979, Galíndez regained his light heavyweight title by beating Rossman in a 10th-round technical knockout in New Orleans. In his next fight on November 30, the recently married Galíndez relinquished the title to Marvin Johnson. On June 14, 1980, Galíndez lost to Jesse Burnett before retiring because of two operations to repair his detached retinas. His career record in the ring was 52-9-4, with 32 wins by knockout. He was inducted into the International Boxing Hall of Fame in 2002.

Following his retirement from boxing, Galíndez pursued his other athletic passion, Formula One racing. He reached the Premier League in Argentina in 1980, taking part in his first race on October 25. During this race, Galíndez was standing in a waiting area while a pit crew conducted repairs to his car. He was struck by a car that had lost control and was killed instantly. He was 31 years old.

Further Reading

Mullan, Harry. *Boxing: The Complete Illustrated Guide.* London: Carlton Books, 2003.
Palmer, Ian. "I Remember Victor Galindez." Tiger Boxing Web site. Available online. URL: http://www.tiger boxing.com/articles/index.php?aid=1001244904. Downloaded on July 5, 2005.
"Victor Galindez." International Boxing Hall of Fame Web site. Available online, URL: http://www.ibhof.com/galindez.htm. Downloaded on July 5, 2005.

Galindo, Rudy
(Val Joe Galindo)
(1969–) *figure skater*

A dominant force in amateur figure skating during the 1980s, Rudy Galindo was a two-time U.S. National Champion, the bronze medalist at the World Skating Championship in 1996, and the first figure skater to acknowledge having HIV/AIDS while still professionally active. He was born Val Joe Galindo on September 7, 1969, in San Jose, California. He began ice-skating after tagging along with his older sister, Laura, as she attended her lessons. His talent was spotted quickly and encouraged by a skating coach, and Galindo began taking lessons. The Galindos—father Jess, mother Margaret, Laura, Rudy, and younger brother George—lived in a San Jose trailer park, and their only source of income was Jesse's job as a cross-country truck driver. The cost of supporting two children in private skating lessons became too heavy to bear for the family. Recognizing Rudy's natural ability and his love for skating, Laura volunteered to give up her training so that Rudy could continue, though she later served as his coach.

Galindo began competing in amateur skating events in 1977 at the age of eight. From 1982 to his last year of amateur competition in 1996, Galindo won two U.S. championships in singles (the 1982 National Novice Men's and the 1996 National Men's) and three in pairs with future women's Olympic gold medalist Kristi Yama-guchi (1986 Junior Pairs and the 1989 and 1990 National Pairs). Galindo also placed third in the National Junior Men's Championships twice (1985 and 1986), as well as finishing in the top three six times in the World Championships, highlighted by the World Junior Men's Championship in 1987 and a bronze medal in the 1996 event that many consider Galindo's best-ever performance.

Galindo announced that he was turning professional later in 1996. He became a popular performer with the Champions on Ice tour and appeared in 33 competitions as a professional ice-skater from 1996 through 2001, dazzling audiences with ambitious and athletic routines and exciting showmanship, featuring his fan-favorite "Village People Medley." During this period, Galindo became the first top skater and one of the most prominent athletes ever to publicly identify him-self as a homosexual. Although he suffered some opposition, both within and outside the world of skating due to the proclamation of his sexuality, Galindo explained, "Society has accepted me for who I am. I guess it must have something to do with how truthful I am."

In 2002, Galindo disclosed that he was HIV-postive. He has effectively managed this condi-tion through medication and a healthy lifestyle, though avascular necrosis, which leads to death of bone due to lack of circulation, led to double hip-replacement surgery in 2003. Galindo returned to the ice a year later and performed his complete rou-tine with the Champions on Ice tour without miss-ing a performance. He continues to perform and is very active in efforts to raise money and awareness in the battle against AIDS.

In 1996, Galindo, along with four other dis-tinguished San Jose–area skaters (Brian Boitino, Debbie Thomas, Peggy Fleming, and Yamagu-chi), was honored with a public art project in San Jose's Guadalupe River Park & Gardens entitled *Five Skaters.* The project features five 20-feet-tall columns, each with an abstract portrait of one of the skaters made from small mosaic tiles.

Comments from all the skaters adorn the floor of the project. Galindo's included: "When I was eight, I started skating at the East Ridge Mall in San Jose . . . I've had my share of ups and downs . . . I never imagined when I started skat-ing that one day I'd win the Junior World Title and the U.S. Pairs Championship twice . . . I guess I'm a survivor."

Further Reading

"Don't Dream It. Do It." Rudy Galindo Web site. Avail-able online. URL: http://www.rudy-galindo.com/. Downloaded on January 13, 2006.

Galindo, Rudy. *Icebreaker: The Autobiography of Rudy Galindo.* New York: Pocket Books, 2003.

Smith, Pohla. "Skating Preview: Skater Changes Atti-tudes and His Fortunes." *Pittsburgh Post-Gazette Magazine,* 18 April 1999.

García, Francisco
(1981–   ) *basketball player*

The highest-selected Dominican-born player in the history of the National Basketball Association (NBA) draft, Francisco García led the 2004–05 University of Louisville Cardinals in scoring, assists, steals, and blocks, helping the team advance to the Final Four of the National Collegiate Ath-letic Association (NCAA) Basketball Tournament. He was born on December 31, 1981, in Santo Domingo, Dominican Republic. García grew up in that nation's capital and largest city playing baseball and only rarely applying his lanky body and athletic talent in basketball.

García moved with his mother, Miguelina, and younger brother, Héctor López, to New York City when he was 15. García soon had a new favor-ite sport, explaining, "When I moved to the Bronx, I had played a little basketball. But I got there (to New York) and everyone was always playing in the streets and in tournaments."

Few played better than García, who showed so much promise that he earned scholarships to two prep schools, Chesire Academy in Connecticut as a junior and Winchendon School in Massachusetts as a senior. As a senior, he averaged more than 18 points, seven rebounds, and five assists per game, and he was rated among the top 40 seniors in high school basketball by *ESPN*, *Sports Illustrated,* and the *Sporting News.* García accepted a scholarship to play basketball at the University of Louisville for renowned coach Rick Pitino.

García contributed to the Cardinals as a freshman, finishing the session with averages of 11 points, three rebounds, and two assists per game. Though standing only 6'7" and playing primarily at small forward, García led the team in blocked shots, ranking 10th in Conference USA (C-USA). He also demonstrated a quick and smooth long-range shooting ability, connecting on 43 percent of his three-point shot attempts, which placed him third in the conference. García's freshman year was highlighted with a school record, eight three-pointers (in 11 attempts) off the bench in a nationally televised Louisville victory over Cincinnati. Following the season, García was named C-USA Freshman of the Year.

García spent the summer of 2003 helping the Dominican Republic to a surprise silver medal performance in the Pan-American Games held in Santo Domingo. He continued his outstanding play, despite the emotional difficulty of dealing with his brother Hector's murder in the Bronx during his sophomore season at Louisville. García took advantage of Coach Pitino's up-tempo system to lead the team with averages of 16.4 points (fourth in C-USA), 4.7 assists (third in C-USA), and 1.9 steals (fourth in C-USA).

Despite his scoring prowess, García consistently showed his unselfishness by handing out at least three assists in 23 of the team's 28 games, including the school record 15-assist performance versus Murray State that broke a 27-year-old mark. García overcame two ankle injuries as a sophomore to become only the 15th player in Louisville's illustrious history to score at least 800 points in his first two seasons.

García considered entering the NBA draft following his sophomore season but decided to return to Louisville, where he led the Cardinals to their first final four appearance in 19 years. He was a first team all C-USA selection and one of 10 players chosen for the John Wooden All-American Team. He averaged 16 points, four rebounds, four assists, and two steals during the regular season and 21 points, four assists, and two blocked shots in the four Louisville victories, leading to their final four match up with the University of Illinois, which the Cardinals lost 72-57.

In June 2005, García became the highest-drafted Dominican-born player in the NBA draft, when he was selected with the 23rd pick of the first round by the Sacramento Kings. (Dominican Felipe López had been selected 24th by the Minnesota Timberwolves in 1998.) Saying, "[it] is a dream come true," and noting that the Kings "[go] right with my style of play," García signed with Sacramento, hoping that his versatility, long-range shooting skill, and passing ability would help the Kings continue to be a perennial playoff team.

Though García struggled with his consistency as a rookie, he played in 67 of Sacramento's 82 regular season games and averaged almost six points and three rebounds a game, helping the Kings reach the playoffs, where they lost to the San Antonio Spurs in six games.

Further Reading

"Francisco Garcia: Playing Through Pain." Slam Web site. Available online. URL: http://slamonline. com/magazine/inyourface/Garcia78/. Downloaded on January 14, 2006.

Swett, Clint. "Garcia Is Kings' Ticket into Latino Market." *Sacramento Bee,* 7 November 2005, p. A1.

"32: Francisco Garcia." University of Louisville Athletics Web site. Available online. URL: http:// uoflsports.collegesports.com/sports/m-baskbl/mtt/ garcia_francisco00.html. Downloaded on January 14, 2006.

Garcia, Jeff
(Jeffrey Garcia)
(1970-) *football player*

An overlooked professional prospect despite a record-setting college career, Jeff Garcia was a star in the Canadian Football League (CFL) and later earned three consecutive Pro Bowl selections as quarterback for the San Francisco 49ers. He was born Jeffrey Garcia on February 24, 1970, in Gilroy, California, located just south of San Jose. By the time he was nine, he had suffered the loss of two younger siblings in separate accidents. Reflecting on these devastating tragedies, Garcia later commented, "I really didn't know how to react. There was a huge loss, a huge void in my life." One way Garcia attempted to deal with these tragedies was to immerse himself in athletics. He was a basketball and football star at Gilroy High School.

Despite his success as the quarterback of Gilroy's football team, an injury during his senior year and his marginal height (6') and arm strength led to a lack of college scholarship offers. Instead, Garcia attended Gavilan College in Gilroy, where his father, Bob, was the athletic director and football coach. Garcia was named junior college honorable mention All-American after throwing for more than 2,000 yards and 18 touchdowns and rushing for 584 yards and four touchdowns. After only one year at Gavilan, Garcia received an athletic scholarship from San Jose State.

Garcia continued to excel at San Jose State, where he was the starting quarterback in each of his three seasons. In his first start, Garcia tied a school record by throwing five touchdown passes. He finished his career at San Jose State ranked first in school history with 7,274 yards of total offense and third in passing yards (6,545) and completions (504). He earned co–most valuable player honors for his performance in the East-West Shrine All-Star Game in 1993, yet because of concerns about his lack of size and throwing power, he was not selected in the 1994 National Football League (NFL) draft.

Undaunted, Garcia began his career in the CFL, where he joined the Calgary Stampeeders as the backup quarterback to former Heisman Trophy winner Doug Flutie. Garcia took over the starting position when Flutie was injured early in the 1995 season, and he quickly demonstrated a dynamic combination of quick, accurate passes and instinctive, touch running that he had shown as a high schooler and collegian. Garcia enjoyed a productive season, highlighted by a game against Edmonton in which he threw for 546 yards and six touchdowns. He finished the season having completed more than 63 percent of his passes for a total of 3,358 yards and 25 touchdowns.

Inspired by Garcia's play, Calgary traded Flutie to Toronto. Garcia quickly rewarded the team's faith in him over the next three seasons, racking up league-leading statistics, victories, and All-Star accolades. In 1996, he finished third in the league with 4,225 yards passing and 25 touchdown passes, and he continued to dazzle everyone with his rushing. In 1997, Garcia threw for more than 4,500 yards and finished seventh in the league in rushing. In 1998, he passed for 4,276 yards and 28 touchdowns and rushed for 575 yards and six touchdowns. He was named Most Valuable Player of the CFL's championship game, the Grey Cup, leading the Stampeeders to the title on the final play of the game.

In 1999, the 28-year-old Garcia became a rookie in the NFL after signing a free-agent contract with his favorite team as a boy, the San Francisco 49ers. He earned the backup quarterback position behind starter Steve Young, who, combined with his predecessor, Joe Montana, had led the 49ers to all five of the team's Super Bowl championships. Garcia became the starter for a rebuilding 49ers squad after Young suffered a concussion early in the season. Garcia was the target of much criticism as the team struggled, though he provided a glimpse of his future success by completing almost two-thirds of his passes for eight touchdowns and only three interceptions over the final five games of the season.

In his first full season as a starter in 2000, Garcia stunned critics by throwing for a team record 4,278 yards and finishing second in the NFL with 31 touchdown passes. In 2001, Garcia led the surprisingly quick resurrection of the 49ers by helping the team achieve a 12-4 record, including four wins that resulted from fourth-quarter comebacks, and he became the first quarterback in team history to throw for more than 30 touchdowns in consecutive seasons.

In 2002, Garcia again started every game for the 49ers and became the first quarterback in team history to complete 300 or more passes in three consecutive seasons. He led five fourth-quarter comeback victories, highlighted by a stellar performance that helped overcome a 24-point deficit in a playoff victory over the New York Giants. He also earned his third consecutive selection to the Pro Bowl.

Garcia's last season in San Francisco, 2003, was a disappointing one. Forty-niners coach Steve Mariucci had been fired. Struggling with nagging injuries, Garcia started 13 games and threw for fewer than 3,000 yards and 20 touchdowns. The 49ers finished 7-9 and decided to release the highly paid Garcia to save money. He then signed with the Cleveland Browns before the 2004 season, where he endured his worst season, playing in only 11 games as the team finished with a 4-12 record.

Following his release by the Browns, Garcia returned to his former coach, Steve Mariucci, by signing with the Detroit Lions prior to the 2005 season. Though signed as a backup, Garcia explained, "My attitude is to not come in here and be a number two. My attitude is to make the position better . . . if I have the opportunity to step on the field—well, like in times past, I'm going to be prepared and ready to take advantage of it." Garcia did take over as the Lions' quaterback in the middle of the 2005 season, but he struggled with injuries and ineffectiveness before being sent back to the bench.

In March 2006, Garcia signed a free-agent contract with the Philadelphia Eagles. Late in the 2006 season, Garcia replaced injured star quarterback Donovan McNabb. Garcia's stellar play helped lead a resurgent Eagles team to the National Football Conference East Division title. Garcia then led Philadelphia to a playoff victory over the New York Giants before losing in the second round to the New Orleans Saints.

Further Reading

"Jeff Garcia." National Football League Player's Association Web site. Available online. URL: http://www.nflplayers.com/players_network/players_network.aspx?ID=26956. Downloaded on July 5, 2005.

Pasquarelli, Len. "Garcia Opts to Back Up Harrington." ESPN Web site. Available online. URL: http://sports.espn.go.com/nfl/columns/story?columnist=pasquarelli_len&id=2011425. Downloaded on July 5, 2005.

Viet, To. "In the Zone with Jeff Garcia, San Francisco 49ers Quarterback." OYE Magazine Web site. Available online. URL: http://www.oyemag.com/Jeff.html. Downloaded on October 29, 2006.

Garciaparra, Nomar
(Anthony Nomar Garciaparra)
(1973–) *baseball player*

The unanimous winner of the 1997 American League (AL) Rookie of the Year Award, Nomar Garciaparra is a five-time All-Star shortstop and two-time batting champion who helped the Boston Red Sox earn three playoff appearances between 1998 and 2003. He was born Anthony Nomar Garciaparra on July 23, 1973, in Whittier, California. He was known by his unusual middle name, which was given to him by his parents, Sylvia and Ramon, because it is his father's name spelled backward.

The intense approach that would later mark Garciaparra's professional career was evident when he was a child playing tee ball, leading some parents to nickname him "No Nonsense Nomar." By the age of nine, Garciaparra was already a standout on the baseball field, making the all-star team in a little league composed mainly of kids three and four years older than he was. Though his slender frame and occasional injuries led some to call him "Glass," Garciaparra continued to excel in baseball, football, and soccer at St. John Bosco High School in Bellflower, California.

Following his graduation from high school in 1991, Garciaparra turned down athletic scholarship offers from numerous colleges and a contract from the Milwaukee Brewers (which chose him in the fifth round of Major League Baseball's amateur draft) to play baseball at Georgia Institute of Technology (Georgia Tech). Garciaparra was the starting shortstop and a first team All-Atlantic Coast Conference performer all three years he played at Georgia Tech, helping the team reach the College World Series Tournament for the first time in the school's history in 1993. In 1992, Garciaparra was part of the U.S. baseball team, which failed to win a medal at the Barcelona Olympics.

After his junior season at Georgia Tech, Garciaparra was selected by the Boston Red Sox as the 12th pick of the first round in the 1994 Major League Baseball draft. He signed a contract with the Red Sox that included a nearly $1 million bonus. He quickly demonstrated his overall skills, keen hitting ability, agile defensive acumen, a strong throwing arm, and speed on the base pads in the minor leagues. In his second professional season, he led AA Trenton (New Jersey) in runs and triples and set a team record with 35 stolen bases. He injured his knee early in 1996 while playing at AAA Pawtucket (Rhode Island) but returned to hit .343 with 16 home runs for the Red Sox's top minor league affiliate. He was called up to Boston late in 1996 and connected for three hits, including a home run in his first start.

In 1997, Garciaparra enjoyed one of the greatest rookie seasons in Major League Baseball history. After earning the starting shortstop job in spring training, Garciaparra led the AL in hits with 209 and batted .306, with 44 doubles, 11 triples, 30 home runs, 98 runs batted in (RBIs), and 22 stolen bases. He also set an AL rookie record with a 30-game hitting streak. Following the sea-

son, Garciaparra became only the sixth player to receive every vote for AL Rookie of the Year, and he ranked eighth in Most Valuable Player (MVP) voting. In 1998, Garciaparra had another stellar season, helping lead the Red Sox to the playoffs by ranking in the top 10 in the AL in batting average (.323), RBIs (122), home runs (35), and hits (195), earning him second place in MVP voting.

Although he was often overlooked in favor of fellow AL shortstops Derek Jeter of the New York Yankees and ALEX RODRIGUEZ of the Seattle Mariners, Garciaparra continued to strengthen his case that he was the greatest at his position in 1999. Despite missing almost 30 games due to injury, he won his first batting title by hitting .357 and again drove in more than 100 runs. His performance in the 1999 playoffs was even more impressive, when he hit .417 with two home runs in a four-game series victory over the Cleveland Indians and batted .400 with two home runs in Boston's five-game loss to the Yankees in the American League Championship Series.

In 2000, Garciaparra again overcame injuries, this time to his back, to win the AL batting title. His .372 batting average was the highest by a right-handed hitter in the AL since Joe DiMaggio batted .381 in 1939. His 2001 season was cut short in its first month when he broke his wrist, which required surgery. In 2002, the man revered in Boston as "NO-MAH!" and famed for his routine of adjusting his wristbands before each pitch, was able to play an injury-free season. He led the AL in doubles (56) and again ranked in the top 10 in batting (.310), hits (197), and RBIs (120), making the All-Star team for the fourth time.

Healthy again in 2003, Garciaparra displayed his all-around excellence, batting .301, hitting 28 home runs, driving in 105 runs, and providing steady defense. His contribution was a key part of a potent Red Sox offensive attack that combined for 237 home runs and more than 900 runs, leading Boston to a wildcard berth in the AL playoffs. After disposing of the Oakland A's in the AL division series, in which Garciaparra batted .300, the

Red Sox fell to their rival, the New York Yankees, in a heartbreaking seven-game series.

Following that season, Garciaparra was bothered by the contract the Red Sox offered him and by the team's effort to trade him in a three-team deal that would have brought Alex Rodriguez to Boston. Though his marriage to soccer star Mia Hamm in 2003 brought happiness to his personal life, his professional relationship with the Red Sox and his teammates became strained, particularly after his 2004 season began with many games missed because of injuries. Boston traded Garciaparra to the Chicago Cubs on July 31, 2004, in a four-team trade that brought the Red Sox a new starting shortstop and first baseman.

Garciaparra's fortunes did not follow those of his former team. Though he batted .297 for the Cubs, the high expectations his acquisition brought were not met when they failed to make the playoffs, and hopes for his role on the team in 2005 were damaged when he suffered a severe groin injury early in the season. Meanwhile, the Red Sox became the first Major League Baseball team to rally from three games down to win a playoff series, when they defeated the Yankees four games to three before sweeping the St. Louis Cardinals to win their first World Series championship in 86 years. After suffering a severe hamstring injury early in 2005, Garciaparra finished the year with the Cubs before signing a free-agent contract with the Los Angeles Dodgers prior to the 2006 season.

After being inactive due to injuries in the first month of the 2006, Garciaparra returned to lead the National League (NL) in batting through the first half of the season. He finished the season with a .303 batting average, 20 home runs, and 93 RBIs. Garciaparra's production helped the Dodgers win the NL wild card playoff berth, and it earned him the NL Comeback Player of the Year award.

Further Reading

Livingstone, Seth. "A Rookie Nomar: Shortstop Playing Like a Veteran." *USA Today Baseball Weekly,* 5 November 1997, p. 8.

"Nomar Garciaparra." Major League Baseball Web site. Available online. URL: http://mlb.mlb.com/ NASApp/mlb/team/player_career.jsp?player_id=114596. Downloaded on January 14, 2006.

Silverman, Michael. "Breaking Up Is Hard to Do: Though Once It Seemed Nomar Garciaparra and the Red Sox Would Live Happily Ever After, Their Relationship Has Eroded to the Point That Staying Together Seems Unlikely." *Sporting News,* 2 August 2004, p. 10.

Garrincha
(Manoel Francisco dos Santos)
(1933–1983) *soccer player*

A member of two World Cup champion teams that lost only one of the 60 games in which he competed for the Brazilian national squad, Garrincha overcame a childhood leg disability to become widely regarded as the greatest dribbler in soccer history. He was born Manoel Francisco dos Santos on October 28, 1933, in Pau Grande, Brazil. The midwife who performed Garrincha's delivery quickly noticed that his legs were crooked, with the left leg bent out and the right leg bent in. As a boy, dos Santos's swaying walk and thin frame led one of his brothers to call him "Garrincha"— Portuguese for "little songbird"—the nickname he would be known by for the rest of his life.

Garrincha grew up in Pau Grande and began working in a factory when he was 14 years old. He played on the factory soccer team on Sundays but generally showed little interest in following or pursuing the sport professionally. By the age of 19, Garrincha's brilliance on the soccer field—though often unrefined and unconventional—led him to begin playing professionally for Botafogo in Brazil.

In his first game with Botafogo, he scored three goals to lead his team to victory and continued to play 581 games for the team, scoring 232 goals. Garrincha's unique ability to confuse and frustrate beleaguered defenders with his dribbling led the crowd to shout "Ole!" Typical of the reaction opponents had after challenging Garrincha was that of a fullback, who upon his substation shouted to his coach, "There's nothing you can do, it's impossible!"

Although his right leg remained six centimeters (more than two inches) shorter than his left leg following a childhood surgery, Garrincha was a fan favorite for his dazzling array of quick, coordinated, and unpredictable footwork and ball skills that regularly left opponents baffled. In addition to Botafogo, Garrincha played for two other teams in Brazil and a Colombian club, but he enjoyed his greatest glory playing for the Brazilian national team during the late 1950s and early 1960s. He made his international debut in the 1957 South American Championship but did not play in the first two games of the 1958 World Cup in Sweden. After many of Garrincha's teammates begged the Brazilian coach to play him, the talented forward teamed with young rising star PELÉ in tallying two assists in Brazil's 5-2 championship game victory over Sweden.

At the 1962 World Cup, Garrincha helped the Brazilians overcome the loss of the injured Pelé by scoring two goals in a 4-2 semifinal win over the host Chilean team. Though he received a red card during that contest for unsportsmanlike conduct, Garrincha was able to play in the final, where Brazil defended its World Cup title by defeating Czechoslovakia 3-1.

Following his performance at the 1958 and 1962 World Cups, Garrincha became an international star and a revered hero throughout Brazil. However, injuries on the field and personal problems—mainly alcohol abuse—off the field contributed to his stunning downfall. He left his wife and eight children to pursue a wild life of affairs and drinking that led to financial struggles, car accidents, and health and legal difficulties.

Garrincha played on Brazil's 1966 World Cup team that failed to reach the quarterfinals, and soon professional teams became reluctant to take a chance on the former star who could not control his drinking. Throughout the 1970s, Garrincha vainly sought steady playing and coaching jobs. He died destitute in the alcoholics ward of a Rio de Janeiro hospital in January 1983 at the age of 49.

Further Reading

Castro, Ruy. *Garrincha: The Triumph and Tragedy of Brazil's Forgotten Footballing Hero.* London: Yellow Jersey Press, 2005.

"Garrincha (Brazil)." Planet World Cup Web site. Available online. URL: http://www.planetworldcup. com/LEGENDS/garrinch.html. Downloaded on January 14, 2005.

Gasol, Pau
(1980–) *basketball player*

The third overall selection in the 2001 National Basketball Association (NBA) draft, Pau Gasol won the NBA Rookie of the Year Award in 2002 and in 2006 became the first Spaniard and first member of the Memphis Grizzlies to be named to an NBA All-Star team.

He was born on July 6, 1980, in Barcelona, Spain. Both of Gasol's parents had played professional basketball in Spain, and each worked in the medical field, his father, Augusti, as a hospital administrator and his mother, Marisa, as a doctor. Gasol began playing organized basketball at the age of seven. Although he was a tall child, Gasol often played guard as a youth, allowing him to develop the excellent ball handling and passing skills that would later mark his NBA career.

In 1992, the Olympics were held in Gasol's hometown of Barcelona, and the 12-year-old Gasol became enamored of the U.S. basketball team—nicknamed "The Dream Team"—which featured NBA legends Michael Jordan, Larry Bird, and Magic Johnson and won the gold medal. Gasol, soon standing at well over 6', began to play basketball more often and with greater desire for a future in the game. At the age of 17, Gasol began studying medicine at the University of Barcelona, though he continued to hone his basketball skills, leading Spain to the European Junior Championship in 1998.

As he approached 7' and now playing forward, Gasol became one of the most highly regarded young players in the world following impressive seasons in Spain's top professional league in 1999–2000 and 2000–01. Though his statistics of 11 points, five rebounds, and 24 minutes played per game were not awe inspiring, Gasol was recognized by fans and scouts—including increasing numbers of NBA talent evaluators—as an unusually gifted, unselfish, and intelligent player with nearly unlimited potential.

Based on such evaluations, Gasol made himself available for the 2001 NBA draft. He was selected with the third overall pick by the Atlanta Hawks and traded later that evening with two other players to the Memphis Grizzlies in exchange for Hawks star forward Shareef Abdur-Rahim. Though many questioned the wisdom of Memphis executives for trading the struggling team's best player for an unknown, skinny European, Gasol quickly proved his worth. He scored 27 points in his first regular season game and consistently frustrated opponents by using his size to overcome smaller players and his quickness to get around bigger players. Gasol was the brightest light in the Grizzlies 23-59 2001–02 season, finishing the year with averages of almost 18 points and nearly nine rebounds a game. He led all rookies in scoring, rebounds, blocked shots, and shooting percentage and was the overwhelming winner of the NBA Rookie of the Year Award.

The 2002–03 Memphis team improved to post a 30-52 record thanks mainly to the continued outstanding play of Gasol, who started all 82 games, averaged 19 points and nine rebounds a game, and posted a team-high 32 double-doubles (game with double-digit points and rebounds.) With Gasol leading the way, the Grizzlies made the playoffs for the first time in their nine-year history in the 2003–04 season. The wiry Gasol led the team in per-game scoring (17.7), rebounds (7.7), and blocked shots (1.69), helping the Grizzlies surge to a 50-32 record. Memphis then was swept in four games by the San Antonio Spurs in the first round of the NBA playoffs.

The 2004–05 season was another solid one for Gasol and the Grizzlies, though the team was again defeated 4-0 in the playoffs, this time by the Phoenix Suns. Prior to the 2005–06 season, Memphis made several acquisitions in an attempt to get the team deeper into the playoffs, including signing veteran point guard Damon Stoudamire. While acknowledging Gasol's talent and well-earned leadership on the team, Stoudamire reflected on Gasol's reputation as a "soft" player who avoids physical play, saying, "His initials are PG, but I want him to be rated R."

Indeed, Gasol, who declined to play on the Spanish national team the previous summer to recuperate from nagging injuries, did play more physically in 2005–06. Now adorned with a bushy beard, Gasol averaged career highs in points (20.4), rebounds (8.9), and assists (4.6.) His breakthrough performance earned him a spot on the Western Conference All-Star team, becoming the first Grizzlie player to do so (the team played in Vancouver from 1995–2001). Despite Gasol's excellence, Memphis again failed to win a playoff game, falling to the Dallas Mavericks in a first-round, four-game sweep.

Further Reading

"Pau Gasol." Jock Bio Web site. Available online. URL: http://www.jockbio.com/Bios/Gasol/Gasol_bio.html. Downloaded on June 18, 2006.

"Pau Gasol." National Basketball Association Web site. Available online. URL: http://www.nba.com/playerfile/pau_gasol/index.html. Downloaded on June 18, 2006.

Wade, Don. "Stepping Up to Stardom: Offensively Gifted Grizzlies Forward Pau Gasol Is Trying to Take His Game to the Next Level—and It Might Be Almost There." *Sporting News,* 4 February 2005, p. 32.

Ginobili, Manu
(Emanuel Ginobili)
(1977–   ) *basketball player*

The leading scorer on Argentina's gold medal–winning basketball team at the 2004 Olympics and a star performer for the National Basketball Association (NBA) 2002 and 2005 champion San Antonio Spurs, Manu Ginobili is the first NBA All-Star from South America and has helped lead the explosive contribution of international players in American basketball in the 21st century. He was born Emanuel Ginobili on July 28, 1977, in Bahía Blanca, Argentina. A descendant of Italian immigrants, he grew up in that beach town, a four-hour drive from Buenos Aires and famed in the soccer-crazed nation for its passion for basketball.

The youngest of three boys born to his parents, Raquel and Jorge, Ginobili often followed his older brothers to their basketball practices and games. Ginobili was considered a decent player as an adolescent but attracted more attention after sprouting 10 inches in his teens to grow to 6'3" tall.

With aggressive drives for the basket and a graceful ability to hang in the air before dunking, shooting, or passing that would later lead him to stardom in the NBA, Ginobili began his professional career at the age of 18 with Andino in the Argentina League in 1995–96. The next year, he began a two-year stint with Estudiantes Bahía Blanca in Argentina, leading the league in scoring and helping the team win the league championship in the 1997–98 season.

Ginobili's skill, leadership, and growth (eventually to 6'6") led to interest among European scouts. In the 1998–99 season, Ginobili played with the Italian League team Basket Viola Reggio Calabria, averaging almost 17 points a game and displaying a unique combination of scoring, defense, effort, and savvy on the court. In his second year with Reggio, Ginobili was named the Italian League Player of the Year. Also in Italy, Ginobili refined "the flop," a defensive maneuver in which he would fall backward when pushed or bumped, inspiring Italian fans and often drawing foul calls on his opponents.

In summer 1999, Ginobili's success ignited interest in NBA executives, including R. C. Buford of the San Antonio Spurs, who selected the left-handed dynamo in the second round of the 1999 NBA draft with the 57th overall pick. While the Spurs retained his American rights, Ginobili stayed in Italy with Reggio in 1999–2000 and Virtus Kinder Bologna in 2000–01. During that season, Ginobili won the Italian League Most Valuable Player (MVP) Award and the MVP award of the Euro League finals after leading Kinder to the tournament championship.

Ginobili followed that season with another MVP performance for Kinder in 2001–02. Confident that Ginobili was now ready for the NBA, the Spurs then signed him to a one-year, $2.9 million contract for the 2002–03 season. In the summer prior to that season, Ginobili led Argentina's national team into the World Basketball Championship Tournament in Indianapolis. After Argentina won the first four games of the tournament, Ginobili led the team to victory over the German squad featuring NBA star Dirk Nowitzki. Although Ginobili suffered a sprained right ankle while launching a three-pointer over Nowitzki in that game, he overcame the pain to lead Argentina to a stunning 87-80 semifinals win over the United States that broke the American 58-game winning streak in international contests. Ginobili's ankle injury limited him to only 12 minutes in the final game, which Argentina won over Yugoslavia in overtime.

The ankle injury sustained in the world championships restricted Ginobili for much of his rookie season in San Antonio, but the defending NBA champion Spurs were able to be patient with Ginobili as they cruised to a strong start. By January, Ginobili was healthy enough to gain regular playing time, and in March, he was named NBA Rookie of the Month after coming off the bench to average more than 10 points, three assists, three rebounds, and two steals a game.

In the playoffs, Ginobili was San Antonio's third leading scorer in the Spurs second-round series win over the Los Angeles Lakers, and he scored 21 points in a critical game for a win over the Dallas Mavericks that helped the Spurs advance to the NBA finals, where they defeated the New

Jersey Nets in six games. An NBA Champion in his first year in the league, Ginobili finished his rookie season with averages of eight points, two rebounds, two assists, and one steal per game.

He returned to Argentina over the summer and was greeted as a hero by fans who made his number 20 Spurs jersey a popular fashion statement. Ginobili met the nation's president, Nestor Kirchner, was named by a leading newspaper as the country's outstanding athlete, and required regular security protection for himself and his family to guard against becoming a high-profile victim of kidnappers.

Ginobili became a starter for the 2003–04 Spurs and played well before being moved to the bench by coach Gregg Popovich, who hoped Ginobili's spirited play would provide a spark for his backup unit. Applying his full intensity in fewer minutes without being concerned about fatigue, Ginobili continued to provide strong production from the bench, finishing the season with averages of almost 13 points, five rebounds, four assists, and two steals per game. The Spurs fell in the second round of the playoffs to the eventual Western Conference champion Los Angeles Lakers, but Ginobili's value to San Antonio was rewarded after the season with a six-year contract worth $52 million.

Ginobili spent the summer of 2004 solidifying his place as one of Argentina's greatest athletic legends. He led Argentina's national team to a decisive semifinal victory over the United States in the Athens Olympics with 29 points before scoring 16 points and dishing out six assists in the gold medal–winning game over Italy.

In 2004–05, Ginobili returned to San Antonio's starting lineup and enjoyed a stellar season, becoming the first South American ever to earn All-Star Team recognition and finishing with averages of 16 points, 4.4 rebounds, 3.9 assists, and 1.6 steals a game. His outstanding team-oriented, selfless play helped make him one of the most popular players in the NBA and dented the common perception of foreign players as only offensively oriented and reluctant to engage in physical con-

Manu Ginobili helped lead the San Antonio Spurs to the National Basketball Association championships in 2003 and 2005 and Argentina to an Olympic gold medal in 2004. *(Rafael Suanes/WireImage.com)*

tact. During the season, Ettore Messina, Ginobili's coach in Bologna said of his former star, "Manu has incredible control of his body in the air. He's like a snake sometimes, he can bend, move and do the strangest things. He's not afraid of contact." Spurs superstar big man Tim Duncan added, "With his controlled chaos, he changes the game for us." San Antonio's coach Popovich, recognizing the lift Ginobili's spirited play provided, noted, "You have to let Manu be Manu."

Ginobili averaged nearly 23 points per game in San Antonio's four wins as he teamed with Duncan, originally from the Virgin Islands, and point guard Tony Parker from France, to power the Spurs to a thrilling seventh-game win in the NBA finals over the Detroit Pistons. The championship was the Spurs' second in the past three years, and it clearly announced what many basketball fans already suspected—that the imprint of international players in American basketball was profound and here to stay. Ginobili, hailed widely for his excellence on the court as well as his humility and charm off it, explained this himself earlier in 2005, saying, "If you want the best league in the world, you need the best players in the world."

Further Reading

Ballard, Chris. "A Hero in Hiding: As an Olympic Idol and the Highest-paid Athlete in Argentina, the Spurs' Manu Ginobili Is an Inspiration to His People, but an Object of Extreme—Sometimes Dangerous—Scrutiny." *Sports Illustrated,* 8 November 2004, p. 58.

"Manu Ginobili." Jock Bio Web site. Available online. URL: http://www.jockbio.com/Bios/Ginobili/Ginobili_bio.html. Downloaded on January 14, 2006.

"Manu Ginobili." National Basketball Association Web site. Available online. URL: http://www.nba.com/playerfile/emanuel_ginobili/bio.html. Downloaded on January 14, 2006.

Manu Ginobili Web site. Available online. URL: http://usa.manuginobili.com/index.php. Downloaded on January 14, 2006.

Robbins, Liz. "Be like Manu: Spurs' Ginobili Predictably Unpredictable." *New York Times,* 20 February 2005, 8-1.

Gomez, Lefty
(Vernon Gomez)
(1908–1989) *baseball player*

The pitching ace of the New York Yankees dynasty teams of the 1930s, Lefty Gomez was an All-Star for seven consecutive seasons (1933–39), led the American League (AL) in wins and earned run average (ERA) twice and strikeouts three times, and won all six of his decisions over the course of five World Series. He was born Vernon Gomez on November 26, 1908, in Rodeo, California. Gomez grew up in the small town located fewer than 50 miles north of Oakland, distinguishing himself as an outstanding pitcher on the sandlots of the town and at Richmond High School. He was known for his high leg kick, left-handed delivery, and overwhelming velocity despite his very lanky 6'2", 170-pound body. In 1929, at the age of 20, Gomez was pitching for the minor league San Francisco Seals when he was purchased for $35,000 by the New York Yankees.

Gomez made his Yankees debut in 1930, appearing in only 15 games and recording a 2-5 record. The next year, he enjoyed the first of his four 20-win seasons as a starting pitcher for one of the greatest championship dynasties in American professional sports history: the New York Yankees of the 1930s. His record in 1931 was 21 and nine, and his 2.67 ERA ranked second in the AL. Gomez was dominant again in 1932, winning 24 games and losing only seven, while recording 176 strikeouts, third-best in the AL. He also won in his only appearance in the 1932 World Series, striking out eight batters in a complete game 5-2 victory over the Chicago Cubs, helping the Yankees sweep the series 4-1.

In 1933, Gomez began a string of seven consecutive seasons in which he was named to the AL All-Star team. During these seven seasons, Gomez paired with teammate Red Ruffing to form one of the best left-handed/right-handed starting combinations in baseball history, considered by many experts comparable to or better than the Los Angeles Dodgers' tandem of Sandy Koufax and Don Drysdale in the 1960s and the Atlanta Braves' duo of Tom Glavine and Greg Maddux in the 1990s. Gomez twice claimed the Pitching Triple Crown—once by leading the AL in wins (26), ERA (2.33), and strikeouts (158) in 1934 and again in 1937 with 21 wins, an ERA of 2.33, and 194 strikeouts. Only Walter Johnson, Lefty

Grove, and Roger Clemens have matched Gomez in repeating as a Triple Crown pitcher.

During this seven-year span, Gomez was also able to emerge as one of baseball's greatest World Series pitchers. Building on his victory in the 1932 World Series, Gomez added five more victories without suffering a defeat in helping the Yankees win the World Series in 1936 over the New York Giants, in 1937 again defeating the Giants, and in 1938 over the Chicago Cubs. He also pitched one inning in the Yankees' 1939 World Series victory over the Cincinnati Reds.

Admired for his ability to pitch with impressive power and, despite a series of arm injuries, clever finesse, Gomez was also beloved for his wit, humor, and humility. Though largely overshadowed by such legendary teammates as Babe Ruth, Lou Gehrig, and later Joe DiMaggio, Gomez was renowned and appreciated for his steady play and joyous personality. Gomez, who married Broadway performer June O'Dea in 1933, often provided quotations that earned him the nickname "Goofy" on Yankees teams famed for their businesslike decorum. An example of this was his explanation following a victory: "I want to thank all my teammates who scored so many runs and Joe DiMaggio, who ran down so many of my mistakes." When Gomez changed his pitching style due to injury, he jokingly offered, "I'm throwing as hard as I ever did, but the ball is just not getting there as fast."

Gomez's arm problems led to an injury-stunted 3-3 record in 1940. He bounced back to go 15-5 in 1941 before struggling with a 6-4 record in 1942. Following his release by the Yankees, Gomez pitched one game (a loss) for the Washington Senators in 1943. He retired from baseball with 189 victories, third-best in the glorious history of the New York Yankees. He also has the distinction of owning a winning record over every AL opponent he ever faced.

After a short period of service in the U.S. military, Gomez whose winning personality made him a popular public speaker, worked as a sales representative for Wilson Sporting Goods. He was elected by the Veterans Committee to the Baseball Hall of Fame in 1972. Gomez died in Greenbrae, California, on February 17, 1989, at the age of 80.

Further Reading

"Lefty Gomez." Baseball Library Web site. Available online. URL: http://www.baseballlibrary.com/baseballlibrary/ballplayers/G/Gomez_Lefty.stm. Downloaded on January 14, 2006.

"Lefty Gomez." National Baseball Hall of Fame Web site. Available online. URL: http://www.baseballhalloffame.org/hofers_and_honorees/hofer_bios/gomez_lefty.htm. Downloaded on January 14, 2006.

"Vernon 'Lefty' Gomez." Latino Legends in Sports Web site. Available online. URL: http://www.latinosportslegends.com/lgomez.htm. Downloaded on January 14, 2006.

Gomez, Scott
(1979–   ) *hockey player*

An agile playmaker and skilled puck handler who was a first-round selection of the 1998 National Hockey League (NHL) draft, Scott Gomez helped power the New Jersey Devils to the Stanley Cup Championship in 2000, the same year he was awarded the Calder Trophy, given to the league's top rookie. He was born on December 23, 1979, in Anchorage, Alaska. The son of a Mexican-American construction worker, Carlo, and a Colombian-American homemaker, Delia, Gomez grew up in Alaska's biggest city, becoming a standout hockey player at Anchorage East High School. As a freshman in high school, Gomez dominated his competition by scoring 30 goals and racking up 48 assists in only 28 games. As a sophomore, he totaled 56 goals and 49 assists in 27 games for an astounding average of almost four points a game.

At the age of 15, Gomez began playing for the Anchorage North Stars of the Anchorage Adult

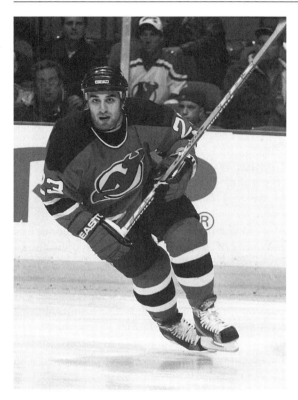

Scott Gomez, seen here in a 2003 game, helped lead the New Jersey Devils to two Stanley Cup Championships in his first four seasons. *(Andy Marlin/WireImage.com)*

Hockey League (AAHL). Though he was playing against adults rather than other high school students, Gomez continued to put up impressive offensive statistics. In his one year in the AAHL, Gomez scored 70 goals and had 67 assists in 40 games. The next season, he played in the British Columbia Hockey League in western Canada, where he averaged two points a game for the South Surrey Eagles and was named the league's top rookie.

After enjoying an outstanding season in 1997–98 for the Tri-City (Washington) Americans in the Western Hockey League (WHL), Gomez was selected by the New Jersey Devils with the 27th pick of the first round in the 1998 NHL draft. He spent another year with Tri-City, scoring 30 goals

and notching 78 assists in just 58 games, earning recognition on the WHL West All-Star team.

Gomez made his NHL debut on October 2, 1999, and scored his first goal two weeks later in a Devils victory over the New York Islanders. In November 1999, Gomez posted an eight-game scoring streak spanning almost three weeks and earned Rookie of the Month honors. In December, with his parents in the stands at New York City's Madison Square Garden, Gomez scored his first hat trick (three goals in a game by an individual player) of his career in a Devils 3-3 tie with the New York Rangers.

Later in the season, Gomez played in the All-Star Game and strung together another extended scoring streak of seven games. He finished his stellar rookie season with a team high 51 assists, a rookie class leading 70 points, and the Calder Trophy, awarded to the NHL's top first-year player. Gomez capped this phenomenal year by scoring 10 points in the playoffs, which culminated in the Devils' Stanley Cup Championship over the Dallas Stars.

In his second season of 2000–01, the 20-year-old Gomez continued to excel. He helped lead the Devils to an Atlantic Division title with a club record of 48 wins and 111 total team points. His 49 assists ranked second on the Devils, who won the Eastern Conference title before falling to the Colorado Avalanche in the Stanley Cup finals. In 2001–02, Gomez again ranked second on the Devils in assists before breaking his hand late in the season. Without their talented center, the Devils lost in the first round of the playoffs.

Gomez and the Devils had another standout year in 2002–03. He led the team in assists, including five in one game, a 6-0 March 30 victory over the New York Islanders. In the playoffs, Gomez led the Devils to another Stanley Cup Championship when they defeated the Mighty Ducks of Anaheim. The next season, Gomez again played a key role in leading the Devils to another 40-plus win campaign (their eighth consecutive) by sharing the NHL lead with 56 assists. Late in the season,

Gomez scored his 300th career point at the age of 24, though his six assists in the five games of the Devils first-run playoff series versus the Philadelphia Flyers were not enough to prevent New Jersey's elimination.

A labor dispute between the NHL Players Association and the owners of the league's teams led to the cancellation of the 2004–05 season. Before the impasse was finally settled in summer 2005, Gomez returned to his home state to play for the Alaska Aces of the East Coast Hockey League. Instead of the nearly $3 million he would have earned if the NHL had been playing, Gomez earned $500 a week playing in front of the many friends and family he had in Alaska. Aces coach Davis Payne noted of his new star player, "This all speaks volumes to what kind of person Scotty is. He doesn't have to be doing this, but he wants to enjoy the game, wants to play hockey, be part of a hockey team and give back to his community." Gomez scored a goal and tallied an assist in his first game in Alaska and, despite suffering a broken pelvis late in the season, led the league in scoring.

With the labor dispute finally settled prior to the 2005–06 season, Gomez returned to the Devils and picked up where he left off before the work stoppage. He played in all 82 of New Jersey's regular season games, scoring 33 goals and tallying 51 assists, placing him in the top 25 in the league in each of those categories. Due largely to Gomez's production and leadership, the Devils won the Atlantic Division with a record of 46-27-9 before losing in the Eastern Conference semifinals to the eventual Stanley Cup champion Carolina Hurricanes.

Further Reading

Farber, Michael. "Devil May Care: The Sensational Scott Gomez, a Rare Latino from Alaska, Has Brought Rookie-of-the-year Talent and Much Needed Levity to Stodgy New Jersey." *Sports Illustrated,* 6 March 2000, p. 42.

Nevala, Matt. "Gomez Is Now an Alaska Ace: NHL Star to Skate at Home during Lockout." *Alaska Daily News,* 26 October 2004.

"Scott Gomez." National Hockey League Web site. Available online. URL: http://www.nhl.com/players/8467351.html. Downloaded on January 14, 2006.

Gómez, Wilfredo
(Bazooka)
(1956–   ) *boxer*

A world champion in three boxing categories and the owner of a record 17 title defenses of his junior featherweight crown, Wilfredo Gómez was one of the most prolific punchers in boxing history, earning 42 of his 44 victories by knockout. He was born on October 29, 1956, in Las Monjas, Puerto Rico. He grew up in the barrios of Las Monjas and discovered boxing as a means to defend himself. He said of his childhood, "I was fighting so much, it's like I was born to fight."

Though he never fought at more than 5'5" and 135 pounds, Gómez's overwhelming power and ferocious style earned him the nickname "Bazooka" and led to an amateur career highlighted by 90 wins in 95 bouts and a world amateur title in 1974 as well as a place on the Puerto Rican boxing team in the 1972 Olympics in Munich, Germany, where he was eliminated in the first round by an Egyptian fighter.

Gómez made his professional debut on November 16, 1974, against Jacinto Fuentes in Panama City. Over the next two years, Gómez fought throughout Central America and Puerto Rico, winning his following 15 contests all by knockout or technical knockout. Though initially competing as a bantamweight, Gómez had moved up to junior featherweight when he defeated Dong Kyun Yum in a 12th-round knockout, to win that division's World Boxing Council (WBC) championship. En route to making 17 title defenses, all by knockout, Gómez defeated Japanese boxing star Royal Kobayashi in Japan and handed CARLOS ZÁRATE his first loss in 53 professional fights.

Gómez suffered his first professional loss in a knockout to boxing legend SALVADOR SÁNCHEZ on August 21, 1981, in Las Vegas. Less than five months later, he began another winning streak of nine fights, winning the first eight by knockout and the ninth in a unanimous decision over the iron-jawed Juan Laporte, bringing Gómez the WBC featherweight title. His reign ended in his next fight, an 11th-round knockout loss to Azumah Nelson.

Another climb in weight class was again accompanied by another championship, when Gómez won a close and controversial majority decision over Rocky Lockridge on May 19, 1985, to earn the World Boxing Association (WBA) junior lightweight crown. Again, as when he won the featherweight crown, Gómez's hold on the title would be short lived, as he lost his first title defense to Alfredo Layne in a ninth-round knockout on May 24, 1986. Gómez retired shortly after that bout, though he returned to win only one fight in both 1988 and 1989.

Gomez retired in Venezuela and discovered that battles outside the ring proved tougher than those he usually pummeled inside it. He struggled with alcohol and cocaine addiction, was arrested for drug possession, and was involved in spousal abuse that contributed to the breakup of his three marriages. Though he has reportedly overcome his substance abuse and reconciled with one of his former wives, Gómez struggles with physical problems resulting from a life in the ring, including a neurological disorder that affects his speech and short-term memory.

Gómez's career record was 44-3-1, with 42 wins coming by knockout. He was inducted into the International Boxing Hall of Fame in 1995. Asked how he would like to be remembered, Gómez responded, "As a world champion for Puerto Rico who gave all his power to boxing."

Further Reading

Myler, Patrick. *A Century of Boxing Greats: Inside the Ring with the Hundred Best Boxers.* London: Robson Books, 2000.

"Wilfredo Gomez." International Boxing Hall of Fame Web site. Available online. URL: http://www.ibhof.com/gomez.htm. Downloaded on July 5, 2005.

Further Viewing

Bazooka: The Battles of Wilfredo Gomez. London: One Eyed Films, 2003.

Gonzales, Pancho
(Ricardo Alonso Gonzáles)
(1928–1995) *tennis player*

An intense competitor renowned for his pure and powerful serve and his often gruff personality, Pancho Gonzales (sometimes spelled Gonzalez) emerged from humble beginnings to win two U.S. amateur championships before dominating the pro tennis tour in the 1950s and early 1960s and, at the age of 41, winning the longest match in the history of Wimbledon. He was born Ricardo Alonso Gonzales on May 9, 1928, in Los Angeles. He grew up in the South Central section of Los Angeles, one of seven children in his family, rebelling against the direction of his house painter father, Manuel, and mother, Carmen, by hustling pool and teaching himself how to play tennis on the public courts of the city with a 51-cent racket he had received as a Christmas gift. Gonzales became one of the top boy tennis players in Los Angeles despite being perceived as an outsider due to his Mexican heritage and lower-class economic status. He quit high school after two years to devote himself full time to tennis but was banned from junior tournaments because he was a dropout. At the age of 15, Gonzales was arrested for burglarizing houses and spent a year in juvenile detention before joining the navy. Within a few years, Gonzales's AWOLs (absent without leave) and poor conduct led to a dishonorable discharge from military service.

Gonzales returned to Los Angeles and began playing tennis again, sharpening his attacking style on the fast concrete courts of Los Angeles and quickly reassuming his dominant status among amateur players in southern California. Now married and known mainly by the name "Pancho," Gonzales entered the 1948 U.S. Championships in Forest Hills, New York, ranked number 17 and emerged as champion following a straight set win over South African Eric Sturgess.

The next year the 6'3" Gonzales, famed for his blistering and accurate right-handed serve, defended his U.S. Championship in a thrilling five-set victory over Ted Schroeder. Riding the wave of his success, Gonzales accepted the $75,000 contract offered by top pro Bobby Riggs in 1950 and began his professional career.

In the 1950s, before the open era of tennis, only amateurs were allowed to play in the prestigious tournaments such as Wimbledon and the U.S. Championships. Few believed that even the winners of those events were the best in the game. That distinction belonged to the professionals who conducted barnstorming tours in which they were matched against newly signed and highly touted challengers, such as Gonzales was in 1950. Gonzales began his pro career by playing against 28-year-old Jack Kramer, who was widely considered the best player in the world. In his first pro season, Gonzales lost 96 of 123 matches.

Gonzales's poor showing against Kramer damaged his reputation and jeopardized his pro career. He spent most of the next four years—his early prime as a player—dabbling in hot rod racing, bowling, dog breeding, and running a tennis shop in Los Angeles that soon failed. In 1954, Kramer invited Gonzales to join a round-robin tour he had organized for top pros including Don Budge and PANCHO SEGURA. Gonzales was a consistent winner in these matches, earning a seven-year contract from Kramer. Gonzales dominated the pro tour for the rest of the 1950s, winning every U.S. pro title from 1954 through 1961, besting the attempts of talented challengers, including

Segura, Tony Trabert, ALEX OLMEDO, and Ken Rosewall.

Although Gonzales's talent and ability to attract tennis fans was undeniable, so too was his irascible nature on the court. He once used his racket to destroy the microphone of a field umpire who refused to overrule a call during a match and recklessly shattered a wall clock when he smacked a ball in frustration. He often had strained relationships with tennis promoters and members of the media. Gonzales's booming voice was regularly heard in arguments with officials, opponents, and even spectators, though these incidents only seemed to focus his intensity and improve his play. The Australian tennis great of the 1960s and 1970s Rod Lever explained of Gonzales, "We hoped he wouldn't get upset; it just made him tougher. Later when he got older, he would get into arguments to

Pancho Gonzales, at 41 years old, competes in the longest match in the history of Wimbledon, eventually defeating his opponent. *(EMPICS)*

stall for time and rest, and we had to be careful it didn't put us off our games."

Gonzales's testy personality extended beyond the court as well. He was married and divorced six times, the final marriage to Rita Agassi, the sister of future tennis star Andre Agassi and Gonzales's student when she was a teen. Only a few of Gonzales's eight children (one of whom died after being thrown from a horse) remained close to him throughout his life. He was, said friend and competitor Olmedo, "a lonely wolf."

By the time the open era allowing pros to play in tournaments such as Wimbledon and the U.S. Open came about, Gonzales was in his early 40s and already inducted into the International Tennis Hall of Fame. He defeated second-seeded Tony Roche and reached the quarterfinals in the first U.S. Open in 1968 but struggled to keep up physically with the great young players of the time. Despite his obvious signs of age (prominent streaks of gray hair and sunbaked wrinkles on his face), the 41-year-old grandfather made tennis history in 1969 by defeating 25-year-old Charlie Pasarell in the longest match in Wimbledon history, by the amazing scores of 22-24, 1-6, 16-14, 6-3, 11-9. The five-hour, 12-minute match (extended over two days), which also set a Wimbledon record for most games played, led to the adoption of tiebreaking rules in tennis, considered one of the most significant structural changes to the game during the 20th century.

The remaining years of Gonzales's career did not bring any major championships, though they did include wins over stars Arthur Ashe, Rod Laver, John Newcombe, Stan Smith, and teenager Jimmy Connors. After his playing days were done, Gonzales was a tournament director at Caesars Palace in Las Vegas, Nevada, from 1970 to 1985 before being fired and living a spartan existence in a small house near the Las Vegas airport.

Gonzales attended the 1994 U.S. Open and was in his hotel room in New York City when severe back and abdominal pain caused him to visit a doctor upon his return to Las Vegas. Gon-

zales was diagnosed with cancer in his stomach, esophagus, chin, and brain. Pancho Gonzales—who Romanian tennis star and manager Ion Tiriac called responsible for "the beginning of professional tennis as we know it . . . the father of everything we have today"—died less than a year later, on July 3, 1995.

Further Reading

"Pancho Gonzales." International Tennis Hall of Fame Web site. Available online. URL: http://www.tennisfame.org/enshrinees/pancho_gonzales.html. Downloaded on January 15, 2006.

Price, S. L. "The Lone Wolf: Pancho Gonzales May Have Been the Best Tennis Player of All Time, but His Fits of Rage Offended Almost Everyone in the Game, Cost Him Six Marriages and Alienated Him from All but the Last of His Eight Children." *Sports Illustrated,* 24 June 2002, p. 68.

"Ricardo 'Pancho' Gonzales." Latino Legends in Sports Web site. Available online. URL: http://www.latinosportslegends.com/pancho_gonzales_bio.htm. Downloaded on January 15, 2006.

González, Gerardo   *See* GONZÁLEZ, KID GAVILAN

González, Juan
(Igor, Juan Gone)
(1969–)   *baseball player*

The all-time major league leader in home runs among Puerto Rican baseball players, Juan González ranked in the top 10 in the American League (AL) in runs batted in (RBIs) nine times during the 1990s and won two AL Most Valuable Player (MVP) awards, helping power the Texas Rangers to three AL West Division titles between 1996 and 1999. He was born on October 16, 1969, in Vega Baja, Puerto Rico. He grew up in Vega Baja, about 25 miles from the Puerto Rican capital of San Juan, in the Alto de Cuba neighborhood notorious for its drugs and poverty. González acquired the nickname "Igor" because of his fondness for a professional wrestler named the "Mighty Igor," but by his teens the nickname seemed appropriate because of his prodigious power with youth league teams, where he batted clean-up behind future New York Yankees centerfielder BERNIE WILLIAMS in games that occasionally pitted him against future Texas Rangers teammate IVÁN RODRÍGUEZ. When González was 16 years old, he and his mother convinced his father to allow him to sign a contract with the Texas Rangers for a bonus of $75,000.

González began his minor league career standing an imposing 6'3" and weighing 170 pounds. The powerful right-handed hitting outfielder quickly rose up through the Rangers system, receiving a call up to the majors just over a month shy of his 20th birthday. Two years later, González earned the starting left field job with the Rangers and responded by hitting .264 with 27 home runs and 102 runs batted in (RBIs). The next season, the 22-year-old González led the AL in home runs with 43 and drove in 109 runs, despite striking out 143 times with only 35 walks.

In 1993, González honed his bat speed and long, quick swing while gaining strength from four years of intensive weight training, which added more than 50 pounds to his frame, to lead the AL again in home runs with 46 while driving in 118 runs and improving his batting average to .310. However, the weight training that helped produce González's prodigious power numbers also played a role in back and neck injuries that prevented him from playing in almost half of the Rangers' games during 1994 and 1995. González also endured personal struggles, including the exposure of a messy divorce from his third wife and a tabloid-making subsequent marriage to a famous Puerto Rican singer, Olga Tañón.

González enjoyed a dominant season in 1996 despite missing 28 games with a torn leg muscle, leading the Rangers to their first playoff appearance by batting .314, with 47 home runs and 144

RBI. Now known by a new nickname, "Juan Gone," which referred to his home run power, González was awarded the AL MVP following the season, and though Texas fell in four games to the New York Yankees in the AL division series, González impressed by batting .438, hitting home runs in each game, joining Reggie Jackson (1977) and Ken Griffey, Jr. (1995), as the only players in major league history to hit five home runs in a single postseason series. González's 1997 season again featured a significant injury (torn ligaments in his left thumb, which cost him 29 games), though he managed to have 42 home runs and drive in 131 runs.

Like 1996, 1998 was a power-fueled success for González and the Rangers. His 101 RBIs at the All-Star Break made him only the second player (joining Hank Greenberg, who accomplished the feat in 1935) to reach the century mark in that category by baseball's midsummer classic. He remained on pace to break Hack Wilson's major league record of 191 RBIs into August, though he finished the season with 157 RBIs, which was the most for an AL player since 1949. González's historic RBI total and his .318 batting average and 45 home runs earned the 28-year-old hitting star another MVP award. The Rangers again lost to the Yankees in the playoffs, with González managing only one double in 12 at-bats.

With the exception of a solid 1999 season with Texas and an outstanding 2001 season playing for the Cleveland Indians, the rest of González's career was a disappointment marked by a wide variety of injuries. Prior to the 2000 season, González was traded to the Detroit Tigers but missed 47 games and was unhappy, rejecting Detroit's lucrative long-term contract offer to sign instead with Cleveland for just one season.

After his success in 2001, González rejoined the Rangers as a free agent but missed more than half the team's games over two years while on the disabled list. In 2004, González played for the Kansas City Royals, missing many games with an assortment of injuries and hitting only five home runs in 33 games. Again in Cleveland in 2005,

González's season ended when he injured his hamstring during just one three-pitch at-bat.

Further Reading

"Juan Gonzalez." Major League Baseball Web site. Available online. URL: http://mlb.mlb.com/ NASApp/mlb/team/player_career.jsp?player_ id=114932&y=1989. Downloaded on January 15, 2006.

Pearlman, Jeff. "The Power of Juan: After a Miserable Season in Detroit, Juan Gonzalez Has Gone Gaga over Cleveland, Where He Has Hit It Big for the Division-leading Indians." *Sports Illustrated,* 2 September 2001, p. 56.

Verducci, Tom. "Puerto Rico's New Patron Saint." *Sports Illustrated,* 5 April 1993, p. 60.

González, Kid Gavilan
(Gerardo González)
(1926–2003) *boxer*

A dynamic and popular welterweight champion during the early 1950s, Kid Gavilan González earned his legacy as a powerful and instinctive boxer and as the inventor of the half hook, half uppercut known as the bolo punch, which he said was developed by years of cutting sugarcane with a machete in his native Cuba. He was born Gerardo González on January 6, 1926, in Camagüey, Cuba. González grew up in Camagüey, the cattle capital of Cuba located about 300 miles east of Havana. González had very little schooling, spending most of his youth shining shoes, peddling newspapers, cutting sugarcane, and working at an ice factory while pursuing his dream of becoming a boxer.

His first amateur fight took place in a cockfighting ring in Palo Seco. González, then a 90-pound flyweight, overwhelmed his opponent in another bout just one week later. By the age of 15, González was one of the top amateur boxers in Cuba. He turned professional at the age of 17 under the tutelage of Fernando Balido, the owner

of a fruit stand called El Gavilán (the sparrow hawk), and soon the nickname "Kid Gavilán" was applied to González to market the store and reflect the powerful instincts of the young fighter.

Kid Gavilan won his first pro bout on June 5, 1943, in a decision over Antonio Díaz in Havana. His quick hands, durable body, and exciting showmanship helped him win 28 of his next 30 fights over the next three years, including a perfect record in his three fights in New York City in late 1946. In 1947, Kid Gavilan was ranked among the top 10 welterweights in the world, and in 1948, he was widely considered the top challenger to the legendary champion Sugar Ray Robinson. Kid Gavilan lost his first bout to Robinson in 1948 and lost again to Robinson in a title bout a year later. Robinson would later claim that the two toughest wins of his career were those against Kid Gavilan.

Kid Gavilan won the world welterweight crown after Robinson moved to the middleweight category by defeating Johnny Bratton in a decision on May 18, 1951, in New York City. The charismatic Kid Gavilan wore his distinctive white trunks and boots and punished opponents with his trademark flashy and wide bolo punch in seven successful title defenses and several nontitle fights over the next three years. Kid Gavilan lost the welterweight crown on October 20, 1954, in a decision to Johnny Saxton in Philadelphia. The controversy surrounding the decision was echoed by 20 of the 22 ringside reporters, who believed that Kid Gavilan had earned the victory.

A fan favorite throughout his career, Kid Gavilan was a celebrated regular at many restaurants and nightclubs and often suffered financially and personally due to his excessive drinking. He was an active supporter of charities and struggling family members, though he also left his wife and children—who later depended on public aid—and racked up a debt of tens of thousands of dollars to the Internal Revenue Service.

Kid Gavilan never regained a championship bout. He boxed from 1954 through 1958 showing flashes of his iron chin but also demonstrating the effect of his hard living in more than 100 fights. During those last years, Kid Gavilan won only 10 of his final 26 bouts and ended his career with a record of 107-30-6.

After his retirement, Kid Gavilan's attempts to succeed as an entertainer in nightclubs ended in failure as he discovered that his fans only truly wanted to see him perform in the ring. He returned to Cuba, where he became a devout Jehovah's Witness and was harassed by officials of Cuban dictator Fidel Castro's regime. Having lost his farm, nearly broke, and almost blind from cataracts in his eyes, Kid Gavilan exiled himself to Miami, where he lost jobs as a member of Muhammad Ali's staff and as a trainer due to his drinking and his undisciplined lifestyle.

Kid Gavilan, who was inducted into the International Boxing Hall of Fame in 1990, lived out his final days in a Miami nursing home, making occasional personal appearances at boxing-related events. He died of a heart attack on February 13, 2003. His funeral, which was paid for by fighters, boxing historians, and friends, attracted hundreds from the fight community who came to pay their respects to the beloved former champion, at rest in his coffin with a bold white boxing robe across his chest.

Further Reading

Cassidy, Robert, Jr. "New Headstone for Kid Gavilan." Sweet Science Web site. Available online. URL: http://www.thesweetscience.com/boxing-article/2128/video-report-new-headstone-kid-gavilan/. Downloaded on January 15, 2006.

Encinosa, Enrique. "Kid Gavilan: The Sparrow Hawk." Cyber Boxing Zone Web site. Available online. URL: http://www.cyberboxingzone.com/boxing/w0403-ee.html. Downloaded on January 15, 2006.

"Gavilan, Kid (Gerardo Gonzalez)." Hickok Sports Web site. Available online. URL: http://www.hickoksports.com/biograph/gavilankid.shtml#other. Downloaded on Janaury 15, 2006.

Gonzalez, Tony
(Anthony Gonzalez)
(1976–) *football player*

A tall, graceful, and durable former college basketball player whose dependable hands helped him become the all-time leading pass catcher for the Kansas City Chiefs, Tony Gonzalez leads active tight ends in receptions, receiving yards, and touchdown catches and already ranks among the most prolific players of his position in the history of the National Football League (NFL). He was born Anthony Gonzalez on February 27, 1976, in Torrance, California. Gonzalez grew up in Huntington Beach, California, a town nicknamed "Surf City" for its ample and picturesque Pacific coastline located in Orange County, south of Los Angeles. Gonzalez's unique ethnic background traces its roots to his paternal grandfather, who immigrated to the United States from the Portuguese Islands of Cape Verde off the coast of Africa, as well as his combination of Jamaican, Mexican, Native American, African-American, and European ancestors.

Gonzalez did not excel in sports until he enjoyed success as a basketball player in eighth grade. Gonzalez lettered in both basketball and football at Huntington Beach High School. As a senior, Gonzalez caught 62 passes for 945 yards and 13 touchdowns in football and averaged 26 points in basketball to earn numerous honors, including Orange County Co-Athlete of the Year in 1993, an award he shared with future golfing great Tiger Woods.

Gonzalez accepted an athletic scholarship from the University of California—Berkeley (Cal). He played both football and basketball at Cal, using his sturdy and agile 6'5" frame to catch 45 passes and three touchdowns as a tight end on the gridiron and averaging six points and four rebounds per game on the hard court after his first two seasons. Gonzalez flourished as a junior with new football coach Steve Mariucci, earning First Team All-America selection at tight end with 46 receptions for 699 yards and five touchdowns. Gonzalez

Tony Gonzalez set the National Football League single-season record for most receptions by a tight end in 2004. *(Kirby Lee/WireImage.com)*

also helped Cal to the Sweet Sixteen of the 1997 National Collegiate Athletic Association (NCAA) basketball tournament by replacing the team's injured leading scorer and Pac 10 Conference Most Valuable Player to score a season high 23 points in a second-run defeat of Villanova University.

Following his stellar junior year, Gonzalez entered the 1997 NFL draft with one year of college eligibility remaining. The Kansas City Chiefs traded with the Houston Oilers to move up five spots to select Gonzalez with the 13th pick of the first round. Gonzalez played in all 16 Chiefs games as a rookie, catching 33 passes, making two touchdowns, and winning distinction as the team's top first-year player. In his second season, Gonzalez started all 16 games and ranked second in the Chiefs with 59 receptions.

Gonzalez missed the season opener in 1999 (the only game he missed in his first nine pro seasons) with a knee injury but managed to start the remaining 15 games to lead Kansas City with 76 catches, 849 yards, and four touchdown receptions, becoming the first Chiefs tight end to make a Pro Bowl appearance and earn consensus First Team All-Pro accolades. In 2000, Gonzalez firmly established himself as an NFL star and one of the league's most potent offensive weapons by leading all NFL tight ends with 93 receptions for 1,203 yards and nine touchdowns, which were capped by his trademark one-handed slam dunk of the football over the goalpost crossbar. In only his fourth campaign, Gonzalez had already eclipsed the Chiefs' record for receptions by a tight end, and he became the first tight end in history to record four consecutive 100-yards receiving games.

Although Gonzalez is most admired for his combination of sure hands, speed, and sharp route running, he is also a very effective blocker, providing the Chiefs with another critical component of the tight end position. In 2001, Ozzie Newsome, a former Cleveland Browns tight end and a member of the Pro Football Hall of Fame, reflected on how Gonzalez's unique skill was affecting football by noting, "He's really something special. He can do so many different things that he's really revolutionizing the position. When I played people said I was athletic, but this guy is something else."

In the 2001–02 and 2002 seasons, Gonzalez continued his outstanding play by averaging 68 catches and almost 850 receiving yards and earning two more Pro Bowl invitations. In 2003, Gonzalez was a Consensus All-Pro, snagging 71 passes for a team high 916 receiving yards and scoring 10 touchdowns. With his 417th career reception, Gonzalez became the all-time Chiefs' reception leader as he led Kansas City to a 13-3 record in the American Football Conference (AFC) West Division title, before falling in the playoffs to the Indianapolis Colts.

In his eighth season (2004), Gonzalez showed no evidence of slowing down his pursuit of becoming known as one of the greatest tight ends of all time. He led Kansas City with a single season franchise record and all-time record for tight ends of 102 receptions for 1,258 yards and 12 touchdowns. His 102 receptions led the entire NFL, making Gonzalez only the third tight end since the NFL–American Football League (AFL) merger and the first since Todd Christensen of the Oakland Raiders in 1986 to accomplish that feat. With 1,258 yards in receptions, Gonzalez ranked second all time in a single season among tight ends, placing Gonzalez among and beyond the accomplishments of tight end greats Newsome, Mike Ditka, Kellen Winslow, and Shannon Sharpe.

Gonzalez followed that remarkable campaign with solid efforts in 2005 and 2006, playing in 31 of 32 games and catching 151 passes for 1,805 yards, including seven touchdowns. Following the 2006 season, the Chiefs signed Gonzalez to a five-year contract worth more than $30 million. As an active player, Gonzalez is currently ineligible to gain what will surely be a place in the Pro Football Hall of Fame, though his number 88 jersey arrived in Canton, Ohio—the home of the Hall of Fame—following the last game of the Chiefs' 2004 season, a 24-17 loss to the San Diego Chargers, when Gonzalez caught 14 passes for 144 yards to set the single-season NFL mark for catches by a tight end.

Further Reading

"Gonzalez's Record-Setting Jersey Arrives in Canton." Pro Football Hall of Fame Web site. Available online. URL: http://www.profootballhof.com/history/release.jsp?release_id=1375. Downloaded on January 15, 2006.

Montville, Leigh. "Chief Weapon: Kansas City's Athletic Tight End, Tony Gonzalez, Used Some of His Basketball Skills to Develop into One of the NFL's Premier Players at His Position." *Sports Illustrated,* 27 December 1999, p. 44.

"Tony Gonzalez—#88." Kansas City Chiefs Web site. Available online. URL: http://www.kcchiefs.com/player/tony_gonzalez/. Downloaded on January 15, 2006.

Gramática, Martín
(Automatica Gramatica)
(1975–   ) *football player*

The kicker for the Super Bowl XXXVII champion Tampa Bay Buccaneers, Martín Gramática also holds the National Collegiate Athletic Association (NCAA) record for the longest field goal made (65 yards) without a tee. He was born on November 27, 1975, in Buenos Aires. Gramática was an outstanding soccer player as a youth in Argentina and never played organized football until his senior year of high school in La Belle, Florida. During that one year as a kicker on La Belle High School's football team, Gramática connected on 10 field goals, including a 52 yarder, and all 22 of his extra point attempts, earning an athletic scholarship to Kansas State University as a kicker.

Gramática was a four-year starter for the Kansas State Wildcats. In his first two college seasons, he converted 13 of 17 field goal attempts, with two of his misses coming from more than 50 yards. Gramática missed the entire 1996 season due to injury but was granted a medical "redshirt," which allowed him to retain two years of eligibility. Gramática made the most of these two years, establishing himself as one of the best kickers in the country. In 1997, he was a consensus All-American and the winner of the Lou Groza Award, given to the best college kicker, after connecting on 19 of 20 field goal attempts, including all three of his attempts beyond 50 yards. In 1998, he helped the Wildcats contend for a national championship by converting more than 70 percent of his field goal attempts. In addition to his accuracy, Gramática demonstrated the power of his right foot by forcing touchbacks on more than half of his kickoffs. He finished his college career ranking second in Big 12 Conference history in scoring with 348 points.

A 1999 National Football League (NFL) draft preview noted of Gramática, "One of the finest kicking specialists to come out of the collegiate ranks in the last 20 years, [he] has a smooth, fluid motion, putting all of his leg power behind his attempts."

The Tampa Bay Buccaneers surprised many by selecting Gramática in the third round of the draft, far higher than kickers are typically selected.

In his rookie season of 1999, Gramática converted 27 of 32 field goal attempts, including three of four beyond 50 yards, and all 25 of his points after touchdown attempts. He also accounted for all six Tampa points in their 11-6 loss to the St. Louis Rams in that season's National Football Conference (NFC) championship game.

A fan favorite in Tampa for his kicking proficiency and demonstrative celebrations, he was dubbed "Automatica Gramática" because of his dependability. In 2000, Gramática was named to the Pro Bowl after another outstanding season in which he connected on 28 of 34 field goal attempts, including five of seven from beyond 50 yards, and all 42 of his extra point attempts.

A strong 2001 season by Gramática was followed by his 2002 performance, in which he again hit more than 80 percent of his field goal attempts and 100 percent of his extra point attempts. He also made a critical 48-yard field goal in Tampa's 27-10 win over the Philadelphia Eagles in the NFC championship game, which brought the Bucaneers their first-ever Super Bowl appearance. In Super Bowl XXXVII, Gramática kicked two field goals and six extra points in Tampa's 48-21 rout of the Oakland Raiders.

Gramática's steady dependability eluded him in the 2003 season, in which he converted only four of 11 attempts beyond 40 yards and missed his first extra point as a professional, leading to a loss to the Carolina Panthers. Nagging injuries led to another disappointing season for Gramática in 2004, resulting in his release by Tampa late in the season. He was picked up by the Indianapolis Colts, where he served as a kickoff specialist before he was again released.

After not playing in 2005, Gramática signed with the New England Patriots prior to the 2006 season with hopes that he could make the roster and replace Adam Vinatieri, who left the Patriots for a lucrative deal with Indianapolis. Gramática was cut by the Patriots, though he played briefly for the

Colts in 2006 when Vinatieri was injured, before finishing the season with the Dallas Cowboys.

Further Reading
"Martin Gramatica." National Football League Players Association Web site. Available online. URL: http://www.nflplayers.com/players_network/players_network.aspx?strSection=bio&ID=27075. Downloaded on July 3, 2005.

"NFL Draft: Martin Gramatica, Kicker." *Milwaukee Journal Sentinel* Web site. Available online. URL: http://www.jsonline.com/packer/stat/apr99/st-gramatica.asp. Downloaded on July 3, 2005.

Guerin, Bill
(William Guerin)
(1970–) *hockey player*

The fifth overall pick in the 1989 National Hockey League (NHL) draft by the New Jersey Devils, Bill Guerin soon emerged as one of hockey's most powerful forwards, helping lead the Devils to their first Stanley Cup Championship in 1995 and later earning the Most Valuable Player (MVP) award in the 2001 NHL All-Star Game while a member of the Boston Bruins. He was born William Guerin on November 9, 1970, in Worcester, Massachusetts. Guerin's Irish-American father and Nicaraguan mother soon moved the family to the western Massachusetts town of Wilbraham, where, like countless other boys in his area, Guerin dreamed of one day playing for the Boston Bruins. He possessed outstanding speed as a young hockey player, particularly for someone who was larger than almost all the other players. When he was 14 years old, Guerin began playing for the Springfield (Massachusetts) Junior Blues, a team in the New England Junior Hockey League (NEJHL). In four years in the NEJHL, Guerin averaged almost a goal and an assist per game and earned a scholarship to play hockey at Boston College.

Guerin continued to excel once at Boston College. As a freshman in 1989–90, he scored 14 goals and tallied

11 assists in 39 games, helping Boston College win the Hockey East Conference championship and earn a trip to the "Frozen Four," the semifinals of the National Collegiate Athletic Association (NCAA) Hockey Tournament. The next season, Guerin scored 26 goals and notched 19 assists in 38 games as Boston College repeated as the Hockey East champions and returned to the NCAA tournament.

Following his stellar sophomore season, Guerin was the fifth player selected in the first round of the 1991 NHL draft by the New Jersey Devils. He spent most of the 1991–92 season with the Devils' minor league affiliate in Utica (New York), though he did appear in five games for New Jersey. The next season, the 6'2", 200-pound Guerin played in 65 of New Jersey's 82 games, scoring 14 goals and earning 20 assists. In the 1993–94 season, Guerin increased his totals to 25 goals and 19 assists as the Devils reached the Eastern Conference finals, where they lost a thrilling series to the eventual Stanley Cup champion New York Rangers.

Although Guerin missed more than 30 games in the 1994–95 season due to injury, he played a key role in helping New Jersey win their first Stanley Cup Championship. Guerin remained an important part of New Jersey's success until he was traded to the Edmonton Oilers early in the 1997–98 season.

During a break in the season for the winter Olympics in Nagano, Japan, Guerin contributed three assists as a member of the U.S. team that failed to medal. Also during that season, Guerin helped raise money to provide relief for people in his mother's native Nicaragua who had suffered from the devastating effects of Hurricane Mitch.

Guerin was one of Edmonton's top players from the time of his arrival until the struggling Oilers traded him early in the 2000–01 season to his beloved Boston Bruins for a talented young player and Boston's top two draft choices. Guerin thrived in Boston, scoring 28 goals and compiling 35 assists in 64 games. He gained his first selection to the NHL All-Star game, where his three goals and two assists helped the North American Team defeat the World Team 14-12 and earned Guerin the game's MVP award.

Guerin enjoyed another standout season in 2001–02 for the Bruins with 41 goals and 25 assists. In early 2002, he returned to the winter Olympics, representing the United States in Salt Lake City, where the American team won the silver medal by defeating Russia before losing to Canada in the gold medal game.

Despite his strong performance and fan support in Boston, the Bruins did not come close to matching the lucrative contract offer Guerin received from the Dallas Stars prior to the 2002–03 season. With Dallas, Guerin averaged 30 goals and 30 assists in his first two seasons, both of which resulted in All-Star Game appearances for Guerin and playoff berths for the Stars.

Guerin struggled when the NHL resumed play in 2005–06 after losing an entire season due to a labor dispute, scoring only 13 goals in 70 games with Dallas. The 35-year-old Guerin then agreed to a free-agent deal with the St. Louis Blues for the relatively modest terms of one year and $2 million. Guerin experienced a resurgence with the Blues, averaging over a point a game in the first half of the 2006–07 season (18 goals, 31 assists) and earning selection to the NHL Western Conference All-Star team.

Further Reading

"Bill Guerin." National Hockey League Web site. Available online. URL: http://www.nhl.com/players/8456464.html. Downloaded on January 14, 2006.

"The Great 8." ESPN Web site. Available online. URL: http://espn.go.com/nhl/columns/buccigross_john/1448821.html#great8. Downloaded on January 14, 2006.

Guerrero, Vladimir
(1976–) *baseball player*

The 2004 leader of the American League (AL) Most Valuable Player (MVP) award, Vladimir Guerrero is a consummate "five tool" baseball player, whose speed, defense, throwing arm, and consistent ability to hit for both average and power has led him to become one of the most respected players of his generation. He was born on February 9, 1976, in Nizao Bani, Dominican Republic. He grew up in Don Gregorio, a hilly village about 40 miles southwest of the capital, Santo Domingo. Guerrero's formal education ended after fifth grade. He spent his youth herding cattle and planting produce on his grandfather's farm to help provide income for his parents and five siblings and, in his free time, playing a form of baseball called "*la placa*" (the plate). In *la placa,* license plates were used as home plates, sticks served as bats, and lemons wrapped in rags sufficed as balls. Each hitter had to keep his stick touching the license plate as the pitch approached, which Guerrero later credited for his ability to hit very low pitches.

Like his three older brothers before him (including Wilton, who played professionally for eight years), Guerrero attracted interest from Major League Baseball scouts. In 1993, he signed a contract with the Montreal Expos for $2,000 at the age of 17, after hitching a ride to a tryout on the back of a motorcycle, carrying two mismatched spikes (baseball shoes) with a sock stuffed into one that was too large.

The 6'3", 200-plus-pound Guerrero rocketed off the Expos farm system by displaying the all-around power and skill that would later mark his major league career. By 1995, he was considered the best prospect in the Expos organization and one of the top young players in any team's system. In 1996, Guerrero was selected as the *Sporting News* Minor League Player of the Year, Eastern League Most Valuable Player, and Baseball America's AA Player of the Year after leading the Harrisburg Senators to the league championship. At age 20, Guerrero was the youngest position player in the Eastern League and the youngest player ever to win that league's batting crown.

In 1997 spring training, Guerrero became the only Expos rookie to make the opening day roster. Days before the season's first game, however, Guerrero broke his left foot after following

a pitch off of it. He played only 90 games that season because of an assortment of injuries to one of his hamstrings and hands as well as his back. He still managed to post impressive statistics, hitting 302 with 11 home runs and 40 runs batted in (RBIs).

Guerrero had recovered from his injuries of the previous season to blast opposing pitchers in 1998. He missed only three games and batted .324 with 202 hits, 38 home runs, and 109 RBIs. Only two players in major league history—Hall of Famers Mel Ott and Joe DiMaggio—have matched or surpassed those numbers before turning 23 years old.

He continued to amaze in 1999, when he was named to his first All-Star team by batting .316 with 42 home runs and 131 RBIs and finished among the top 10 performers in the major leagues in 11 different categories. His 31-game hitting streak that season was the longest in the majors during the 1990s and made Guerrero the youngest of four players in history to have 30 home runs and a 30-game hitting streak in the same season. (Rogers Hornsby, 1922; Joe DiMaggio, 1941; and Nomar Garciaparra, 1997, were the others.)

In 2000, Guerrero continued to rewrite the Expos record book by batting .345 (third in the National League [NL]), hitting 44 home runs (fifth in the NL), and driving in 123 RBIs (fourth in the NL). Despite playing for an Expos team that did not contend for the playoffs and drew little attention, Guerrero was voted by fans to start in the All-Star Game. Guerrero's 12 assists from right field ranked in the top 10 in the majors and helped solidify his well-earned reputation as having one of the strongest and most accurate arms of any outfielder. Guerrero posted another stellar season in 2001, batting .307 with 34 home runs and 108 RBIs, and showcased his complete skill set by stealing 37 bases.

Guerrero played all but one game in 2002, leading the major leagues in hits (206) and ranking in the top five in batting (.336), home runs (39), RBIs (111), and stolen bases (40), as he was again voted to start in the All-Star Game.

Although Guerrero's throwing arm discouraged runners from challenging him, he managed to throw out 14 men on the base paths, a tie for first in the major leagues. In 2003, Guerrero missed 50 games due to persistent back pain caused by a herniated disc. Despite missing almost a third of the season, Guerrero finished second on the Expos in RBIs (79) and finished the season with a .330 batting average.

With the conclusion of the 2003 season came the end of Guerrero's five-year contract. With the future of the Expos' franchise uncertain and countless teams interested in acquiring him, Guerrero decided to explore the free-agent market and eventually signed a five-year, $70 million contract with the Anaheim Angels. He won the 2004 American League (AL) MVP award after batting .337, belting 39 home runs and driving in 126 runs. In the season's final week with the Angels trailing the Oakland A's by three games in the AL West, Guerrero led the Angels to the division title by batting .536, hitting six home runs, and driving in 11 RBIs. Said Angels relief pitcher Troy Percival, "Flat and simple, he put us on his back unlike any player I've ever seen."

Guerrero followed his MVP performance with another outstanding season in 2005. He batted .317, belted 32 home runs, and drove in 108 runs to lead the Angels to the American League West Championship. The Angels defeated the New York Yankees in the American League division series before falling in five games to the eventual World Series champion Chicago White Sox in the American League Championship Series. Guerrero continued his excellent play in 2006, finishing fifth in the AL in batting average (.329) and hits (200) and seventh in RBIs (116).

Despite these heroics, Guerrero's admirers remained most impressed with his rare combination of unassuming nature and all-world talent. Of his shy star outfielder, Angels manager Mike Scioscia noted, "It really impresses you to see a guy with the incredible amount of natural talent that he has worked so hard to be an elite player and still

be approachable, still have perspective and care about winning as he does." Perhaps the greatest praise of Guerrero comes from his former Expos and Angels teammate ANDRÉS GALARRAGA who explained, "He swings like [ROBERTO] CLEMENTE. Bad pitches, he's still driving into the gap. He can reach everything inside and outside. I ask him how he hit a pitch and he doesn't know. That's the kind of hitter he is."

Further Reading
D'Hippolito, Joseph. "Vladimir Guerrero 2004 Player of the Year." *Baseball Digest,* January–February 2005.
Santiago, Esmerelda. "The Quiet Warrior." *Sports Illustrated,* 30 August 2004, p. 74.
"Vladimir Guerrero." Major League Baseball Web site. Available online. URL: http://mlb.mlb.com/NASApp/mlb/team/player.jsp?player_id=115223. Downloaded on January 15, 2006.

Guevara, Ana
(Ana Gabriela Guevara)
(1977–) *sprinter*

The silver medalist in the women's 400-meter race at the 2004 Olympics in Athens, Ana Guevara is the most successful track and field athlete in Mexican history. She was born Ana Gabriela Guevara on March 4, 1977, in Nogales, Mexico. She grew up the oldest of five children in a middle-class neighborhood in this small city located just over the south-central border of Arizona. Guevara excelled in athletics at a young age, gaining her greatest joy and recognition playing basketball. During her first year in college, she decided that her career in basketball did not provide a hopeful future, yet she remained determined to continue competing in athletics. She left college to focus on training in track and field, specifically the 400 meters.

Within five years, Guevara had ascended to the top of female runners in Latin America and soon proved to rank among the best in the world. In 2002, she won every individual race she participated in on the international circuit, earning third place in the race for Athlete of the Year from the International Association of Athletics Federations (IAAF), track and field's world governing body.

In 2003, Guevara won the gold medal at the World Championships in St-Denis, France, after placing sixth in 1999 and third in 2001. Her winning time in the 400 meters, 48.89 seconds, was more than a second better than her third-place mark two years earlier. This championship capped an impressive and steady improvement in

Ana Guevara celebrates her gold medal–winning effort in the 400 meters at the 2003 World Championships in Paris. *(EMPICS)*

Guevara's performance and helped establish her as Mexico's most popular female athlete and as the widely expected favorite to win the gold at the 2004 Olympics in Athens.

Guevara, whose streak of 28 consecutive victories would not conclude until a few months before the Olympics, embraced her status as a star and role model, repeatedly explaining that she hoped her achievements would inspire Mexican women in a nation that often rejected their athletic contributions. Indeed, Guevara had already had a major impact on traditional attitudes, evidenced by her enormous popularity among Mexicans of both genders. In homes and bars, millions of Mexicans gathered on the evening of August 24, 2004, to watch Guevara go for the gold.

Guevara trailed for most of the 400-meters finals. Rounding the final turn, however, Guevara moved inside versus Tonique Williams-Darling of the Bahamas, briefly pulling even, before Williams-Darling pulled away over the final 50 meters for the victory. Guevara finished second, .15 seconds behind, with a time of 49.56 seconds. Though clearly disappointed and fatigued, Guevara nonetheless responded to the cheers in the stadium by taking a victory lap around the track while carrying a sombrero and a Mexican flag.

An hour after the race, Guevara received a call from Mexican president Vicente Fox congratulating her on a "great race." Later that evening, Guevara recognized the high expectations placed on her and the nature of athletic competition, explaining that she was happy with the silver medal and candidly added, "I couldn't have done any more . . . this is the way things are in sport. Sometimes you have spectacular races and you win. Sometimes you don't." In early 2005, Guevara expressed her dedication to compete in the 2008 Olympics in Beijing, China, in either the 400-meters or 800-meters competition.

Further Reading

"Ana Guevara." Athens 2004 Olympics Web site. Available online. URL: http://www.athens2004.com/

en/ParticipantsAthletes/newParticipants?pid=360
638. Downloaded on July 1, 2005.

Hansen, Greg. "Sonoran Hero Claims Silver: Fans in
Nogales Celebrate Guevara's Shining Moment."
Arizona Daily Star, 25 August 2004.

Zeigler, Mark. "Guevara's Best Good Enough for a
Silver: Mexico's First Athens Medal Might Disap-
point Some Fans." *San Diego Union Tribune,* 25
August 2004.

Guillén, Ozzie
(Oswaldo Guillen)
(1964–   ) *baseball player*

A three-time All-Star shortstop who spent 13
years of his 16-year career playing for the Chicago
White Sox, Ozzie Guillén became the first for-
eign-born manager to win the World Series when
he led the 2005 White Sox to the franchise's first
World Series championship in 88 years. He was
born Oswaldo Guillén on January 20, 1964, in
Oculare del Tuy, Venezuela. He grew up in Guarenas, a working-class city of 200,000 people about
50 miles from the Venezuelan capital of Caracas,
a skinny and hyperactive kid raised with his four
siblings by his school administrator mother, Victo-
ria. Guillén was a standout athlete, particularly in
volleyball, playing on Venezuela's national youth
team. But aside from his childhood girlfriend,
Ibis, who later became his wife, Guillén's true love
was baseball, which he played in the fields and
streets of Guarenas.

Guillén's skills on the baseball diamond drew
attention from Major League Baseball teams,
including scouts from the San Diego Padres, who
signed the 16 year old to a contract in 1980. His
speed, hustle, defense, and passion evoked comparisons to his Venezuelan shortstop predecessors
Chico Carrasquel, LUIS APARICIO, and DAVEY
CONCEPCIÓN and earned Guillén's status as one
of the top players in the Padres' foreign system.
Although they valued him highly, the Padres

traded Guillén to the Chicago White Sox as part
of a seven-player deal on December 6, 1984, that
brought 1983 American League (AL) Cy Young
Award winner LaMarr Hoyt to San Diego.

The left-handed hitting Guillén was the starting shortstop on 1985's opening day for the White
Sox, and he played in almost all of the team's games
that season. His .273 batting average and slick
fielding helped spark the White Sox to an 11-game
improvement from the previous year and earned
him the 1985 AL Rookie of the Year Award.

Guillén remained with the White Sox through
the 1997 season, setting a franchise record by
starting 13 consecutive opening days at shortstop.
From 1985 through 1991, the 5'11", 150-pound
Guillén was an iron man, playing in more than
95 percent of the White Sox games. During this
period, Guillén also became one of the most dangerous bunters and base runners in the AL, swip-
ing an average of almost 20 bases a season and
ranking among the top 10 in the AL in triples
four times. This offensive production, combined
with his steady defense, which earned him a Gold
Glove award in 1990, led to three All-Star Game
appearances for Guillén.

An injury in 1992 limited Guillén to only 12
games. He came back in 1993 to help the White
Sox to the AL West title and enjoyed a career high
.288 batting average in 1994. Guillén finished his
stint as a White Sox player following the 1997 season, and he spent the next three seasons with the
Baltimore Orioles, Atlanta Braves, and Tampa Bay
Devil Rays, respectively. He retired after the 2000
season with 1,764 hits and an at-bat-per-strikeout
ratio of 13:1, a remarkable statistic indicating his
outstanding bat control.

Following his playing days, Guillén became
a coach with the Montreal Expos and Florida
Marlins, where he was third base coach for the
Marlins' 2003 World Series championship squad.
Prior to the 2004 season, Guillén returned to Chi-
cago when he was hired to be the manager of the
White Sox.

In 2005, Guillén led the White Sox to a 99-63 record and a four-game sweep of the Houston Astros in the World Series, giving the White Sox their first World Championship since 1917. Following this dream season, Guillén was named the 2005 AL Manager of the Year.

Further Reading

Dellios, Hugh. "Hometown Recalls Hyperactive Guillen." *Chicago Tribune,* 28 October 2005, p. A1.

"Ozzie Guillen." Baseball Reference Web site. Available online. URL: http://www.baseball-reference.com/g/guilloz01.shtml. Downloaded on January 15, 2006.

H

Hernandez, Keith
(1953–) *baseball player*

A smooth swinging, five-time All-Star whose 11 consecutive Gold Glove awards led many to consider him the greatest defensive first baseman in baseball history, Keith Hernandez won the 1979 National League (NL) batting title, shared that season's NL Most Valuable Player (MVP) award, and in 1986 played a critical role in the thrilling World Series championship for the New York Mets. Hernandez was born on October 20, 1953, in San Francisco. He spent most of his youth in the blue-collar coastal town of Pacifica about 20 miles south of San Francisco. Of his youth in Pacifica, Hernandez recalled, "It was a great place to grow up. Got home from school, cut through the fence, and ran through the artichoke fields . . . [there was] a neighborhood of around 15 kids. We followed the creek back up to the mounds. Almost Huck Finn kind of stuff. And we played ball."

Few children anywhere played baseball better than Hernandez. He and his older brother Gary (who later starred at the University of California and played in the minor leagues) learned the fundamentals and nuances of baseball from their father, John, a Spanish-American fireman. John Hernandez had been a standout high school first baseman in San Francisco and highly touted prospect in the Brooklyn Dodgers system before he was hit by a pitch in the early 1940s, causing damage to his eyesight that prevented his advancement to the majors. John was a demanding father who immersed himself in the athletic lives of his sons, requiring them to take written tests on baseball strategy and analyzing film of their little league games to improve their swings.

The family moved to nearby Millbrae, California, when the introverted and sensitive Hernandez was in his early teens. He excelled on the baseball field and was a standout guard on the basketball team and starting quarterback on the football team at Capuchino High School. With his father's support, Hernandez quit Capuchino's baseball team early in his senior season following a dispute with the coach. As a result, major league teams became concerned about Hernandez's attitude, and he was not selected in the 1971 major league draft until the St. Louis Cardinals picked him in the 40th round. Hernandez signed with the Cardinals for $30,000 and shot up in their system, earning a brief call to St. Louis as a 20-year-old during the 1974 season and comparisons to legendary Cardinals left-handed Stan Musial.

Hernandez made the Cardinals' opening day roster in 1975 but struggled in the first half of the season, leading to a demotion to the team's AAA affiliate in Tulsa, Oklahoma. After recapturing his brilliant left-handed hitting stroke in the minors, Hernandez returned to the majors for good in 1976, batting .289. With the support and guidance of his teammate and future Hall of Famer Lou Brock, Hernandez continued to improve in 1977, batting .291, with 15 home runs and 91 runs batted in (RBIs), as well as becoming more vocal on the field, where his defensive skills shone.

In 1978, Hernandez's offensive production dropped, though he earned the first of his 11 Gold Glove awards at first base, given to each league's top defensive player at their position. The following year, 1979, would prove to be Hernandez's best year statistically, as he hit 11 home runs, drove in 105 runs, and exploded to lead the NL in batting with a .344 average. His keen eye at the plate also helped Hernandez rank in the top three in high base percentage, a feat he repeated for the next five seasons. At the end of the season, Hernandez shared the NL MVP with Willie Stargell of the Pittsburgh Pirates.

From 1980 through 1982, Hernandez ranked in the top 10 in the NL in batting average. In 1982, he helped lead the Cardinals to their first playoff appearance in 14 years. He batted .333 in the Cardinals' sweep of the Atlanta Braves in the National League Championship Series (NLCS) and drove in eight runs as St. Louis defeated the Milwaukee Brewers in seven games in the World Series. However, on June 15, 1983, St. Louis traded Hernandez to the New York Mets for two unacclaimed pitchers. The puzzlingly lopsided trade in favor of the Mets was better understood in 1985 when Hernandez testified before a highly publicized Pittsburgh grand jury investigating a drug dealer who supplied baseball players with illegal narcotics that he had used cocaine regularly between 1980 and early 1983.

Initially, Hernandez resisted the trade to the Mets, a team that had finished in last place in the NL East in five of the previous six seasons. After batting .306 with the Mets in 1983, Hernandez signed a lucrative five-year contract to stay in New York. He was rejuvenated by the cultural attrac-

tions of his new city and valued his role as the clear and admired leader on a young and improving Mets team that featured future stars Dwight Gooden, Daryl Strawberry, and Lenny Dykstra. Describing Hernandez's ability to position infielders, advise pitchers, and encourage hitters, Mets pitcher Ed Lynch commented, "If Einstein starts talking about the speed of light, you better listen to him."

With Hernandez as the Mets' first-ever team captain, the team enjoyed its best five-year span in franchise history. In 1984, with Hernandez batting .311, with 15 home runs and 94 RBIs, the Mets made a 22-game improvement to win 90 games and finish in second place in the NL East. In 1985, Hernandez batted .309 as the Mets won 98 games, again finishing second in the division.

In 1986, Hernandez displayed steady excellence, batting .310 with 13 home runs and 83 RBIs, helping the Mets win a franchise record 108 games. After defeating the Houston Astros in the NLCS, Hernandez made the second out in the bottom of the 10th inning in the World Series against the Boston Red Sox before the Mets staged a remarkable rally to even the series 3-3. The next night, with the Mets trailing 3-0, Hernandez hit a single with the bases loaded to drive in two runs and spark the Mets to an 8-5 victory and the World Series championship.

Hernandez had a productive 1987 season before injuries and age took their toll. He appeared in fewer than half the games over two more seasons with the Mets before finishing his career by playing 43 games for the Cleveland Indians in 1990.

Since his playing days ended, Hernandez has worked as a broadcaster of Mets games, written a children's book about a little league baseball player, and guest-starred as himself on a classic two-part episode of the popular sitcom *Seinfeld*. Though his chances of being elected into baseballs' Hall of Fame appear slim due to his impressive but unspectacular offensive statistics,

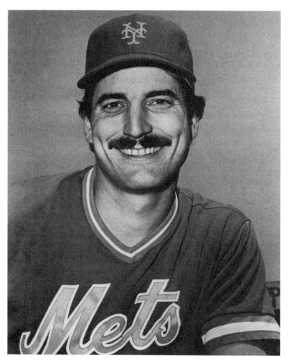

Keith Hernandez led the 1986 World Series champion New York Mets in batting with a .310 average. *(National Baseball Hall of Fame Library)*

Hernandez's place as one of the purest hitters of his generation and one of the greatest fielding first baseman of any generation are secure. Also secure is his imprint on his past teammates, four of whom (David Cone, Ron Darling, Bob Ojeda, and Roger McDowell) changed their numbers to Hernandez's number 17 after leaving the Mets to pay tribute to him.

Further Reading

Hernandez, Keith, and Mike Bryan. *Pure Baseball: Pitch by Pitch for the Advanced Fan.* New York: Harper Perennial, 1995.

"Keith Hernandez." Baseball Reference Web site. Available online. URL: http://www.baseball-reference. com/h/hernake01.shtml. Downloaded on January 15, 2006.

Nack, William. "He's Still Not Home Free." *Sports Illustrated,* 13 October 1986, p. 104.

Hernández, Willie
(Guillermo Hernández)
(1954–   ) *baseball player*

The second relief pitcher in baseball history to win the Cy Young Award and Most Valuable Player (MVP) award in the same year, Willie Hernández emerged from relative obscurity in 1984 to help lead the Detroit Tigers to a World Series championship. He was born Guillermo Hernández on November 14, 1954, in Aguada, Puerto Rico. Hernández grew up in that town on the island's northwest coast, excelling at baseball, his value enhanced because he was left-handed.

In 1973, at the age of 18, Hernández was signed by the Philadelphia Phillies. Following three mediocre years in the Phillies minor league system, Hernández was picked up by the Chicago Cubs prior to the 1977 season.

Hernandez made the 1977 Cubs roster as a middle reliever and appeared in 67 games, earning an 8-7 record, with four saves and an impressive earned run average of 3.03. He remained with the Cubs fulfilling the same role over the next five-plus years before being traded back to the Philadelphia Phillies on May 22, 1983.

His role expanded in Philadelphia, and he responded with eight wins and seven saves over the season's final four months, ranking third in the National League in games pitched (74). Late in spring training in 1984, the Phillies traded Hernández and first baseman Dave Bergman to the Detroit Tigers for John Wockenfuss and Glenn Wilson.

Though little attention was given to the trade in Philadelphia or Detroit, it turned out to be one of the best acquisitions in Tigers history. Detroit began the 1984 season with nine consecutive wins, a record 17 consecutive victories on the road, and a 35-5 record, the best 40-game start in Major League Baseball history.

The most consistently outstanding performer on this talent-rich team that included Jack Morris, Kirk Gibson, Lou Whitaker, and Alan Trammell, was the newcomer Hernández. Under the tutelage of Tigers pitching coach Roger Craig, Hernández mastered the screwball, a pitch that is thrown with the same motion as a fastball and curves in the direction opposite to that of a normal curve ball, breaking sharply down and away from right-handed batters.

Detroit manager Sparky Anderson called on Hernández in a major league–leading 80 games during 1984, during which Hernández posted phenomenal statistics: a 9-3 record, 1.92 earned run average, 32 saves in 33 chances, and 112 strikeouts and only 36 walks in 140 innings. Hernández closed out the Tigers' American League East Division–clinching game versus Milwaukee and the American League Championship Series against Kansas City and was on the mound in Tiger Stadium on October 14 when Detroit defeated the San Diego Padres for the team's first World Series championship since 1968. His dominance was recognized with the 1984 Cy Young Award and MVP award, joining Hall of Famer Rollie Fingers as the only relief pitchers ever to win those awards in the same year.

Hernández finished his career with five more seasons in Detroit, in which he was unable to come close to duplicating the magic of 1984. Though he tallied 88 saves over those years, he blew a high percentage of his save opportunities. His struggles on the field led to tense relationships with fans and media, dropping to a low in a highly publicized incident when he dumped a bucket of ice water on Detroit sports writer Mitch Albom.

After undergoing elbow surgery in 1989, Hernández left baseball, returning in 1991 to pitch for the AAA affiliate of the Toronto Blue Jays and coming back again in spring training of 1995 as a replacement player during a players' strike for the New York Yankees. The strike was settled before the season, and Hernández never again pitched in the majors.

Living on a farm in the Dominican Republic in 2004, Hernández returned to Detroit for the 20th reunion of the Tigers' 1984 championship team. He was warmly received by the fans and reflected on his and the team's glorious 1984, saying, "They're the memories you want to keep for the rest of your life."

Further Reading

Cantor, George. *Wire to Wire: Inside the 1984 Detroit Tigers Championship Season*. Chicago: Triumph Books, 2004.

"Willie Hernandez." Baseball Reference Web site. Available online. URL: http://www.baseball-reference.com/h/hernawi01.shtml. Downloaded on July 3, 2005.

Hilario, Maybyner Rodney   *See* NENÉ

K

Kid Chocolate *See* SARDINAS, KID CHOCOLATE

Kid Gavilan *See* GONZÁLEZ, KID GAVILAN

Kuerten, Gustavo
(Guga Kuerten)
(1976–) *tennis player*

A three-time French Open champion, Gustavo Kuerten became in 2000 the first South American player to finish a season ranked number one in the world in the Association of Tennis Professionals (ATP) rankings. He was born on September 10, 1976, in Florianopolis, Brazil. Often referred to by the diminutive form of Gustavo—Guga—he began playing tennis at the age of six, emulating his father, Aldo, who was a tennis umpire and former amateur player in Brazil.

Kuerten's father died of a heart attack while umpiring a match in Florianopolis when Kuerten was only eight. Though staggered by his father's death and the struggles to meet the needs of his younger brother, who suffered severe brain damage at birth, Kuerten was supported by his family as he began traveling around the world to play in junior tournaments at the age of 14. Kuerten began his professional career four years later.

By 1996, Kuerten was the second-ranked Brazilian player and a key member of Brazil's Davis Cup team that reached the semifinals in 1996. In 1997, Kuerten, ranked number 66, stunned the tennis world by defeating three former French Open champions (Brad Muster, Yevgeny Kafelnikov, and Sergi Bruguera) on his way to winning the French Open on the famous clay courts of Roland Garros Stadium in Paris.

Kuerten had difficulty meeting the lofty expectations that accompanied his surprise win at the French Open and his top 20 ranking. He bounced back in 1999, reaching the quarterfinals at the French Open and becoming the first Brazilian to reach the quarterfinals at Wimbledon since 1967. His successful momentum grew in 2000, culminating in his second French Open title and the number one ranking in the world, breaking an eight-year American reign of tennis's top spot. Kuerten's second consecutive top five finish that year marked the first time that feat had been accomplished by a South American player since GUILLERMO VILAS did it in 1977–78.

Kuerten's best year was 2001, as he won his third French Open, joining former greats Bjorn Borg, Ivan Lendl, and Mats Wilander as the only men to have won three or more French Open titles in the open era. Following his victory, Kuerten drew a heart on the clay to express his appreciation for the support of French fans. He also won five other titles, four of which came on his favorite surface, clay, on which his solid serve, heavy topspin, ground strokes, and effective baseline style of play allowed him to wear down opponents. He finished the year again ranked number one and earned more than $4 million in winnings.

Kuerten underwent arthroscopic hip surgery in 2002 and has not returned to his previous level of excellence, though he has remained among the top 50 ranked players in the world through 2004. Despite the numerous layoffs in competition caused by his various injuries, Kuerten has continued to perform well at Roland Garros, reaching the fourth round in 2002 and 2003 and the quarterfinals in 2004, including a victory over top seed Roger Federer.

Although he did not win any tournaments in 2005 and 2006, Kuerten remains among Brazil's most popular athletes. He has been celebrated with an official postage stamp and the Brazilian Cross of Merit, one of the highest honors bestowed on Brazilian citizens. He has also been recognized by UNESCO (United Nations Education, Scientific and Cultural Organization) for his off-court work, including his donation of hundreds of thousands of dollars to agencies that serve the severely disabled.

Further Reading

"Gustavo Kuerten." Association of Tennis Professionals Web site. Available online. URL: http://www.atptennis.com/en/players/playerprofiles/Highlights/default.asp?playernumber=K293. Downloaded on July 3, 2005.

Wine, Steven. "Former Champ Kuerten Knocks Off No. 1 Federer." *Oakland Tribune,* 30 May 2004.

L

Laguna, Ismael
(1943–) *boxer*

A boxer with a unique mix of power and finesse, Ismael Laguna was the first Panamanian to become world champion and the lightweight champion in 1965 and 1970. He was born on June 28, 1943, in Colón, Panama. He grew up in this populous city on Panama's northern coast as one of 10 children in his family and helped support his parents and siblings as a boy by working as a butcher's assistant. By his early adolescence, he had developed the athletic skills and mental toughness that would later mark his boxing career, and by the age of 17, he began fighting professionally.

Laguna's first bout was a second-round knockout of Antonio Morán in Colón on January 8, 1961. He then won 26 consecutive fights, including the Panamanian featherweight title, before suffering his first loss to Antonio Herrera in Bogotá, Colombia, on June 8, 1963. He won 12 of his next 13 bouts, leading to his first shot at the title, an April 10, 1965, fight in Panama City versus CARLOS ORTIZ for the lightweight title. The smaller Laguna used his distinctively stiff jabs to stagger Ortiz and his quick feet to avoid punishment to earn a split decision victory. After the fight, Ortiz admired Laguna's strategy and skill, remarking, "He doesn't stick around to get hit, and I wasn't fast enough to catch him."

Laguna relinquished the title to Ortiz in a unanimous decision seven months later. He quickly embarked on a quest to regain it by taking on some of the toughest fighters of his era. He met Ortiz for the lightweight title for the third time on August 16, 1967, and lost this rubber match by unanimous decision.

Still, Laguna pursued the crown over the next three years by winning 14 of his next 15 fights before getting another opportunity to win the lightweight title in a bout against Mando Ramos in Los Angeles on March 3, 1970. Laguna stunned the southern California native Ramos and the 15,000 spectators cheering him by delivering a steady flurry of crisp jabs to open major cuts on Ramos's eyes and gained a ninth-round technical knockout victory.

Again, Laguna's grasp on the title would be short lived, as he lost a split decision to Ken Buchanan on September 26, 1970, in San Juan, Puerto Rico. He fought only three more times, winning twice, before losing again to Buchanan at New York City's Madison Square Garden on September 13, 1971.

Following that bout, Laguna retired from boxing. Unlike many of his boxing peers, he never returned to the ring and wisely maintained his wealth, enjoying retirement in the suburbs of Panama City.

Further Reading
"Ismael Laguna." International Boxing Hall of Fame Web site. Available online. URL: http://www.ibhof.com/laguna.htm. Downloaded on July 3, 2005.

"Ismael Laguna in the Hall of Fame." World Boxing Association Web site. Available online. URL: http://www.wbaonline.com/event/halloffame/Ilaguna.htm. Downloaded on July 3, 2005.

McIlvanney, Hugh. *The Hardest Game: McIlvanney on Boxing.* New York: McGraw Hill, 2001.

Leônidas
(Leônidas da Silva, O Homem Borracha, Diamante Negro)
(1913–2004) *soccer player*

An acrobatic center-forward who popularized the dazzling "bicycle kick," Leônidas was Brazil's first great soccer star, helping establish that nation's craze for the sport and its appreciation for a uniquely flamboyant, skillful, and joyous style of play. He was born Leônidas da Silva on September 6, 1913, in Rio de Janeiro, Brazil. The son of a Portuguese sailor father and Afro-Brazilian mother, he reflected the multiethnic nature of Brazil.

As a young teen, Leônidas often skipped school to play with a local soccer club, where he quickly developed a reputation as an athletic prodigy. He was small for the position of center-forward, but he overcame this with remarkable quickness and agility, earning the nickname "O Homem Borracha" (the Rubber Man).

Leônidas began playing soccer full time in 1930, before it was a professional sport in Brazil. Two years later, he was selected to play on the Brazilian national team. In 1933, he enhanced his growing fame as a soccer sensation by scoring twice in a game against Uruguay's national team. The second of these goals was accomplished using a bicycle kick, in which Leônidas stood with his back to the goal before leaping into the air, flipping backward just as the pass arrived, and kicking it back over his head and shoulders as he tumbled upside down to the turf.

His popularity led to perks regularly enjoyed by prominent athletes of subsequent generations, including a generous salary. Leônidas, often called

"Diamante Negro" (Black Diamond), endorsed a chocolate bar by the same name, which remains popular in Brazil. His success and charisma on the field have been credited by many with helping Brazilians accept the diverse multiethnic heritage of the nation and embrace a shared sense of national identity and pride through soccer.

This pride swelled during the 1938 World Cup tournament in France. In the first round game, Leônidas scored four goals in a 6-5 victory over Poland, including a game winner delivered without the aid of a shoe, which had come off in the muddy turf. In the semifinal game against Italy, Brazil's overconfident coach chose to rest Leônidas for the expected finals match. However, Brazil lost to Italy in the semifinals. Leônidas returned to the lineup, scoring two goals in a third-place game win over Sweden. Though Brazil's team returned without the World Cup, the nation had been captivated by soccer, and Europe had been finally introduced to a new image of Brazil, an image of talent and artistry crafted largely by Leônidas.

Leônidas became embroiled in controversy in 1941 when he was convicted of using forged documents to escape mandatory military service. He spent eight months in jail before returning to the soccer field. He was a key contributor to the Flamengo team of São Paulo in the 1940s that won five titles during the seven seasons he was on the team. Yet his reputation was tarnished enough that he was never again selected to play for the Brazilian national team.

Leônidas retired in 1949 and then spent many years coaching and providing radio commentary during soccer games. In 1974, the 60-year-old Leônidas began to suffer from Alzheimer's disease. He spent the next 30 years living privately in São Paulo, where he died of complications from Alzheimer's and diabetes on January 24, 2004, at the age of 90.

Further Reading
Gardner, Lee. "The Beautiful Game: Leonidas da Silva." *Baltimore City Paper.* 29 December 2004.

"Global Gleanings: 2004" Global Game Web site. Available online. URL: http://www.theglobal-game.com/gln0104.htm. Downloaded on July 3, 2005.

"Leonidas." Planet World Cup Web site. Available online. URL: http://www.planetworldcup.com/LEGENDS/leonidas.html. Downoladed on July 3, 2005.

Lima, Vanderlei de
(Vanderlei Cordeiro de Lima)
(1969–) *marathon runner*

The leader in the 2004 Olympic marathon with only three miles left in the race, Vanderlei de Lima was attacked by a spectator yet managed to win the bronze medal and a special award recognizing his outstanding competitive spirit. He was born on August 11, 1969, in Cruzeiro do Oeste, Brazil. De Lima helped his family by doing small jobs on farms and dreaming of a career as a professional soccer player. A physical education teacher recognized de Lima's running skills and stamina and encouraged him to become a competitive runner.

In 1992, de Lima began working with Brazilian running coach Ricardo D'Angelo. Though not initially a marathon runner, de Lima quickly improved his long-distance abilities, winning the Reims Marathon in France in fall 1994. Two years later, de Lima qualified for the Brazilian Olympic team after running a South American record time of 2:08:38 in the Tokyo Marathon. De Lima struggled with his shoes and the tough, hilly marathon course at the 1996 Olympics in Atlanta, finishing with a disappointing 47th place.

He continued to strengthen his worldwide reputation as a top marathoner over the next few years, taking second place at the 1998 Tokyo Marathon and finishing fifth in the New York Marathon that same year. In 1999, de Lima won the marathon at the Pan-American Games in Winnipeg, Canada. He again encountered frustration at the Olympics, finishing 75th at the 2000 Sydney games. De Lima maintained Olympic hopes, continuing to compete and excel, again winning the Pan-American Games marathon gold in 2003 in Santo Domingo, Dominican Republic.

De Lima qualified for his third Olympic team in 2004, preparing with his longtime coach D'Angelo for that year's race in Athens with high-altitude training in Colombia. Finally, on August 30, as tradition dictates, the marathon was held on the last day of Olympic competition.

De Lima began the race strongly and continued to run well past the midway point. His lead was shrinking heading into the final three miles when he was suddenly accosted and shoved into the curbside throng by Cornelius Horan, a defrocked Irish priest. Horan, dressed in a kilt, a green beret, and matching knee-high socks and wearing a sign with biblical references attached to his back, was quickly grabbed by a Greek spectator before being corralled by the police.

De Lima managed to continue the race, but he was clearly knocked out of his rhythm. He drew loud cheers from the crowd as he became the third runner to enter Panithinako Stadium for the final paces of the race. Smiling broadly, de Lima spread his arms like wings and weaved from side to side as he crossed the finish line.

After accepting the bronze medal, de Lima said, "I have achieved my goal, no matter what happened, and I am happy to be on the medal podium with these athletes." The International Olympic Committee soon awarded de Lima with the Pierre de Coubertin medal in recognition of his "exceptional demonstration of fair play and Olympic values."

Sports Illustrated writer S. L. Price suggested that de Lima be named the winner of the magazine's prestigious Sportsman of the Year (eventually awarded to the Boston Red Sox), noting of de Lima, "On that day, in the honest heat of the race, his message couldn't have been clearer: Let everyone else feel sad: I am alive. I am in the Olympics. Attack me? I'll just go harder. Throw me off rhythm? I'll finish. You can't bring me down. In fact, I am going to fly."

Further Reading

"Attack on Race Leader Mars Men's Marathon." MSNBC Web site. Available online. URL: http://www.msnbc.msn.com/id/5859225/. Downloaded on July 8, 2005.

Price, S. L. "My Sportsman Choice: Vanderlei de Lima." *Sports Illustrated* Web site. Available online. URL: http://sportsillustrated.cnn.com/2004/magazine/specials/sportsman/2004/11/09/price.lima/. Downloaded on July 8, 2005.

"Vanderlei de Lima—The Story of a Man That Goes Beyond One Strange Incident." International Association of Athletics Federation. Available online. URL: http://www.iaaf.org/news/Kind=2/newsId=28044.html. Downloaded on July 8, 2005.

Lobo, Rebecca

(1973–   ) *basketball player*

The 1995 National Collegiate Athletic Association (NCAA) Women's Basketball Player of the Year when she led the University of Connecticut to an undefeated season in the NCAA Championship, Rebecca Lobo later won an Olympic gold medal and was among the first stars of the fledgling Women's National Basketball Association (WNBA). She was born on October 6, 1973, in Hartford, Connecticut. Lobo, who derives her Cuban heritage from her father, is the youngest of three children in her family and was raised by schoolteacher parents Ruth Ann and Dennis in Southwick, Massachusetts. A tall, enthusiastic girl, Lobo enjoyed sports, particularly basketball because of its effect on her frame of mind, explaining, "Sometimes I played because I wanted to get out of a bad mood, sometimes because I was worried about an upcoming test. Sometimes basketball was just a great way to forget myself."

Lobo excelled in academics and athletics at Southwick Tolland Regional High School, gradu-

ating second in her class and starring on the field hockey, softball, track, and basketball teams. Standing at a towering 6'4" and having mastered a variety of skillful moves as a result of years of dedicated practice, Lobo shone the brightest on the basketball court, where she set a Massachusetts career-scoring goals record. Included in that record tally was a 62-point performance in her senior year.

With more than 100 athletic scholarships offered to her in her senior year, Lobo chose to attend the University of Connecticut (UConn) because of its proximity to her home and its reputation as a women's basketball powerhouse. Though she often found herself at odds with UConn's

Rebecca Lobo led the University of Connecticut women's basketball team to an undefeated record and the national championship in 1995. *(U.S. Olympic Committee)*

combative coach Geno Auriemma, Lobo prospered, helping lead the team to the NCAA quarterfinals in her junior year.

In the next season, 1994–95, Lobo was the leading scorer and top rebounder for UConn as they inspired sold-out home crowds and rolled to an undefeated 28-0 record and an average margin of victory of 35 points prior to the NCAA tournament. Reflecting on his star player's all around skill, Auriemma said, "What is she great at? I can't say any one thing. But the sum of all the parts is unreal." Lobo finished her senior year averaging more than 17 points, 10 rebounds, three blocks, and three assists per game, leading UConn to a 70-65 win over the University of Tennessee in the final game, completing a perfect record, and bringing the national championship to UConn. As a result of her performance and leadership, Lobo received an ESPY Award from the ESPN network as 1995's Outstanding Women's Athlete and the Women's Basketball Player of the Year by the NCAA.

After graduating with a B.A. in political science, Lobo played for the 1996 U.S. basketball team, which won the gold medal at the Atlanta Olympics. She decided against playing professionally in Europe in order to stay in the United States and participate in the inaugural season of the WNBA. She was assigned to the New York Liberty and averaged 12 points, seven rebounds, two blocks, and two assists a game, earning second team all WNBA honors.

Because of her solid play and charming, down-to-earth personality conveyed in interviews and public appearances, Lobo's image was regularly featured in WNBA promotions, as well as endorsement deals from major corporations such as General Motors and Reebok. Some people complained that Lobo was receiving more attention than her play warranted, though she defended herself in 1998 from these accusations by explaining, "It's not all about the numbers . . . I rely on my teammates . . . set screens and get rebounds . . . in the next three years, I will be one of the best players in the league."

Unfortunately, a tear of her interior cruciate ligament in her left knee suffered in the first minute of the first game of the 1999 season prevented that prediction from becoming reality. Lobo missed the entire season and was progressing in her rehabilitation when she again tore the same ligament. Another surgery and rehabilitation kept Lobo out of action for the entire 2000 season as well. Lobo was never able to recapture her previous ability and finished her career coming off the bench for the Houston Comets in 2002 and Connecticut Sun in 2003.

Following her retirement, Lobo married *Sports Illustrated* reporter Steve Rushin in 2003 and gave birth to a baby girl, Siobhan, in 2005. She has remained a prominent figure in women's basketball as an analyst of WNBA games and has been an active supporter of several causes, including breast cancer research and the Hispanic Scholarship Fund.

Further Reading

Lobo, Ruth Ann, and Rebecca Lobo. *The Home Team: Of Mothers, Daughters, and American Champions.* New York: Kodansha America, 1997.

"Rebecca Lobo." Women's National Basketball Association Web site. Available online, URL: http://www.wnba.com/playerfile/rebecca_lobo/bio.html. Downloaded on January 15, 2006.

Rushin, Steve. "My Big Fat Sports Wedding." *Sports Illustrated,* 21 April 2003, p. 19.

Telander, Rick. "The Post with the Most—Connecticut Basketball Star Rebecca Lobo." *Sports Illustrated,* 20 March 1995, p. 98.

Lopez, Al
(Alfonso Ramon Lopez)
(1908–2005) *baseball player*

One of the most durable and defensively skilled catchers in baseball history, Al Lopez was the first full-time Latino manager of a major league team, leading the Cleveland Indians and the Chicago

White Sox to the World Series and finishing his managerial career ranked in the top 10 in career winning percentage. He was born Alfonso Ramon Lopez on August 20, 1908, in Tampa, Florida. Lopez's parents, Cuban immigrants who were born in Spain, raised their children in Tampa's Ybor City, a lively and multiethnic community, renowned in the early 20th century as the "cigar capital of the world."

Encouraged by his older brother Emilio, who played for amateur teams, Lopez pursued his goal of playing in the major leagues with intensity, graduating at age 16 from Tampa's Jefferson High School. He immediately began playing professionally for Tampa in the Florida state league. A little more than three years later, on September 22, 1928, Lopez made his major league debut with the Brooklyn Robins, failing to reach base in 12 at-bats.

Lopez returned to Brooklyn from the minor leagues in 1930, becoming the team's starting catcher. In 1933, Lopez, a solid but unspectacular hitter, led Brooklyn (renamed the Dodgers in 1932) in hitting with a .301 batting average and for the second consecutive year led National League (NL) catchers in assists, solidifying his reputation as an outstanding defensive backstop and astute pitch-caller for his pitchers. Later he reflected on his reputation for understanding pitchers' strengths and batters' tendencies, noting, "It's tough to be pitching and having to worry about what a catcher's going to call. If the catcher has a reputation of being a rockhead [unintelligent], the pitcher's gonna have to worry that much more."

Another strong season in 1934 earned Lopez the first of his two All-Star Game appearances. Following a dip in offensive production, Brooklyn traded Lopez to the Boston Braves. Lopez spent four years with the Braves before they traded him to the Pittsburgh Pirates during the 1940 season. He spent the next six years with the Pirates, the last two playing primarily as a late game defensive replacement. In 1947, Lopez spent his last season with the Cleveland Indians.

Lopez finished his career with modest offensive totals (.261 batting average, 1,547 hits, 51 home runs, and 652 runs batted in). However, his career catching marks set standards of excellence for decades. Lopez owned the record for most games caught (1,918) from 1947 until 1990, when future Hall of Famer Gary Carter eclipsed that total. He caught more than 100 games in a season 12 times and led NL catchers in fielding percentage three times.

But Lopez's greatest contribution to baseball came from the dugout. After three years as manager of the Indians' minor league affiliate Minneapolis team, Lopez replaced fan favorite Lou Boudreau as manager of the Cleveland Indians. Lopez's first three seasons at the helm of the Indians resulted in 90-plus wins each year and second-place finishes to the pennant winning New York Yankees. In 1954, Lopez led the Indians to a 111-43 record, establishing an American League (AL) mark for most wins in a season that stood until 1998. In the 1954 World Series, the Indians met the New York Giants, losing game one following Giants center fielder Willie Mays's remarkable spinning catch and went on to lose the series four games to none.

Lopez had two more winning seasons in Cleveland, again finishing second to the Yankees both years before he resigned and took the managerial position with the Chicago White Sox in 1957. After two more second-place finishes to the Yankees, Lopez's "GoGo" Sox of 1959, known (like many Lopez-led teams) as scrappy overachievers, won the AL pennant, then lost the World Series to the Los Angeles Dodgers four games to two.

Lopez managed the White Sox through the 1965 season, finishing with a winning record each year, though never returning to the World Series. He returned to manage the White Sox in the middle of the 1968 season and retired from managing due to health concerns on May 2, 1969. His managerial résumé ranks among the best in baseball history, including a .584 winning percentage (fourth-best among managers in the 20th century) and the distinction as the only manager to interrupt the Yankees' AL pennant winning dynasty of 1949 to 1964.

In 1977, Lopez was enshrined in the National Baseball Hall of Fame. Lopez was known for enjoying a daily game of gin rummy at the Palma Ceia Country Club in his native Tampa until he died at the age of 97 on October 29, 2005, three days after his former team, the Chicago White Sox, won their first World Series championship in 88 years.

Further Reading

"Al Lopez." Baseball Library Web site. Available online. URL: http://baseballlibrary.com/baseballlibrary/ballplayers/L/Lopez_Al.stm. Downloaded on July 3, 2005.

"Al Lopez." National Baseball Hall of Fame Web site. Available online. URL: http://www.baseballhalloffame.org/hofers_and_honorees/hofer_bios/Lopez_Al.htm. Downloaded on July 3, 2005.

Johnston, Joey. "Al Lopez Dies." *Tampa Tribune* Web site. Available online. URL: http://tampatrib.com/sportsnews/MGB6PBKLFFE.html. Downloaded on June 20, 2006.

Kalas, Larry. "Strength Down the Middle: The Story of the 1959 Chicago White Sox." Fort Worth, Tex.: Mereken Land & Production Co., 1999.

Lopez, Nancy
(1957–) *golfer*

A four-time Ladies Professional Golf Association (LPGA) Player of the Year (1978, 1979, 1985, and 1988) and a 1978 LPGA Rookie of the Year, Nancy Lopez overcame country club discrimination to win 48 LPGA events and become, at the age of 30, the youngest player ever inducted into the LPGA Hall of Fame. She was born on January 6, 1957, in Torrance, California. Soon after she was born, her family moved to Roswell, New Mexico, where her father, Domingo, opened an auto repair shop. Lopez was introduced to golf when she tagged along with her parents to local courses after her father had suggested that her mother, Marina,

begin playing to ease persistent chest pains. When she was eight years old, Lopez's father gave her a golf club and encouraged her to pursue what was becoming her favorite sport.

Though Lopez took no professional lessons, she was taught by her father, who instructed her to "play happy." When she demonstrated her unique talent on the links, winning the Youth State Championship at the age of 10, her father dug a big hole in the backyard and filled it with sand so she could practice her wedge shots. He also sought to preserve Lopez's hands by allowing her to skip certain household chores and purchased orthodontic braces for her despite the difficulty affording them, because he believed his daughter's smile would be important when she achieved fame as a golfer.

Lopez's extraordinary power, poise, and touch helped her win the New Mexico Women's Amateur Tournament when she was only 12 years old. Lopez then proved to be one of the top young female golfers in the United States by winning the U.S. Golf Association Junior Girl Championship at the ages of 15 (1972) and 17 (1974). She led the otherwise all-boys golf team at Goddard High School in Roswell to state titles in 1973 and 1974, and in 1975, she remarkably finished second while playing as an amateur at the U.S. Women's Open.

Lopez accomplished all these feats despite not being a member of the Roswell Country Club, where she practiced. She later explained that her ethnicity prevented her family from joining the club: "I thought we weren't members of the country club because we couldn't afford it. Now I think it was discrimination."

Following her graduation from high school, Lopez became the first woman to receive a scholarship to play golf at the University of Tulsa. In her first season (1976), Lopez won the Association of Intercollegiate Athletics for Women (AIAW) National Championship, was named an All-American, and was honored as the University of Tulsa's Female Athlete of the Year. Following her sophomore year at Tulsa, Lopez left school to join the professional tour.

Lopez played in six tournaments during the 1977 season and finished second twice. She was stunned by her mother's sudden death early in 1978 following an appendectomy but later credited that tragedy for inspiring her to become mentally tougher and more aggressive on the golf course.

As a 21-year-old in 1978, Lopez took the women's golf world by storm by winning nine of the 26 tournaments in which she played, including her first pro victory at the Bent Tree Classic in Sarasota, Florida. She also enjoyed a streak of five consecutive tournament victories during May and June. One of those five wins was the LPGA Championship, in which Lopez ran away from the field, winning by six strokes over runner-up Amy Alcott and setting a course record at King's Island in Ohio. During her legendary 1978 season, Lopez became the first (and remains the only) woman to win the LPGA's Rookie of the Year, Player of the Year, and Vare Trophy (for best scoring average) in the same year.

Throughout Lopez's amazingly successful debut, golf fans admired her fresh-faced charisma. Her performance helped invigorate women's golf and served as an inspiration for countless young players, particularly Latinos and other ethnic minorities. Lopez's opponents also took notice, evidenced by women's golf legend Judy Rankin's comment, "They've got the wrong person playing Wonder Woman."

In 1979, Lopez married Cincinnati sportscaster Tim Melton. She continued her spectacular play by winning eight tournaments, repeating as the Player of the Year and Vare Trophy recipient, and becoming, at 22 years old, the youngest women to reach 10 career victories. She won only three tournaments in both 1980 and 1981 as she coped with the separation and ultimate divorce from her husband.

In May 1982, Lopez married professional baseball player Ray Knight, won two events, and recorded the first hole in one of her professional career. In 1983, she cut back on the number of tournaments she played as she gave birth to the

Nancy Lopez follows through on a swing in 1978, when she won the Ladies Professional Golf Association Rookie of the Year and Player of the Year awards. *(EMPICS)*

first of her three daughters, though she still was able to win two tournaments and pass the $1 million career earnings mark.

Lopez remained one of the top contenders and draws on the women's tour throughout the 1980s and into the 1990s, though two more pregnancies and later a variety of injuries limited her participation in tournament events. She won five tournaments including the LPGA Championship in 1985 on her way to her third Player of the Year and Vare Trophy. In 1988, Lopez won three tournaments and her fourth and last Player of the Year award. During the 1990s, Lopez won six tournaments, the last coming at the Chic-Fil-A Charity Championship in 1997.

Still admired as a pioneer and legend in women's golf, Lopez occasionally plays in charity tournaments and senior events, though there is no full-fledged women's golf senior circuit. She lives in Georgia with her husband and youngest daughter, not far from her older daughters, who attend Auburn University in Alabama.

Further Reading

"Career Highlights—Nancy Lopez." Ladies Professional Golf Association Web site. Available online. URL: http://www.lpga.com/player_career.aspx?id=500. Downloaded on January 15, 2006.

Hilton, Lisette. "Lopez Is LPGA's Knight in Shining Armor." ESPN Classic Web site. Available online. URL: http://espn.go.com/classic/biography/s/Lopez_Nancy.html. Downloaded on January 15, 2006.

"Nancy Lopez." Latino Legends in Sports Web site. Available online. URL: http://www.latinosportslegends.com/Lopez_Nancy-bio.htm. Downloaded on January 15, 2006.

Wicker, Brian. "Queen of the LPGA; Nancy Lopez's Skill and Aw-shucks Style Has Made Her an Enduring Folk Heroine among Golf Fans." *Minneapolis Star-Tribune,* 16 August 1998.

Lopez, Steven
(1978–   ) *tae kwon do fighter*

A gold medalist at the 2000 and 2004 Olympics, Steven Lopez is the most successful American tae kwon do fighter in history. He was born on September 11, 1978, in New York City. His parents, Julio and Ordina, came to the United States in the early 1970s from Nicaragua, where Lopez's father had worked as an engineer for a government overthrown in a recent revolution. The Lopez family first settled in Spanish Harlem of New York City before moving to Houston, Texas.

Lopez and his siblings were regularly engaged in physical activity, including early morning runs organized by their father. At the age of five, he began taking tae kwon do (Korean for "the way of the fist and the foot") lessons in the family's two-

Steven Lopez won gold medals in tae kwon do in the 2000 Olympics in Sydney and the 2004 Olympics in Athens. *(U.S. Olympic Committee)*

car garage under the tutelage of his 14-year-old brother, Jean, who would eventually win medals in more than 30 national and international tae kwon do competitions in the 1990s. From Jean's training, Lopez developed an aggressive and adaptable fighting style, including powerful kicking aptitude with either foot.

In 1999, Lopez won the gold medal at the Pan-American Games in Winnipeg, Canada. The following year, tae kwon do made its debut as an Olympic sport at the 2000 games in Sydney. Lopez competed in the featherweight division, advancing to the gold medal match against South Korean Sin Joon-Sik. In the third and final round, Lopez scored a point with a back kick to Joon-Sik's face in the final minute to win the gold medal.

Lopez won the 2001 tae kwon do world championships in South Korea and the 2003 world championships in Germany and then turned his attention again to the Olympics. For the 2004 Olympics in Athens, Greece, Lopez moved up to the welterweight class. Most crowds at first-round matches were quiet, but Lopez had to deal with a raucous and openly hostile crowd in his initial match against Raid Rasheed of Iraq. Though Lopez presented his opponent with a U.S. tae kwon do T-shirt before the match, most spectators, opposed to the American invasion of Iraq in 2003, chanted "Iraq!" repeatedly as Lopez cruised to victory. After his win, Lopez commented, "I think that was expected. It's too bad you can't keep politics outside of the Olympics."

Lopez advanced to the gold medal round, where he met Bahri Tanrikulu of Turkey. He backed Tanrikulu into a corner and kicked him in the gut to take the lead in the second of three rounds on his way to a decisive victory. Lopez and his brother/coach, Jean, jogged a lap around the arena carrying an American flag, while the rest of his family, including younger siblings who are now each elite level tae kwon do competitors, cheered. A few weeks later, following his second consecutive gold medal, Lopez was honored with a citywide celebration in his suburban Houston hometown of Sugar Land, Texas.

Lopez then set his sights on an Olympic gold medal at the 2008 games in Beijing, China. His brother and coach, Jean, like many other tae kwon do fans, believes he will accomplish this goal, explaining, "Steven's tenacity, his composure, along with his God-given talent and the hard work he puts in make him overwhelming. He is by far the Michael Jordan, the Lance Armstrong of our sport."

Further Reading
Barron, David. "Houstonian Steven Lopez Is Already Considered America's Premier Practitioner of Tae-kwondo, but He Has a Chance to Achieve Something Greater." *Houston Chronicle,* 27 August 2004, p. J3.

Bleiker, Cecil. "Steven Lopez Repeats as Olympic Gold Medalist in Taekwondo at the 2004 Olympic Games in Athens, Greece." U.S. Olympic Team Web site. Available online. URL: http://www.usoc.org/73_26294.htm. Downloaded on July 3, 2005.

"Martial Matters: Lopez Tops in Taekwondo." *Washington Post,* 29 August 2004, p. E15.

Luque, Dolf
(Adolfo Domingo De Guzmán Luque)
(1890–1957) *baseball player*

The first Cuban-born player to reach the major leagues and one of the top pitchers of the 1920s, Dolf Luque enjoyed a stellar career in which he twice led the majors in earned run average (ERA) and garnered 194 wins, including his final major league victory in the 1933 World Series. He was born Adolfo Domingo De Guzmán Luque on August 4, 1890, in Havana, Cuba. He grew up playing on the baseball fields of Cuba's capital, standing out as a small (5'7", 160 pounds) and feisty competitor with a wicked curve ball.

Luque signed with the Boston Braves and came to the United States in 1912 to pitch in the minor leagues. Luque posted an impressive 22-5 record in the minors in 1913 but appeared in only four games over the next two seasons for the Braves.

Luque did not appear again in a major league game until 1918, when he posted a 6-3 record with the Cincinnati Reds. Splitting time as a starter and a reliever in 1919 and 1920, the right-handed Luque won 23 and lost only 12. In 1919, he pitched in relief during two World Series games, striking out six and allowing only one hit in five innings as the Reds defeated the Chicago White Sox.

In 1921, Luque's success out of the bullpen and as a spot starter led the Reds to make him primarily a starting pitcher, a role that he would retain for the rest of the 1920s. In 1921, the durable Luque pitched more than 300 innings and ranked third in the National League (NL) with 25 complete games, while racking up a record of 17-19.

In his frustrating 1922 season, Luque went 13-23 and was a central figure in an ugly brawl between the Reds and the New York Giants that began when Luque responded to ethnic taunts hurled at him by slugging the Giants' Casey Stengel. It was later learned that Stengel was actually sitting next to the player who was slurring Luque. Before the brawl ended, Luque had threatened Giants players with a baseball bat and had to be removed by policemen from Cincinnati's Crosley Field.

Luque put the struggles of 1922 behind him in 1923, his best season in the majors, leading the league with a 27-8 record and 1.93 ERA. Two years later, despite having a losing record of 16-18, Luque again led the NL in ERA with a mark of 2.63. He continued to serve as a workhorse of the Reds rotation for the next four years, ending the 1920s having ranked in the top 10 in the NL in strikeouts six times, complete games five times, shutouts four times, and ERA six times.

In February 1930, Luque was traded to the Brooklyn Dodgers, where he played for two years before moving on to the New York Giants. With the Giants, Luque pitched almost exclusively in relief, enjoying a 19-12 record over four seasons, the last two of which he was the oldest player in the NL. His greatest moment with the Giants came in 1933, when he pitched four and one-third shutout innings of relief to earn the victory in the fifth and final game of the Giants 1933 World Series championship over the Washington Senators.

Luque retired from Major League Baseball in 1935 but returned to Cuba to pitch for four more seasons, including his final appearance at the age of 54 for the Cienfuegos club in 1945. Luque managed in the Cuban League and won several pennants, earning a reputation as a cantankerous but effective teacher whose understanding of the nuances of pitching helped future successful hurlers, including Sal "the Barber" Maglie and fellow Cuban CAMILO PASCUAL. Luque died in Havana on July 3, 1957, and was inducted into the Cincinnati Reds Hall of Fame in 1967.

Further Reading

"Dolf Luque." Baseball Reference Web site. Available online. URL: http://www.baseball-reference.com/l/luquedo01.shtml. Downloaded on January 15, 2006.

Robinson, James G. "Luque Loses His Cool." Baseball Library Web site. Available online. URL: http://www.baseballlibrary.com/baseballlibrary/features/flashbacks/05_28_1921.stm. Downloaded on January 15, 2006.

Wolinsky, Russell. "Dolf Luque and Camilo Pascual: Two Cuban Curveballers." National Baseball Hall of Fame Web site. URL: http://www.baseballhalloffame.org/library/columns/rw_050718.htm. Downloaded on January 15, 2006.

M

Maradona, Diego
(Diego Armando Maradona)
(1960–) *soccer player*

A stout and quick attacking midfielder renowned for his technical brilliance and controversial character, Diego Maradona led Argentina's national soccer team to the 1986 World Cup championship and is widely considered the greatest player ever produced by that nation. Diego Armando Maradona was born on October 30, 1960, in Villa Florito, Argentina. He grew up in that shantytown just south of Buenos Aires and quickly became a standout soccer player.

When he was only 10 years old, Maradona was discovered while playing for his local team by a talent scout and soon began playing for Los Cebollitas, the junior team of Buenos Aires–based Argentinos Juniors. Maradona also developed a penchant for showmanship as a ball boy during intermissions of professional games, entertaining thousands of spectators with displays of his remarkable dribbling skills.

In 1976, Maradona began his professional career with the Argentinos Juniors at the age of 15. He remained with that club until 1981, compiling 116 goals in 166 games. Despite this auspicious beginning, Maradona suffered a bitter setback in 1978 when, because of his youth, he was not selected to be a member of the 1978 Argentine national team that won that year's World Cup, held in Argentina. At the age of 18, he captained

the World Youth Cup winners and continued his success with stellar play that led him to be voted South American Player of the Year in 1979 and 1980. At the end of the 1981 season and for the 1982 season, Maradona played for the team he had cheered as a youth, the Boca Juniors, with whom he scored 28 goals in 42 games and solidified his reputation as one of the top young soccer talents in the world.

Following his stint with the Boca Juniors club, Maradona played in his first World Cup. The defending champion Argentine team struggled in the 1982 tournament held in Spain and was eliminated in round 16, following a loss in which Maradona was ejected for kicking an opponent.

Later in 1982, Maradona's rights were transferred to FC Barcelona for a then–world record fee of more than $8 million. With Barcelona, Maradona scored 38 goals in 58 games through 1984 and helped the team win the 1983 Copa del Rey (Spain's annual national championship). However, Maradona's time with FC Barcelona was marked by struggles with hepatitis and an injury resulting from a controversial tackle by Real Madrid's Andoni Goikoetxea that left Maradona with back problems and two screws in his left ankle.

After the 1984 season, Maradona's rights were purchased by the Italian Club SSC Napoli for another record fee. Maradona spent the prime years of his career starring for Napoli, leading the

Diego Maradona is seen at the 1986 World Cup in Mexico, where he led Argentina to the championship. *(EMPICS)*

team to its first-ever championship in 1986–87 and another in 1989–90. During his time with the team, stretching from 1984 through 1991, Maradona played in 259 games and scored 115 goals, becoming the top paid soccer player in the world and recipient of several million additional dollars from endorsements. Images of Maradona, his short, strong body topped by thick, dark hair and his body adorned in the number 10 light blue-and-white jersey of Napoli were ubiquitous throughout Naples and southern Italy. He was beloved particularly by the poor, who related to the soccer star's slum-dwelling background and his gritty defiance of obstacles.

In addition to his greatness on the soccer field, Maradona also attracted attention for his headline-making lifestyle. He spent money extravagantly, was the focus of a long-standing (and ultimately successful) paternity suit, and was rumored to be linked to the local mafia. Though praised by soccer legend PELÉ as "the best player on Earth," Maradona was often blasted by critics who said he did not have the class or sportsmanship of the Brazilian great.

Maradona reached the apex of his career in 1986 playing for the Argentine national team during the World Cup tournament in Mexico. Maradona led Argentina to a quarterfinals match with England, a contest made even more contentious by the recently concluded Falkland Islands War between the two nations. Maradona opened the game's scoring by striking the ball with his hand. Despite English protest and the shouts of thousands of fans who noticed the illegal hand touching, officials allowed the goal, termed "the hand of God goal" when Maradona answered a postgame reporter's question about the tally, explaining with a smile, "Even if there was a hand, it must have been the hand of God." Later in Argentina's win over England, Maradona scored again by using strong bursts of speed and nimble ball control to weave through the English defense for a goal. Maradona followed this performance with two goals in a semifinals win over Belgium and an assist in the championship game victory over West Germany, bringing an elated Argentina the World Cup title.

At the 1990 World Cup in Italy, Maradona again led Argentina to a final-game contest with West Germany, but this time the Argentines lost. Soon after this World Cup, Maradona's career tumbled. In 1991, he was suspended for 15 months after testing positive for cocaine. He played through 1997 for Sevilla FC (1992–93), Newell's Old Boys (1993), and Boca Juniors (1995–97). Maradona was suspended in 1994 for using a banned substance during the World Cup tournament in Brazil, in which the Argentines were eliminated in the second round. On October 30, 1997, Maradona's 37th birthday, he announced his retirement from soccer.

Maradona enjoyed postplay glory in 2000 when he was voted Player of the Century in an official Fédération Internationale de Football Association (FIFA) Internet poll, though FIFA infuriated Maradona (who stormed out of the awards ceremony) by allowing Pelé to share the award as a result of his overwhelming support from an unannounced vote by former coaches, journalists, and FIFA officials. Maradona spent much of the ensuing years in and out of rehabilitation centers in Cuba and Switzerland while struggling with his addiction to cocaine, a massive heart attack in 2004, and obesity.

In 2005, Maradona emerged noticeably thinner following gastric bypass surgery and resumed his high profile, hosting the popular Argentine television show *La Noche del Diez,* which featured a five-hour interview of Cuban leader Fidel Castro. Also on his show that same year, Maradona for the first time admitted that the "hand of God" goal was illegal and intentional.

Further Reading

Burns, Jimmy. *Hand of God: The Life of Diego Maradona, Soccer's Fallen Star.* Guilford, Conn: Lyons Press, 2001.

"Diego Maradona (Argentina)." Planet World Cup Web site. Available online. URL: http://www.planetworldcup.com/LEGENDS/maradona.html. Downloaded on January 15, 2006.

Gammon, Clive. "Diego's Downfall; Soccer's Hero Takes a World-class Tumble." *Sports Illustrated,* 10 June 1991, p. 14.

"Maradona Calls Famous Goal 'Bit of Mischief.'" ESPN Soccer Net Web site. Available online. URL: http://soccernet.espn.go.com/news/story?id=340282&cc=5901. Downloaded on January 15, 2006.

"Split Decision: Pele, Maradona Each Win FIFA Century Awards after Feud." CNN/*Sports Illustrated* Web site. Available online. URL: http://sportsillustrated. cnn.com/soccer/news/2000/12/11/pele_maradona/. Downloaded on Janaury 15, 2006.

Marichal, Juan
(Juan Antonio Marichal, the Dominican Dandy)
(1937–) *baseball player*

The first Dominican to be inducted into the National Baseball Hall of Fame, Juan Marichal was a dominant right-handed pitcher whose distinctive high leg kick and masterful command of a dazzling array of pitches helped him become the winningest pitcher of the 1960s. Juan Antonio Marichal was born on October 30, 1937, in Laguna Verde, Dominican Republic. He grew up in this countryside community, where he attended school, helped his family with farming chores, and spent most of his remaining time playing baseball.

Marichal was a standout shortstop on his local team until he attended a game featuring the Dominican national team, during which the boy became enamored with the sidearm pitching delivery of one of the team's pitchers. He soon enjoyed success on the mound, including winning both games of a double-header against the Dominican Military Aviation (air force) team. The next day, two military officials appeared at the Marichal home and ordered Marichal to report to the air force base in Santo Domingo, where he immediately became a member of the Dominican Military Aviation baseball team.

Marichal continued to excel with his new club, attracting a great deal of interest from major league scouts. A gentleman's agreement between Marichal's admired older brother, Gonzalo, and a scout from the New York Giants led Marichal to sign with the team in fall 1957. After two and a half stellar years in the minors, during which he adopted his distinctive high leg kick and overhand delivery, the 21-year-old Marichal made his major league debut on July 19, 1960, for the San Francisco Giants (moved in 1958) against the Philadelphia

Phillies. Serving notice of his future dominance, Marichal struck out the first two batters and did not allow a base runner until the seventh inning, striking out 12 and giving up only one hit in a 2-0 Giants victory.

Marichal finished 6-2 with an earned run average (ERA) of 2.66 in 1960 and after a 13-10 season in 1961, earned the first of his eventual nine spots on the National League (NL) All-Star team in 1962. He ended that year with an 18-11 record and four shutout innings in the World Series, which the Giants lost to the New York Yankees 4-3.

In 1963, Marichal ranked among the top five in the NL in wins (25; first), innings (321.3; first), shutouts (five; fifth), and strikeouts (248; fourth). Among these 25 wins were an 89-pitch no-hitter of the Houston Colt .45s and a 16-inning complete game 1-0 victory over future Hall of Famer Warren Spahn and the Milwaukee Braves.

From 1964 through 1966, Marichal, often called "the Dominican Dandy," ascended to the elite of major league pitchers, ranking with Sandy Koufax of the Los Angeles Dodgers and Bob Gibson of the St. Louis Cardinals as baseball's best hurlers. He compiled records of 21-8 in 1964, 22-13 in 1965, and 25-6 in 1966, with ERAs below 2.50 each season. Marichal's remarkable accuracy was reflected in his strikeout-to-walk ratio over the course of those seasons of 5:1. During these three seasons and in all but one (1972) of Marichal's 14 seasons with the Giants, he helped the team to a winning record.

However, this astounding run of excellence featured the darkest day of Marichal's career, August 22, 1965, in a game between the Giants and their rival, the Los Angeles Dodgers. Escalating animosity between the NL's two top teams reached a boiling point when, with Marichal at bat, Dodgers catcher Johnny Roseboro whizzed a return throw to the mound by Marichal's head. Marichal and Roseboro exchanged hostile words until the catcher took off his mask, and Marichal struck him over the head with his bat, setting off one of the ugliest melees in Major League Baseball history. The bloody Roseboro suffered a concus-

sion and later sued Marichal, though he eventually dropped the lawsuit and forgave the Giants star.

Marichal was slapped with a $1,750 fine (the largest in major league history at the time) and a nine-game suspension by Major League Baseball. Marichal eventually apologized, reflecting after his career ended, "I did good things for the game, but I wish I could take back that one incident, I regret it."

Marichal closed out the 1960s with a three-year run from 1967 through 1969 that witnessed him racking up a record of 61-30, with 15 shutouts, and ERAs that progressively dropped from 2.76 to 2.43 to 2.10. His superior skills were respected by the greatest of his opponents. All-time major league home run king Hank Aaron said of Marichal, "He can throw all day within a 2" space, in, out, up, or down. I've never seen anyone as good at that." Pittsburgh Pirates legend ROBERTO CLEMENTE added, "It doesn't matter what he throws; when he's got it, he beats you."

In 1970, Marichal suffered a severe reaction to penicillin that led to chronic arthritis and a back injury resulting from attempting to return too soon. He finished the 1970 season with a record of 12-10 but rebounded in 1971 with less power and increased guile to go 18-11 with 18 complete games. He would never finish a season with a winning record again, though he followed a 6-16 season in 1972 with a complete game four-hit loss to the Pittsburgh Pirates in the National League Championship Series, won by the Pirates three games to one. Marichal went 11-15 in 1973, his final season as a Giant, before spending 1974 with the Boston Red Sox and, with the vocal support of former Dodger Roseboro, two starts in 1975 with the Los Angeles Dodgers.

Marichal retired following the 1975 season with a career mark of 243 and 142, one of only eight right-handed pitchers to have 100 or more career wins than losses. In the late 1970s, Marichal lived in San Francisco and the Dominican Republic, where he had a banana and rice farm. In 1983, Marichal became the first Dominican

Juan Marichal, shown winding up with his distinctive high leg kick, dominated batters throughout the 1960s and early 1970s. *(National Baseball Hall of Fame Library)*

www.latinosportslegends.com/Marichal_Juan-bio.htm. Downloaded on January 15, 2006.

"Juan Marichal." Baseball Reference Web site. Available online. URL: http://www.baseball-reference.com/m/maricju01.shtml. Downloaded on January 15, 2006.

"Juan Marichal." National Baseball Hall of Fame Web site. Available online. URL: http://www.baseballhalloffame.org/hofers_and_honorees/hofer_bios/marichal_juan.htm. Downloaded on January 15, 2006.

Olbermann, Keith. "Going the Distance." *Sports Illustrated,* 11 May 1998, p. 102.

Ortiz, Jorge L. "Alive and Kicking: Marichal's Legend to Be Immortalized by SBC Park Statue." *San Francisco Chronicle,* 19 May 2005.

Marta
(Marta Vieira da Silva)
(1986–   ) *soccer player*

A teenage sensation who helped lead Brazil's women's soccer team to the silver medal at the 2004 Olympics, Marta has earned the distinction bestowed upon that soccer-crazed nation's greatest male players—being referred to by a one-word nickname. She was born Marta Vieira da Silva on February 19, 1986, in Dois Riachos, Brazil. She became involved in soccer at the age of seven mainly by playing *futsal,* an indoor version of soccer that emphasizes quick opportunistic strikes.

As a 12-year-old girl in Dois Riachos, Marta watched on television as the Brazilian women finished third in the first Women's World Cup, played in 1999 in the United States. Of that experience she later recalled, "I said then: 'One day I will be there playing.'"

In 2002, the 16-year-old Marta took a giant step toward joining Brazil's national women's team by being named to Brazil's squad participating in the inaugural Under-19 Women's World Championship in Canada. In her first game, Marta tallied two assists in Brazil's 5-3 win over Mexico.

inducted into the National Baseball Hall of Fame before working as a scout for the Oakland A's. In 1996, Marichal was asked to serve as the Dominican Republic's minister of sports, physical education, and recreation.

In 2005, the 67-year-old Marichal returned to San Francisco from the Dominican Republic to attend a ceremony before a Giants game where a statue featuring his indelibly unique pitching delivery was unveiled. This event and monument reaffirm his excellence on the mound, role as a hero to scores of future Dominican professional pitchers, and undisputed place as the greatest pitcher in San Francisco Giants history and one of the greatest in the history of Major League Baseball.

Further Reading

"Juan Antonio (Sanchez) Marichal." Latino Legends in Sports Web site. Available online. URL: http://

In Brazil's next game, the 5'3", 125-pound Marta used a commanding combination of speed, power, and grace to lift her team to a 1-0 victory over Germany. She went from intriguing observers to astonishing them with a three-goal performance in Brazil's 4-0 win over France. In her next game, Marta had a long and impressive solo sprint to the goal in the game's fourth minute, helping lead Brazil to a 4-3 win over Australia. Her goal late in Brazil's next game against Canada forced overtime, when the Brazilians finally fell.

A Fédération Internationale de Football Association (FIFA) article recalling the tournament later noted, "Day after day the press . . . buzzed with whispers and applause over the sultry skills and bustling delicate bravado of young Marta. Her name was on everyone's lips and FIFA President Joseph S. Blatter may well have been thinking of the teenager when he said 'the technical and tactical level of the [soccer] has been astonishing.'"

Wearing the honored number 10 donned by Brazilian women's soccer pioneer Sissi, the 17-year-old Marta moved on to star on the 2003 Brazilian Women's World Cup team that competed in the United States. She scored a goal in each of Brazil's first two games, a 3-0 win over South Korea and a 4-1 victory over Norway. Following Brazil's 1-1 tie with France, Marta scored Brazil's only goal in a 2-1 loss to Sweden in the quarterfinals that eliminated Brazil from title contention.

In the 2004 Olympics in Athens, Greece, many media reports focused on Marta, portraying her as a music-loving teenage phenomenon who was spearheading the growing passion in Brazil for

Brazilian soccer sensation Marta (center) outruns two Americans in the 2004 Olympics women's soccer final, won by the United States 2-1. *(EMPICS)*

women's soccer. Her performance at the Olympics validated this attention. After scoring the decisive goal in Brazil's opening 1-0 victory over Australia, Australian coach Adrian Santrac remarked, "We already knew Marta is a world class player who has the ability to change a game. She is all left-foot, like Maradona, and she's difficult to stop."

The Brazilians lost their next game 2-0 to the United States before Marta scored three goals in a 7-0 drubbing of Greece, and she notched a goal and assist in a 5-0 rout of Mexico. After a win over Sweden, Brazil advanced to the gold medal game versus the United States.

In that game, Marta's deft dribbling and relentless pursuit of the net brought Brazil to a hard-fought 2-1 loss and the silver medal. Prior to this game, Marta commented on the newfound flair and confidence in Brazilian women's soccer that also reflected her influence, saying, "Style, movement, class, and rhythm, that's how we learn to play in Brazil . . . we are learning more in every game and getting better every day." Marta is working to apply that style as she prepares for the 2007 Women's World Cup to be played in China.

Further Reading

"Marta." Women's World Cup 2003 Web site. Available online. URL: http://fifaworldcup.yahoo.com/03/en/t/pl/190358.html. Downloaded on July 2, 2005.

"Marta Magic Mesmerises Matildas." Fédération Internationale de Football Association Web site. Available online. URL: http://www.fifa.com/en/comp/index/0,2442,102526,00.html?comp=OFW&year=2004&articleid=102526. Downloaded on July 2, 2005.

Martínez, Dennis
(José Dennis Martínez, El Presidente)
(1955–) *baseball player*

The first Nicaraguan ever to play Major League Baseball, Dennis Martínez pitched for 23 seasons, overcoming alcoholism to become only the 13th man (and first Latin American) to hurl a perfect game, and finished his career with 245 victories, surpassing the previous mark of most wins by a Latin American pitcher held for more than 20 years by Hall of Famer JUAN MARICHAL. He was born José Dennis Martínez in Granada, Nicaragua, on May 14, 1955. Martínez grew up in Granada, Central America's oldest colonial city, until he signed a contract with the Baltimore Orioles organization on December 10, 1973.

Martínez quickly moved up the Orioles' minor league system before making his major league debut in Baltimore's Memorial Stadium at the age of 21 on September 14, 1976. In that game, Martínez struck out the first three batters he faced and pitched five and two-thirds innings of relief to earn the victory over the Detroit Tigers.

Martínez was named the International League Pitcher of the Year for his excellence at the highest level of minor league baseball following the 1976 season. He continued to pitch well during his full rookie season of 1977, ranking second among all first-year pitchers with 14 wins.

From 1978 to 1982, Martínez used his hard-throwing style to establish himself as one of the best young pitchers in baseball. With the exception of an injury-plagued 1980 season in which he went 6-4, Martínez averaged 15 wins a year during this period, leading the American League (AL) in games started (39), innings pitched (292.3), and complete games (18) in 1979 and wins (14) in 1981. He was the starting pitcher for Baltimore in game four of the 1979 World Series versus the Pittsburgh Pirates and appeared in relief during the Orioles' decisive game-seven loss.

In 1983, Martínez was entering the stage of his career in which most great players enjoy their most productive years. However, personal problems prevented him from playing an important role for the Orioles, who would become the 1983 World Series champions. Martínez's battle with alcoholism led to his career-worst record of 7-16. Martínez's struggles led Baltimore manager Earl

Weaver to keep the formerly reliable and effective pitcher off the mound throughout the Orioles' five-game World Series victory over the Philadelphia Phillies.

Things got worse for Martínez later in 1983. On December 3, he was arrested and briefly placed in jail on charges of drunk driving. He remained with Baltimore during the 1984 and 1985 seasons, pitching as a starter and, during his many slumps, being shuffled to the bullpen as a reliever. During these two seasons, he had a record of 19-20 and his earned run average (ERA) continued to hover above the high 5.00 level. Frustrated by his poor performance, nagging injuries, and personal problems, the Orioles traded Martínez to the Montreal Expos on June 16, 1986, for a lightly regarded minor league shortstop. Martínez surprised no one by continuing to struggle through the 1986 season with his new team.

Few, if any, however, anticipated the remarkable resurrection of his career that began in 1987 following his successful treatment for alcoholism. During his stint in Montreal (1987–93), Martínez was the ace of the Expos's pitching staff, and he was among the consistently best pitchers in baseball. In seven seasons, he displayed a potent combination of guts, savvy, and a sinking fastball to win 97 games, losing only 66. He was named to the National League (NL) All-Star team in 1990, 1991, and 1992. In 1991, at the age of 36, Martínez led the NL in ERA (2.39), shutouts (five), and complete games (nine). The normally frugal Expos rewarded Martínez with a salary that season of more than $3 million, which ranked among the 10 highest in baseball.

Martínez's greatest on-field accomplishment occurred on July 28, 1991, in Los Angeles. Pitching in front of more than 45,000 fans of the first-place Los Angeles Dodgers, Martínez pitched a perfect game—retiring all 27 batters without allowing one to reach base—becoming only the 13th man and the first Latin American to achieve this feat in the history of Major League Baseball. Already revered in his homeland, Nicaragua, as "El Presidente" for his athletic achievement and national pride, Martínez was now recognized throughout the baseball world as one of the top pitchers and admired for his unique comeback story.

On September 28, 1993, in his last game as a member of the Expos, Martínez defeated the Florida Marlins to become only the seventh pitcher and again the first Latin American in baseball history to win at least 100 games in each of the American and National Leagues. He shares this distinction with such pitching legends as Cy Young and Nolan Ryan.

On December 2, 1993, one day shy of the 10th anniversary of his drunk driving arrest, Martínez signed a three-year contract with the Cleveland Indians worth more than $12 million. In his three years with Cleveland, Martínez anchored the Indians' pitching staff, winning 32 games while losing only 17. In 1995, the 40-year-old Martínez helped lead the Indians to their first AL pennant since 1954. Martínez's game-six victory over the Seattle Mariners in the American League Championship Series, a win he would later describe as his best ever, brought the Indians to the World Series. He started two games in that series, losing game two before pitching five shutout innings in Cleveland's game-six loss that earned the championship for the Atlanta Braves.

Martínez had another winning season with Cleveland in 1996, during which he became the oldest player in baseball, a distinction he would hold for two more seasons. Now a grandfather, Martínez began the 1997 season with a new team, the pennant-contending Seattle Mariners, but he was released after suffering a 1-5 record. He briefly retired from baseball before signing on for one last campaign with the Atlanta Braves prior to the 1998 season.

Most of the attention given to Martínez during his last season was focused on his pursuit of the career-wins record for Latin American pitchers of 243, held by Dominican great Marichal. Martínez was used almost exclusively as a middle reliever for the Braves when the score was often lopsided, making opportunities for wins scarce. He started only five games that season, though one of those starts was a complete game shutout over the Milwaukee Brewers on June 2 that tied Marichal's win record.

For almost two months, Martínez was not able to earn another win. Finally, on August 9, 1998, he became the Latin American career leader in pitching victories when the Braves defeated the San Francisco Giants, the team for whom Marichal enjoyed almost all his success. Martínez would add another victory in September, bringing his total to 245. The last appearance by Martínez in a game was fittingly a victory over the San Diego Padres in game four of the National League Championship Series, which the Braves lost in six games.

After the 1998 season, Martínez formally announced his retirement at a press conference in Nicaragua's capital city, Managua. Nicaragua's president, Arnoldo Alemán, who had renamed the national baseball stadium after Martínez in 1997, called him "the maximum glory of national sport." Since retiring, Martínez has lived in Nicaragua, where he has often been urged to run for political office, and Florida, where he serves as the president of the Dennis Martinez Foundation, an organization that provides aid for underprivileged children and disaster relief in Nicaragua and throughout Latin America.

Further Reading

Buckley, James, Jr. *Perfect: The Inside Story of Baseball's Seventeen Perfect Games.* Chicago: Triumph Books, 2005.

"Dennis Martinez." Baseball Library Web site. Available online. URL: http://baseballlibrary.com/baseballlibrary/ballplayers/M/Martinez_Dennis.stm. Downloaded on July 1, 2005.

"Dennis Martinez." Baseball Reference Web site. Available online. URL: http://www.baseball-reference.com/m/martide01.shtml. Downloaded on July 1, 2005.

Knisley, Michael. "The Wait of a Nation—Nicaraguan Pitcher Dennis Martinez of the Atlanta Braves Sets Major League Record for Most Wins by a Latin American." *Sporting News,* 10 August 1998, p. 22.

Loverro, Thom. *Oriole Magic: The O's of '83.* Chicago: Triumph Books, 2004.

Martinez, Edgar
(Papi)
(1963–) *baseball player*

The all-time career leader among designated hitters in batting average, home runs, and runs batted in (RBIs), Edgar Martinez spent his entire 18-year career playing for the Seattle Mariners, becoming one of baseball's most feared hitters and most respected players. He was born on January 2, 1963, in New York City. His parents divorced two years later, and he moved to Dorado, Puerto Rico, where he lived with his grandparents. In 1971, Martinez watched on television as Puerto Rican legend ROBERTO CLEMENTE led the Pittsburgh Pirates to the World Series championship. Martinez later recalled, "After that series, I went outside my house and I started playing in the backyard, and I was hooked on baseball after that." When Martinez was 11 years old, his parents reconciled and summoned him and his siblings back to New York City to live with them. Martinez refused, instead staying with his grandparents in Dorado, where he graduated from high school.

Martinez signed as an undrafted free agent with the Seattle Mariners on December 19, 1982. He moved slowly and steadily up the Mariners' farm system before making his major league debut as a third baseman on September 12, 1987. Martinez appeared in fewer than 100 games for the Mariners from 1987 to 1989, largely because of his inconsistent defense.

However, Martinez's booming bat led Seattle to name him their starting third baseman in 1990, and he did not disappoint, finishing with a .302 batting average and 27 doubles. After a solid 1991 season, Martinez broke out in 1992, leading the American League (AL) in batting average (.343) and doubles (46). Following this season, he was rewarded with a three-year, $10 million contract. When asked by reporters to name the first thing he planned to buy with his newfound wealth, Martinez reflected his soft-spoken and classy reputation by responding, "Heart medicine for my grandmother."

Injuries to his hamstring in 1993 and wrist in 1994 halted his playing time and production. But in 1995, Martinez enjoyed the greatest season of his career, leading the AL in batting average (.356), runs (121), and on-base percentage (an astounding .479). His batting title gave him the distinction of being the first AL right-handed hitter to win two batting average crowns in more than 50 years. That same year, 1995, was also the first in a seven-year span in which Martinez, now almost exclusively a designated hitter, made five All-Star teams, ranked in the top 10 in AL batting average five times, and ranked in the top 10 in walks 10 times.

The highlight of Martinez's stellar 1995 season came on October 8 in Seattle's Kingdome during the decisive fifth game of the Mariners' first-ever playoff appearance, a division series against the New York Yankees. With the Mariners trailing the Yankees 6-5 in the 11th inning, Martinez delivered a clutch line drive double to drive in two runs, setting off a wild celebration at home plate and creating the greatest moment in the city's sports history. His .571 batting average and 10 RBIs earned Martinez the series' Most Valuable Player award.

Though often overshadowed by star teammates Ken Griffey, Jr., Randy Johnson, and ALEX RODRIGUEZ, Martinez continued to play a major role in the Mariners' success over the next few years. From 1996 to 2001, Seattle made the playoffs three times, including a major league best ever 116-win season in 2001, with Martinez using his pigeon-toed batting stance and keen eye to rank among baseball's top offensive threats. Though the Mariners never made it to the World Series, Seattle fans remained enamored of the man endearingly nicknamed "Papi"—Spanish for "Daddy."

Martinez remained productive from 2002 through 2004, though injuries and age limited his contribution. He announced his retirement during the 2004 season and was met with an outpouring of gratitude from the baseball fans and the city he had played in for almost two decades. He became the first Puerto Rican to receive the Roberto Clemente Award, given annually by Major League Baseball to the player who best demonstrates excellence on the field and in the community.

On the season's final Saturday, a sellout crowd at Seattle's Safeco Field, including the city's mayor, the state's governor, baseball's commissioner, and Puerto Rican Hall of Famer ORLANDO CEPEDA, honored Martinez with speeches and celebration. This occasion was made even more special with the announcement that the award for the AL's outstanding designated hitter would be renamed the Edgar Martinez Award.

Teammate Bret Boone captured the spirit of the fans and views of many who played with Martinez by saying, "He epitomized what a professional is . . . stats aside, he is one of the best men I've ever known." Martinez lives in the Seattle area with his wife, Holli, and their children, and he is the owner of Caribbean Apparel, Inc.

Further Reading

"Edgar Martinez." Baseball Library Web site. Available online. URL: http://baseballlibrary.com/baseballlibrary/ballplayers/M/Martinez_Edgar.stm. Downloaded on July 1, 2005.

"Goodbye Mr. Baseball." *Seattle Times,* 4 October 2004, A1.

Thiel, Art. *Out of Left Field: How the Mariners Made Baseball Fly in Seattle.* Seattle, Wash.: Sasquatch Books, 2003.

Martínez, Pedro
(Pedro Jaime Martínez)
(1971–) *baseball player*

A three-time Cy Young Award winner, whose whip-like delivery of a wicked repertoire of pitches helped him win more than 70 percent of his decisions through his first 14 seasons, Pedro Martínez helped lead the 2004 Boston Red Sox to the franchise's first World Series championship since 1918. He was born Pedro Jaime Martínez on October 25, 1971, in Manoguayabo, Dominican Republic. He grew up in the small town, about 30 miles from Santo Domingo, one of six children born to his mother, Leopoldina, who worked as a maid, and his father, Paulino, a janitor who had been a star pitcher in the Dominican leagues during the 1950s.

Martínez was a very good student in school and also enjoyed baseball, following his older brother, Los Angeles Dodgers signee Ramón, to workouts at the Dominican Training Academy established by the team. Though he stood well under 6' and was extremely thin, Martínez had a smooth, compact pitching motion that consistently delivered pitches with good movement in the 80-to-90-miles-an-hour range. In July 1988, at the age of 16, Martínez signed a professional contract with the Los Angeles Dodgers.

Martínez rocketed through the minor leagues, baffling hitters with the command and poise of a much more experienced pitcher and the power and velocity of a man who weighed much more than 140 pounds. In 1991, Martínez was named by the *Sporting News* the minor league player of the year, and he made his major league debut with the Dodgers the following year as a 20 year old, striking out eight batters in eight innings.

The last man cut from the Dodgers' 25-man roster following spring training in 1993, Martínez was called up to Los Angeles early in the season and held the role as a middle reliever, with an impressive record of 10 wins and five losses and an earned run average (ERA) of 2.61, while striking out 119 batters in only 107 innings. Martínez was eager to

Pedro Martínez delivers a pitch in 2004, when he helped lead the Boston Red Sox to their first World Series championship in 86 years. *(Larry Goren/WireImage.com)*

prove himself as a starting pitcher and asked Dodgers manager Tommy Lasorda for opportunities to begin games. When Martínez did not perform well in those starts, many in the Dodgers organization decided that Martínez would likely never be a dependable starting pitcher. Believing they could fill his role in the bullpen and anxious to add a proven offensive star, the Dodgers traded Martínez to the Montreal Expos for Delino DeShields prior to the 1994 season.

In Montreal, Martínez was a starting pitcher on a promising club managed by FELIPE ALOU, a former teammate of Martínez's father in the Dominican Republic. Martínez enjoyed a great first season in Montreal, finishing 11-5 and ranking third in the National League (NL) in strikeouts per nine innings (8.83). The Expos had a six-game lead in the National League East when a labor dispute ended the season, and the team then proceeded to allow several of their top players to leave via free agency prior to the 1995 season in order to preserve a low payroll.

Despite the purging of Montreal's talent, Martínez continued to excel. In 1995, he ranked fifth in the NL in wins (14) and strikeouts (174), pitched into the seventh inning or beyond in 24 of his 30 starts, and carried a perfect game into the 10th inning in a June 3 game at San Diego. Martínez followed with another strong campaign in 1996 before dominating NL hitters in 1997, finishing 17-8, with an ERA of 1.90 and 305 strikeouts. By racking up more than 300 strikeouts and holding his ERA under 2.00, Martínez became the first pitcher to achieve that feat since Steve Carlton had in 1972 and the first right-handed pitcher to do so since Walter Johnson had in 1912.

Martínez won the 1997 NL Cy Young Award and at a postseason banquet presented the award to former major league star and Dominican pitcher JUAN MARICHAL, who, despite a Hall of Fame career, never won the award. Marichal was visibly emotionally moved but soon gave the award back to Martínez.

As the 1998 season approached, the Expos informed other teams that Martínez, who was in line for a huge contract following the season, was available in trade for top inexpensive prospects. The Expos then sent Martínez to the Boston Red Sox for young pitchers Carl Pavano and Tony Armas, Jr. Martínez signed a six-year, $75 million contract with Boston before throwing a pitch for his new team but did not disappoint the city's ravenous baseball fans when the season began. He struck out 11 in seven shutout innings in an opening-day win over the Oakland A's and finished the season with a 19-7 record, 2.89 ERA, and 251 strikeouts, helping Boston reach the playoffs, where they fell to the Cleveland Indians.

In 1999, Martínez enjoyed one of the greatest individual seasons for a pitcher, leading the American League (AL) in wins (23), ERA (2.07), and strikeouts (313) and earning the AL Cy Young Award. He also had a memorable start in the All-

Star game in Boston's Fenway Park, striking out the first four batters he faced, including SAMMY SOSA and Mark McGwire. The Red Sox again won the AL wildcard and reached the American League Championship Series (ALCS), where they lost to the New York Yankees in five games, despite Martínez's 12-strikeout victory in game three.

Over the next two years, Martínez battled shoulder problems but managed to tally 25 wins against only nine losses. In 2000, his AL-leading 1.74 ERA and 284 strikeouts, along with his 18-6 record, earned him a third Cy Young Award. In 2001, Martínez, now physically thicker and pitching with even more intelligence and savvy, again led the AL in ERA (2.26) and strikeouts (239), finishing the year with a 20-4 record.

In 2003, arm trouble again limited Martínez's appearances, though it did little to restrain his effectiveness, as he ended up with a record of 14-4 and an ERA of 2.22. The Red Sox reached game seven of the ALCS versus their archrival, the New York Yankees, with Martínez on the mound nursing a 5-2 lead. Though tiring, Martínez told Boston manager Grady Little that he was able to continue pitching, but the Yankees rallied, knocked out Martínez, and won the game in extra innings. Following the game, Martínez defended his manager's controversial decision, explaining, "I'm the ace of the team . . . this is no time to say 'I'm tired.' There is no reason to blame Grady . . . if anybody look[s] at somebody and point the finger, they can point it at me because I was the one pitching."

Martínez and the Red Sox would gain sweet redemption in 2004 when they came back from a three-game deficit to defeat the Yankees in a seven-game ALCS and then rolled to their first World Series championship in 88 years in a four-game sweep of the St. Louis Cardinals, including a Martínez win in game three. Following the season, the Red Sox, concerned with Martínez's advancing age, frequency of nagging injuries, and drop in production in 2004 (16-9, 3.90 ERA), decided not to match or exceed the free-agent contract offer made by the New York Mets of four years and $53 million.

Martínez signed with the Mets and in 2005 maintained his standing as one of baseball's best pitchers, finishing in the top five in the NL in wins (15), ERA (2.82), and strikeouts (208). Martínez struggled with injuries and ineffectiveness in 2006, finishing the year with a mediocre 9-8 record and a career-worst 4.48 ERA.

Despite his subpar season, Martínez entered 2007, at the age of 35, with a career record of 206-92, with 2,998 strikeouts and a 2.81 cumulative ERA—statistics that will certainly earn him a place in baseball's Hall of Fame and status as one of the most masterful pitchers of his era.

Further Reading

Callahan, Gerry. "Rocket Redux." *Sports Illustrated,* 20 April 1998, p. 38.
"Pedro Martinez." Jock Bio Web site. Available online. URL: http://www.jockbio.com/Bios/Pedro/Pedro_bio.html. Downloaded on January 15, 2006.
"Pedro Martinez." Major League Baseball Web site. Available online. URL: http://newyork.mets.mlb.com/NASApp/mlb/team/player.jsp?player_id=118377. Downloaded on January 15, 2006.
Rosenthal, Ken. "Ace in a Hole: Years of Overuse Have Left Pedro Martinez, the King of Mound Two Years Ago, at a Crossroads in his Career." *Sporting News,* 4 March 2002, p. 34.

Further Viewing

Faith Rewarded—The Historic Season of the 2004 Boston Red Sox (DVD). New England Sports Network, 2004.

Méndez, José
(El Diamante Negro)
(1887–1928) *baseball player*

A dominant right-handed pitcher in the Negro Leagues until he injured his arm and became a standout shortstop, José Méndez is the first Latino baseball legend. He was born on March 19, 1887, in Cárdenas, Cuba. Méndez grew up amid the poverty common in this northern coastal city just east of Havana. Though slight of build and standing only 5'8", Méndez threw remarkably hard and by his late teens became admired within Cuba as "El Diamante Negro" (the Black Diamond) because of his rare ability and his dark skin. Méndez's skin color prevented major league teams from pursuing him as he played in the early 1900s, almost four decades before Jackie Robinson became the first black person to play in Major League Baseball.

In 1907, at the age of 20, Méndez played his first season in the Cuban Winter League, compiling a 15-6 record as a pitcher. He then played with the Cuban Stars in the Negro Leagues and went 44-2. Many of those victories came against semiprofessional clubs, though most came against the high level of competition found among Negro League teams in the United States.

After becoming a professional, Méndez spent all of his winters until 1914 pitching in Cuba against American major league teams, which regularly trained in that nation, earning victories over talented and highly touted pitchers, including future Hall of Famers Christy Mathewson and Eddie Plank. During this time, Méndez demonstrated a keen pitching intellect, a baffling ability to change speeds, a sharp breaking curve, and a devastating fastball that reportedly killed a teammate when Méndez accidentally hit him with a pitch in the chest during batting practice. Legendary New York Giants manager John McGraw noted that if Méndez were white he would be worth a $50,000 contract, a whopping figure for the time, explaining, "Jose Mendez is better than any pitcher except Mordecai Brown and Christy Mathewson."

From 1912 to 1916, Méndez played for the All-Nations of Kansas City. This team was the most racially mixed of its time, with a roster composed of blacks, whites, Hawaiians, Japanese, Native Americans, and Latinos. The All-Nations team was a barnstorming club rather than a league team, playing exhibitions against top competition, including the Negro League's Indianapolis ABCs, against whom All-Nations won three of four games in 1916.

Although Méndez's accomplishments slowed following arm injuries in 1914, he achieved his greatest fame late in his career after J. L. Wilkinson, owner of the Negro League's powerhouse Kansas City Monarchs, signed him to a contract. From 1920 through 1926, Méndez managed, pitched, and played shortstop. With Méndez at shortstop, the Monarchs won three consecutive pennants from 1923 to 1925. In the first Negro League World Series in 1924, Méndez pitched in four games against the Hilldale Giants of the Eastern Colored League, winning two of them without suffering a loss. He won the deciding game by pitching a complete game shutout.

On October 31, 1928, Méndez died of pneumonia in Havana, Cuba, at the age of 41. He was inducted into the Cuban Baseball Hall of Fame in 1939.

Further Reading

Dixon, Phil. *The Negro Baseball Leagues: A Photographic History.* Mattituck, N.Y.: Ameron House Publishing, 1992.

"Jose 'Black Diamond' Mendez." Negro League Baseball Players Association Web site. Available online. URL: http://www.nlbpa.com/mendez_jose.html. Downloaded on July 1, 2005.

"Jose Mendez." Baseball Library Web site. Available online. URL: http://baseballlibrary.com/baseball-library/ballplayers/M/Mendez_Jose.stm. Downloaded on July 1, 2005.

Mendoza, Saúl
(1967–) *wheelchair athlete*

The most prolific competitor in the history of wheelchair racing, Saúl Mendoza has participated in more than 300 events, winning more than 200, including the Los Angeles Marathon seven times.

Saúl Mendoza is seen here following his silver medal performance in the 1,500 meters at the 2004 Olympics in Athens. *(Mexsport/WireImage.com)*

He was born on January 6, 1967, in Mexico City. Mendoza was struck with polio at six months of age, which caused him to permanently lose the use of his legs.

Despite his disability, which forced him to rely on crutches and wheelchairs for mobility, Mendoza was a physically active child, excelling in wheelchair basketball as a teenager. His natural speed and graceful aggressiveness on the basketball court led him to transition to the increasingly popular field of wheelchair racing.

At the age of 18, Mendoza won his first major event, the 1985 Mexican Marathon. He continued to train intensively, building up tremendous upper-body strength while learning the nuances of successful wheelchair racing. In his first paralympic competition, in Seoul, South Korea, in 1988, Mendoza won a silver and two bronze medals. Mendoza would eventually win a total of six medals over the course of five paralympic games.

Mendoza has also enjoyed enormous success competing at the Olympics, where wheelchair racing was an exhibition event in 2000 and 2004. In the 2000 games in Sydney, Australia, Mendoza won the gold in the 1,500-meter race with a record time of 3.06.75 (minutes and seconds). In the 2004 games in Athens, Greece, Mendoza again represented Mexico in the 1,500-meter race and brought home a medal, this time a silver.

With a relentless training regimen that often finds him logging more than 200 miles a week, Mendoza has been able to distinguish himself as a marathoner as well. Beginning in 1997, he won the first of seven Los Angeles Marathons. Mendoza's ability to climb over hills and through rough pavement have helped him win two New York City Marathons, in 2001 and 2004.

Mendoza, a two-time recipient of Mexico's Premio Nacional del Deporte (National Sporting Prize), is a vigorous advocate for increased athletic opportunities for disabled athletes and when he is not competing, is a popular motivational speaker. He resides with his wife near San Antonio, Texas, but remains a Mexican citizen, explaining, "I have many things that I like about the United States, but I have green, white, and red [Mexico's national colors] very deep in my heart. I am going to continue to represent Mexico and bring positive recognition to my country."

Further Reading

Hammond, Rich. "Mendoza Rolls, Makes It Four in a Row." *Los Angeles Daily News*, 6 March 2000.
"Saul Mendoza." Paralympics Web site. Available online. URL: http://www.paralympic.org/release/Main_Sections_Menu/Paralympic_Games/Past_Games/A thens_2004/Athletes_Profiles/athlete_twenty.html. Downloaded on January 15, 2006.

Miñoso, Minnie
(Saturnino Orestes Armas Miñoso)
(1922–   ) *baseball player*

A Negro League All-Star before becoming the first black player on the Chicago White Sox (and the only player to appear in games in five different decades), Minnie Miñoso was a leading offensive threat throughout the 1950s, winning three American League (AL) stolen base titles and earning top-10 rankings in on-base percentage every year from 1953 through 1960. He was born Saturnino Orestes Armas Miñoso on November 29, 1922, in Havana, Cuba. He grew up in Havana and, like many other young men at that time, worked cutting sugarcane with a machete while striving to play professional baseball.

Miñoso's lean strength, skillful bat control, and dangerous speed helped him become one of the island nation's standout baseball players. He played with Puerto Vallarta in the Mexican League and with Marianao in the Cuban Winter League, before joining the New York Cubans of the Negro League.

In 1947, the 24-year-old Miñoso helped lead the New York Cubans to their first Negro League World Series championship. This was also the year Jackie Robinson of the Brooklyn Dodgers became the first black player in Major League Baseball, which helped open the door for other promising black players such as Miñoso to sign major league contracts. Miñoso signed with the Cleveland Indians organization prior to the 1948 season, and he made his major league debut with the team in 1949, hitting a home run in only his second start.

Miñoso played in only nine games in 1949 and spent all of the 1950 season in the minor leagues. He began the 1951 season with the Indians before being traded to the Chicago White Sox, where he became the first black to play in the club's history. He also enjoyed the opportunity to be a full-time player, splitting time between the outfield and third base while shining offensively, batting .326 with 10 home runs, 76 runs batted in (RBIs), and 31 stolen bases, tops in the AL. Miñoso made the AL

All-Star team and was named the AL Rookie of the Year by the *Sporting News,* though the baseball writers gave the award to Gil McDougald of the New York Yankees despite his inferior production.

From 1952 through 1957, Miñoso, now primarily a left fielder, was the most consistent offensive star on the exciting "Go-Go Sox" team of the 1950s. Though Chicago failed to win a pennant during this period, they had a winning record each year largely due to Miñoso's play, which earned him All-Star appearances in 1952, 1953, 1954, and 1957.

Miñoso led the AL in stolen bases in 1952 and 1953, triples in 1954, and doubles in 1957. He was famous and beloved in Chicago for doing anything to get on base. His keen eye allowed him to rank in the top 10 in the AL in walks four times, and his physical bravery helped him lead the AL in hit-by-pitches every year from 1951 through 1961, with the exception of 1955, when he finished fourth. Miñoso's 192 career hit-by-pitches placed him eighth in major league history.

Prior to the 1958 season, Miñoso was traded back to the Cleveland Indians, where he had two excellent seasons, driving in 103 runs in 1958 and belting a career-high 24 home runs in 1959. Though Miñoso was not part of the 1959 AL champion Chicago team, White Sox owner Bill Veeck awarded him a championship ring in appreciation for his enormous contribution in helping build the team's success.

Miñoso was traded back to the White Sox after the 1959 season and spent two more solid years in Chicago in 1960 and 1961 before he was traded to the St. Louis Cardinals. He played sparingly for St. Louis in 1962, the Washington Senators in 1963, and the White Sox again in 1964.

White Sox owner Veeck brought the fan-favorite Miñoso back to the team in 1976, and he became, at the age of 53, the oldest player in major league history to collect a hit when he singled off California's Sid Monge. Veeck encouraged Miñoso to return to the White Sox in 1980, where he went hitless in two pinch-hit appearances and became the only major league player to appear in games in five different decades.

Miñoso has worked as a goodwill ambassador for the White Sox since that final game in 1980. In 2004, a life-sized statue depicting the familiar right-handed stance of Miñoso leaning out above an unseen home plate was unveiled in the left center field concourse at the White Sox's U.S. Cellular Field. Following the ceremony, the 81-year-old Miñoso commented, "I have a little arthritis now but I am the same guy I was in 1951. I am so happy they would do something like this for me. It will make me happy forever."

Further Reading

Kuenster, John. "Minnie Minoso Added an Unforgettable Touch to the Game." *Baseball Digest,* January–February 2005.
"Minnie Minoso." Baseball Library Web site. Available online. URL: http://www.baseballlibrary.com/baseballlibrary/ballplayers/M/Minoso_Minnie.stm. Downloaded on January 15, 2006.
"Minnie Minoso." Baseball Reference Web site. Available online. URL: http://www.baseball-reference.com/m/minosmi01.shtml. Downloaded on January 15, 2006.

Miranda, Patricia
(1979–   ) *wrestler*

A women's wrestling trailblazer and the bronze medalist in the first-ever Olympics women's wrestling competition at the 2004 games in Athens, Greece, Patricia Miranda is a two-time world champion silver medalist and a Phi Beta Kappa graduate of Stanford University, where she participated on the men's wrestling team. She was born on June 11, 1979, in Manteca, California. Miranda was the second of four children born to her father, Jose, a physician who had immigrated to the United States from Brazil, and her mother, Lia, who died of a brain aneurysm when Miranda was only 10 years old.

Although she had not been successful in sports previously, Miranda tried out for Saratoga (California) High School's wrestling team when she was 13.

She endured the taunts of competitors, opponents' parents, and even the disapproval of her own father, who initially resisted having his daughter participate in what was then almost exclusively a boys' sport. Of her father's resistance, Miranda later said, "That was the wrong thing to do. Trying to make me quit basically assured that I wouldn't."

Miranda wrestled throughout high school, holding up her end of a deal made with her father that allowed her to compete as long as she excelled academically. Her teammates (all boys) named her captain in her junior and senior years, during which she won about half her matches.

Following her graduation from high school in 1998, Miranda enrolled at Stanford University, where she was welcomed to the wrestling team by the coach and, later, his successor. She spent five years at Stanford and did not wrestle in a meet until her final year, when she replaced a teammate who was unable to meet the 125-pound weight requirement and another who was struggling academically. Though she never weighed more than 120 pounds while competing, the 5'-tall Miranda competed in college wrestling's lowest weight class (125 pounds), earning a record of 3-13. Also at Stanford, Miranda began dating teammate Levi Weikel-Magden, who became her husband in 2004.

While at Stanford and following her graduation, Miranda began to excel in international competition against other women. She won two silver medals as a member of the U.S. women's team competing at the world championships. In 2003, Miranda won the gold medal at the Pan-American Games in the Dominican Republic. Miranda, who earned a bachelors in economics and a masters in international policy from Stanford, then deferred enrollment at Yale University Law School in order to concentrate on training for the 2004 Olympics in Athens, where women's wrestling made its debut as an Olympic sport.

Wrestling at 105.5 pounds, Miranda won her first three matches to reach the semifinals. She then lost to eventual gold medalist Irini Merlini of Ukraine before rebounding to defeat Angélique Berthenet of France to win the bronze medal, the first medals awarded in women's wrestling in the history of the Olympics.

Miranda's success garnered much attention for women's wrestling in the United States, where she was named 2004 USA Wrestling Woman of the Year by USA Wrestling, the national governing body for amateur wrestling. She also became popular in her father's native Brazil, where she was the focus of many interviews during which she spoke fluent Portuguese. Jack McCallum of *Sports Illustrated* selected Miranda as his choice for that magazine's prestigious Sportsperson of the Year.

Miranda's prominence and her advocacy for women's wrestling is expected to help the sport grow in popularity. Miranda lives with her husband in New Haven, Connecticut, where she is a law student at Yale University.

Further Reading

Abbott, Gary. "Patricia Miranda Named 2004 Wrestling Woman of the Year." InterMat Wrestling Web site. Available online. URL: http://www.intermatwrestle.com/news/newsdisplay.aspx?ID=3070. Downloaded on January 15, 2006.

McCallum, Jack. "My Sportsman Choice: Patricia Miranda." *Sports Illustrated* Web site. Available online. URL: http://sportsillustrated.cnn.com/2004/magazine/specials/sportsman/2004/11/12/patricia.miran da/index.html. Downloaded on June 20, 2006.

Mihoces, Gary. "Miranda a Leader in Debut of Women's Wrestling." *USA Today* Web site. Available online. URL: http://www.usatoday.com/sports/olympics/athens/wrestling/2004-08-08-focus-miranda_x.htm. Downloaded on October 30, 2006.

Montoya, Alvaro
(1985–) *hockey player*

A star goaltender at the University of Michigan and for the first American hockey team ever to win the World Junior Championships, Alvaro Montoya was selected by the New York Rangers as the sixth pick of the first round in the 2004 National Hockey League (NHL) draft. He was born on February 13, 1985, in Chicago, Illinois. Montoya was introduced to hockey at age three when his mother, Irene, a physician who had fled Fidel Castro's dictatorship in Cuba with her family when she was a child, took him to a local hockey rink.

Montoya soon began playing youth hockey as a goalie, and by the time he was 14 years old, he was one of the top junior goaltenders in the United States. He transferred from his suburban Chicago private school to attend high school in Fort Worth, Texas, where he played in the North American Hockey League. He graduated from high school in Ann Arbor, Michigan, where he joined the U.S. National Under-17 team.

Montoya remained in Ann Arbor to accept an athletic scholarship at the University of Michigan. As a freshman, Montoya led all National Collegiate Athletic Association (NCAA) Division 1 goalies in games and minutes played. He also tallied an impressive 30-10-3 record and a stingy 2.33 goals against average, leading Michigan to the "Frozen Four" in the 2003 NCAA hockey tournament.

In the 2003–04 season, Montoya continued his stellar play by posting a 26-12-2 record and a 2.23 goals against average. In 2004, he helped bring the United States its first-ever gold medal at the International Ice Hockey Federation Under-20 World Championship. In that tournament, Montoya started all six games for Team USA while earning two shutouts and a 1.33 goals against average.

In spring 2004, Montoya was chosen by the New York Rangers as the sixth pick of the first round in the NHL draft. However, Montoya returned to school and played for Michigan while a labor dispute cancelled the 2004–05 NHL season. Montoya displayed flashes of his effective use of size, quickness, instincts, and poise in going 25-6-3 as a junior, though his goals against average rose to 2.69. He also was not as solid in goals during the NCAA tournament and the World Junior Championships that followed.

In summer 2005, Montoya signed a contract with the Rangers with the hope that he would be able to earn the starting job for the 2005–06 season. Rangers supporters in New York welcomed the addition of the handsome, charismatic Montoya, who chatted in English and Spanish with fans and media at his introductory press conference, where he explained that despite his high draft position and confidence in his ability, he was taking nothing for granted. He said, "The competition is great. I've always said to be the best player you have to beat the best." Montoya then spent the 2005–06 season with the Rangers' minor league teams in Hartford, Connecticut, and Charlotte, North Carolina. He played well but suffered a dislocated left shoulder late in the season. Montoya began the 2006–07 season with Hartford preparing for what many believe will be his imminent call to join the Rangers.

Further Reading

Adams, Alan. "Mom's Love Guides Montoya." National Hockey League Web site. Available online. URL: http://www.nhl.com/intheslot/read/juniors/wjc2004/montoya123003.html. Downloaded on January 15, 2006.

"Al Montoya." New York Rangers Web site. Available online. URL: http://www.newyorkrangers.com/team/playerinfo.asp?playerid=306. Downloaded on January 15, 2006.

"Alvaro Montoya." Hockey's Future Web site. Available online. URL: http://www.hockeysfuture.com/prospect.php?pid=3935. Downloaded on January 15, 2006.

Montoya, Juan Pablo
(1975–) *auto racer*

The youngest champion in the history of the Championship Auto Racing Team (CART) series and the winner of the 2000 Indianapolis 500 in his first attempt at that prestigious race, Juan Pablo Montoya has become one of the top Formula One drivers in the world, placing in the top five in the drivers' championship every year since 2002. He was born on September 20, 1975, in Bogotá, Colombia. Montoya's architect father, Pablo, raced carts as a hobby and introduced his son to racing when Montoya was six years old.

When he was nine, Montoya won the children's national cart championship in Colombia. Two years later, he won that country's national championship in the junior division.

Montoya advanced in the racing world through his teams, winning consecutive cart junior world championships in 1990 and 1991 before competing in Formula Three, winning that circuit's British crown in 1996. In 1998, Montoya won the Formula 3000 Series (a preparatory circuit for the Formula One series) championship and signed a multiyear testing contract with the prestigious Williams Formula One Team.

The Williams Team sent Montoya to the United States to compete in the 1999 CART tournament. Montoya won seven races that year and earned the championship in his rookie season, becoming, at age 24, the youngest driver ever to win a title in that series. In 2000, Montoya became the youngest driver to win the Indianapolis 500 by claiming victory in his first year of participation in that event, the first rookie to do so in 34 years.

On March 4, 2001, Montoya made his much-anticipated Formula One debut at the Australian Grand Prix. Within a month, he stunned world champion Michael Schumacher with a daring maneuver at the Brazilian Grand Prix, though a subsequent collision prevented him from winning that race. Montoya finished his rookie season in Formula One in sixth place in the championship rankings, with a victory in the Italian Grand Prix and three other second-place finishes.

In 2002, Montoya's racing skills brought him to the postrace podium seven times (four second-place and three third-place finishes), which earned him third place in the championship rankings. Wins in Monaco and Germany in 2003 helped Montoya gain another third-place season ranking.

The following year, 2004, was disappointing for the popular Montoya, as he finished fifth overall despite a victory at the Brazilian Grand Prix.

Montoya switched to the McLaren Racing Team in 2005. He enjoyed great success by winning the British and Italian Grand Prix events but was frustrated by inconsistency that resulted from injury, tactical errors, and his team's mechanical failures.

However, Montoya's desire to win, which has earned him the admiration of fans as well as a reputation for volatility, did not diminish. Following a race in which an aggressive move put his team's success in jeopardy, Montoya commented, "I am here to try and win races. If the team wants someone to finish second, they need to hire a different driver."

Montoya stunned most racing fans in July 2006 when he announced that he was leaving Formula One racing to complete in the National Association of Stock Car Auto Racing (NASCAR) circuit. Montoya's departure for NASCAR was further evidence of its booming popularity and was viewed by many as potentially critical in the circuit's growth outside the United States.

Further Reading

"Ask Juan Pablo." Team McLaren Web site. Available online. URL: http://www.mclaren.com/features/driver/ask_Juan-Pablo.php. Downloaded on June 20, 2006.

"Juan Pablo Montoya." Sporting Life Web site. Available online. URL: http://www.sportinglife.com/formula1/drivers/montoya.html. Downloaded on January 15, 2006.

Juan Pablo Montoya Web site. Available online. URL: http://www.jpmontoya.com/Templates/home.aspx?Page_ID=182, Downloaded on January 15, 2006.

Knutson, Dan. "Montoya Continues to Search for Consistency." ESPN Web site. Available online. URL: http://sports.espn.go.com/rpm/news/story?series=f1&id=2143630. Downloaded on January 15, 2006.

Monzón, Carlos
(1942–1995) *boxer*

A middleweight boxing champion throughout most of the 1970s who won the last 81 bouts of his career over a 13-year span, Carlos Monzón fought with a powerful intensity and dynamic flair, though his legacy as an all-time great in the ring is tainted by his violent and tragic life outside it. He was born on August 7, 1942, in Santa Fe, Argentina. Monzón grew up in the slums of Santa Fe, one of 12 children in his family.

At age six, he began selling newspapers, shining shoes, and delivering milk to earn money. By his early teens, he began boxing at a local club under the tutelage of trainer Amilcar Brusa, who later described his pupil as "a skinny kid with rage in his eyes." Brusa taught Monzón the strategies and techniques of boxing, bailed him out of jail twice following arrests for assault, and guided him to 73 wins in 87 amateur bouts.

At age 20, Monzón made his professional boxing debut on February 6, 1963, winning a second-round knockout over Ramón Montenegro in Rafala, Argentina. After going 15-2 in his next 17 fights, Monzón lost a decision to Alberto Massi on October 9, 1964. He would never lose another bout. In 1966, Monzón claimed the Argentine middleweight title by defeating Jorge José Fernández in Buenos Aries, and the next year he won the South American middleweight title by again defeating Fernández in Buenos Aries.

Despite his dominance in Argentina, where all his fights had taken place, Monzón was still largely an unknown throughout the boxing world. He was not ranked among the middleweight division's top 10 until 1969. On November 7, 1970, Monzón fought outside Argentina for the first time to meet Nino Benvenuti in Rome for the World Boxing Counsel (WBC) and World Boxing Association (WBA) middleweight title. In what would later be named by *Ring Magazine* the 1970 Fight of the Year, Monzón used his long reach and hard jabs to pummel Benvenuti as the champion's worn-down attempts to respond harmlessly grazed off Monzón's granitelike chin. Monzón finished the heavily favored Benvenuti before thousands of stunned Italian fans with a left hook and a right hand to the head in the 12th round to become the middleweight champion of the world.

Monzón retained that title for the remainder of his career spanning almost seven years—the longest continuous reign in the history of the middleweight division. His title defenses feature victories over five former world champions, including Benvenuti, Emile Griffith, and JOSÉ NÁPOLES. Angelo Dundee, Nápoles's trainer, said following their bout, "Monzón is the complete fighter. He can box, he can hit, he can think, and he is game all the way."

Monzón's undefeated streak, which eventually reached a remarkable 81, remained intact despite a chronically sore right hand and a shoulder that housed a bullet fired at him by his wife during a 1972 argument. The mental discipline Monzón demonstrated in the ring was largely absent outside it, where the champion became famous for his extravagant playboy lifestyle that often found him in Paris nightclubs and on movie sets rather than in gyms. Before his only fight in the United States, a 1975 win over Tony Licata, Monzón reflected on his unique approach, explaining, "After the fight I will smoke a cigarette, drink a cold glass of wine, and go make a movie."

Monzón's fame and good looks did help him land acting roles in movies even while he was still active in the ring. Monzón became an international celebrity, and he was especially revered in his native Argentina, particularly among the poor and middle class, though some members of the upper class of Argentine society never fully embraced him because of his indigenous heritage.

The last bout of Monzón's career occurred on July 30, 1977, when he won a unanimous decision over Rodrigo Valdez in Monte Carlo. Saying that he had proved that he was definitely "one of the great ones," Monzón retired to his 1,750-acre ranch in Argentina, hoping to establish a full-time career in movies. However, no longer accompanied by the aura of a world boxing championship, Monzón's acting opportunities diminished.

Divorced from his first wife, Monzón married dancer Alicia Muñiz in 1979. After nine turbulent years together, he strangled her and threw her off a balcony to her death. He was convicted in her killing and sentenced to 11 years in prison. In 1991, while serving time, Monzón was inducted into the International Boxing Hall of Fame.

On January 8, 1995, while returning to jail from a weekend furlough, Monzón died when the car he was driving went out of control, flipped, and crashed in a one-vehicle accident on a desolate highway in Santa Rosa de Calchines, Argentina.

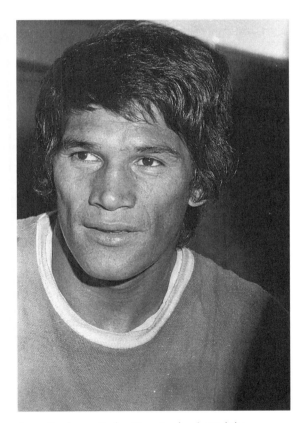

Argentine boxer Carlos Monzón dominated the middleweight division throughout much of the 1970s. *(Associated Press)*

It has never been conclusively determined whether the crash was a suicide or an accident. More than 30,000 people attended Monzón's funeral in Santa Fe. A year later, the people of the city honored Monzón by erecting a statue depicting their beloved sports hero.

Further Reading

"Carlos Monzon." International Boxing Hall of Fame Web site. Available online. URL: http://www. ibhof.com/monzon.htm. Downloaded on January 15, 2006.

"Juan Carlos Monzon." Boxing Records Archive Web site. Available online. URL: http://boxing.about.com/ gi/dynamic/offsite.htm?site=http://boxrec.com/ boxer%5Fdisplay.php %3Fboxer%5Fid=009002. Downloaded on January 15, 2006.

Smith, George Diaz. "Boxing: RSR Looks Back at Carlos Monzon." Ringside Report Web site. Available online. URL: http://www.ringsidereport. com/Smith5182005.htm. Downloaded on January 15, 2006.

Morales, Pablo
(1964–   ) *swimmer*

The star of three consecutive National Collegiate Athletic Association (NCAA) championship swim teams at Stanford University and a three-time medalist at the 1984 Olympics, Pablo Morales was the captain of the U.S. men's swim team at the 1992 Olympics, where, at age 27, he became the oldest swimming gold medalist in Olympic history. He was born on December 5, 1964, in Chicago, Illinois. Almost immediately, Morales began taking swimming lessons—"Before [he was] walking"—his mother would later describe.

When Morales was two years old, he moved with his Cuban immigrant parents and older sister to Santa Clara, California, where the swimming lessons continued. His future as one of the world's greatest swimmers was not evident when, as a six-year-old, he failed more than half of the 17 categories

Pablo Morales finished his illustrious career by serving as captain of the U.S. men's swim team and winning two gold medals at the 1992 Olympics in Barcelona. *(U.S. Olympic Committee)*

ley, and 4 × 100-medley relay. He captained the 1987 team to Stanford's third consecutive NCAA championship and played a key role on the Stanford water polo team that also won three straight NCAA titles from 1985 through 1987.

Morales also excelled in national and international competition during his college years of 1983 through 1987. In 1984, he qualified for the U.S. Olympic team in three events, establishing the world record in the 100-meter butterfly at the Olympic trials. At the 1984 Olympic games in Los Angeles, California, Morales won the gold medal as a member of the 4 × 100-meter relay team with a then-world record of 3:39.30 (minutes and seconds). He also earned silver medals in the 100-meter and 200-meter butterfly events. Morales concluded a spectacular year by being named World Swimmer of the Year by *Swimming World Magazine.*

Following his success in 1984, Morales remained among the world's elite swimmers. In 1985, he won gold medals in the 100-meter butterfly and 200-meter individual medley at the Pan-Pacific games, and he repeated as champion in the 100-meter butterfly at the Pan-Pacific games two years later. At the world championship games in Madrid, Spain, in 1986, Morales won the gold medal in the 100-meter butterfly and 4 × 100-meter relay. His world championship trials time that year set the world record for the 100-meter butterfly at 15.84 seconds, a record that stood for almost 10 years.

In 1988, Morales was expected to qualify for the U.S. Olympic team in three different events yet failed to qualify for any. He left competitive swimming for three years while attending Cornell University Law School but returned to the pool in 1991 to make one more attempt at Olympic glory. Although many doubted he would make the team after his long layoff at the relatively advanced age of 26, Morales qualified for the 100-meter butterfly and 4 × 100-meter medley relay.

The widespread admiration of Morales within the swimming community and his reputation for

in his swim class. However, at age 10, Pablo became the national 10-and-under leader in the 50-yard butterfly. He repeated as the national age group leader at age 12 and 14. When Morales was 16, he went to the junior national competition in Mission Viejo, California, where he won the 100- and 200-meter butterfly titles.

Following his standout high school swimming and academic career at Bellarmine Prep in San Jose, California, where he broke Mark Spitz's 16-year-old high school 100-yard butterfly record, Morales accepted an athletic scholarship to attend Stanford University. At Stanford, Morales won a record 11 NCAA titles in the 100-yard butterfly, 200-yard butterfly, 200-yard individual med-

leadership and likeability were reflected by the excited reactions of his fellow swimmers after he qualified for the team, of which he was soon named captain. American swimmer Melvin Stewart said of Morales following the 1992 trials, "I was rooting for the guy . . . and I had to race him."

Morales finished his remarkable comeback by capping his career with two gold medals at the 1992 Olympics in Barcelona, Spain. Following this success, Morales retired from competitive swimming and graduated from law school. Morales then became a swim coach at Stanford University (assistant, 1997–98), San Jose State University (women's team, 1998–2001), and the University of Nebraska (2001–present). Now married and the father of three sons, Morales was inducted into the International Swimming Hall of Fame in 1998.

Further Reading

Henrichs, Tod. "Olympic Legend Pablo Morales Now Coaches." United States Olympic Team Web site. Available online. URL: http://www.usoc.org/132_29693.htm. Downloaded on January 16, 2006.

Montville, Leigh. "Bravo, Pablo—Pablo Morales Leads U.S. Swimmers at 1992 Olympics." *Sports Illustrated,* 3 August 1992, p. 34.

"Pablo Morales (USA)." International Swimming Hall of Fame Web site. Available online. URL: http://www.ishof.org/98pmorales.html. Downloaded on January 16, 2006.

Moreira, Ronaldo de Assis *See* RONALDINHO

Mulanovich, Sofía
(1983–) *surfer*

The first South American surfer of either gender to win a World Championship Tour (WCT) title and an Association of Surfing Professionals (ASP) world championship, Sofía Mulanovich shocked the surfing world in 2004 by bringing a title to Peru in a sport dominated by Americans and Australians. She was born on June 24, 1983, in Lima, Peru. Inspired by the waves outside her childhood home in Punta Hermosa, Mulanovich followed her grandfather and parents, Herbert and Inés, into surfing at age nine. Mulanovich's first coach, Robert Meza, recalled of her first lesson, "She tried to stand up but fell the first few times. But before the day was over, she stood up and went for a long ride. Not many can do that on their first day."

Mulanovich, who traces Serbian-Croatian descent on her father's side, began competing at age 12. Because few girls were entered in local tournaments, she usually competed against, and often defeated, boys. When she was 14, Mulanovich visited surfing mecca Hawaii for the first time and watched some of the world's top female surfers. Reflecting on her growing passion to surf, after returning to Peru, Mulanovich recalled, "I started surfing more and watching more surfing videos. I began begging my mom to let me stay home from school when the waves were good."

Her wishes to surf rather than attend class were ignored by her parents, though Mulanovich did begin competing professionally at 17. In 2002, she began competing in the world qualifying series, the junior pro tour, finishing second overall. The next year, Mulanovich moved up to the WCT, where only the top 18 surfers compete, finishing an impressive seventh.

In 2004, the 21-year-old Mulanovich enjoyed a stunningly dominant year, including victories in three consecutive competitions (in France, Tahiti, and Fiji). With each victory, the popularity of surfing in Peru, a nation with a coastline three times the length of California's, grew.

Her personal following boomed as well, as Peruvians cheered her successes and embraced the increasingly prominent advertisements, articles, and appearances featuring Mulanovich's familiar blond hair, pearl earrings, and expressive smile. Following a second place finish at the Roxy Pro at Haleiwei, Hawaii, that clenched the WCT crown, Mulanovich joyously explained, "I've done this for my country and for all South Americans . . . for the future? I don't know. I'm just stoked I'm world champion this year."

Many other surfing observers feel that Mulanovich, who finished second in suffing's WCT rankings in 2005 and ranked among the top five late in the 2006 season, is simply being humble with such statements. Fernando Aguerre, co-owner of a major surfing apparel company, noted, "Anybody who reaches the top of anything, it takes a lot of work and persistence . . . Sofia is obsessed with what she wants. She could be at the top of women's surfing for the next ten years. She's not going to waste that opportunity."

Further Reading

Bridges, Tyler. "Surfer on the Verge of History." *Miami Herald,* 1 November 2004, p. 13A.

Myers, Nathan. "Interview with Sofia Mulanovich— 2004 Women's World Cup Champion." *Surfing Magazine* January 2005.

"Sofia Mulanovich Is World Champion & Queen of Surfing." Wahine Surfing Web site. Available online. URL: http://www.wahinesurfing.com/article.asp?id_article=72. Downloaded on July 2, 2005.

Muñoz, Anthony
(Michael Anthony Muñoz)
(1958–) *football player*

The third overall pick in the 1980 National Football League (NFL) draft despite suffering multiple knee injuries in college, Anthony Muñoz was named to 11 consecutive pro bowl squads, led the Cincinnati Bengals to the team's only two Super Bowl appearances, and is widely considered the greatest offensive lineman of the 1980s and among the best at his position in the history of professional football. He was born Michael Anthony Muñoz on August 19, 1958, in Ontario, California, about 45 miles east of Los Angeles. He grew up in Ontario, one of five children raised by his mother, Esther, who provided for the family by packing eggs into cartons on a nearby farm after Muñoz's father left

the family when the future football star was a preschooler. Muñoz was a large and athletic child, regularly playing his favorite sport of baseball with older children from the time he was five years old. He was too big to participate in Pop Warner youth league football but did play at Chaffey High School, starting as an offensive lineman and earning an athletic scholarship from the University of Southern California (USC).

Muñoz signed an agreement with USC that he could skip spring football training so he could play for the Trojans baseball team. However, a knee injury sustained on the football field prevented Muñoz from playing college baseball except for his sophomore year of 1978, when he pitched on USC's National Collegiate Athletic Association's (NCAA) national championship baseball team. Muñoz was a standout offensive tackle on the USC football team despite his battle with injuries and was considered a top NFL prospect heading into his senior year.

In the first game of his senior year, Muñoz's left knee was struck by an opponent's helmet, causing an injury that required reconstructive surgery. Remarkably, Muñoz returned to the field four months later on New Year's Day 1979 to play in USC's 17-16 Rose Bowl victory over Ohio State University. Attending that game in the Rose Bowl were Cincinnati Bengals founder and general manager Paul Brown and his sons, Mike and Pete, who also worked in Cincinnati's front office.

Knowing they held the third pick in the upcoming 1980 NFL draft, the Brown family paid close attention to Muñoz and discussed whether the team could risk selecting him so high considering his history of knee trouble. Muñoz's dominance of Ohio State defenders convinced them they should. Explained Mike Brown, "The three of us sat there and laughed out loud. [Muñoz] was so big and so good it was a joke."

Cincinnati selected the 6'6", 270-pound Muñoz with the third pick of the 1980 draft and quickly reaped the rewards of his prodigious ability in leadership. A mainstay at left tackle, Muñoz was primarily responsible for protecting quarterbacks

Anthony Muñoz, shown in this 1984 photo, is widely regarded as one of the best offensive linemen in the history of football. *(NFL/WireImage.com)*

Ken Anderson and later Boomer Esiason, as well as opening up rushing lanes for Bengals running backs. Muñoz's agility, quickness, strength, and savvy combined with his fundamentally sound technique allowed him to manhandle opposing defensive ends. He also demonstrated impressive durability by starting 164 of 168 games from 1980 through 1990 and athletic versatility by catching seven passes, including four touchdowns, on rarely called tackle eligible plays.

Over the course of Muñoz's 13-year career, he served as the physical and spiritual anchor on the Bengals three American Football Conference (AFC) Central Division championship teams. He also helped lead Cincinnati to two AFC championships

(1981 and 1988) and Super Bowls XVI and XXIII, where the Bengals fell each time to the San Francisco 49ers. Muñoz's excellence earned him 11 straight selections by his playing peers to the Pro Bowl. Muñoz was also highly respected for his community and charitable work off the field and was honored in 1991 with the NFL Man of the Year Award.

By the early 1990s, Muñoz's chronic shoulder pain and a subsequent knee injury led him to announce his retirement prior to the end of the 1992 season. At the final game of that season, fans at Cincinnati's Riverfront Stadium paid tribute to Muñoz during a special halftime ceremony. Found among the celebration was a banner on which was written: "Muñoz: Next Stop Canton."

The prediction expressed on the banner was proven correct when Muñoz was inducted into the Pro Football Hall of Fame in Canton, Ohio, on August 1, 1998. Muñoz and his wife of more than 25 years, Dede, live in the Cincinnati area, where he is active with his Anthony Muñoz Foundation, which supports leadership activities for young people.

Further Reading

"Anthony Muñoz." Latino Legends in Sports Web site. Available online. URL: http://www. latinosportslegends.com/Munoz.htm. Downloaded on January 16, 2006.

"Anthony Muñoz." Pro Football Hall of Fame Web site. Available online. URL: http://www.profootballhof. com/hof/member.jsp?player_id=158. Downloaded on January 16, 2006.

Gordon, Hannah. "Where Are They Now: Anthony Muñoz." National Football League Web site. Available online. URL: http://www.nfl.com/ news/story/6797317. Downloaded on June 19, 2006.

Greenberg, Jay. "The King of the Block: Anthony Muñoz Sets a Standard for Lineman on and off the Field." *Sports Illustrated,* 10 September 1990, p. 79.

N

Nadal, Rafael
(1986–) *tennis player*

The French Open champion in 2005 and 2006, Rafael Nadal won tennis's all-time record for most consecutive victories on clay courts. He was born on June 3, 1986, in Manacor, Spain. Nadal grew up in this picturesque town on the island of Majorca located near the eastern coast of Spain sharing the same last name of his uncle Miguel Angel, who was known as "the Beast" during his illustrious career as a soccer player with Real Majorca and FC Barcelona.

Rafael was an excellent soccer player as well, though he also enjoyed tennis, which he began playing at the age of four under the tutelage of his uncle Toni Nadal, his first and only coach. When he was 12 years old Nadal decided to devote his immense athletic skill and effort to tennis.

Nadal quickly proved to be one of the top tennis players in Spain and among the best teenage players in the world. At the age of 14, Nadal defeated his childhood hero and fellow Spaniard, Carlos Moya (who was ranked in the top 10 in the world at the time), in an exhibition match. Nadal turned pro at 15 and made his debut at the prestigious Wimbledon tournament at the All England Tennis Club as a 17-year-old in 2003, becoming the youngest player to reach the third round at that tournament since Boris Becker accomplished that feat in 1984.

Another highlight of Nadal's young and already successful career took place in a December 3, 2004, Davis Cup match between Spain and the United States on the red clay court of Seville's Olympic Stadium. Powered by 27,000 boisterous, flag-waving Spanish fans, the 18-year-old Nadal, then ranked 51st in the world, defeated American Andy Roddick, who was ranked second in the world, in four sets.

Nadal followed that triumph with an astonishing 2005, winning matches in Brazil, Mexico, Monaco, Spain, and Italy, all on clay courts that favored his consistent baseline volleying and top-spinning style. In his first appearance at the French Open, Nadal stunned even those who admired his promise and skill by rolling through early rounds, celebrating his 19th birthday by defeating number-one-ranked Roger Federer in the semifinals and beating Mariano Puerta in four sets to win the French Open championship.

His French Open victory made Nadal only the seventh man to win a Grand Slam tournament (which also includes the Australian Open, Wimbledon, and U.S. Open) in his first appearance at the event and the first to do so since Andre Agassi won the Australian Open in 1995. It also marked the first time a teenager won a men's Grand Slam event since Pete Sampras won the U.S. Open in 1990. The French Open title brought Nadal's 2005 championship total to six, a number that had not been matched by a teenage male since Agassi won six events as an 18-year-old in 1988.

Nadal was eliminated in the second round at Wimbledon in 2005 and in the third round of the 2005 U.S. Open, but despite these setbacks, it was clear he was one of the top players in the world. Respected for his quickness, stamina, and competitive zeal and noted for his distinctive style of white head band, below-the-knee length shorts, and sleeveless shirts that displayed his muscular arms, Nadal attracted attention from foes, fans, and the sporting press as one of the world's most exciting young athletes.

He bolstered his reputation further in the 2006 French Open. Nadal's first-round victory was his 54th consecutive win on a clay court, breaking a record set by Guillermo Vilas in 1977. His finals triumph over number-one-ranked Federer in four sets ended Federer's streak of three consecutive Grand Slam tournament wins, and it was his first loss in eight matches in a Grand Slam final. Federer remained the top-ranked player in the world after the match, though Nadal—who had given Federer his only four losses in 48 matches in 2006—was now ranked number two.

Though Nadal, who still lives on his home island of Mallorca with his parents, sister, and uncles, already has a record of achievement envied by successful veteran tennis players, his future appears even more brilliant. Reflecting the thoughts of many who have played and watched Nadal, his vanquished opponent in the 2005 French Open final, Puerta, said, "Rafael Nadal is going to be a legend of tennis."

Further Reading

"Rafael Nadal." Association of Tennis Professionals Web site. Available online URL: http://www.atptennis.com/en/players/playerprofiles/Highlights/default.asp?player number=N409. Downloaded on June 18, 2006.

Sheppard, Whit. "Nadal Among Great Teenage Athletes." ESPN Web site. Available online. URL: http://sports.espn.go.com/sports/tennis/french06/news/story?id=2476698. Downloaded on June 18, 2006.

Wertheim, L. Jon. "A King Ruled by a Prince: Second-ranked Rafael Nadal Defended His French Open Title by Continuing His Domination of No. 1 Roger Federer and Spoiling His Rival's Grand Slam Bid." *Sports Illustrated,* 19 June 2006, p. 56.

Nájera, Eduardo
(1976–) *basketball player*

A versatile forward whose rebounding and defensive tenacity have made him the greatest Mexican-born player in the history of college and professional basketball, Eduardo Nájera helped lead the University of Oklahoma to four consecutive National Collegiate Athletic Association (NCAA) basketball tournaments and later became a valuable player in the National Basketball Association (NBA). He was born on July 11, 1976, in Meoqui, Mexico. Eduardo grew up in Meoqui in the northern Mexican state of Chihuahua, the seventh child of parents Servando and Rosa and spent much of his youth playing basketball with his five older brothers at a schoolyard across the street from his house.

A tall but unrefined basketball player in his early teens, Nájera quickly honed his game in high school. At 17, he signed a contract for $3,000 per month to play basketball in a professional league in Chihuahua. When he was 19, Nájera moved to San Antonio, Texas, where he learned English, completed high school, and attracted the recruiting attention of several of the top college basketball programs. In 1996, Nájera accepted an athletic scholarship to play basketball at the University of Oklahoma.

Nájera enjoyed an outstanding career at Oklahoma, demonstrating significant individual improvement each year while playing a critical role in helping the school reach the NCAA tournament in each of his four years. Nájera finished second in voting in the Big XII Conference's Freshman of the Year following the 1996–97 season, in which he averaged seven points and six rebounds in less than 25 minutes of action per game period. As a sophomore, he ranked third on the team in scoring (10.5) and rebounding (5.4). In his junior year, the 6'8" and sturdily built Nájera increased his averages to almost 16 points and more than eight rebounds per contest, earning second team all-conference recognition.

Following his junior season at Oklahoma, Nájera led the Mexican national basketball team to a surprising fourth-place finish at the World University Games in Spain. Nájera followed with his senior season at Oklahoma, averaging 18 points and nine rebounds per game and leading him to be named to the all Big XII first team, earning recognition as a third team All-American. Nájera also received the Chip Hilton Player of the Year Award from the Basketball Hall of Fame, an award given to a player who has demonstrated personal character on and off the court.

Despite Nájera's excellence in college, his lack of speed concerned NBA scouts. He was bypassed in the 2000 NBA draft until the Houston Rockets selected him in the second round with a 38th overall pick. The Rockets traded Nájera that evening to the Dallas Mavericks, where he played sparingly as a rookie, though he did become the second Mexican to play in the NBA and the all-time Mexican leader in games played.

In his second season of 2001–02, Nájera joined other international players on the Mavericks, including Canadian Steve Nash and German Dirk Novwitzski to power the Mavericks to the Western Conference semifinals. Nájera averaged seven points and six rebounds playing primarily off the bench and started 11 games, in which the Mavericks went 10-1.

Prior to the 2002–03 season, Dallas rewarded Nájera for his rugged and consistent play by signing him to a six-year, $24 million contract. Nájera continued to produce over the next two seasons in Dallas but was limited by a variety of injuries. Following the 2003–04 season, Dallas traded Nájera to the Golden State Warriors, where he played only 42 games before they traded him to the Denver Nuggets.

Nájera's health improved, and his minutes played increased in Denver in 2004–05, where his tough inside presence and solid defense contributed to the Nuggets' late-season resurgence that resulted in a playoff berth. Nájera continued his rugged play off the bench in 2005–06, again helping the Nuggets reach the playoff, where they were eliminated by the Los Angeles Clippers.

Further Reading

"Eduardo Najera." National Basketball Association Web site. Available online. URL: http://www.nba.com/playerfile/eduardo_najera/?nav=page. Downloaded on January 16, 2006.

Ridgell, Patrick. "Eduardo Najera: You Can't Keep a Good Man Down." *Latino Leaders,* December 2002.

Nalbandian, David
(1982–   ) *tennis player*

A finalist in the 2002 Wimbledon tennis championship, David Nalbandian reached the quarterfinals or beyond in half the grand slam tennis tournaments (Wimbledon, U.S. Open, Australian Open, and French Open) from 2002 through 2005. He was born on January 1, 1982, in Córdoba, Argentina. The youngest son of parents Norbert and Alda, Nalbandian began playing tennis with his two older brothers on a cement court in his backyard, which was built by his Armenian immigrant grandfather.

Nalbandian was an excellent all-around athlete and avid sports fan who enjoyed fishing, watching rally races, and cheering the River Plate's soccer team. When he reached his early teens, Nalbandian was among the top young tennis players in Argentina. At the age of 16, he defeated future number-one player in the world Roger Federer for the 1998 U.S. Open Junior Boys title and in 1999, he was the runner-up in the French Open Juniors championship and a semifinalist at the Wimbledon Juniors tournament.

Nalbandian took his versatile game to the professional level in 2000. The next year, he enjoyed success in various Association of Tennis Professionals (ATP) tournaments, reaching the quarterfinals in tournaments in Colombia and Chile, the semifinals at tournaments in Croatia and Poland, and the finals in a tournament in Italy. This string of successes boosted Nalbandian's rating to number 47 in the world.

In 2002, Nalbandian continued his steady climb to tennis's elite by winning his first ATP event, defeating Jarkko Nieminen in Portugal. He followed this by storming through Wimbledon as a 20-year-old number 28 seed, reaching the finals, where he lost to Lleyton Hewitt. Nalbandian completed his stellar year by winning the ATP title in Basel, Switzerland, finishing the year ranked number 12 in the world.

Over the next two years, Nalbandian experienced a mix of great tennis and disappointing injuries. In 2003, he advanced to the Australian Open quarterfinals and the semifinals of the U.S. Open, though rest as a result of some abdominal injuries forced him to miss many tournaments in the fall.

In 2004, Nalbandian powered his way to the Australian Open quarterfinals without losing a set, before falling to eventual champion Federer in a tightly contested four-set match. Nalbandian overcame an ankle injury to make it to the semifinals at the French Open, but a stomach muscle injury caused him to miss Wimbledon and led to a second-round loss in the U.S. Open.

Healthy again in 2005, Nalbandian kept his standing among the top tennis players in the world by winning the ATP event in Munich, Germany, and reaching the quarterfinals in the Australian Open, Wimbledon, and U.S. Open. In 2006, Nalbandian reached the semifinals of the Australian Open and the French Open, but failed to emerge from the early rounds at Wimbledon and the U.S. open.

Further Reading

"David Nalbandian." Association of Tennis Professionals Web site. Available online. URL: http://www.atptennis.com/en/players/playerprofiles/Highlights/default.asp?playernumber=N301. Downloaded on January 16, 2006.

"David Nalbandian Interview." Cincinnati Tennis Tournaments Web site. Available online. URL: http://www.cincytennis.com/1009/news/news1887_rx.asp. Downloaded on June 20, 2006.

Ramsay, Alix. "David Nalbandian, the Secret Charmer, Reveals All." *Tennis Life,* 29 July 2005.

Nápoles, José
(Mantequilla)
(1940–) *boxer*

A two-time welterweight boxing champion over a span of more than seven years during the 1960s and early 1970s, José Nápoles fled communist Cuba for Mexico in 1962 and became a beloved sports hero throughout Latin America. He was born on April 13, 1940, in Santiago de Cuba. Nápoles grew up in this coastal city on the far southeast of the island nation and became a standout amateur boxer by the time he was a teenager. He crossed Cuba, moving to the capital city of Havana before making his professional boxing debut at the age of 18 on August 2, 1958, in a first-round knockout of Julio Rojas in Havana.

Each of Nápoles's first 18 fights, in which he compiled a 17-1 record, took place in Havana. However, Fidel Castro, who had taken control of the Cuban government in the 1959 revolution, reversed his early support of Cuba's rich boxing tradition with his 1962 national decree 83a that outlawed professional sports. Faced with this obstacle to his ambition, the talented Nápoles decided to flee Cuba that same year and settle in Mexico City.

After almost a year and a half without a bout due to his relocation, Nápoles returned to the ring on July 21, 1962, knocking out Enrique Camarena in Mexico City. Over the course of the next four years, Nápoles, nicknamed "Mantequilla" (Butter) because of his smooth fighting style, became one of the top lightweight contenders. However, he was unable to secure a title fight largely due to the impression held among potential opponents' managers that Nápoles would crush their boxers.

Having earned 26 wins in 29 bouts since his move to Mexico, Nápoles moved up to the welterweight division in 1967. He dominated his competition, going undefeated in his 12 fights from 1968 to early 1969 before meeting Curtis Cokes for the World Boxing Counsel (WBC) and World Boxing Association (WBA) welterweight titles on April 18, 1969, in Englewood, California. Nápoles pounded Cokes, bloodying his nose and mouth and swelling his eyes before the fight was called in the 13th round in favor of Nápoles.

Nápoles held the crown for more than a year and a half, defending his title by again defeating Cokes, Emile Griffith, and others before losing to Billy Backus on December 2, 1970, in Syracuse, New York, after sustaining a severe cut above his left eye. Nápoles regained the title seven months later by knocking out Backus on June 3, 1971. He then won 16 of his next 17 fights, his only loss coming when he moved up in class to fight middleweight champion CARLOS MONZÓN in 1974.

Nápoles's second welterweight championship reign of more than four and a half years came to an end on December 6, 1975, when he lost to John Stracey in Mexico City. Nápoles retired after this bout with a career record of 77-7, with 54 knockouts. In 1990, Nápoles was inducted into the International Boxing Hall of Fame. He currently lives in Chihuahua, Mexico, where he works as a boxing trainer.

Further Reading

"Jose Angel Napoles." Boxing Record Archive Web site. Available online. URL: http://www.boxrec.com/boxer_display.php?boxer_id=009025. Downloaded on January 16, 2006.

"Jose Napoles." International Boxing Hall of Fame Web site. Available online. URL: http://www.ibhof.com/napoles.htm. Downloaded on January 16, 2006.

Nascimento, Edson Arantes do   *See* PELÉ

Negron, Esmeralda
(1983–   ) *soccer player*

The most valuable player on the first Ivy League team to reach the Final Four of the National Collegiate Athletic Association's (NCAA) women's soccer tournament, Esmeralda Negron is the leading scorer in the history of Princeton University soccer. She was born on January 15, 1983, in Harrington Park, New Jersey. Encouraged by her father, whom she has described as "[not] really seeing a difference in the way [to] raise a girl or a boy,"

Negron began playing soccer in a recreational league in first grade. Though she also participated in basketball, softball, and gymnastics, Negron decided to focus on soccer because she enjoyed the constant motion the sport provided. Negron excelled at soccer at Northern Valley/Old Tappan High School in New Jersey, where she was recruited by several colleges before choosing to attend Princeton University.

In her first season of 2001, Negron had an immediate impact on the success of Princeton's women's soccer team, the Tigers, which had won only a single Ivy League championship since 1982. An athletic, team-oriented forward, she scored six goals that season, five of which were game winners, helping the Tigers earn the Ivy League title and a bid to the NCAA women's soccer tournament. In her sophomore year of 2002, Negron scored eight goals, had nine assists, and was named First Team All-Ivy League, as Princeton repeated as conference champions.

As a junior in 2003, Negron was named Ivy League Player of the Year after she tied a 22-year-old school record for most goals in a season (13) and came within one point of tying the school record for most points in a season (31). Negron followed this stellar performance by playing on the U.S. Under-21 national team that won the world championship in Iceland in 2003.

Negron's greatest achievement occurred in 2004, her senior season at Princeton. In the final game of the regular season, Negron scored three goals in a 7-0 win over Cornell University that gave the Tigers another Ivy League title. Her performance in that game also established Princeton women's soccer marks for single-season goals (14), points in a season (36), and career points (96) and tied the school's career goals record (41).

In the 2004 NCAA tournament, Negron led Princeton to the first Final Four appearance by an Ivy League team. The Tigers lost to the University of California–Los Angeles (UCLA) 2-0, finishing their season with a school-best record of 19-3.

Negron graduated from Princeton with a bachelor's degree in Spanish in 2005. She played with a club team in France in 2005–06 before returning to the United States with hopes to make the U.S. national team.

Further Reading

"Esmeralda Negron." Princeton University Athletics Web site. Available online. URL: http://goprincetontigers.cstv.com/sports/w-soccer/mtt/negron_esmeralda00.html. Downloaded on July 1, 2005.

"Negron's Record-Setting Night Leads No. 8 Princeton to Ivy Women's Soccer Title." Princeton University Athletics Web site. Available online. URL: http://goprincetontigers.cstv.com/sports/w-soccer/recaps/102904aaa.html. Downloaded on July 1, 2005.

"Wildcats Add Attacking Duo." New Jersey Wildcats Web site. Available online. URL: http://www.njwildcats/com/home/137044.html. Downloaded on June 20, 2006.

Nenê
(Maybyner Rodney Hilario)
(1982–) *basketball player*

The seventh overall selection in the 2002 National Basketball Association (NBA) draft, Nenê has become one of the league's top young power forwards, helping lead the Denver Nuggets to consecutive playoff appearances (2004–05) for the first time in 10 years. He was born Maybyner Rodney Hilario on September 13, 1982, in São Carlos, Brazil. He acquired the nickname "Nenê" (Portuguese for "baby") because he was the youngest person in his family, who lived in São Carlos, an industrial city of 200,000 located about 150 miles north of São Paulo.

Nenê was always the tallest kid in his class and enjoyed soccer and handball, though he did not play basketball until he was 14 years old, at which time his teacher recommended that he attend a local school for the sport. Within three years, Nenê had almost reached his eventual height of 6'10", and he left home to play professional basketball in São Paulo.

The following year the 18-year-old Nenê played for the Vasco da Gama squad in Rio de Janeiro. He then played for the bronze medal–winning national team at the 2001 Goodwill Games in Brisbane, Australia, where he made an impression with his size, quickness, and shot blocking ability, which was evident when he rejected future NBA All-Star Jermaine O'Neal three times in one possession period.

With the help of a Cleveland-based agent and a Portuguese-Canadian basketball talent scout, Nenê traveled to the United States in spring 2002 to showcase his skill for NBA teams. A few months later, Nenê completed his remarkable assent from solid contributor in the Brazilian league to a first-round selection in the NBA draft when he was chosen by the New York Knicks with the seventh overall pick. He was traded minutes later to the Denver Nuggets.

As a rookie with Denver in 2002–03, Nenê struggled early in the season but closed the year strongly, finishing with an average of almost 11 points, six rebounds, and more than one and a half steals per game, earning recognition on the NBA's All-Rookie first team. In the 2003–04 season, Nenê started all 77 games in which he played, averaging almost 12 points and six and a half rebounds per game and ranking sixth in the NBA in field goal percentage (52 percent). Despite this statistical production from Nenê and the vast improvement of his team, many fans and people within the Nuggets organization had hoped for more from the talented, big, young man.

Prior to the 2004–05 season, the Nuggets acquired power forward Kenyon Martin from the New Jersey Nets, who sent Nenê to the bench. Though his minutes declined and he missed a third of the season due to a knee injury, Nenê was an important contributor to another Denver playoff-bound squad, using his solid body and increasingly refined moves around the basket to average almost 10 points and six rebounds a game, while continuing to provide consistent and intimidating defense.

At the beginning of the 2005–06 season, Nenê was prepared to help the Nuggets continue their dramatic improvement and determined to demonstrate that the belief in his potential shown by the team three years earlier was well placed. Unfortunately, Nenê suffered a severe knee injury just three minutes into his first appearance of the season. Although the injury ended Nenê's season, the Nuggets were so confident that he would make a full recovery that they signed him to a six-year, $60 million contract prior to the 2006–07 season.

Further Reading

Lopez, Aaron J. "Nene Plans to Be Well-healed." *Rocky Mountain News,* 3 November 2005.

"Nene." National Basketball Association Web site. Available online. URL: http://www.nba.com/playerfile/nene/bio.html. Downloaded on January 16, 2006.

"Nene 31." Nene Web site. Available online. URL: http://www.nene31.com/en/view.asp?id=45&id_ss=67. Downloaded on January 16, 2006.

Nocioni, Andrés
(El Chapu)
(1979–   ) *basketball player*

As a key member of Argentina's gold medal–winning basketball team at the 2004 Olympics,

Andrés Nocioni enjoyed a stellar rookie season with the National Basketball Association (NBA) and provided all-out hustle and intensity to help the Chicago Bulls reach the playoffs in 2005 for the first time since the franchise's championship dynasty ended in 1998. He was born on November 30, 1979, in Santa Fe, Argentina. Nocioni, the second son of a farm equipment salesman and housewife, grew up in Santa Fe playing basketball with his older brother and other boys who were older and taller than he was. Because of his relentless energy and drive, Nocioni was nicknamed "El Chapu" after the popular Latin American television comic superhero El Chapulin Colorado, who epitomized scrappy overachievement.

Though known mainly for his outstanding effort on the basketball court, Nocioni has demonstrated versatile athletic skills. At age 15, just a few weeks after helping his team win a South American youth tournament, Nocioni made his professional debut in Argentina's national basketball league.

His style of play, featuring aggressive defense, hard-nosed drives to the basket, and an insatiable desire to win, earned Nocioni a contract to play professionally in Spain when he was only 19 years old. In 1999 the 6'7" forward became a member of the Argentine national team and contributed to the team's success, including silver medals in the 1999 South American championship and 2002 world championships (where Argentina became the first team to defeat a dream team of American professionals in international competition) and a bronze medal in the 1999 Pan-American Games.

Nocioni played for Tau Cerámica in Spain in one of Europe's strongest professional leagues. His steady improvement and overall excellence led many, including fellow Argentine and NBA star MANU GINOBILI, to encourage Nocioni to try his hand in the NBA. But Nocioni preferred to be patient, explaining, "The NBA will come at the proper time. I'll go when I'm ready."

After his 17 points and nine rebounds per game average earned him the most valuable player in his league, Nocioni made the move to the United

States, signing a three-year, $8 million contract with the Chicago Bulls. Following his departure from Spain, Nocioni's coach with Tau Cerámica said, "We cannot replace Andrés Nocioni. Andrés' competitive attitude and his willingness to sacrifice go hand-in-hand with his great fundamentals and winning mentality."

Before playing for the Bulls, Nocioni enjoyed a significant role on Argentina's 2004 Olympic team in Athens that powered its way past the favored U.S. team and all others to capture the gold medal. After a slow start in Chicago, Nocioni played primarily off the bench to average more than eight points and almost five rebounds a game, playing in all but one game in the 2004–05 season. The highlight of his rookie season was an astounding 25 points, 18 rebounds, and four assists performance in Chicago's win over the Washington Wizards in game one of the Eastern Conference first-round playoff series. Nocioni continued to play well in the series, though Chicago fell to Washington in six games.

In the 2005–06 season, Nocioni's role on the Bulls grew as he started more than half the team's games. He raised his averages to 13 points and more than six rebounds a game while serving as Chicago's toughest and most effective defensive player. As he did the previous season, he elevated his impact in the playoffs, leading the team in scoring (22.3 points) and rebounds (nine) per game as the Bulls lost a first-round series to the eventual NBA champion Miami Heat in six games.

After only two seasons in the NBA, Nocioni had firmly established himself as a valuable player with a unique brand of grittiness. Reflecting this, Bulls coach Scott Skiles noted, "Nocioni . . . [is] one of those you love to have on your team, but you hate to play against." And Chicago general manager John Paxson explained, "Andrés plays with a passion that . . . all players should play with. He brings his best efforts every night. He's Chicago—he's tough, and he'll never give up."

Further Reading

"Andrés Nocioni." National Basketball Association Web site. Available online. URL: http://www.nba.com/playerfile/andrés_nocioni/bio.html. Downloaded on January 16, 2006.

Lee, Michael. "Wizards Get Bulldozed: Chicago's Rookie Nocioni Outshines Arenas in Opener." *Washington Post,* 25 April 2005, p. D1.

"Nocioni: All Heart, All Hustle, All the Time." Chicago Bulls Web site. Available online. URL: http://www.nba.com/bulls/news/nocioni_feature_050106.html. Downloaded on January 16, 2006.

Ochoa, Lorena
(1981–   ) *golfer*

A dominant amateur golfer who was named the National Collegiate Athletic Association's (NCAA) Player of the Year in both of her two seasons at the University of Arizona, Lorena Ochoa earned the Ladies' Professional Golf Association (LPGA) Rookie of the Year award in 2003 and in 2004 became the first Mexican-born player ever to win an LPGA event. She was born on November 15, 1981, in Guadalajara, Mexico. Ochoa grew up in Tapalpa, a mountainous town about 100 miles south of Guadalajara, the third of four children born to her real estate developer father, Javier, and artist mother, Marcela. Ochoa's introduction to golf came at age five and resulted from her childhood home's proximity to a golf course, where she would practice with her siblings after dinner. Ochoa soon started formal golf training and, at age nine, began a record streak of five consecutive junior world championships (Tiger Woods owns the boys' record with four straight titles). Because there are few young golfers in Mexico and because she demonstrated great ability at a young age, Ochoa then began competing and succeeding in boys' tournaments when she was 11 years old.

Although she had been to the United States only a few times and spoke little English, Ochoa chose to attend and play golf at the University of Arizona in 2000. In just two years at Arizona, Ochoa amassed an impressive record of achieve-

ments. In her first year, she had four event wins and finished second in the 2001 NCAA championship after losing to current LPGA tour player Candy Hannemann in the playoff. Ochoa was also named NCAA Player of the Year and NCAA Freshman of the Year. In her sophomore season (2001–02), Ochoa's eight wins in a row set an NCAA record for consecutive victories. She finished tied for second in the NCAA championship and again earned recognition as the NCAA Player of the Year.

In 2002, Ochoa left the University of Arizona to begin competing in the LPGA tour. Though only 20 years old, Ochoa was a major sports star in Mexico, where President Vicente Fox awarded her the Premio Nacional del Deporte (National Sports Award) and television film crews regularly chronicled her visits to Guadalajara and her play at the local country club.

An eight-time Mexican national champion in women's golf, Ochoa's skills and quiet charm have helped make her one of the most celebrated female athletes in that nation's history. Explained her former longtime coach Rafael Alarcón, "In Mexico the masses don't even know what golf is, but if you ask any taxi driver in Mexico City, he'll know who Lorena Ochoa is."

As a professional, Ochoa—occasionally referred to as the Tiger Woods of Mexico—continued to excel. She made the cut in four of her five tournaments in 2002 and finished among the top 10 twice. In 2003, she made 23 of 24 cuts, with eight top-10 finishes, including five in the top three.

In 2004, Ochoa made the cut in all 27 tournaments in which she played, finishing among the top 10 18 times and the top three eight times, including wins in the Franklin American Mortgage Championship and the Wachovia LPGA Classic. Ochoa also achieved her first professional hole in one in 2004 and brought her single-season winnings total to more than $1 million. Ochoa's unique combination of power and finesse helped her climb in the LPGA rankings in 2005, when she finished behind LPGA superstar Annika Sorenstam for second place among women golfers in the world. Ochoa continued her excellent play in 2006, winning six tournaments and ending Sorentstam's five-year reign as the winner of the Vare Trophy, which is awarded to the top female golfer in the world. Ochoa's stellar 2006 was capped when she was named Associated Press Female Athlete of the Year—the first Mexican to be so recognized—and by receiving the National Sports Prize, the highest honor bestowed by the Mexican government on that nation's athletes.

Further Reading

Callahan, Tom. "Here Comes Lorena." *Golf Digest,* January 2003.

"Career Highlights: Lorena Ochoa." Ladies Professional Golf Association Web site. Available online. URL: http://www.lpga.com/player_career.aspx?id=519. Downloaded on January 16, 2006.

Lorena Ochoa Web site. Available online. URL: http://www.lorenaochoa.com/home.asp?idioma=ENG. Downloaded on January 16, 2006.

Yen, Yi-Wyn. "Lady in Waiting: It's Only a Matter of Time before Lorena Ochoa Does on the LPGA Tour What She's Doing at Arizona." *Sports Illustrated,* 1 April 2002, p. 73.

Oliva, Tony
(Antonio Oliva, Tony-O)
(1938–   ) *baseball player*

The only baseball player in major league history to win batting titles in his first two seasons and only the second (joining Joe DiMaggio) to be named to the All-Star team in his first eight seasons, Tony Oliva was the 1964 American League (AL) Rookie of the Year and spent his entire 15-year career with the Minnesota Twins, leading the team to three playoff appearances. He was born Antonio Oliva on July 20, 1938, in Pinar del Río, Cuba. He grew up on his family's farm in Pinar del Río treasuring Sundays, when he and his friends traveled around the countryside in search of baseball games against teams from other towns. His graceful and natural hitting stroke and imposing size (6'2" and 190 pounds) impressed professional baseball scouts, and Oliva signed a contract with the Minnesota Twins organization in 1961. He quickly became known as "Tony-O," though he was also sometimes referred to as "Pedro" because of a false story claiming Oliva had used his brother's passport to enter the United States and that Pedro was actually his given name.

Oliva wasted no time in justifying the faith placed in him by the Twins. In 1961, he won the silver Louisville Slugger award as the top hitter in all of professional baseball after batting .410 for Wytheville (Virginia) of the Appalachian League, where he led all batters in hits, total bases, runs batted in (RBIs), and sacrificed flies. Oliva spent most of 1962 in the minors before making his major league debut on September 9, 1962. In his two brief stints with the Twins in 1962 and 1963, Oliva collected seven hits in only 16 at-bats.

In 1964, Oliva enjoyed one of the greatest rookie seasons in the history of Major League Baseball. Playing in all but one of the Twins' games, Oliva led the AL with a .323 batting average, 217 hits, 109 runs, and 374 total bases. He ranked among the top 10 in the league in homeruns (32), RBIs (94), and triples nine. Oliva's excellence earned him the first of his eight consecutive All-Star game appearances and unanimous support for the 1964 AL Rookie of the Year award.

Oliva continued his outstanding play in his second season of 1965 despite getting off to a dismal start that found his batting average hovering in the .200s in mid-May. He again led the AL in batting average (.321) and hits (185), helping the Twins win the AL pennant. In the World Series, Oliva's game two double off Los Angeles Dodgers pitching ace Sandy Koufax helped lift the Twins to a 5-1 victory, though Minnesota ultimately fell to the Dodgers 4-3. Following the 1965 season, Oliva finished second in voting for the AL Most Valuable Player award.

From 1966 through 1967, Oliva remained a consistent force in the Twins' lineup and among the best players in the majors, with two-year averages of .299 batting, 21 homeruns, and 85 RBIs. Oliva's excellence in right field also earned him his first and only Gold Glove award, a feat made particularly impressive because of his defensive struggles earlier in his career. Although Oliva continued to produce solid offensive numbers in 1968, he missed about a quarter of the season due to knee injuries, which would later plague and ultimately shorten his career.

Another stellar year for Oliva was 1969, though it was marked by many highs and lows. During a midseason 14-game hitting streak, Oliva collected 20 hits in only 59 at-bats, including a string of eight consecutive hits. That streak was interrupted by Oliva's contraction of chicken pox, which led to a week off and then a two-week slump. Despite this difficulty, Oliva finished the 1969 season with a .309 batting average (third in the AL), and he again led the AL in hits and doubles.

Oliva knocked in his career high of 107 runs in 1970 while batting .325 (third in the AL) and followed that performance by leading the AL in batting with an average of .337 in 1971, despite missing almost 40 games because of another knee injury. Oliva's hitting acumen also benefited his roommate on the road, a young future Hall of Famer—ROD CAREW.

Injuries prevented Oliva from playing in all but 10 games during the 1972 season. Oliva's career was prolonged by the AL's adoption of a designated hitter, which allowed the injury-hampered Oliva to do what he did best—smoothly and powerfully hit the ball—without having to play defense. He played through the 1976 season and finished his career with a lifetime .304 batting average, 1,917 hits, 220 homeruns, and 947 RBIs.

Oliva's postplaying years remained dedicated to the Twins. He served as the team's first base coach and batting instructor between 1977 and 1991, helping improve the batting techniques of future Hall of Famer Kirby Puckett and others who brought Minnesota World Series championships in 1987 and 1991. The Twins retired Oliva's number 6 during the 1991 season, though his expressed wish that he be inducted into the National Baseball Hall of Fame has not yet been fulfilled.

Further Reading

La Velle, Neil E., III. "On the Brink . . . Again." *Minneapolis Star-Tribune*, 27 February 2000.

Thielman, Jim. *Cool of the Evening: The 1965 Minnesota Twins*. Minneapolis, Minn.: Kirk House Publishers, 2005.

"Tony Oliva." Baseball Reference Web site. Available online. URL: http://www.baseball-reference.com/o/olivato01.shtml. Downloaded on January 20, 2006.

Olivares, Rubén
(El Púas)
(1947–) *boxer*

A bantamweight and featherweight boxing champion renowned for his vicious left hook, Rubén Olivares won a remarkable 75 percent of his fights by knockout, becoming one of Mexico's most accomplished and celebrated sports figures. He was born on January 14, 1947, in Mexico City. Olivares grew up in the rough and tumble Tepito section north of the center of Mexico City, distinguishing himself as an outstanding boxer as a boy. After a successful career as an amateur boxer, the 5'9", 118-pound Olivares brought his lightning quick hands and aggressive approach, which earned him the nickname "El Púas" (Spikes), to professional rings.

Olivares's first pro bout took place on January 4, 1965, and resulted in a first-round knockout win. He followed that with 21 consecutive knock-outs over a span of more than two years. The first opponent to make it through a fight with Olivares and remain on his feet, Felipe Gonzáles, lost by a unanimous decision on March 8, 1967. Less than five months later, Germán Bastidas earned a draw with Olivares.

Following that fight, Olivares began another astounding winning streak, with almost all of his wins coming by knockout. Included in this run of success were knockouts over Gonzáles and Basti-das and a knockout of boxing icon KID GAVILAN GONZÁLEZ. Also during this time was Olivares's first fight in the United States, a third-run techni-cal knockout of Bernabé Fernández in Inglewood, California, on August 28, 1968.

Now possessing a well-earned reputation as a tremendous puncher with a wicked left hook, Oli-vares pursued the world bantamweight title. In his first chance at the title, Olivares knocked out Lio-nel Rose on August 22, 1969, in Inglewood to win the World Boxing Association (WBA) and World Boxing Council's (WBC) bantamweight champi-onships. After winning this fight, Olivares's record stood at a near perfect 51-0-1 with 49 knockouts.

Olivares had worn the bantamweight crown for more than a year when he met Chucho Castillo in Inglewood on October 16, 1970. Six months earlier, Castillo had knocked down Olivares before losing a unanimous decision to him. But on this night, Castillo opened a severe cut over Olivares's left eye and finished off the champion in a 14-round technical knockout.

Less than six months later, Olivares met Cas-tillo in the rubber match of their championship trilogy. Though knocked down in the sixth round, Olivares rose from the canvas and controlled the bout, defeating Castillo in a unanimous decision and regaining the WBA and WBC bantamweight titles. Olivares relinquished the title less than a year later to countryman Rafael Herrera in an eighth-round knockout.

The remainder of Olivares's career featured a step up in weight class and a brief reign as the North American Boxing Federation's feather-weight champion following a technical knockout of BOBBY CHACON. However, Olivares also dem-onstrated that he was not nearly the boxer he had been in his younger years, winning only 20 of his final 33 fights.

After he retired from boxing, Olivares appeared as an actor in several Mexican movies, often por-traying the good-natured, working-class persona he had possessed as a boxing champion. Olivares's final record was 88-13-3. He was inducted into the International Boxing Hall of Fame in 1991.

Further Reading

"Ruben Olivares." Boxing Records Archive Web site. Available online. URL: http://boxing.about.com/ gi/dynamic/offsite.htm?site=http://boxrec.com/ boxer%5Fdisplay.php %3Fboxer%5Fid=009002. Downloaded on January 20, 2006.
"Ruben Olivares." International Boxing Hall of Fame Web site. Available online. URL: http://www. ibhof.com/ruben.htm. Downloaded on January 20, 2006.

Oliveira, Sócrates Brasileiro Sampaio de Souza Vieira   *See* SÓCRATES

Olmedo, Alex
(Luis Alejandro Rodríguez Olmedo, the Chief)
(1936–   )   *tennis player*

A college singles and doubles tennis champion at the University of Southern California (USC), Alex Olmedo was the 1959 Wimbledon singles and Australian National singles champion before spending five years as a top attraction on the tour-ing professional tennis circuit. He was born Luis Alejandro Rodríguez Olmedo on March 24, 1936, in Arequipa, Peru. A descendant of Incan ances-try, Olmedo first played tennis at age nine when he borrowed his father's racquet to play on the courts of Arequipa, a city located on the outskirts of the western range of the Andes Mountains. By age 17, Olmedo had demonstrated enough promise as a tennis player that local patrons collected $700 to finance a boat to Havana, a flight to Miami, and a bus to Los Angeles, where Olmedo worked at a tennis shop by day and studied English at night school.

Olmedo soon enrolled at USC and played tennis there for three years. At USC, Olmedo, nicknamed "the Chief" because of his regal Incan bearing, won National Collegiate Athletic Association (NCAA) championships in singles and doubles in 1956 and 1958. Later in 1958, U.S. Davis Cup team captain Perry Jones named the agile Olmedo to the team, claiming that despite not being an American citizen, Olmedo's more than three years of continuous residence in the United States made him eligible, particularly because Peru had no Davis Cup team. Olmedo's powerful serve led to victories in one doubles and two singles matches, giving the United States the championship over a powerful Australian squad.

In 1959, Olmedo was featured on the cover of the September 7, 1959, issue of *Sports Illustrated*. During this year, he won the U.S. indoor singles and doubles titles, the Australian championships, and Wimbledon over Australian star Rod Laver. He also made it to the finals of the U.S. championships in singles and doubles.

However, this otherwise successful year was tarnished by his poor play in the 1959 Davis Cup loss to Australia, which Olmedo later explained was the result of exhaustion and being forced to return for a preparation tournament by the United States Lawn Tennis Association. He finished the year ranked as the number two amateur player in the world.

In 1960, Olmedo turned professional and joined the ranks of other tennis greats, including PANCHO GONZALES, Ken Rosewall, and Tony Trabert, who barnstormed from city to city in the days before the open era. In his first year as a pro, Olmedo defeated Trabert for the U.S. pro singles title. Olmedo retired from full-time play as a pro in 1965, though he did return to Wimbledon in 1968 to team with doubles partner PANCHO SEGURA, winning an early round, four-set match over Abe

Segal and Gordon Forbes that featured the longest set (32-30) in the history of the prestigious tournament. Since 1965 Olmedo has worked as a teaching pro at the Beverly Hills Hotel, where his clients have included actors Katharine Hepburn, Chevy Chase, and Robert Duvall. Olmedo, who was inducted into the International Tennis Hall of Fame in 1987, still works at the Beverly Hills Hotel, proudly noting, "It's the first and only job I ever had."

Further Reading

"Alex Olmedo." International Tennis Hall of Fame Web site. Available online. URL: http://www. tennisfame.org/enshrinees/alex_olmedo.html. Downloaded on January 20, 2006.

Fernando, Luis. "Alex Olmedo, Tennis Champion: September 7, 1959." *Sports Illustrated,* 7 September 1998, p. 14.

Ortiz, Carlos
(1936-) *boxer*

A Puerto Rican immigrant to New York City who was introduced to boxing as a way to avoid juvenile delinquency, Carlos Ortiz was the lightweight boxing champion for most of the 1960s. He was born on September 9, 1936, in Ponce, Puerto Rico. Ortiz moved with his family to New York City when he was a child, where he regularly became involved in street fights.

When he was 10 years old, Ortiz was picked up by the police for causing problems in Macy's department store. An officer explained to Ortiz that day that the police would not pursue further punishment if he would join the local Madison Square Boys' Club. Ortiz later explained, "I started working in the street to gain money for the dues . . . [the club] was beautiful. . . . [in the club] there was a noise in the beyond that I heard. It was the sound of a light [punching] bag. When I heard that noise it mesmerized me."

Ortiz continued to train at the Madison Square Boys' Club, showing dedication and skill that made him one of New York City's top amateur boxers. The 5'7", 136-pound Ortiz made his professional debut as an 18-year-old on February 14, 1955, winning a first-round knockout over Henry Bell. Ortiz proceeded to win his next 19 bouts before his fight against Lou Filippo was ruled a no-decision, because Filippo was unable to continue when Ortiz hit him after the bell ending the ninth round.

By the beginning of 1959, Ortiz had compiled a 28-2 record. After another victory, Ortiz gained his first title fight in a June 12, 1959, matchup with Kenny Lane for the vacant world light welterweight title. Fighting in storied Madison Square Garden, just steps from where he trained and blocks from where he had lived as a child, Ortiz defeated Lane with a technical knockout in the second round, avenging an earlier loss. Ortiz's hold on this crown was short lived, however, as he lost in a controversial decision to Italian Duilo Loi in Milan on September 1, 1960.

Following another loss to Loi, Ortiz focused on the more prestigious lightweight championship, which he gained by winning a unanimous decision over Joe Brown in Las Vegas on April 21, 1962. Ortiz won his next nine fights, including four title defenses, until dropping a 15-round decision to Ismael Laguna on April 10, 1965, in Laguna's hometown of Panama City, Panama.

Seven months later, Ortiz regained the title from Laguna by winning a unanimous decision in San Juan, Puerto Rico. He kept the championship for more than two and a half years, beating several top fighters including Laguna and Sugar Ramos.

Ortiz lost a split decision to Carlos Teo Cruz in Cruz's hometown of Santo Domingo, Dominican Republic, on June 29, 1968, and he never again reigned as champion. Ortiz retired in 1969 but returned two years later, winning nine fights before losing his last bout in a six-round technical knockout to Ken Buchanan in Madison Square Garden.

Ortiz's final record was 61-7-1. He was inducted into the International Boxing Hall of Fame in 1991, the first Puerto Rican native to earn that honor. He lives near New York City and remains an avid boxing fan.

Further Reading

"Carlos Ortiz." Boxing Records Archive Web site. Available online. URL: http://www.boxrec.com/boxer_display.php?boxer_id=008387. Downloaded on January 20, 2006.

"Interview with Carlos Ortiz: 'If I Could Box Today, I Would.'" Doghouse Boxing Web site. Available online. URL: http://www.doghouseboxing.com/Newman/Newman031504.htm. Downloaded on January 20, 2006.

Osuna, Rafael
(1938–1969) *tennis player*

A small, quick, and clever U.S. national singles champion and two-time Wimbledon doubles champion, Rafael Osuna remains the greatest Mexican tennis player of all time despite having his life tragically cut short at age 30 in a plane crash. He was born on September 15, 1938, in Mexico City. Osuna honed his tennis skills on the courts of Mexico's capital until he became a member of the nation's Davis Cup team as a 19-year-old in 1958, helping Mexico reach the quarterfinals.

In 1960, Osuna, a 21-year-old freshman at the University of Southern California (USC), became the first Mexican to win a championship at Wimbledon, when he teamed with fellow USC player Dennis Ralston to win that prestigious tournament's doubles title. Osuna and his Davis Cup doubles partner Antonio Palafox won the U.S. Nationals doubles championship in 1962 and finished as finalists in 1960 and 1963. He again won the Wimbledon doubles title in 1963, this time playing with Palafox.

As a collegian, Osuna effectively befuddled opponents with his serving and aggressive play that seemingly put him in more than one place at a time to win the National Collegiate Athletic

Association's (NCAA) singles championship in 1962. Osuna became the first player since World War I to win the NCAA doubles championship three times, teaming with Ramsey Earnhart in 1961 and 1962 and Dennis Ralston in 1963 to win those titles.

Osuna's greatest achievement in international competition came in 1962, when he led the Mexican Davis Cup team past the United States, Yugoslavia, Sweden, and India before the team lost to reigning champion Australia. During this 1962 Davis Cup run, Osuna was 5-1 in singles, demonstrating his propensity for clutch play in winning two emotionally and physically draining five-set marathons over Jack Douglas of the United States and Jan-Erik Lundquist of Sweden.

Osuna was ranked among the top 10 amateur players in the world in 1962, 1963 (when he was ranked number one), and 1964. He continued to participate on the Mexican Davis Cup team throughout the 1960s. In 1969, he spearheaded Mexico's surprise triumph over Australia by winning his singles and doubles matches. Sadly, these would be Osuna's final matches. On June 6, 1969,

less than two weeks after these victories, a plane he was traveling on crashed near Monterrey, Mexico, killing everyone on board.

Osuna became the first Mexican to be enshrined in the International Tennis Hall of Fame when he was inducted posthumously in 1979. He has been further honored by the Intercollegiate Tennis Association, the governing body of college tennis, which annually presents the Rafael Osuna Award to the men's player who "displays sportsmanship, character, excellent academics, and has had outstanding tennis accomplishments."

Further Reading

"Rafael Osuna." International Tennis Hall of Fame Web site. Available online. URL: http://www.tennisfame.org/enshrinees/rafael_osuna.html. Downloaded on January 20, 2006.

"2005 ITA Regional Award Winners for NCAA Division I Tennis." Intercollegiate Tennis Association Web site. Available online. URL: http://www.itatennis.com/05d1menswinners.htm. Downloaded on January 20, 2006.

P

Palmeiro, Rafael
(1964–) *baseball player*

A smooth swinging, left-handed hitting first baseman who ranked among the American League's (AL) top 10 in home runs every year from 1993 through 2003, Rafael Palmeiro surpassed the 3,000 career hit mark before becoming the highest-profile player in Major League Baseball history to be suspended for steroid use. He was born on September 24, 1964, in Havana, Cuba. Palmeiro was seven when his family fled Cuba for Miami, Florida.

Under the guidance of his demanding bricklaying father, José, Rafael developed two traits that would later mark his professional career—his sweet batting stroke and self-critical approach. Palmeiro later said of his father, who admitted that he often told his son he would never become a major leaguer, "He was very critical of me at times, but he did it for my own good. I think he knew I could handle it."

In 1982, Palmeiro's excellence on the baseball diamond earned him a scholarship to play baseball at Mississippi State University. He was a three-time All-American for Mississippi State, though his quiet personality led him to be overshadowed by his boisterous and acclaimed teammate Will Clark, who would later star for the San Francisco Giants.

Palmeiro was drafted in the first round of the 1985 amateur draft by the Chicago Cubs. He continued his success in the minors and made his major league debut on September 8, 1986, with the Cubs. In part-time duty in 1987, Palmeiro batted .276 with 14 home runs and became a full-time outfielder for Chicago in 1988, finishing that season with an impressive .307 batting average and ranking second in the National League (NL) with 41 doubles.

Following the 1988 season, the Cubs, who had a young star, Mark Grace, whose hitting style mirrored Palmeiro's, traded Palmeiro to the Texas Rangers as the key component of a nine-player deal. Palmeiro spent five seasons with the Rangers, playing in all but 16 of the teams' games while becoming one of baseball's best hitters. Batting in the middle of a potent lineup that included such stars as JOSE CANSECO, IVÁN RODRÍGUEZ, and JUAN GONZÁLEZ, Palmeiro was named to the AL All-Star team in 1988 and 1981 and ranked in the top three in the AL in hits three times (1988, 1990, and 1991).

In 1993, Palmeiro broke through as a dangerous power hitter, belting 37 home runs and 105 runs batted in (RBIs). After that season, Palmeiro signed a five-year, $27.5 million free-agent contract with the Baltimore Orioles. Following an injury-plagued 1994 campaign, Palmeiro was the offensive muscle of an Orioles team that twice advanced to the postseason (1996 and 1997). From 1995 through 1998, Palmeiro averaged 40 home runs and almost 120 RBIs, and his athletic grace at first base earned him two Gold Glove awards (1997 and 1998).

Though respected and well liked by his Baltimore teammates, Palmeiro developed a reputation as a notorious pessimist and worrier. Orioles third baseman Cal Ripken, Jr., noted, "We have a kind of running joke around here. The more Raffy complains and the worse he looks, the better he's going to do." Palmeiro's former manager with the Rangers, Bobby Valentine, remembered that when Palmeiro was told before a season that he would hit .300, "Raffy would say, 'Maybe, but I still can't hit like Tony Gwynn.'"

Despite such disparaging comments about his own play, Palmeiro was admired by fellow players and desired by teams mainly for the production resulting from what a *Sports Illustrated* reporter described as his "controlled, almost surgical at bats." Evidence of this was provided after the 1998 season, when the free-agent Palmeiro returned to the Rangers, signing a five-year, $44 million contract.

From 1999 through 2003, the remarkably durable Palmeiro continued to rack up hits and amazing power numbers, averaging 41 home runs and more than 120 RBIs a season and helping the Rangers win the AL West championship in 1999. However, prior to the 2004 season, Palmeiro returned to Baltimore and batted a career low .258 with diminished power totals.

In March 2005, Palmeiro testified before a U.S. congressional panel investigating steroid use in baseball and emphatically refuted rumors that his power surge was the result of performance-enhancement drugs—as alleged by former teammate Canseco in his book *Juiced*—saying, "I have never used steroids period." Needing only 78 hits to reach the coveted milestone career mark of 3,000 when the 2005 season began, Palmeiro doubled on July 15 in Seattle to become only the 26th major leaguer to accomplish that feat and only the fourth to have 3,000 hits and at least 500 career home runs (joining Willie Mays, Hank Aaron, and Eddie Murray).

Less than three weeks after his historic accomplishment, Palmeiro was suspended for 10 days by Major League Baseball for testing positive for steroids. Stunned, embarrassed, and expressing confusion regarding how he tested positive, Palmeiro

played only seven more games in 2005, attempting to drown out the boos from fans in Toronto by using earplugs. After a postsuspension slump in which he got only two hits in 26 at-bats, Palmeiro did not appear at another game. Neither the Orioles nor any other major league team offered him a contract after the season.

The controversy over Palmeiro's positive test for steroids shook baseball and severely tainted his legacy of consistency and excellence. Connecticut congressman Christopher Shays captured the thoughts of many, explaining, "He [Palmeiro] ended up being the most outspoken against steroid use and even this guy is in a situation where he's been suspended. It just blows me away. Obviously it calls into question every accomplishment he's had."

Of how he will be remembered, Palmeiro said, "I hope people look at my whole career . . . I respect the Hall of Fame, and if they think that I'm worthy enough, I would be very honored. And if they don't, I gave it all I had to this game."

Further Reading
Hille, Bob. "Raffy and Texas, Then and Now." *Sporting News,* 13 September 1999, p. 48.

Johnette, Howard. "A Star in the Shadows." *Sports Illustrated,* 8 September 1997, p. 42.

"Rafael Palmeiro." Baseball Reference Web site. Available online. URL: http://www.baseball-reference.com/p/palmera01.shtml. Downloaded on January 20, 2006.

"Steroid Shocker: Palmeiro Suspended." MSNBC Web site. Available online. URL: http://www.msnbc.msn.com/id/8788193/. Downloaded on January 20, 2006.

Palomino, Carlos
(1949–   ) *boxer*

The welterweight boxing champion for most of the late 1970s, Carlos Palomino holds the distinction of being one of the few college graduates ever to hold the boxing crown. He was born on August 10, 1949, in San Luis de Colorado, Mexico. Palomino moved to Los Angeles with his family when he was eight years old and excelled as a baseball player in youth leagues. He initially disliked boxing because his father, Pablo, had frequently forced him to spar in his backyard with one of his four brothers.

However, Palomino took up boxing again while serving in the U.S. Army from 1971 to 1972. In 1972, Palomino was the All-Army welterweight champion. Later in 1972, he won the National Amateur Athletic Union (AAU) championship when he defeated future Olympic gold medalist "Sugar" Ray Seales.

Palomino's first professional fight took place on September 14, 1972, when he won a decision over Javier Martínez in Los Angeles. Palomino did not lose a bout until nearly two years later, when he lost to Andy Price in San Diego. During this period, he graduated from California State University–Long Beach with a bachelor's degree in recreational administration.

Following his loss to Price, Palomino put together a 10-0-2 streak leading to his first championship title opportunity on June 22, 1976, versus welterweight champion John Stracey in London. Fighting in front of 8,000 boisterous Stracey fans, Palomino dropped the champion twice in the 12th round before the referee stopped the fight and declared Palomino the winner, making him the new World Boxing Council (WBC) welterweight champion.

Palomino was an active champion, successfully defending his title seven times over almost two years with his well-rounded, technically sound balance of attack and defense. Palomino lost the crown to Wilfred Benitez on January 14, 1979, in San Juan, Puerto Rico. Five months later, Palomino lost a unanimous decision to Roberto Durán in New York City, after which Palomino retired from boxing.

Despite being out of boxing, Palomino remained highly visible due to his forays into acting. He appeared as himself on the popular televi-sion sitcom *Taxi* and in a series of commercials for Miller Lite beer. He also had small roles in several cable television movies during the 1980s and 1990s, as well as roles in individual episodes of the highly acclaimed television dramas *Hill Street Blues* and *NYPD Blue*.

In 1997, approximately 17 years after he left the ring, Palomino returned to boxing, explaining that doing so would help his heart heal following his father's recent death. He won four of five bouts in the Los Angeles area against lightly regarded competition before retiring again with a career record of 31-4-3. Palomino, who works as a boxing trainer in the Los Angeles area, was inducted in the International Boxing Hall of Fame in 2004.

Further Reading

"Carlos Palomino." Boxing Records Archive Web site. Available online. URL: http://www.boxrec.com/boxer_display.php?boxer_id=000406. Downloaded on October 31, 2006.

Lidz, Frank. "From the Ring to the Screen." *Sports Illustrated,* 7 November 1988, p. 23.

"Shadowboxer." California State University–Long Beach Web site. Available online. URL: http://www.csulb.edu/~univmag/12-1-97/palomino.html. Downloaded on January 22, 2006.

Parra, Derek
(1970–   ) *speed skater*

The gold medal winner in the 1,500-meter speed skating event at the 2002 winter Olympics, Derek Parra emerged as an unlikely champion, his undersized stature and working-class upbringing in southern California inspiring speed skating fans and competitors. He was born on March 15, 1970, in San Bernardino, California, about 60 miles southeast of Los Angeles. Parra's parents, Gilbert and Maria, divorced when Parra was a toddler, and his father, a prison guard in San Bernardino, raised him and his brother, Gilbert, Jr.

As an adolescent, Parra was a regular at San Bernardino's Stardust Roller Rink, where he spent hours racing on inline skates, earning tickets for hot dogs and soda by winning competitions. While in high school, Parra scraped together enough money to attend the U.S. Olympic Training Center in Colorado Springs, where he received instruction from renowned roller-skating coach Virgil Dooley.

Parra graduated from high school in 1988 and moved to Florida to train with Dooley, following the coach to Maryland, and eventually Delaware, where Parra lived from 1990 to 1996. During this time, Parra (5'4", 145 pounds) dominated the world of competitive inline skating, winning 18 titles and setting several world records for speed. Disappointed that inline skating was not chosen to be a sport for the 1996 Olympics in Atlanta, Georgia, Parra turned his intense dedication to speed skating on ice, despite having previously worn ice skates only once in his life.

After experiencing extraordinary success in inline skating, Parra struggled with his new sport, explaining, "It was very frustrating coming to the ice and being a nobody, especially after being the best in the world . . . I knew I could do it, but the results weren't coming as fast as I wanted them." Parra posted strong enough times to make the 1998 U.S. Olympic speed skating team as an alternate, but he did not compete in any events.

Parra decided to continue his Olympic quest and spent the next four years training in Milwaukee, Minnesota, and Utah as part of a joint program of the U.S. Olympic Committee and Home Depot stores that provided a half-time job for full-time pay in return for allowing himself to be featured in the stores' commercials. This mutually beneficial arrangement paid off when Parra won a world speed skating medal, coming in second in the 1,500-meter race in 2001.

When the 2002 winter Olympics in Salt Lake City, Utah, began, Parra—who married in 1999 and was now the father of a baby girl—was considered a long shot in the 5,000-meter competition, a race usually won by skaters much larger than the upstart American. However, Parra set an American record in the event and won a silver medal. In the 1,500-meters event, Parra set a world record of 6:17.98 to win the gold medal. Reflecting the respect Parra earned among his opponents, 1,500-meter silver medalist Jochem Uytdehaage said, "I knew Derek would skate very fast, and this may sound strange, but I was happy for him to break the record. It was an awesome skate."

Following his gold medal victory, Parra traveled across the United States as a motivational speaker and continued to train with hopes of competing in the 2006 winter Olympics in Torino, Italy. He skated poorly in events leading up to the Olympic trials, citing "suffering" and "depression" resulting from his impending divorce. However, bolstered by the overwhelming support of his teammates, who referred to him as the "backbone" and the "hardest working guy on the team," Parra qualified in the 1,500-meter event to earn a spot on the 2006 U.S. speed skating team.

In Torino, he competed in the 1,500-meters and finished in 19th place. Soon after the conclusion of the Olympics, Parra expressed interest in becoming a coach for the U.S. national speed skating team.

Further Reading

"Derek Parra." Q Sports Web site. Available online. URL: http://www.latinosportslegends.com/interviews/interview_with_derek_parra-081002.htm. Downloaded on January 20, 2006.

"An Interview with 2002 Olympic Gold Medalist, Derek Parra." Latino Legends in Sports Web site. Available online. URL: http://www.latinosportslegends.com/interviews/interview_with_derek_parra-081002.htm. Downloaded on October 31, 2006.

Isaacson, Melissa. "Skater Regains Personal Footing." *Chicago Tribune,* 1 January 2006, p. 61.

Parra, Derek. *Reflections on Ice: Inside the Heart and Mind of an Olympic Champion.* Orlando, Fla: Podium Publishing, 2003.

Pascual, Camilo
(Little Potato)
(1934–   ) *baseball player*

A dominant right-handed starting pitcher of the late 1950s and early 1960s whose fidgety manner on the mound belied his masterful command of a repertoire of deceptive and overwhelming pitches, Camilo Pascual was a five-time All-Star and led the American League (AL) three times in strikeouts, shutouts, and complete games. He was born on January 10, 1934, in Havana, Cuba. Pascual followed his older brother Carlos the same lots of Cupis Capital, sharpening what would become a devastating curveball and a blazing fastball.

As a teenager, the right-handed Pascual played for teams in Cuba before signing with the Washington Senators organization. Soon after his 20th birthday, Pascual made his major league debut for the Senators, compiling a 4-7 record.

Nicknamed "Little Potato" (his brother Carlos, who had pitched briefly for the Senators, had been known as "Big Potato"), Pascual struggled on some very weak Senators teams, completing his fourth season with a career record of 20 and 54. However, in 1958, Pascual began demonstrating the skill that would make him one of the best pitchers well into the next decade. Despite an 8-12 record that year, Pascual's 3.15 earned run average (ERA) ranked ninth in the AL.

In 1959, Pascual established himself as the ace and workhorse of the Senators staff, making the AL All-Star team and finishing the year ranked second in strikeouts (185), second in ERA (2.64), fourth in wins (17), and first in shutouts six and complete games (17). Pascual began the 1960 season by pitching one of his finest games, performing before President Dwight Eisenhower and setting a franchise record for strikeouts in a single game (15) in a 10-1 win over the Boston Red Sox.

In 1961, the Senators relocated and became the Minnesota Twins. Beginning in 1961 over the next three seasons, Pascual went 56-36, leading the AL in strikeouts each year, in shutouts in 1961 and

1962, and in complete games in 1962 and 1963, despite pitching with chronic shoulder soreness. Pascual's remarkable durability was most evident in 1962 when he pitched 12 innings three days after pitching a complete game victory.

The 1964 season was witness to an unusual incident that highlighted Pascual's symbolism as a hero to Cuban exiles during the intense time of the cold war. At an April 28 game at Yankee Stadium in New York City, eight Cubans protesting communist dictator Fidel Castro's rule ran onto the field and draped Pascual with a Cuban flag, holding a banner that read "United to Liberate Cuba." Pascual, who left Cuba in 1961 and would not be reunited with his family until they immigrated to the United States in 1964, was shaken by this demonstration of affection but went on to pitch the Twins to a six-hit complete game victory over the Yankees.

Despite his excellence on the mound, Pascual was renowned for appearing fidgety during game periods. A reporter covering a Pascual-pitched game in 1964 in Baltimore noted that it took the Twins pitcher 20 minutes to pitch to just five batters because of his in-between-pitch rituals, which included adjusting his cap, pulling up his pants, removing his glove and knobbing at the baseball, peering behind at his outfielders, and wiping his forehead.

Pascual's last great season was 1964, when he helped improve the Twins' club by going 15 and 12 and ranking second in the AL in strikeouts and complete games. When the Twins were swept by the Los Angeles Dodgers in the 1965 World Series, Pascual started game three and suffered a loss.

He pitched for the Twins in 1966 for a new Washington Senators franchise from 1967 to 1969, before appearing briefly for the Cincinnati Reds (1969), Los Angeles Dodgers (1970), and Cleveland Indians. Pascual finished his career with a record of 174 and 170 with 2,167 strikeouts.

Following his retirement, Pascual remained in baseball by serving as the Twins pitching coach from 1978 to 1980 and recently served as a Caribbean regional scout with the Los Angeles Dodgers.

Further Reading

Amato, Jim. "Camilo Pascual: The Forgotten 'Strikeout King.'" At Home Plate Web site. Available online. URL: http://www.athomeplate.com/bytes2.shtml. Downloaded on January 20, 2006.

"Camilo Pascual." Baseball Reference Web site. Available online. URL: http://www.baseball-reference.com/p/pascuca02.shtml. Downloaded on January 20, 2006.

Thielman, Jim. *Cool of the Evening: The 1965 Minnesota Twins.* Minneapolis, Minn.: Kirk House Publishers, 2005.

Wolinsky, Russell. "Dolf Luque and Camilo Pascual: Two Cuban Curveballers." National Baseball Hall of Fame Web site. Available online. URL: http://www.baseballhalloffame.org/library/columns/rw_050718.htm. Downloaded on January 20, 2006.

Pedroza, Eusebio
(1953–   ) *boxer*

The featherweight boxing champion for more than seven years, Eusebio Pedroza successfully defended his title 19 consecutive times between 1978 and 1985, the longest such streak since heavyweight legend Joe Lewis's 24 straight defenses ended in 1948. He was born on March 2, 1953, in Panama City, Panama. Pedroza grew up in the city's Marañón district among the dilapidated shacks originally built for Panama Canal workers.

By his late teens, Pedroza had sprouted to a height of almost 5'9", though he weighed only about 120 pounds. Pedroza's toughness, boxing acumen, and unusually long reach led him to become a professional boxer when he was 20 years old.

Pedroza's first pro fight took place on December 1, 1973, in a fourth-round knockout of Julio García in Santiaga de Veraguas, Panama. Pedroza won his next eight bouts before being knocked out by Alfonso Pérez in Panama City on January 18, 1975. He rebounded to win his next five fights, leading to his first title opportunity on April 3, 1976, versus Alfonso Zemora for the World Boxing Association's (WBA) bantamweight championship. It was only Pedroza's 16th pro fight, and his inexperience showed as he was knocked out in the second round.

After a loss in his next fight, Pedroza won three straight, leading to an April 15, 1978, bout in Panama City with Cecilio Lastra for the WBA featherweight title. Pedroza defeated Lastra by technical knockout and followed this win with a division record 19 consecutive successful title defenses, including victories over Royal Kobayashi, RUBÉN OLIVARES, and Rocky Lockridge.

Pedroza wore the featherweight crown for more than seven years. During this period, he became celebrated in Panama, but he was not nearly as famous or wealthy as fellow countryman ROBERTO DURÁN. Fighting in a less prestigious division and reluctant to participate in the extravagant lifestyle of many boxing champions, Pedroza was a member of Panama's National Assembly during the latter part of his championship reign.

Despite a relative lack of attention, Pedroza was well respected as a hard, aggressive puncher and intelligent boxer, though his detractors claimed he was prone to dirty tactics, such as low blows. Veteran Panamanian journalist Alfonso Castillo echoed praise of Pedroza, noting, "He is . . . a most competitive boxer. He can brawl as well as box and still maintain his distance . . . His reach is so long. He'll study his man for maybe two or three rounds, then let down his guard just so he can counterpunch like Ali."

Pedroza relinquished the featherweight title on June 8, 1985, losing a unanimous decision to Barry McGuigan in London. He lost his next bout, retired for more than five years, and returned in late 1991, winning three of four fights over the next year, after which he retired. Pedroza's final record was 42-6-1, with 25 knockouts.

In 1999, Pedroza was enshrined in the International Boxing Hall of Fame. A resident of Panama, he has worked for the Panamanian government in various capacities, including as the chief of general services, an agency that provides utilities to poor citizens.

Further Reading

"Eusebio Pedroza." Boxing Archives Web site. Available online. URL: http://boxing.about.com/gi/dynamic/offsite.htm?site=http://boxrec.com/boxer%5Fdisplay.php %3Fboxer%5Fid=009002. Downloaded on January 20, 2006.

"Eusebio Pedroza." Latino Legends in Sports Web site. Available online. URL: http://www.latinosportslegends.com/Pedroza.htm. Downloaded on January 20, 2006.

Gammon, Clive. "A Champ with Lots of Clout." *Sports Illustrated,* 20 May 1985.

Pelé
(Edson Arantes do Nascimento, Dico, O Rei)
(1940–) *soccer player*

The most celebrated soccer player in the history of the sport and a man widely regarded as the greatest ever, Pelé used his uncanny combination of speed, ball control, and powerful shooting ability to help lead Brazil to three World Cup championships and applied his charisma and passion for what he termed "the beautiful game" to spark the popularity of soccer throughout the world. He was born Edson Arantes do Nascimento on October 23, 1940, in Três Corações, Brazil. He grew up in this poor town of about 50,000 people located in southeastern Brazil. His father was a former soccer player, Dordinho, whose career was hindered by a broken leg. His mother, Dona Celeste, who was painfully aware of the precarious nature of a career as a professional soccer player, cautioned her son to pursue another path.

Under the tutelage of his father, the boy known as "Dico" demonstrated his enormous soccer talent in games with other boys before he was 10 years old. During one of these games,

someone inexplicably called him "Pelé," a name that had no meaning in Portuguese or any other language. Initially, Pelé thought the name was an insult and insisted that the other boys stop using it. But the name stuck largely because its mysterious derivation and meaning matched the singular skill of the man to whom it was applied.

At the age of 11, Pelé was discovered by Brazilian pro Waldemar de Brito. De Brito brought Pelé to the directors of the Santos football club, telling them, "This boy will be the greatest soccer player in the world." Pelé soon began playing for a minor league club and made his professional debut with Santos in 1956 at age 16. In his first full season with Santos, Pelé led the league with 32 goals and was soon selected to be a member of Brazil's national team set to compete at the 1958 World Cup in Sweden.

Despite the fact that Pelé missed the first two games of the tournament with a knee injury, no one else would have a greater impact on that year's World Cup. He scored the game winning–goal in a quarterfinals win over Wales, had three goals in the semifinals win over France, and scored two goals in the championship victory over Sweden. Following that win, which brought Brazil its first World Cup championship, Pelé's teammates carried the 17-year-old phenomenon off the field on their shoulders.

Brazil's World Cup championship invigorated the nation, significantly altered its international image, and profoundly affected professional soccer. Of Pelé, anointed "O Rei" (the King) by Brazilian playwright Nelson Rodrigues, Brazilian journalist João Luiz de Alburquerque wrote, "He was the light at the end of the tunnel. All the poor said, 'Hey, if this guy made it, I can make it.' He brought the rest of Brazil with him."

Respectful of his importance to the Brazilian people and highly compensated between his salary and the money he made from frequent and well-attended Santos exhibition games, Pelé consistently rejected the lucrative offers to play for the most prestigious teams in Europe, further enhancing his legendary status in Brazil and fortifying pride in their national identity among the people.

Pelé continued his excellence throughout the 1960s, though battles with injuries limited his influence in the 1962 and 1966 World Cup tournaments. In the 1962 World Cup in Chile, Pelé played with an injured groin, restricting his participation to only the first two games of the tournament, though Brazil was able to repeat as champion. In 1966, hard tackles on Pelé by Bulgarian and Portuguese defenders led to injury and kept the Brazilian star out of all but two contests as Brazil fell in the first round.

Although his contributions in the World Cups of the 1960s were minimal, Pelé's legend continued to grow as he dominated professionally in Brazil with his speed, agility, ball control, and knack for succeeding in clutched situations. His habit of dominating defenses was captured by the French newspaper *L'Équipe,* which described a 1960 performance of Pelé's by noting, "We have now seen the supreme work of art. Pele infiltrated through his opponents like Novocain through a sick man's tissues." Pelé's performance on the field also helped him extend his influence off of it, which was never more evident than in 1969, when a visit to Africa by Pelé and the Santos team led to a two-day ceasefire in the war between Nigeria and the secessionist Biafra.

Pelé also heaped praise and adulation on himself. Commenting on how he ended up becoming a soccer player, Pelé said, "I was born for soccer, just as Beethoven was born for music." When a reporter asked him if his fame was comparable to that of Jesus Christ, Pelé responded, "There are parts of the world where Jesus Christ is not so well known." Such statements were rarely interpreted as the arrogant boss of self-importance but rather were usually perceived as accurate characterizations of reality because of Pelé's undeniable talent and engaging personality.

Pelé provided more evidence of his greatness in the 1970 World Cup in Mexico. Playing with

Pelé celebrates scoring the opening goal of Brazil's 4-1 victory over Italy in the 1970 World Cup final. *(EMPICS)*

a team considered by many soccer experts as the best ever, Pelé scored a goal in the opening game win over Czechoslovakia, earned the only assist in a scintillating 1-0 victory over defending champion England, and scored two more goals in a 3-2 win over Romania. After defeating Peru and Uruguay, Brazil reached the finals against Italy to determine which nation would become the first to win a third World Cup championship. Powered by three Pelé goals, Brazil won 4-1.

Following the 1970 World Cup title, Pelé retired from the Brazilian national team, and in 1974, he retired from playing professionally in Brazil. After a bad business deal left him in debt, Pelé returned to the soccer field in 1975 after signing a lucrative three-year contract to play with the New York Cosmos in the flagging North American Soccer League (NASL). Perhaps persuaded by the Cosmos' general managers' assessment that in Spain or Italy all he could do was win a championship, but in the United States he could "win a country," Pelé quickly helped infuse the NASL with excitement and fan support, as well as helping to ignite an enormous increase in soccer participation among American youths.

Pelé retired after leading the Cosmos to the NASL championship in 1977 and a final exhibition between the Cosmos and Santos, in which he played a half period for each team. His final statistics are unequaled in their excellence, including 1,281 goals in 1,363 games, one eight-goal game, six five-goal games, 30 four-goal games, and 92 three-goal games.

Pelé has remained an active ambassador for soccer in retirement in addition to being a highly sought after and well-paid endorser of many products. He has written autobiographies, composed music, done some acting, served as Brazil's minister of sport, and has been a successful businessman in Brazil. Pelé has also been an energetic advocate for poor youth around the world in his role at the United Nations Children's Fund (UNICEF). Pelé was named soccer player of the century by the Fédération Internationale Football Association (FIFA) and finished second to Muhammad Ali as sportsman of the century according to *Sports Illustrated*.

Pelé's transcendent influence on soccer is perhaps best reflected in the words of Franz Beckenbauer, who played with Pelé in New York and remains the only person ever to win a World Cup as both a player and a coach: "I have had many great moments in my career, but the greatest honor was to play with Pelé."

Further Reading

Harris, Harry. *Pele: His Life and Times.* New York: Welcome Rain Publishers, 2003.

Hersh, Hank. "SI Flashback: Soccer's Greatest Genius." *Sports Illustrated* Web site. Available online. URL: http://sportsillustrated.cnn.com/centurys_best/news/1999/05/19/siflashback_pele/. Downloaded on January 20, 2006.

Kierby, Gentry. "Pele, King of Futbol." ESPN Classic Web site. Available online. URL: http://espn.go.com/classic/biography/s/Pele.html. Downloaded on January 20, 2006.

"Pele." Fédération Internationale de Football Association World Cup Web site. Available online. URL: http://fifaworldcup.yahoo.com/06/en/p/cp/bra/pele.html. Downloaded on January 20, 2006.

Pele and Robert L. Fish. *Pele, My Life and the Beautiful Game.* New York: Doubleday, 1977.

Pérez, Tony
(Atanasio Perez)
(1942–   ) *baseball player*

A clutch-hitting run-producing mainstay of the Cincinnati Reds "Big Red Machine" teams of the 1970s, Tony Pérez drove in more than 100 runs in seven seasons, helping Cincinnati win five division titles, four pennants, and two World Series championships. He was born Atanasio Pérez on May 14, 1942, in Camagüey, Cuba. Pérez grew up among the sugarcane fields of Camagüey idolizing Cuban baseball star MINNIE MIÑOSO and hoping to follow his path to playing professionally. Pérez overcame his rail thin physique (6'2", 147 pounds) as a teenageer by demonstrating an impressive ability to hit. This skill earned the 17-year-old Pérez a ticket out of the sugar processing factory and onto the roster of the Havana Sugar Kings, the Cuban minor league affiliate of the Cincinnati Reds.

In 1960, Pérez was sent to play for the Reds' minor league team in Geneva, New York. Like many other Latino players, Pérez struggled with being so far away from home and having to adjust to a new culture. He later reflected, "To hear words like 'cut off man,' 'go to first,' 'go to third,' simple things like that . . . I had to learn how to play the game all over again in English." However, by his second year with Geneva, Pérez had added power to his body that resulted in outstanding offensive statistics.

Pérez made his major league debut as a first baseman on July 26, 1964. The right-handed hitting Pérez platooned at first base through 1966, boasting solid but unspectacular numbers. He won the full-time first base job in 1967 spring training and proved that he was worthy by batting .290, with 26 home runs and 102 runs batted in (RBIs). Pérez earned the first of his seven career All-Star game appearances and launched a 15th-inning home run off Oakland's Jim "Catfish" Hunter to lead the National League (NL) to victory in the All-Star game, which earned him the contest's Most Valuable Player award.

Pérez's 102 RBIs in 1966 began a string of 11 consecutive seasons with more than 90. Pérez continued his success in 1968 (.282 batting average, 18 home runs, 92 RBIs) and in 1969 (.294, 37, and 122) as he joined other rising Cincinnati stars including Johnny Bench and Pete Rose in forming a potent line-up. Powered by Pérez's .317 batting average, 40 homeruns, and 119 RBIs, the 1970 Reds earned only their second postseason appearance in 30 years, eventually falling to the Pittsburgh Pirates in the National League Championship Series.

A sub-par year for both Pérez and the Reds in 1971 was followed by one of the greatest five-year runs ever enjoyed by a major league team, as Cincinnati won four division titles (1972, 1973, 1975, and 1976), three pennants (1972, 1975, and 1976), and two World Series championships (1975 and 1976). At the foundation of this success was the steady batting and leadership of Pérez, who averaged 28 home runs and 98 RBIs during these years.

The words of his Hall of Fame teammate catcher Johnny Bench and his Reds manager and future Hall of Famer Sparky Anderson reflect the admiration he garnered. Bench explained, "Tony cast the net over the entire team with his attitude. He was always up, always had a sense of humor." Anderson added, "He's the best clutch hitter I've ever seen."

Highlighting the Big Red Machine dynasty in the 1970s were the World Series championship seasons of 1975 and 1976. Pérez's knack for timely hitting was on display in both years. His sixth-inning home run off Bill Lee of the Boston Red Sox helped Cincinnati rally from a 3-0 deficit in the decisive game seven of the World Series for a 4-3 victory. In 1976, he batted .312 as the Reds demolished the New York Yankees 4-0.

Despite his vital importance to the Reds' success, Cincinnati traded Pérez to the Montreal Expos in an effort to save money and infuse youth following the 1976 season. Pérez had three productive seasons in Montreal from 1977 through 1979, before signing as a free agent with the Boston Red Sox.

He enjoyed a solid 1980 campaign in Boston but suffered through injuries and slumps over the next two seasons. Pérez was then a part-time player for the NL champion Philadelphia Phillies in 1983, before returning to Cincinnati, where he played the last three seasons of his 23-year career.

Pérez retired with the most home runs (379) and RBIs (1,652) by a Latino major leaguer (the home run total was later surpassed by JOSE CANSECO). He remained in the game as a coach and served as interim manager for the Reds in 1993 and the Florida Marlins in 2001. In May 2000, the Reds retired his number 24 jersey, and a few months later, he was inducted into the National Baseball Hall of Fame in Cooperstown, New York.

Further Reading

Fimrite, Ron. "Adios to a Big Red Machinist." *Sports Illustrated,* 29 September 1986, p. 34.

"Induction Speeches: Tony Perez." National Baseball Hall of Fame Web site. Available online. URL: http://www.baseballhalloffame.org/hof_weekend/2000/speeches/perez_tony.htm. Downloaded on January 20, 2006.

"Tony Perez." Baseball Reference Web site. Available online. URL: http://www.baseball-reference.com/p/pereztoO1.shtml. Downloaded on January 20, 2006.

"Tony Perez." Latino Legends in Sports Web site. Available online. URL: http://www.latinosportslegends.com/tonyperez.htm. Downloaded on January 20, 2006.

Perez, Yuliana
(1981–   ) *sprinter*

A top triple jumper and long jumper for Cuba despite being born in the United States, Yuliana Perez overcame a tragic childhood to eventually become an American track and field competitor at the Olympics. She was born on July 21, 1981, in Tuscon, Arizona. By the time Perez was three years old, her father (who had immigrated to the United States from Cuba during the Mariel boat lift of 1980, in which Cuban dictator Fidel Castro allowed thousands of criminals and mental patients to escape to the United States) was in a Georgia prison, and her mother, also a Cuban immigrant, had been murdered in a drive-by shooting in San Diego, California. After two unhappy years living in foster homes in the United States, Perez was sent to Cuba to live with her paternal grandfather in 1986.

In Cuba, Perez developed into one of the island nation's greatest female athletes. As a member of the Cuban national track and field team, Perez won a silver medal at the 1997 Junior Pan-American Games. However, when Perez refused to renounce her U.S. citizenship as a condition for a spot on the 2000 Cuban Olympic team, she was kicked off the team and expelled from high school because she was considered a defection risk.

At age 18, Perez convinced the officials in the Swiss Embassy in Havana to give her a passport so that she could return to the United States. She then left Cuba and returned to Tucson, where she worked as a waitress. While riding a Tucson city bus, Perez struck up a conversation with the bus driver, Guillermo Diaz, who happened to be a runner and a friend of the Pima Community College jump coach, Mariel Pena. Within days, Perez met with Pena and the Pima track and field head coach, and she quickly received a scholarship. Perez explained, "I was reborn."

As a freshman at Pima, Perez won the national junior college triple jump and long jump championships. A few weeks later, Perez shocked national observers by finishing second in the triple jump at the USA Outdoor Championships, ahead of American record-holder Sheila Hudson. Perez continued to excel over the course of the next few years, winning the USA Outdoor Triple Jump championship in 2002 and 2003. Also in 2003, Perez finished second in the triple jump at the Pan-American Games in the Dominican Republic.

Perez qualified for the 2004 Olympics by clearing 46'8¼" in the triple jump in June 2003. But in 2004, after refusing a track scholarship to the University of Arizona so that she could train in Arkansas to live near her boyfriend (former college triple jump champion Melvin Lister), Perez performed poorly at the Olympic trials in Sacramento, California.

Still seeking her confidence after her recent sub-par performances and struggling with a hamstring injury, Perez finished a disappointing 12th in the triple jump competition trials at the 2004 Olympics in Athens, Greece, with a jump of less than 45 feet. Though discouraged by the outcome in 2004, Perez remains focused on the 2008 Olympics in Beijing, China, and her ultimate goal of a triple jump of 50 feet.

Further Reading
Hansen, Greg. "Perez Reaches Out for Help." *Arizona Daily Star,* 18 July 2004.
"Perez, Yuliana." U.S. Olympic Team Web site. Available online. URL: http://www.usoc.org/26_1359. htm. Downloaded on January 20, 2006.

Pérez del Solar, Gaby
(Gabriela Pérez del Solar)
(1968–   ) *volleyball player*

The player widely considered the greatest South American ever to compete in women's volleyball, Gaby Pérez del Solar led Peru to the silver medal at the 1988 Olympics before enjoying a stellar professional career in Europe. Gabriela Pérez del Solar was born on June 8, 1968, in Lima, Peru. She was a very tall and lanky girl whose early athletic efforts were marked more by clumsiness than by excellence. By the time Pérez del Solar was 18, she had sprouted to a height of 6'4" and had refined her volleyball skills to the point that she earned a spot on the Peruvian national women's volleyball team.

In her first major international event, the 1986 World Championships in Czechoslovakia, the woman affectionately referred to as "Gaby" became a sensation due to her height and unique blocking ability. Though one of the youngest players in the entire tournament, Pérez del Solar played a critical role in Peru's surprising bronze medal–winning performance.

Pérez del Solar continued to boost her reputation as one of the world's top young volleyball players in 1987, when she led the Peruvian team to a silver medal at the Pan-American Games in Indianapolis, Indiana. Though only 20 years old, Pérez del Solar had extended her game beyond that of being a great blocker to become a powerful offensive force and outstanding all-around player and emotional leader.

These qualities were in evidence at the 1988 Olympics in Seoul, South Korea, where Pérez del Solar powered Peru to shocking victories over the United States and Japan, setting up a gold medal match with the Soviet Union. Peru won the first two sets over the heavily favored Soviets and led 12-6 in the third set before losing the match 3-2.

The scrappy success story of the Pérez del Solar–led Peruvian team inspired the people of Peru. However, losses of veteran players prevented the team from repeating previous achievements despite Pérez del Solar's unquestioned dominance. The team finished in fourth place in the 1990 Goodwill Games in Seattle, Washington, and finished a disappointing sixth place in the 1990 World Championships in China.

Peru's hopes of qualifying for the 1992 Olympics in Barcelona, Spain, were dashed in the 1991 World Cup loss to the United States. Pérez del Solar, who began playing professionally in Italy in 1992, played once more for Peru in the 1993 Continental Championship. She was at the top of her game and led Peru to a championship match win over Brazil for women's volleyball supremacy in South America.

Pérez del Solar returned to play professionally in Italy throughout the 1990s. Soon after the turn of the century, she retired returned to Peru, and went into business with her brother constructing and owning a hotel near the famed Inca ruins of Machu Picchu.

Further Reading

Gaby Perez del Solar Web site. Available online. URL: http://www.gabyperezdelsolar.com/bio/gaby_e.html. Downloaded on January 20, 2006.

Smith, Michael. "Women's Volleyball Is Big League in Peru." *Washington Post*, 12 September 1986.

Pincay, Laffit, Jr.
(1946–) *jockey*

The holder of the career victory record among jockeys, Laffit Pincay, Jr., won the Kentucky Derby once and the Belmont Stakes three times and ranked in the top 10 in purse earnings an astounding 24 consecutive years between 1966 and 1989. He was born on December 29, 1946, in Panama City, Panama. His parents divorced when he was a child, and he moved with his father, Laffit Sr., to Venezuela, where the elder Pincay worked as a jockey.

Laffit began working at a horse track as a hot walker (person who walks horses to cool them off after a workout or race) and groom at age 15 without pay to gain experience in horse racing. Over the next two years, he learned to ride and earned his jockey license at age 17. On May 16, 1964, in only his second race, Pincay returned to Panama and won his first victory as a jockey aboard Huelen at Presidente Remon Racetrack. He followed with many other victories, becoming known within just a few years as Panama's top jockey.

In 1966, Pincay was sponsored by legendary thoroughbred owner and breeder Fred Hooper to come to the United States and ride under contract for $500 a month. Though Pincay spoke only Spanish (later explaining that he learned English by watching game shows), he quickly and successfully adjusted to his new country. Racing primarily at Arlington Park in Chicago, Illinois, Pincay won eight of his first 11 races.

With this auspicious beginning, Pincay's American racing career continued in the same vein throughout the 1970s. Racing primarily on the famed southern California race tracks of Santa Anita, Hollywood Park, and Del Mar, Pincay won the Eclipse Award (given to horse racing's best jockey) four times during the decade—1971, 1973, 1974, and 1979.

He was the leading money-winning jockey each year from 1970 through 1974 and in 1979, and he was the leading jockey in races in 1971. Pincay's consistent excellence led to his distinction of being the youngest person ever to earn a place in horse racing's Hall of Fame when he was enshrined in 1975 at age 28.

Pincay's impressive achievements continued throughout the 1980s. He won the Belmont Stakes, the third jewel in horse racing's Triple Crown, three consecutive times from 1982 to 1984 aboard Conquistador Cielo, Caveat, and Swale, respectively. In 1984, Pincay rode Swale to the jockey's only Kentucky Derby victory.

Along with his enormous success, Pincay also dealt with severe adversity during his racing career. Standing 5'1" and usually weighing between 115 and 120 pounds, Pincay was considered relatively large for a jockey. He struggled with his weight for years before finally discovering an effective nutritional plan. During his career, he also endured 11 broken ribs, two spinal fractures, two punctured lungs, and two broken thumbs.

In 1985, at the height of his career, his wife, Linda, committed suicide. Saying that racing was the best way for him to deal with that loss, he was back competing within a month, displaying his combination of strength, finesse, and skillful finishing charges that earned him the reputation as one of horse racing's greatest jockeys of all time.

Pincay continued to race into his early 50s, racking up victories that put him within grasp of Willie Shoemaker's career record of 8,333 wins. On December 17, 1999, at Hollywood Park Racetrack, Pincay rode Irish Nip for his 8,334th win, surpassing Shoemaker, who had held the mark for more than 29 years. Following this record-breaking race, Shoemaker said of Pincay, "He's been a credit to racing. He's conducted himself with dignity all through his career. He races in rain, hail, sleet, and snow. He wouldn't take off like most jocks would. I'm very proud of him." Pincay celebrated his historic feat by forgoing his standard 850-calories-a-day diet to dine on filet mignon, a baked potato, asparagus, cake, and champagne.

Even with such great accomplishments, Pincay's racing career would not end for another three and a half years. On April 29, 2003, at age 56, Pincay announced his retirement as a jockey. Four weeks earlier he had been tossed from his horse, and though he expected to return within a week, it was discovered that he had actually suffered a broken neck. Pincay followed the advice of doctors who believed that his spine was not stable enough to continue racing. His final victory tally in almost 50,000 races over 35 years stands at an all-time record of 9,531.

Further Reading

Harris, Beth. "Neck Injury Forces Jockey Pincay to Retire at 56." *Chicago Sun Times,* 30 April 2003, p. 150.

"Laffit Pincay." National Museum of Racing and Hall of Fame Web site. Available online. URL: http://www.racingmuseum.org/hall/jockey.asp?ID=213. Downloaded on July 1, 2005.

"Pincay Breaks Tie with Shoemaker." ESPN Web site. Available online. URL: http://espn.go.com/horse/news/1999/1210/225163.html. Downloaded on July 1, 2005.

Shulman, Lenny. *Ride of Their Lives: The Triumphs and Turmoil of Today's Top Jockeys.* Lexington, Ky.: Eclipse Press, 2002.

Pineda-Boutte, Leticia
(Leticia Pineda, Lety Pineda)
(1976–) *softball player*

The only collegiate softball player to be named All-American at three different positions (catcher, third base, and first base), Leticia Pineda-Boutte helped lead the University of Arizona to two national championships in the 1990s. She was born Leticia Pineda on March 30, 1976, in Tucson, Arizona. Her father, a former Minor League Baseball player, volunteered as a coach of local children, including his daughter, who was affectionately known as "Lety." She attended Tucson's Desert View High School, where her excellence on the softball diamond earned her an athletic scholarship to attend her hometown college and softball powerhouse, the University of Arizona.

In 1996, Pineda's sophomore season, she was named All-American as a catcher and helped the University of Arizona Wildcats earn the National Collegiate Athletic Association (NCAA) championship. The following season, she was named All-American at third base and again played a critical role in leading Arizona to another national title. In 1998, Pineda's senior season, she was named All-American at first base and helped Arizona reach the college world series tournament.

During her career at Arizona, Pineda totaled some of the most impressive career statistics in college softball history. She hit 52 home runs (10th in NCAA history), and her 240 runs batted in (RBIs) rank sixth all time. Both her .357 career batting average and .687 slugging percentage place her among the top 20 all time in those categories. Her 96 RBIs in 1996 was the fifth-highest season RBI total, and her 20 home runs was among the top-20 single-season marks in NCAA history.

In 1998, she also became the first member of her family to graduate from college after earning a bachelor's degree in humanities. She then played one season for the now-defunct Tampa Bay Firestix in the National Pro Fastpitch Softball

League. Pineda next began her career as a softball coach at the University of Colorado–Colorado Springs, leading that team to its first postseason appearance.

In 2001, she married Shawn Boutte and the next year accepted an assistant coach position with Creighton University in Omaha, Nebraska. While there, she worked primarily with the Creighton pitching staff, which ranked sixth in the nation in earned run average.

In 2004, Pineda-Boutte was hired to be an assistant coach at Purdue University in West Lafayette, Indiana. That same year, she was also inducted into the University of Arizona Hall of Fame.

Further Reading
"Latina Athletes." U.S. Olympic Team Web site. Available online. URL: http://www.usolympicteam. com/11730_31762.htm. Downloaded on July 1, 2005.
"Leticia Pineda-Boutte." Purdue Intercollegiate Athletics Web site. Available online. URL: http://purduesports.cstv.com/sports/wsoftbl/mtt/pinedaboutte_leticia00.html. Downloaded on July 1, 2005.

Piquet, Nelson
(Nelson Piquet Souto Maior)
(1952–) *auto racer*

An intensely competitive maverick whose success on the racetrack and dashing lifestyle made headlines, Nelson Piquet won three Formula One championships during the 1980s. He was born Nelson Piquet Souto Maior on August 17, 1952, in Rio de Janeiro, Brazil. The son of the Brazilian health minister, Estacio Souto Maior, Piquet spent much of his youth in Brazil's capital, Brasília, where he developed an early skill for racing and tennis.

At age 16, Piquet was sent to high school in San Francisco, California, to further his tennis career, but he instead became increasingly interested in racing. He returned to Brazil and soon began racing carts, using his mother Clotilde's maiden name of Piquet to keep his activity hidden from his family. Piquet's secret did not last long, as his consistent winning led to attention in the Brazilian Cart Championship in 1971.

Piquet's father continued to refuse to support his son's racing career, insisting that Nelson attend college. Piquet studied engineering and management but continued to race, winning another Brazilian Cart Championship in 1972 and the nation's Super Vee title in 1976.

In 1976, Piquet decided to move to Europe to race on the Formula Three circuit. His success in the late 1970s in Formula Three led to a transition to Formula One racing with the Brabham Team, whose owner, Bernie Ecclestone, valued Piquet's speed, mistake-free driving, and innovation. Piquet became Brabham's number one driver in 1979, and he won his first Formula One race, the Long Beach Grand Prix, in 1980.

Piquet won the German, San Marino, and Argentine Grand Prix races in 1981 on his way to his first Formula One championship that year. He repeated as champion in 1983, powered by wins in the Italian, Brazilian, and European Grand Prix races. He continued to rank among the most prominent drivers in the world throughout the 1980s and won his third Formula One title in 1987 while racing for the Williams' Team, earning victories in the Hungarian, German, and Italian Grand Prix races.

In 1988, Piquet switched to the faltering Lotus Racing Team and failed to gain a win that year or in 1989. Piquet signed with the Benetton in 1990 and earned wins in Japan and Australia before finishing his career in 1991, gaining his last win in Montreal over longtime rival Nigel Mansell.

Piquet tried Indy Car racing in 1992 but crashed during a qualifying run for the Indianapolis 500 and badly injured his foot. Since 1993, Piquet has competed in a few racing events, mainly in Brazil, though his focus has been on recreation rather than championships.

Since 2000, Piquet, who over the years has gained, squandered, and regained fortunes in various business interests, has been an active supporter of the Formula 1 racing career of his son, Nelson Piquet, Jr. The elder Piquet's legacy as one of Formula One's greatest racers remains strong, reflected in his 23 career wins and 93 top-five finishes in 204 Grand Prix races.

Further Reading
"Drivers: Nelson Piquet." Grand Prix Web site. Available online. URL: http://www.grandprix.com/gpe/drv-piqnel.html. Downloaded on January 20, 2006.

"Nelson Piquet." Motorsport Publishing Group Web site. Available online. URL: http://www.ddavid.com/formula1/piquet_bio.htm. Downloaded on January 20, 2006.

Plunkett, Jim
(James Plunkett)
(1947–   ) *football player*

The winner of the 1970 Heisman Trophy, 1971 American Football Conference (AFC) Rookie of the Year award, and Super Bowl XV Most Valuable Player (MVP) award, Jim Plunkett demonstrated remarkable resilience on and off the field to become, in the words of Oakland Raiders owner Al Davis, "one of the great comeback stories of our time." He was born James Plunkett on December 5, 1947, in San Jose, California. He grew up in nearby Santa Clara and later returned to San Jose.

Plunkett's parents, William and Carmella, each had Mexican and Irish heritage, and both suffered from blindness. Jim was a talented athlete who helped supplement his father's meager earnings as a newsstand vendor by working at a gas station and delivering newspapers. As a senior at San Jose's James Lick High School, Plunkett led his football team to an unbeaten season and accepted an athletic scholarship to attend Stanford University in nearby Palo Alto, a short drive away from his family.

A large (6'3", 200 pounds) and agile quarterback with a strong throwing arm, Plunkett's progress was immediately stalled by surgery for a benign tumor in his neck as a freshman. The next spring, Stanford's coach John Ralston suggested Plunkett change positions to defensive end. Plunkett rejected the idea, and after being red-shirted (not playing but retaining a year of eligibility) in 1967, he earned the starting quarterback job in 1968, setting a Pacific Eight (Pac Eight) Conference record with 2,156 yards passing.

In his junior year, 1969, Plunkett set conference records for touchdown passes (20), passing yards (2,673), and total offense (2,786 yards). Though he was eligible to enter his name in the National Football League (NFL) draft and needed money to help support his now-widowed father, Plunkett remained at Stanford for his senior year, continuing his outstanding play and leading Stanford to an 8-3 record and the Pac Eight Championship.

He capped the season by defeating previously unbeaten, top-ranked, and heavily favored Ohio State University in a 27-17 upset in the 1971 Rose Bowl. A few weeks prior to that Rose Bowl victory, Plunkett was awarded the Heisman Trophy in what was known as "The Year of the Quarterback," receiving more votes than runners up and future NFL stars Joe Theismann and Archie Manning.

Plunkett's legendary college career concluded with him holding the National Collegiate Athletic Association (NCAA) record for passing yards (7,544) and total offense (7,887 yards). His dominance on the gridiron attracted the praise of opposing coaches, including University of California–Los Angeles (UCLA) coach Tommy Prothro, who said, "Plunkett is the best drop back passer I've ever seen in college football. He has real strength and good speed. If you go all out to blitz him, he'll eat you alive." Oregon State University coach Jerry Frei captured the thoughts of countless

others, noting with relief, "I'm just happy to see him graduate."

Plunkett was the first overall selection in the 1971 NFL draft by the Boston (later New England) Patriots. Starting in his first year, Plunkett led the Patriots to a 6-8 record, their best mark in five years, throwing for 2,158 yards and 19 touchdowns and earning the AFC Rookie of the Year award.

The next season was a disaster for Plunkett, as he threw 25 interceptions with only eight touchdowns and often found himself at the bottom of a pile of defenders as the Patriots fell to a record of 3-11. Plunkett suffered several knee and shoulder injuries while playing for mediocre Patriot teams over the next three seasons before he was traded to the San Francisco 49ers prior to the 1976 season.

Quarterback Jim Plunkett is shown here on the sideline during Stanford's 27-17 victory over Ohio State in the 1971 Rose Bowl. *(George Long/LPI/WireImage.com)*

Playing before friends and family in northern California, Plunkett hoped to revive the 49ers, but inconsistency and injuries led to frustration and his release after only two seasons. Now 30 years old and years removed from his last sustained success, Plunkett considered retiring but instead signed a three-year contract with the Oakland Raiders. Serving as a backup, Plunkett did not play in 1978 and threw only 15 passes in 1979. Expecting little or no playing time in his third year in Oakland, Plunkett requested a trade, but that request was rejected by Raiders owner Al Davis.

When Oakland quarterback Dan Pastorini broke his leg in the season's fifth week, Plunkett got a chance to start again. With Plunkett at the helm and under the tutelage of coach and former Raiders quarterback Tom Flores, the Raiders won nine of their 11 remaining regular season games. Plunkett won the NFL's Comeback Player of the Year award before leading Oakland to four post-season wins, including a 34-27 victory over San Diego in the AFC Championship in which Plunkett completed 14 of 18 passes for 261 yards and two touchdowns.

The Oakland Raiders then won Super Bowl XV 27-10 over the Philadelphia Eagles. In that game, Plunkett completed 13 of 21 passes for 261 yards, with three touchdowns and no interceptions, earning the game's MVP award and completing one of the sport's most impressive and inspiring resurrections.

Plunkett battled injuries over the next few seasons but managed to again lead the Raiders (which relocated to Los Angeles in 1982) to the championship as Plunkett passed for 172 yards and a touchdown in a 38-9 rout over the Washington Redskins in Super Bowl XVIII. Plunkett remained with the Raiders from 1984 through 1986 but made only 17 starts due to an assortment of injuries. After missing the entire 1987 season because of injuries, Plunkett was released by the Raiders at age 40 prior to the 1988 campaign, at which point Plunkett retired.

Afterward, Plunkett, who had a reputation for reticence as a player, worked for the Raiders radio broadcasting team and gave speeches to corporate audiences. Though severely hobbled by injuries from his playing days, Plunkett owns a beer distributorship and lives in northern California, the region he was born in and in which he enjoyed his greatest successes as a high school, college, and professional quarterback.

Further Reading

Carter, Bob. "Plunkett Kept Coming Back." ESPN Classic Web site. Available online. URL: http://espn.go.com/classic/biography/s/Plunkett_Jim.html. Downloaded on January 20, 2006.

"Jim Plunkett." Pro Football Reference Web site. Available online. URL: http://www.pro-football-reference.com/players/PlunJi00.htm. Downloaded on January 20, 2006.

Silver, Michael. "Painful Reminders." *Sports Illustrated*, 11 July 2005, p. 130.

"Super Bowl MVPs: Super Bowl XV." Super Bowl Web site. Available online. URL: http://www.superbowl.com/history/mvps/game/sbxv. Downloaded on January 20, 2006.

Poll, Claudia

(1972–   ) *swimmer*

The only Costa Rican ever to win a gold medal at the Olympics, Claudia Poll established three swimming world records and won three Olympic medals before a two-year suspension for steroid use tarnished her reputation as one of the world's best female swimmers. She was born on December 21, 1972, in Managua, Nicaragua. Poll's parents were German immigrants who decided to leave Nicaragua following a devastating earthquake in 1972 and subsequent political instability.

The Polls moved to Caliari, Costa Rica, to raise Claudia and her older sister, Sylvia. Claudia began taking swimming lessons at age seven and demonstrated tremendous talent and dedication in the pool.

By 1988 (the year her older sister, Sylvia, won Costa Rica's first Olympic medal when she earned a silver in Seoul, South Korea), Poll had set seven Central American records in Caribbean swimming competitions. Poll's powerful swimming physique (6'2" and 155 pounds) and her disciplined training techniques helped make her one of the top competitors in the world throughout the first half of the 1990s.

Poll's greatest success to date came at the 1996 Olympics in Atlanta, Georgia, where she earned Costa Rica's first gold medal in Olympic competition by upsetting German world champion Franziska Van Almsick to win the 200-meter freestyle event. Poll returned to the Olympics in Sydney, Australia, in 2000 and won two bronze medals, in the 200-meter freestyle and the 400-meter freestyle.

Between these events, Poll described what she has gained in swimming beyond the medals and accolades: "To have discipline, patience, and constancy are all important things that I have learned. I also learned to win, but the most important thing is that I learned not to win."

In 2002, however, Poll was determined to have used a banned steroid in competition and was suspended for four years. She challenged her punishment, claiming that the testing procedure was faulty and that she was in fact innocent. Her suspension was not overturned, though it was reduced, allowing Poll to compete in the 2004 Olympics in Athens, Greece. At the 2004 Olympics, Poll again participated in the 200-meter and 400-meter freestyle events, finishing in 10th and ninth place, respectively.

Further Reading

"Claudia Poll." Info Costa Rica Web site. Available online. URL: http://www.infocostarica.com/people/claudia.html. Downloaded on January 20, 2006.

"Press Release: Swimming—Doping." Sportrecht Web site. Available online. URL: http://www.sportrecht.org/EU-Recht/PollTAS04-02-03.htm. Downloaded on January 20, 2006.

Pujols, Albert
(José Alberto Pujols)
(1980–) *baseball player*

A clutch hitter whose quick hands, disciplined batting approach, and blistering swing helped him win the 2001 National League (NL) Rookie of the Year and 2005 NL Most Valuable Player (MVP) awards, Albert Pujols has produced offensive statistics in his first five major league seasons that rival or surpass those of all-time baseball greats. He was born José Alberto Pujols on January 16, 1980, in Santo Domingo, Dominican Republic. Pujols was raised primarily by his grandmother, América, though he admired his father, Bienvenido Pujols, who had been a star pitcher in the Dominican Republic.

By age six, Pujols was playing baseball in the dusty fields near his home. At age 16, Pujols moved with his father to New York City, where several relatives had already settled. Within a year, concerns about the expenses and crime of New York City led Pujols and his dad to move to Independence, Missouri, a small town near Kansas City, Missouri, best known for being the hometown of President Harry S. Truman. Pujols attended Fort Osage High School in Independence and starred on the baseball team, standing out because of his size of 6'3" and 200 lbs., impressive work ethic, and powerful stroke.

Following high school, Pujols played for one season at Maplewoods Community College in Missouri. In Major League Baseball's amateur draft, he was selected in the 13th round by the St. Louis Cardinals but did not sign with them until they significantly upgraded their bonus offer. Pujols, a former shortstop, tore through the minor leagues, playing third base and demonstrating an uncanny ability to hit for a high average, as well as power, while showing what would later be known as his trademark discipline at the plate, regularly attracting walks and rarely striking out.

Although the Cardinals expected to place Pujols on their AAA club to begin the 2001

Albert Pujols launches a ninth-inning home run to lead the St. Louis Cardinals to victory in game five of the 2005 National League Championship Series. *(Mike Ehrmann/WireImage.com)*

season, his performance and leadership during spring training earned him a ticket for the majors. He amazed everyone by posting one of the best rookie seasons in Major League Baseball history, leading the Cardinals in games played (161), batting average (.329), home runs (37), runs batted in (RBIs; 130), and runs (112). St. Louis manager Tony LaRussa praised the 21-year-old Pujols late in 2001, saying, "I've had many great players have MVP caliber seasons. Carlton Fisk, Harold Baines, JOSE CANSECO, Mark McGwire, Rickey Henderson . . . but what this kid has done is the greatest performance of any positioned player I've ever had." Pittsburgh Pirates manager Lloyd McClendon added, "I've never seen anything like it. He's quick to the ball with his

bat, he hits to all fields, he rarely goes out of the strike zone, and no situation seems to rattle him." After leading the Cardinals to the playoffs in 2001, Pujols became only the ninth player in history to be unanimously voted NL Rookie of the Year.

In 2002, Pujols continued his dominance as he propelled the Cardinals to the National League Championship Series (NLCS), where they fell to the San Francisco Giants 4-1. Now primarily playing left field after rotating among left field, right field, third base, and first base as a rookie, Pujols batted .314, hit 34 home runs, and drove in 127 runs, finishing second to San Francisco's Barry Bonds in MVP voting. In 2003, Pujols led the NL in batting average (.359), runs (137), hits (212), doubles (51), and total bases (394), again ranking second to Bonds in voting for MVP and earning his second All-Star Game nod.

Prior to the 2004 season, St. Louis signed Pujols to a seven-year, $100 million contract. Displaying the same diligent approach to the game that helped make him one of baseball's most dangerous hitters, Pujols enjoyed another stellar season. Now employing his soft hands and nimble feet as a solid defensive first baseman, Pujols led the NL in runs (133) and total bases (389), while ranking among the top five in batting (.331), home runs (46), and RBIs (123). Pujols was again recognized as an All-Star and eventually finished third in MVP balloting.

Pujols then led the Cardinals to the World Series by batting .500 with four home runs and nine RBIs in the NLCS, as the Cardinals came back from a 3-2 deficit to defeat the Houston Astros in seven games. Despite his .333 batting average in the World Series, Pujols and the Cardinals were swept in four games by the Boston Red Sox.

In 2005, Pujols had another fantastic season, again ranking in the top five in the NL in batting (.330), home runs (41), and RBIs (117) and helping the Cardinals to the best record in the majors. After batting a stratospheric .556 in a NL division series victory over the San Diego Padres, Pujols staved off elimination with St. Louis down 3-1 to the Houston Astros in the NLCS when he launched a prodigious three-run blast with two outs in the ninth inning and the Cardinals trailing 4-2. The Cardinals were eliminated by the Astros in game six, but a few weeks later Pujols's excellence was recognized when he was voted the winner of the NL MVP.

Pujols's 25 home runs and 65 RBIs in just the opening two months of the 2006 season made it clear that the MVP award and the lucrative contract did nothing to diminish his motivation or ability. Although he eventually missed nearly 20 games due to injury, Pujols finished 2006 ranked third in the NL in batting average (.331) and second in home runs (49) and RBIs (137). Powered by the production and leadership of Pujols, the Cardinals won the 2006 World Series, defeating the Detroit Tigers four games to one.

After his first six seasons in the majors, Pujols has established himself not only as a superstar of his era but also one of the best young players in the history of Major League Baseball. His cumulative hits and home run totals after six full seasons outpace those of legends Ted Williams, Hank Aaron, and Joe DiMaggio.

Further Reading

"Albert Pujols." Jock Bio Web site. Available online. URL: http://www.jockbio.com/Bios/Pujols/Pujols_bio.html. Downloaded on January 20, 2006.

"Albert Pujols." St. Louis Cardinals Web site. Available online. URL: http://stlouis.cardinals.mlb.com/NASApp/mlb/team/player.jsp?player_id=405395. Downloaded on January 20, 2006.

"Pujols Signs Cards' Richest Contract Ever." MSNBC Web site. Available online. URL: http://msnbc.msn.com/id/4201009. Downloaded on January 20, 2006.

Verducci, Tom. "Wild Card: While Powering St. Louis Toward a Playoff Berth, MVP Candidate Albert Pujols May Be Having the Greatest Rookie Year Ever." *Sports Illustrated,* 1 October 2001, p. 44.

R

Ramírez, Manny
(Manuel Ramírez)
(1972–) *baseball player*

A prolific hitter who ranks second in career grand slams (21) and placed in the top 10 American League (AL) Most Valuable Player (MVP) voting each year between 1998 and 2005, Manny Ramírez was the MVP of the 2004 World Series, when the Boston Red Sox won their first world championship in 86 years. He was born Manuel Ramírez on May 30, 1972, in Santo Domingo, Dominican Republic. He spent his boyhood in Santo Domingo, the son of a cab driver father, Aristide, and seamstress mother, Onelcida.

When he was 13 years old, Ramírez moved with his family to the heavily Dominican Washington Heights neighborhood of New York City. Though he struggled with learning English and adjusting to a new environment, Ramírez found comfort in playing baseball. A strong right-handed hitter with an explosive swing, Ramírez led George Washington High School to three consecutive Manhattan Division Championships (1988, 1989, and 1990) and as a senior was named the New York City Public Schools High School Player of the Year.

In 1991, the Cleveland Indians selected Ramírez with the 13th overall pick in the major league amateur draft. He weathered minor league pitching and earned a promotion to the major league on September 2, 1993. The next night,

Ramírez thrilled the throngs of Dominican-flag-waving friends and family in attendance at New York's Yankee Stadium by hitting a home run and two doubles. In 1994, Ramírez appeared in only 94 games for the Indians but managed to hit 17 home runs with 60 runs batted in (RBIs), earning second place in AL Rookie of the Year voting.

Ramírez became Cleveland's full-time right fielder in 1995 and remained a key cog of the Indians' powerful lineup through the 2000 season. During those six seasons, Ramírez helped lead the Indians to five straight AL Central Division titles (1995–99) and two AL pennants (1995 and 1997).

Ramírez's ability to hit for average and power made him one of the most dangerous hitters in the majors throughout his years in Cleveland, as he posted yearly batting averages ranging from .294 to .351 and RBI totals ranging from 88 to a 1998 league-leading 165, when he spent much of the season threatening Hack Wilson's major league single-season RBI record of 191 set in 1930.

In addition to his outstanding play, Ramírez was also attractive to fans and media because of his personality, which was regularly described as free spirited, enigmatic, spacy, and flaky. Stories lending credence to such characterizations abounded: He occasionally had mental lapses during games and stood out on the field with dyed, long curly hair and a jersey worn with only the bottom few buttons fastened. He was well liked by teammates, though few felt they really knew him.

Commenting on Ramírez's unique and occasionally puzzling personality, Indians teammate Sandy Alomar, Jr., said, "Manny never gets upset. The rest of us grind and fight ourselves. Manny never worries. If he doesn't get a hit, he thinks 'no problem—next at bat I'll get one.' It's the perfect attitude, but you can only have it when you're as good as he is."

Prior to the 2001 season, the free-agent Ramírez signed an eight-year, $160 million contract with the Boston Red Sox. Although his devastating batting stroke, in which he kept his head tucked patiently before unleashing his quick wrists and exploding through the pitch, produced stellar seasons (including an AL-leading .349 batting average in 2002), Ramírez was not completely embraced by Boston's fans, who often viewed his eccentricities as indicative of apathy and contributing to the team's underachieving ways.

In 2003, Ramírez batted .325, hit 37 home runs, and drove in 104 runs, but Boston lost the American League Championship Series (ALCS) to the New York Yankees in a heartbreaking seventh game. Following that season, Ramírez was dangled in three team trade talks that almost brought ALEX RODRIGUEZ to the Red Sox.

In 2004, Ramírez led the AL in home runs with 43 while batting .308 with 131 RBIs. In the playoffs, Ramírez had seven RBIs in a three-game sweep of the Anaheim Angels, and after the Red Sox came back from a three-game deficit in the ALCS against the Yankees, won the MVP of the World Series by batting .412 with four RBIs in a four-game sweep of the St. Louis Cardinals.

Ramírez posted stellar numbers again in 2005, ranking third in the AL in RBIs, with 144, and joining Hall of Famer Carl Yastrzemski as the only Red Sox players to hit 40 or more home runs in three different seasons. However, as he had done previously, Ramírez requested to be traded from the Red Sox. The team, wary of such requests yet eager to shed his enormous paycheck, was willing to comply, though they recognized the risk. One Red Sox executive explained, "We're talking about

a premier hitter in the prime of his career. That's a lot of offense to replace. It's not easy."

In 2006, as in the past, the Red Sox held on to Ramírez, and he responded with solid offensive production, helping the Red Sox begin the season with one of the best records in Major League Baseball. Injuries slowed Ramírez toward the end of the season as Boston fell out of playoff contention, though he still managed to rank eighth in the AL in home runs (35), batting average (.321), and first in on-base percentage (.439).

Further Reading

"About Manny." Manny Ramirez Web site. Available online. URL: http://www.mannyramirez.com/about.htm. Downloaded on January 20, 2006.

"Manny Ramirez." Boston Red Sox Web site. Available online. URL: http://mlb.mlb.com/NASApp/mlb/team/player.jsp?player_id=120903. Downloaded on January 20, 2006.

Weinreb, Michael. "A Manny among Men." *Sporting News,* 21 June 1999, p. 12.

Further Viewing

Faith Rewarded—The Historic Season of the 2004 Boston Red Sox (DVD). New England Sports Network, 2004.

Ramos, Sugar
(Ultiminio Ramos)
(1941–   ) *boxer*

A featherweight boxing champion with a powerful right hand, Sugar Ramos won his title in a historic but tragic bout that claimed the life of his opponent, Davey Moore. Ultiminio Ramos was born on December 2, 1941, in Matanzas, Cuba. By his early teens, the 5'4" Ultiminio (so named because his parents expected him to be the last of their 15 children) had demonstrated remarkable quickness and toughness in local gyms and was considered a cannot-miss future professional. In his first professional fight when he was only 15 years old, on

October 5, 1957, Ramos defeated René Arce in a second-round knockout in Havana, Cuba.

Ramos went 23-0-1 in his next 24 bouts, fought mainly in Cuba from late 1957 to the end of 1960. He won the Cuban featherweight title in early 1960 but fled the country later in 1961 to escape the communist regime of Fidel Castro, which had taken power two years earlier.

While living and training in Mexico City, Mexico, Ramos continued to rise as a contender for the world featherweight crown. He suffered two losses and a draw in 1961 but bounced back to win all seven of his bouts in 1962 and set up his first title fight, on March 21, 1963.

The match against reigning title-holder Davey Moore was part of a card of three championship fights at Dodger Stadium in Los Angeles, the first such competitions in that stadium's history. There have not been any since. The Ramos-Moore fight was the second of the three. The champion Moore controlled the first few rounds, later described by writer Melvin Durslag as "A study in politeness . . . while a savage war was developing."

In the third round, Ramos became more assertive, delighting the largely Latino crowd by bloodying Moore's mouth and nose and knocking out his opponent's mouthpiece in the fifth round. Moore rallied in the middle rounds, but in the 10th Ramos pummeled Moore with a series of hooks that sent him into the ropes. Ramos continued to drive the champ into the center of the ring, where a left hook drove him to the floor, his head landing against the lowest of the three ropes. Moore got up as the referee reached "three" in his count. Between rounds, Moore's corner conceded the fight, and Ramos exulted in his championship.

After the fight, Moore noted to reporters, "It just wasn't my night," adding that he wanted a rematch with Ramos. Moments later Moore remarked, "Oh my head aches" and slumped into unconsciousness. He soon fell into a coma, and 10 days later he was dead. Ramos, as well as the rest of the boxing world, was stunned, though a neu-rologist report determined that Moore's death was caused not by a blow, but rather by a "million to one" accident in which the rope struck Moore like an expert karate blow.

The backlash against boxing was intense. California governor Pat Brown called for an end to "this so-called sport," and the Vatican newspaper condemned boxing as "morally illicit." Singer-songwriter Bob Dylan wrote "Who Killed Davey Moore," implicating all who support and participate in boxing in Moore's death and repeating the refrain, "Who Killed Davey Moore, why an' what's the reason for?" Some changes to boxing followed this tragedy, including a fourth rope and padding ropes in fights taking place in California.

Moore's death took an emotional toll on Ramos, but he continued to fight despite the constant reminders of the tragic bout. He retained the featherweight title until September 26, 1964, when he lost to VICENTE SALDÍVAR.

Ramos twice challenged CARLOS ORTIZ for the lightweight championship, in 1966 and 1967, but lost both times. Ramos retired at age 27 in 1972 with a career record of 55-7-4 with 40 knockouts. He was inducted into the International Boxing Hall of Fame in 2001.

Ramos lives in the Miami, Florida, area and suffers from boxing-related speech, hearing, and vision problems. One of his children, Santiago Perez, is a rising contender in the middleweight division.

Further Reading

Modesti, Kevin. "A Championship Night 38 Years Ago Brings Back Unwanted Memories." *Los Angeles Daily News,* 26 July 2001.

"Sugar Ramos." Boxing Records Archive Web site. Available online. URL: http://www.boxrec.com/ print.php?boxer_id=012683. Downloaded on January 20, 2006.

"Ultiminio 'Sugar' Ramos." International Boxing Hall of Fame Web site. Available online. URL: http:// www.ibhof.com/ramos.htm. Downloaded on January 20, 2006.

Rentería, Edgar
(1975–) *baseball player*

A speedy base runner and sure-handed fielder who delivered the game-ending hit to win the 1997 World Series for the Florida Marlins, Edgar Rentería is widely considered the greatest Colombian-born player in the history of Major League Baseball. He was born on August 7, 1975, in Barranquilla, Colombia. He grew up in Barranquilla, a populous, bustling Caribbean port city located on Colombia's north-central coast, one of 14 siblings born to Francisco (who died of hypertension before Rentería was one), and Vina. Rentería was raised by his widowed mother and followed his brother Edson (who later reached the AAA level in the Houston Astros organization), into baseball, making a name for himself as a rangy prodigy.

At age 16, Rentería signed a contract with the expansion Florida Marlins, excelling at each stop in the minors. Rentería's first professional hit broke up a no-hitter with one out in the bottom of the ninth inning, foreshadowing a future knack for contributing in the clutch. In 1985 at age 20, Rentería was voted the Marlins' Organizational Player of the Year by the farm systems' managers and field staff after ranking among the Eastern League leaders in hits and stolen bases.

The Marlins called up Rentería to the major league early in the 1996 season. He made his debut on May 10, becoming only the fourth Colombian to play Major League Baseball. During his first season, Rentería put together a 22-game hitting streak, a .309 batting average, and 16 stolen bases in only 18 attempts. His impressive performance earned him second place in voting for the National League (NL) Rookie of the Year.

In 1997, Rentería ranked second among all NL players with 143 singles and led NL shortstops with 242 putouts. With Rentería providing steady play on offense and defense, the Marlins won the NL wildcard and advanced to a playoffs match-up with the San Francisco Giants. In game one of that series, Rentería knocked a two-out, bases-loaded, game-winning single.

The Marlins went on to defeat the Giants 3-0 and dumped the Atlanta Braves 4-2 to advance to the World Series versus the Cleveland Indians. In the bottom of the 11th inning of the decisive seventh game, the 22-year-old Rentería singled off Cleveland pitcher Charles Nagy to drive in the winning run and bring the Marlins their first World Series championship in only their fifth season of play, faster than any expansion team in Major League Baseball history.

Rentería enjoyed another productive season in 1998, including making his first All-Star team but was traded by Florida to the St. Louis Cardinals because he was approaching the end of his contract and was expected to receive more money than the cost-cutting Marlins were prepared to pay. In his five seasons in St. Louis, Rentería played in three All-Star games, won three Gold Glove awards for his excellence at shortstop, and helped the Cardinals advance to the postseason four times, including the 2004 World Series, when he again was the last batter, this time bouncing out to the pitcher as the Boston Red Sox swept St. Louis in four games.

Rentería's next at-bat was with the Red Sox, after he signed as a free agent with them prior to the 2005 season. Despite posting solid offensive statistics (.278 batting average and 70 runs batted in), Rentería had trouble with his new team, committing a career-high 30 errors and not endearing himself to Red Sox fans by struggling to hit in Boston's Fenway Park.

Following the 2005 season, Rentería was traded to the Atlanta Braves for a top prospect. Rentería bounced back from his disappointing year in Boston with a solid season in Atlanta that earned him a spot on the 2006 NL All-Star team.

At age 30, Rentería already had collected almost 1,600 hits, as well as a reputation as an intelligent, hard-working team leader who spends his time and money in the off-season promoting the growth of baseball among underprivileged youth in Colombia through the Team Rentería Baseball Academy. For his efforts and accomplishment, Rentería has received the San Carlos Cross of the Order of the Great Knight, Colombia's highest honor, and he remains one of the nation's most popular figures.

Further Reading

"Edgar Renteria." Atlanta Braves Web site. Available online. URL: http://atlanta.braves.mlb.com/NASApp/mlb/team/player.jsp?player_id=121074. Downloaded on January 20, 2006.

O'Neill, Dan. "Cardinals Look to Edgar Renteria for Leadership." *Baseball Digest,* 1 July 2003.

Reyna, Claudio

(1973–) *soccer player*

A key member of three U.S. World Cup squads and two U.S. Olympic soccer teams, Claudio Reyna is the first American ever named to the Fédération Internationale de Football Association (FIFA) World Cup All-Star team. He was born on July 20, 1973, in Livingston, New Jersey. His father, Miguel, was a former Argentine professional soccer player, and Reyna and his family lived in his father's native Argentina for a brief period.

Reyna grew up in New Jersey, where he twice earned *Parade Magazine's* national Soccer Player of the Year (1989 and 1990) while playing at St. Benedict's Prep in Newark. During his high school career, Reyna's St. Benedict's teams lost only two games (both while he was training with the U.S. Under-23 national team) and won two state championships. He capped his high school accomplishments with the Gatorade National Player of the Year award in 1990.

Reyna then attended the University of Virginia, where he played midfield and became one of the most decorated players in college soccer history. Reyna followed his first season in 1991, in which he was named Soccer America Freshman of the Year and won a National Collegiate Athletic

Association (NCAA) championship, with two more NCAA titles and Soccer America Player of the Year honors in 1992 and 1993.

While still in college, Reyna was the youngest member of the U.S. Olympic soccer team that finished 1-1-1 in Barcelona, Spain. He played every minute of the tournament and assisted on two goals. In 1994, Reyna was the youngest member on the U.S. World Cup team, though he did not play due to a hamstring injury.

In 1994, Reyna began playing professionally in Europe, starting with a stint with the German team Bayer Leverkusen. His sharp vision, pinpoint passing skills, and unselfish style helped him become the first American ever to captain a European team when he was chosen to head the German Wolfsburg team. His career in Europe continued for several more years, including stops with teams in Scotland and England.

Although Reyna has made significant contributions to soccer in Europe, his greatest influence has been as a leader of U.S. national squads. In 1996, he starred on the U.S. Olympic team competing in Atlanta, Georgia, scoring a goal less than a minute into the game against heavily favored Argentina (the U.S. team lost the game, 3-1).

In the 1998 World Cup held in France, Reyna was one of only three U.S. players to play every minute of the tournament, finishing with a goal and two assists. In the 2002 World Cup in South Korea and Japan, Reyna earned an assist and played one of his best matches in a 2-0 win over Mexico, helping the U.S. team advance all the way to the quarterfinals, where they lost to eventual runner-up Germany.

Despite his advancing age and accumulated injuries, including a knee ligament tear in 2003, Reyna committed to play for his fourth U.S. team and World Cup competition at the 2006 tournament in Germany. In 2004, now married to former women's soccer star Danielle Egan and the father of two, and over a decade after his first being named to the U.S. national team, Reyna became only the seventh American to play in 100 international games. Bruce Arena, the U.S. coach and Reyna's college coach, reflected on this achievement, noting, "He is arguably our best player . . . It means a lot to have him on the field. It's a tremendous accomplishment."

Though expected by many soccer experts to make a strong showing, the United States failed to qualify for the second round at the 2006 World Cup in Germany. Following the team's final game, a 2-1 loss to Ghana, Reyna announced his retirement from international play. Said Arena of the longtime American captain Reyna: "When we look down the road, the day we do eventually win a World Cup, I think Claudio is still going to be remembered as one of the greats and one of the pioneers."

Further Reading

"Claudio Reyna." U.S. Soccer Official Web site. Available online. URL: http://www.ussoccer.com/bio/bio.sps?iBiographyID=1715. Downloaded on July 1, 2005.

Connolly, Marc. "U.S. Hopes to Exorcise Demons." ESPN Soccernet Web site. Available online. URL: http://soccernet.espn.go.com/print?id=328841&type=feature&cc=5739. Downloaded on July 1, 2005.

Reyna, Claudio, and Mike Woitalla. *More Than Goals: The Journey from Backyard Games to World Cup Competition.* Champaign, Ill.: Human Kinetics, 2004.

Ríos, Marcelo
(Chino)
(1975–) *tennis player*

The first Latino to rank number one in the world in men's tennis and the only player to receive that distinction without ever having won a Grand Slam tournament, Marcelo Ríos was renowned for his left-handed volleying wizardry and his often surly personality. He was born on December 26, 1975, in Santiago, Chile. Ríos grew up in a wealthy fam-

ily that moved to a house adjacent to a country club when he was nine.

He soon began playing tennis at the country club and quickly demonstrated a precocious mixture of precision and skill on the court. At age 14, Ríos transferred to a sports academy, and within a few years, he established himself as one of the top amateur players in the world. In 1993, Ríos won the U.S. Open juniors title at age 17, and he turned professional within a year.

Ríos won three tournaments in 1995 and another in 1996, helping him become the first Chilean ever to rank in the top 10 in the world in men's tennis. Nicknamed "Chino" (Spanish for Chinese) because of his Asiatic facial features and easily recognized by his dark ponytail, Ríos was one of the smallest players on the tennis tour, standing about 5'9" and weighing 140 pounds. Despite his diminutive size, Ríos was an aggressive volleyer with surprising power whose quick maneuverability and masterful footwork allowed him to respond to difficult shots with whiplike, cleverly placed returns endowed with wicked spin.

Though respected for his tactical excellence and entertaining style of play, Ríos was also disliked and occasionally reviled for what many felt was his nasty disposition. Stretching back to his amateur days, Ríos regularly had run-ins with opponents, officials, the media, and fans.

Ríos was also criticized for his perceived tendency to quit in matches if he was trailing or struggling. Former pro Ion Tiriac described Ríos as "a finely tuned Swiss watch missing a couple of wheels," and fellow tour players often described Ríos as boorish, arrogant, and aloof.

Such characterizations seemed only to inspire Ríos. Prior to his match against a French player in the 1998 French Open, Ríos was asked if having the entire crowd against him would bother him. He responded, "No, I am looking forward to it. I am at my best when it is just me against the world."

Earlier that year, Ríos reached the championship match in the Australian Open—his only finals appearance in a Grand Slam event, but he lost to Spaniard Carlos Moya. It was during this spring of 1998 that Ríos held the number one spot in the Association of Tennis Professionals (ATP) rankings for six weeks, becoming the first Latino to hold that prestigious place.

Injuries severely diminished Ríos's competitive strength beginning in 1999. He advanced as far as the quarterfinals only once (2002 Australian Open) from 1999 through 2003. Still admired in his native country, Ríos announced his retirement in 2004 before traveling throughout Chile in a popular farewell tour.

Further Reading

Lidz, Franz. "The Most Hated Man in Tennis." *Sports Illustrated*, 23 March 1998, p. 40.
"Marcelo Rios." Tennis Corner Web site. Available online. URL: http://www.tenniscorner.net/index.php?corner=M&action=players&playerid=RIM001. Downloaded on January 16, 2006.

Rivelino, Roberto
(Rivelino, Reizinho do Parque)
(1946–) *soccer player*

A key member of Brazil's 1970 World Cup championship soccer team, Roberto Rivelino was renowned for thunderous free kicks, his accurate left-foot shot, and imaginative dribbling skills. He was born on January 1, 1946, in São Paulo, Brazil. The youngster who would later come to be known simply as "Rivelino" played soccer on the streets and community fields of São Paulo as well as *fustal* (indoor soccer, roughly translated from a Portuguese phrase meaning "room soccer").

At age 16, Rivelino began playing professionally for Corinthians in São Paulo, rapidly moving up the club's system and remaining with them until 1974. Despite the team's failings, the loyal Rivelino earned the affection and admiration of his native city's fans, who nicknamed him "Reizinho do Parque" ("Little King of the Park"). Rivelino then moved on to play for the Flumenense club

in Rio de Janeiro, Brazil, where his consistency, durability, strong foot, and quick thinking helped make him enormously popular among the team's fans during his three years there.

Despite his success in Brazil's professional leagues, Rivelino made his greatest impact with his contributions to the Brazilian national team during the 1970s. From 1968 through 1978, Rivelino appeared in 121 games for the Brazilian national team, including all six games for Brazil's 1970 World Cup championship team, a squad many consider the best ever assembled.

In Brazil's first match of that tournament, Rivelino scored three goals, including a booming free kick, in a 4-1 win over Czechoslovakia. Brazil won its next four games over England, Romania, Peru, and Uruguay to reach the final versus Italy. In that game, played before more than 100,000 spectators in Mexico City's Azteca Stadium, Rivelino gained an assist passing to PELÉ, who scored the game's first goal in what would be a 4-1 victory for Brazil.

Rivelino was a key contributor at mid-field and left wing for the Brazilian team that competed in the 1974 World Cup, helping the club to a fourth-place finish. In the 1978 World Cup tournament, Rivelino played sparingly as his playing time was taken by emerging young stars such as ZICO, though the veteran with the distinctive mustache did come off the bench to help Brazil defeat Italy in the third-place match.

In the last stage of his playing days, Rivelino played for three years in Saudi Arabia, helping the El Halal club win two league championships. Rivelino's distinguished career ended at age 35 in 1981. Among his many accomplishments on the field, Rivelino is also credited with scoring the fastest goal ever, unofficially recorded as taking only three seconds. The goal was scored directly from a kickoff pass as the opposition goalkeeper was completing his prematch prayer.

Since retiring, Rivelino has worked as a soccer commentator and currently runs a sports center for youths in São Paulo, which he sees as playing an important social role, explaining, "There isn't anywhere safe any more. I could never have seen myself having a football school like this, it never even struck my mind that there would be a need. But they simply don't have anywhere else."

Further Reading

"Roberto Rivelino (Brazil)." Planet World Cup Web site. Available online. URL: http://www.planetworldcup.com/LEGENDS/rivelino.html. Downloaded on January 16, 2006.

Ragan, Sanjay. "Icons of the World Cup." Sportstar Web site. Available online. URL: http://www.sportstaronnet.com/tss2519/25190530.htm. Downloaded on January 16, 2006.

Rivera, Marco
(1972–   ) *football player*

A mainstay on the offensive line for the Green Bay Packers between 1997 and 2004, Marco Rivera helped lead the team to six playoff appearances. He was born on April 26, 1972, in Brooklyn, New York. He soon moved with his family to Long Island, where he grew up as one of the region's top athletes. At Elmont Memorial High School, Rivera starred in lacrosse, basketball, and football, earning national recognition as a top offensive and defensive lineman and an athletic scholarship to Pennsylvania State University (Penn State).

Rivera was a three-year starter on the offensive line for Penn State. In his junior year of 1994, Rivera started every game and earned second team All-Big 10 honors on a squad that went undefeated (12-0) and led the National Collegiate Athletic Association (NCAA) in scoring with an average of 47.8 points per game and total offense with an average of more than 520 yards per game.

As a senior, Rivera again was named to the second team All-Big 10 as an offensive lineman. Despite his outstanding play as a collegian, concerns among National Football League (NFL) scouts regarding Rivera's shoulder injuries and lack of athleticism caused him to drop all the way to the sixth round of the 1996 NFL draft, where he was selected by the Green Bay Packers.

Like many rookies selected in the later rounds of the draft, Rivera's career began slowly. He did not appear in any of the Packers' games in 1996, and he did not start in any of the 14 contests in which he played in 1997. He became a starting left guard in 1998 after the previous starter left the Packers as a free agent. Rivera missed only one game that season, starting in all the others.

From 1999 through 2004, Rivera started every game for the Packers and became renowned throughout the NFL as one of the toughest and most consistent offensive linemen in football. Despite his success in football, he was embarrassed by a highly publicized drunk driving conviction he received in 2000.

The steady improvement Rivera demonstrated, particularly his ability to adjust to speedy defensive rushers and create rushing lanes for Packers running backs, led to two Pro Bowl appearances. Rivera's contribution to the dominant Packers offensive line helped Green Bay quarterback Brett Favre achieve superstardom and powered the team to six playoff appearances, including three consecutive National Football Conference (NFC) North Division championships from 2002 through 2004.

Rivera was named the Packers recipient of the 2004 Walter Payton Man of the Year Award, given by the NFL to one player on each team to recognize outstanding contributions on and off the field. Prior to the 2005 season, Rivera signed as a free agent with the Dallas Cowboys, where he immediately strengthened the offensive line performance on the improving Cowboys team. In 2006, at age 34, Rivera remained a starter for a Dallas team that earned a wild card berth in the NFC playoffs.

Further Reading

"Marco Rivera—#62." National Football League Players Association Web site. Available online. URL: http://www.nflplayers.com/players/player.aspx?id=23920. Downloaded on January 16, 2006.

McGinn, Bob. "Marco Rivera the Man on the Line for the Packers." *Milwaukee Journal-Sentinel,* 26 November 2003.

Rivera, Mariano
(Mo)
(1969–) *baseball player*

The Most Valuable Player (MVP) of the 1999 World Series and a seven-time All-Star, Mariano Rivera has ranked among the top 10 in saves in nine consecutive seasons, from 1997 through 2005, and his dominance in the playoffs has earned him the distinction as the most successful closer in Major League Baseball postseason history. He was born on November 29, 1969, in Panama City, Panama. Rivera grew up in Puerto Caimito, a fishing village on the southern coast of Panama, where he assisted his fisherman father.

A lean and athletic youth, Rivera played soccer and baseball, though he did not become a pitcher until he was 19. Within a few months, word of his unique skill on the mound reached local scouts for the New York Yankees, who signed Rivera. Less than a year later, Rivera was manhandling opposing batters in the Gulf Coast League with a remarkably low earned run average (ERA) of 0.17, the result of allowing only one earned run in 52 innings.

From 1991 through 1994, Rivera pitched as a starter and a reliever, making a steady climb up the Yankees' farm system despite interruptions as a result of injuries, while demonstrating the pinpoint control, wicked fastball, and unflappable poise that would later mark his major league career. Rivera made his major league debut on May 23, 1995, giving up five earned runs in three and one-third innings in a loss to the California Angels.

He shuttled between New York and the Yankees' minor league affiliate in Columbus, Ohio, for the rest of 1995. Stellar performances, such as an 11th strikeout outing and eight shutout innings in Chicago on July 4 and his shutout work over five and one-third innings in New York's 1995 playoff loss to the Seattle Mariners, convinced the Yankees that Rivera was ready to be a full-time major leaguer.

In 1996, Rivera, or "Mo" to teammates and Yankees fans, shined as a setup man for Yankees relief ace John Wetteland. Pitching primarily in the eighth inning, Rivera used his fluid motion and smooth delivery to go 8-3, with 130 strikeouts in less than 108 innings and a 2.09 ERA. In the playoffs, Rivera allowed only one run in $14\frac{1}{3}$ innings, as the Yankees ultimately defeated the Atlanta Braves in six games for their first World Series championship in 18 years.

With Rivera as their closer beginning in 1997, the Yankees continued their annual sojourn to baseball's postseason. Though teammates such as shortstop Derek Jeter and outfielder BERNIE WILLIAMS usually received more attention from fans and media, no one was more responsible for New York's success than the quiet Rivera, whose demeanor contrasted with the rugged and raucous personalities of other famed closers.

Rivera surrendered a game-winning home run to Cleveland's Sandy Alomar in game four of the 1997 playoffs (which New York lost in five games), but, according to Yankees manager Joe Torre, this failure did not diminish Rivera's resolve. Torre explained, "It [Alomar's home run] was a turning point for him, not just because he became more determined, but because he dismissed it."

Rivera's statistics over the ensuing seasons support Torre's point. From 1998 through 2004, Rivera averaged more than 41 saves per season, leading the major leagues in 1999 (45), 2001 (50), and 2004 (53). Rivera's ERA during these years never rose above a still excellent 2.85 (2000) and sank below the 2.00 mark four times. In addition, the trademark accuracy of his fastball and deceptive-cut fastball helped him achieve a strikeout-to-walk ratio of more than three to one.

Although Rivera was outstanding in the regular season, he was even more dominant against baseball's best in the playoffs, where the Yankees appeared in every season from 1995 through 2004. In these 23 series, Rivera posted a record of 8-1, a miniscule ERA of 0.75, 32 saves, and 85 strikeouts against only 14 walks. Rivera was on the mound when the Yankees won the World Series in 1998 in a four-game sweep of the San Diego Padres, in 1999 in a sweep over the Atlanta Braves, and in 2000 when the Yankees defeated their crosstown rivals, the New York Mets 4-1. Rivera's one win and two saves in 1999 earned him the World Series MVP award.

Rivera's 2004 season ended on a disappointing note. Days after returning from Panama, where he traveled to attend the funeral of his wife's relative who died in an accident at Rivera's house, Rivera twice failed to close out the Boston Red Sox, who eventually made history by becoming the first major league team to win a postseason series after trailing 3-0.

After a bumpy start in 2005, Rivera rallied to enjoy one of his greatest individual campaigns. His 7-4 record, 43 saves, and 80 strikeouts in 78 2/3 innings helped the Yankees again reach the playoffs (where they fell to the Los Angeles Angels)

New York Yankees relief pitcher Mariano Rivera is the all-time World Series saves leader. *(National Baseball Hall of Fame Library)*

and earned Rivera second place in voting for the American League Cy Young Award. He was solid again in 2006, finishing the season with 34 saves and a 1.80 ERA, though the Yankees again lost in the first round of the playoffs, this time to the Detroit Tigers.

Rivera's straightforward effectiveness is reflected in his philosophy of pitching, which belies his pleasant looks and the genial manner that have earned him the respect and affection of millions: "Throw strikes. Go after hitters. When they're in the batter's box they're the enemy . . . if you give them a chance they'll kill you. Don't let them breathe."

Further Reading

Bamberger, Michael. "Strikeouts by the Boatload." *Sports Illustrated,* 24 March 1997, p. 50.

"Mariano Rivera." Major League Baseball Web site. Available online. URL: http://newyork.yankees. mlb.com/NASApp/mlb/team/player.jsp?player_ id=121250. Downloaded on January 16, 2006.

Pierce, Charles. "The Hammer of God." *Esquire,* 1 June 2001, p. 62.

Further Viewing

The New York Yankees Fall Classic Collector's Edition 1996–2001. A&E Home Video, 2005.

Rivera, Ron
(1962–   ) *football player*

A member of the Chicago Bears Super Bowl XX championship team, Ron Rivera spent his entire nine-year National Football League (NFL) career playing for the Chicago Bears, helping lead the team to the playoffs seven times and later becoming their defensive coordinator. He was born on January 7, 1962, in Fort Ord, California. Rivera's father, a native Puerto Rican who was a U.S. Army officer, brought the family with him on his commissions to Germany, Panama, Washington, and Maryland, before settling in central California about 100 miles south of San

Francisco. Rivera attended Seaside High School and excelled at football, earning an athletic scholarship to the University of California–Berkeley (Cal).

Rivera enjoyed a stellar college career in California and remains one of the top defensive performers in the school's history. He started at linebacker in Cal's most famous victory, a 1982 win over Stanford University that ended with what has become known as "The Play," in which Cal shocked Stanford by returning a kickoff on the game's final play for a touchdown following several remarkable laterals.

Rivera was captain of Cal's 1983 squad and a consensus All-American and finished his career as the school's all-time leader in sacks (22) and tackles (336), marks that have since been surpassed. Rivera, however, remains Cal's single-season record holder for most tackles for a loss, with 26.5 in 1983.

In the 1984 NFL draft, Rivera was selected in the second round by the Chicago Bears. During his nine years in Chicago, Rivera was a major contributor on several outstanding Bears teams. In his rookie year, Rivera was a reserve on a Bears team that reached the National Football Conference (NFC) championship game, and the next season he again provided key support from the bench on the Bears team, which went 18-1 and crushed the New England Patriots 46-10 in Super Bowl XX.

Playing alongside star linebackers Mike Singletary and Wilber Marshall, Rivera bolstered the bruising defense of Chicago coach Mike Ditka in 1986, when the Bears had a record of 14-2 but lost in the first round of the playoffs. As a starter on the Bears from 1988 through 1991, Rivera earned a reputation as a tough, consistent, and smart player on teams that averaged more than 10 wins a season.

Injuries and reduced production led Rivera to retire following the 1992 season. By this time, he had accumulated an impressive set of career statistics: 392 tackles (190 solo), nine interceptions, five forced fumbles, four fumble recoveries, and seven quarterback sacks.

After his playing days ended, Rivera was a broadcaster for the Bears and for college football games before he entered coaching as Chicago's defensive quality control assistant in 1997. In 1999, Rivera became the linebackers coach for the Philadelphia Eagles. He spent five years in Philadelphia, guiding the Eagles' linebacking unit to rank among the NFL's best.

In 2004, Rivera returned to the Bears as the team's defensive coordinator and implemented an innovative and aggressive system that helped Chicago's defense become one of the most feared units in football. Powered by Rivera's strong defense, the Bears won the 2005 NFC North Division title in 2005 and 2006.

Further Reading

Bannon, Terry. "He's Puttin' on the Blitz." *Chicago Tribune,* 22 August 2004, p. C1.
"Ron Rivera." Chicago Bears Web site. Available online. URL: http://www.chicagobears.com/team/coachbio.jsp?id=33. Downloaded on January 16, 2006.

Rodriguez, Alex
(Alexander Emmanuel Rodriguez, A-Rod)
(1975–) *baseball player*

A lanky shortstop prodigy from a Miami, Florida, high school who was the first player selected in the 1993 Major League Baseball draft, Alex Rodriguez quickly emerged as one of the top all-around players of his generation, winning two Most Valuable Player (MVP) awards, becoming the youngest player to reach 400 career home runs, and signing the most lucrative contract in the history of American team sports.

He was born Alexander Emmanuel Rodriguez on July 27, 1975, in New York City. Rodriguez spent the first four years of his life living with his parents Victor and Lourdes and two older siblings in a small apartment behind a shoe store owned by his father in the Washington Heights neighborhood of northern Manhattan.

When he was four, his parents moved the family to their native Dominican Republic, where they bought a home located just a block from the Caribbean Sea and opened a pharmacy. Economic woes in the Dominican Republic led the family to return to the United States and settle in Miami when Rodriguez was eight. The next year, Rodriguez's father, who had introduced Alex to his beloved baseball, went to New York City ostensibly to work but never returned. Rodriguez explained in 1998, "I kept thinking that my father would come back, but he never did," adding, "it still hurts."

Rodriguez assimilated with his peers and dealt with the abandonment by his father by immersing himself in basketball, football, soccer, and baseball. A tall, graceful, and exceptionally coordinated youth, Rodriguez played shortstop, like his idol Cal Ripken, Jr., of the Baltimore Orioles, and with financial aid and money earned by his mother, who worked as a waitress and secretary, he was able to attend Miami's Westminster Christian High School.

Rodriguez starred on Westminster's football, basketball, and baseball teams and excelled in the classroom. Following his junior and senior seasons, in which Rodriguez wowed scouts with his hitting, speed, and poise, he received a scholarship to play baseball at the University of Miami and was selected by the Seattle Mariners with the first pick of the 1993 Major League Baseball draft.

Concerned that he did not want to play baseball in the opposite corner of the country, Rodriguez initially balked at Seattle's contract offer during contentious negotiations, eventually choosing to sign with the Mariners for a bonus of $1.3 million. Rodriguez rocketed up through Seattle's farm system and made his major league debut as an 18-year-old on July 8, 1994.

After a brief and unproductive stint with the Mariners in 1994, Rodriguez was a late-season call-up in 1995, helping the Mariners win their first American League (AL) West championship. Rodriguez (not a rookie because he had more than 100 plate appearances in 1995) became Seattle's full-time shortstop in 1996 and responded by leading the AL in batting average (.358) and runs (141), adding 36 home runs and 123 runs batted in (RBIs)

to earn his first All-Star game appearance and a razor-thin second-place finish to JUAN GONZÁLEZ of the Texas Rangers in voting for AL MVP.

In 1997, the right-handed hitting Rodriguez continued to mature physically and began the season well, including hitting for the cycle (single, double, triple, and home run in same game) against the Detroit Tigers in June. Later that month, a collision with a Toronto Blue Jays player resulted in a chest injury that hindered Rodriguez for the remainder of the season, though he still managed to bat .300, with 23 home runs and 84 RBIs. The Mariners again reached the playoffs, but Rodriguez mustered only one RBI in an AL division series loss to the Baltimore Orioles.

From 1998 through 2000, Rodriguez posted phenomenal numbers, joining fellow hitting stars Ken Griffey, Jr., and EDGAR MARTINEZ to make the Mariners one of the most potent teams in the majors. In these three seasons, Rodriguez averaged 42 home runs and 122 RBIs. In 1998, he led the AL in hits (213) and followed JOSE CANSECO and Barry Bonds to become only the third major leaguer in history to hit 40 or more home runs and steal 40 or more bases in the same season.

Rodriguez's 1999 season was hampered by a knee injury, which limited him to only 129 games, yet he still hit 42 home runs and drove in 111 runs. In 2000, Rodriguez finished third in MVP voting and helped the Mariners reach the American League Championship Series (ALCS), where despite his .409 batting average and five RBIs Seattle lost in six games to the New York Yankees.

Prior to the 2001 season, Rodriguez was the focus of intense speculation due to his new free-agent status. Seattle clearly wanted to retain their still young and enormously popular star, referred to across the baseball world as "A-Rod." Rodriguez's near pristine reputation as the handsome, intelligent, and articulate superstar who respected the game and its history was dented when details of requested perks from prospective teams leaked in the press. Rodriguez's image suffered further when he signed a record 10-year, $252 million contract with the last place Texas Rangers.

Although Rodriguez's signing sparked a surge in ticket and merchandise sales for the Rangers, it failed to translate into wins as the Rangers finished in last place in the AL West in 2001, 2002, and 2003. Rodriguez, derisively called "Pay Rod" when negatively received in Seattle as a member of the Rangers, did his part, battering the ball around Texas's cozy ballpark at Arlington to average an astounding 52 home runs and 132 RBIs per season during those three years, winning the AL MVP in 2003 and Gold Glove awards in 2002 and 2003.

After three years, Rangers owner Tom Hicks recognized that his hefty financial gamble on Rodriguez was not paying dividends, and he

The Seattle Mariners selected Alex Rodriguez with the first overall pick of the 1993 amateur draft. *(National Baseball Hall of Fame Library)*

began seeking a trading partner who could absorb the burden of Rodriguez's contract. A deal with the Boston Red Sox that would have sent MANNY RAMÍREZ to Texas was scuttled by the Major League Baseball Player's Association, which did not want Rodriguez to forfeit part of his salary, a condition of the trade. Instead, Texas traded Rodriguez and $60 million to Boston's hated rival, the New York Yankees, in exchange for Alfonso Soriano and a prospect.

Because the Yankees already had a star short-stop—team captain and fan favorite Derek Jeter—Rodriguez moved to third base. Learning a new position and dealing with the intense pressure of high expectations in the nation's media capital of New York City contributed to Rodriguez's slow start in 2004, including a one-hit in 17 at-bats series with six strikeouts in Boston. However, Rodriguez finished the year strong to post solid, if not typically phenomenal, offensive statistics (.286 batting average, 36 home runs, and 106 RBIs).

In the playoffs, Rodriguez batted .421 in a series victory over the Minnesota Twins, and his five runs scored in game three of the ALCS versus Boston helped the Yankees gain a seemingly insurmountable 3-0 over the Red Sox. But he struggled in the remaining four games as Boston became the first major league team to win four consecutive elimination games in the same series. After concluding the series in a two for 17 slump, Rodriguez received and accepted much of the blame for the team's historic and embarrassing collapse.

In 2005, Rodriguez, now a married father of a baby girl, appeared more relaxed, and his play was consistently excellent. In the spring, he surprised many people by describing how recent psychotherapy helped him personally and professionally. He pummeled opposing pitching by leading the AL in home runs (48), finishing second in batting (.321) and fourth in RBIs (130). The Yankees won the AL East but fell to the Los Angeles Angels in the AL Division series, with Rodriguez again struggling with only two hits in 15 at-bats. Following the season, Rodriguez was named the AL MVP.

Although Rodriguez compiled impressive statistics in 2006 (.290 batting average, 35 home runs, 121 RBIs), he was also the recipient of harsh criticism in New York because of his erratic fielding (committing a career-high 24 errors) and his failure to produce in the playoffs. In New York's AL divisional series against the Detroit Tigers, Rodriguez collected only one hit in 14 at-bats, as the Yankees lost three games to one. In the final game of that series, Yankees manager Joe Torre dropped the slumping Rodriguez to eighth in the lineup—his lowest appearance in a lineup in more than 10 years. Following the loss, Rodriguez addressed rampant rumors that his failure to gain the acceptance of New York fans and teammates and his postseason struggles might lead him to be traded by saying, "I 100 percent, unconditionally want to be a Yankee."

Further Reading

"Alex Rodriguez." Jock Bio Web site. Available online. URL: http://www.jockbio.com/Bios/ARod/ARod_bio.html. Downloaded on January 16, 2006.

"Alex Rodriguez." Major League Baseball Web site. Available online. URL: http://newyork.yankees.mlb.com/NASApp/mlb/team/player.jsp?player_id=121347. Downloaded on January 16, 2006.

Callahan, Gerry. "The fairest of them all." *Sports Illustrated,* 8 July 1996, p. 38.

Rosenthal, Ken. "Lightning Rod: The Yankees' Alex Rodriguez Has a Talent for Playing Baseball—and Ticking Off his Peers." *The Sporting News,* 15 April 2005, p. 28.

"Selig Gives Blessing to Mega-Merger." ESPN Web site. Available online. URL: http://sports.espn.go.com/mlb/news/story?id=1735937. Downloaded on January 16, 2006.

Rodríguez, Chi Chi
(Juan Rodríguez)
(1935–   ) *golfer*

The greatest showman in the history of professional golf and the first Puerto Rican ever inducted into the World Golf Hall of Fame, Chi Chi Rodríguez won eight Professional Golf Association (PGA) events in 22 PGA senior tournaments. He was born Juan Rodríguez on October 23, 1935, in Río Piedras, Puerto Rico. As a child, "Chi Chi" helped support his parents and five siblings by working as a water carrier on a sugar plantation.

At age seven, he wandered onto a golf course and soon began working as a caddie. Rodríguez practiced on his own by hitting baseballs with a guava tree stick into tin cans until a member of the club where Rodríguez worked let the boy use his clubs. By the time Rodríguez was 12, his outstanding hand-eye coordination, natural instincts, and intelligence and knowledge of golf strategy led him to become one of Puerto Rico's best youth players.

Rodríguez continued to play golf as he caddied throughout his teenage years. When he was 19, Rodríguez enlisted in the U.S. Army, where he played golf in military tournaments, becoming well known for his long drives despite his small stature (5'7" and 115–130 lbs.).

When his service in the army was completed in 1957, Rodríguez returned to Puerto Rico, where he worked as an assistant golf pro at the Dorado Beach Resort. Over the next three years, Rodríguez received his first formal lessons in golf from the club's pros, and at age 25, he advanced his game sufficiently to set out on the professional golf circuit.

Throughout the 1960s and early 1970s, Rodríguez was among the best players on the PGA tour and was unquestionably one of the favorites among golf fans. Rodríguez won his first tour event at the 1963 Denver Open, which he later described as his biggest thrill. He won four more events in the late 1960s and three tournaments from 1972 through 1979.

Rodríguez was recognized as the most entertaining showman on the tour because of his habit of putting his always-present hat over a hole whenever he made a birdie or an eagle. When word came to Rodríguez that some other golfers found this to be unsportsmanlike, he developed his famous "toreador dance," in which he celebrated a particularly successful effort by pantomiming a bullfight, using his club as a sword to slay the conquered hole.

In 1985, Rodríguez became eligible to play on the PGA Seniors Tour (now known as the Champions Tour) and accumulated 22 victories between 1986. He holds the Seniors Tour's record for most outings, explaining his enthusiasm for the competition by saying, "You have to have a reason to get out of bed each morning."

As Rodríguez approached 70, he still managed to make a few tournament appearances. He continues to maintain an active role in the Chi Chi Rodriguez Youth Foundation, which has supported after-school programs for at-risk youth since 1979.

Further Reading

"Chi Chi Rodriguez." Professional Golf Association Web site. Available online. URL: http://www.pgatour.com/players/intro/132219. Downloaded on January 16, 2006.

Diaz, Jaime. "Chi Chi Has a Last Laugh." *Sports Illustrated,* 23 November 1987, p. 38.

"Juan 'Chi Chi' Rodriguez." Latino Legends in Sports Web site. Available online. URL: http://www.latinosportslegends.com/chi-chi.htm. Downloaded on January 16, 2006.

Rodríguez, Iván
(Pudge)
(1971–   ) *baseball player*

A stocky catcher whose remarkably steady defense and intimidating throwing arm earned him 11 Gold Glove awards, Iván Rodríguez also ranks among the all-time greatest hitters at his position, achieving a career batting average of about .300 and helping him earn the 1999 American League (AL) Most Valuable Player (MVP) award. He was born on November 27, 1971, in Manatí, Puerto Rico. Rodríguez grew up on the island's northern coast in the poverty stricken town of Vega Baja, the younger son of an electrician father, José, and a schoolteacher mother, Eva, who later said of the future star, "From the time he was seven, it's been baseball, baseball, baseball." "Pudge," a nickname he acquired because of his stout stature, was a star on local youth teams, playing several positions including pitcher, where he faced future Rangers teammate JUAN GONZÁLEZ and first attracted attention from major leagues scouts. Rodríguez signed with the Texas Rangers at age 16 and quickly became one of the top minor league catching prospects in baseball.

Rodríguez made his major league debut at age 19 on June 20, 1991, and started 81 of the 102 games in which he appeared that season. He became the youngest Ranger ever to hit a home run and finished the 1991 campaign ranked fourth in voting for AL Rookie of the Year. In 1992, his first full season in the majors, Rodríguez earned the first of 12 appearances on the All-Star team largely because of his precocious defense behind the plate.

After hitting .260 in 1992, Rodríguez improved his batting average to .273 in 1993, .298 in 1994, and .303 in 1995; developed his ability to spring the ball to all parts of the ball park (rarely striking out); and displayed occasional bursts of power. Although he was increasingly becoming an offensive threat, Rodríguez was most feared for his defense and cannon-arm. Texas teammate Will Clark described how Rodríguez caused that "Drop Anchor Effect" on opposing teams, as when they reached first base, they stopped because of well-founded concern that Rodríguez would throw them out if they tried to steal.

In addition to his perennial league-leading percentage of base runners thrown out attempting to steal, Rodríguez also intimidated opposing runners on the base paths by firing the ball in a single quick motion following a pitch to remind straying runners who was catching and often resulting in successful pickoffs. Commenting on this patented move, Rangers backup catcher Dave Valle noted of Rodríguez, "He loves putting fear and trepidation in the minds of opposing players."

Rodríguez permanently established his place as the best all-around catcher since Johnny Bench played for the Cincinnati Reds in the 1970s by batting about .300 every year from 1996 through 2002. This consistent excellence in hitting was accompanied by Rodríguez's growth and power, culminating in a 1999 season in which he belted a career-high 35 home runs and 113 runs batted in (RBIs), while batting .332 to win the AL MVP award. Following this season, which saw the Rangers win their third consecutive AL West Division title, Texas lost for the third straight time in the playoffs to the New York Yankees. In these three postseason series, Rodríguez batted .263 with only three RBIs and 38 at-bats.

Since Rodríguez's MVP season of 1999, his playing time has been restricted by nagging injuries. After the 2002 season, the Rangers elected to allow their star catcher to leave via free agency, but concerns over Rodríguez's physical condition led many teams to offer only one-year deals. He signed a one-year, $10 million contract with the Florida Marlins in January 2003.

In the 2003 season, a rejuvenated Rodríguez played in almost 90 percent of Florida's games, batting .297 with 16 home runs and 85 RBIs, while continuing his stellar defensive play. In the 2003 playoffs, Rodríguez exemplified the heart of the underdog Marlins, batting .353 and closing out game three against the San Francisco Giants with a spectacular block and tag at the plate.

Rodríguez won the National League Championship Series (NLCS) MVP, batting .321 in an exciting seven-game triumph over the Chicago Cubs, in which the Marlins came back from down 3-1. Rodríguez's steady play on offense and defense then helped the Marlins win the World Series in six games over the heavily favored New York Yankees.

Despite his playoff heroics, the Marlins remained wary of resigning Rodríguez to a long-term deal. Instead, Rodríguez signed a four-year, $40 million contract with the Detroit Tigers, a formerly successful franchise that was coming off a near major league record 119-loss season in 2003. With Rodríguez behind the plate in 2004, the Tigers had a 29-game improvement, and Rodrí-

guez won the Tiger of the Year award after batting .334 with 19 home runs and 86 RBIs.

Following a disappointing 2005 season in which Rodríguez struggled through injuries, accusations of former steroid use, and divorce, he bounced back to his previous form in 2006, batting .300, with 13 home runs and 69 RBIs, while maintaining his stellar defense. Rodríguez's production, leadership, and guidance of Detroit's young pitching staff helped the Tigers stun the baseball world by reaching the World Series, where they lost to the St. Louis Cardinals four games to one.

Further Reading

Barnas, Jo Ann. "Born to Lead: Ivan Rodriguez Takes Charge in Detroit." *Baseball Digest,* January 2004.

Chen, Albert. "Masked Marvel: Healthy Again and Close to Home, Ivan Rodriguez, the Finest Catcher of His Era, Was the Marlins' Mainstay." *Sports Illustrated,* 31 October 2003, p. 12.

Geffner, Michael. "Places in the Heart." *Sporting News,* 5 January 1998, p. 56.

"Ivan Rodriguez." Detroit Tigers Web site. Available online. URL: http://detroit.tigers.mlb.com/ NASApp/mlb/team/player.jsp?player_id=121358. Downloaded on January 16, 2006.

Rodriguez, Jennifer
(1976–)   *speed skater*

A roller- and inline skating champion as a teenager, Jennifer Rodriguez won two bronze medals in speed skating in the 2002 winter Olympics and earned a gold medal at speed skating's World Sprint Championships in 2005. She was born on June 8, 1976, in Miami, Florida. Rodriguez first began roller-skating at age four when she attended a friend's birthday party at a roller rink. A year later, she was competing in artistic and speed roller-skating competitions.

Rodriguez won 12 world championship medals in roller-skating and holds the distinction of being the only competitor to win world championship medals in artistic roller-skating (which is similar to figure skating) and speed roller-skating. Rodriguez's success earned her recognition as the 1991–92 Roller-Skating Athlete of the Year.

Rodriguez transitioned to inline skating competition over the next few years and began speed skating on ice in 1996 at the suggestion of her boyfriend and future Olympic speed skater K. C. Boutilette. Her first season on the ice, 1996–97, resulted in a 41st-place finish in the 3,000 meters in the overall World Cup standings.

Rodriguez qualified for the U.S. Olympic team in speed skating in 1998. At that year's winter Olympics in Nagano, Japan, she finished fourth in the 3,000 meters, hundredths of a second away from a medal. Encouraged by her performance and undeterred by her near miss of a medal, Rodriguez commented, ". . . people asked me if I was disappointed that I didn't win a medal, and I was like, 'are you kidding me?' I thought I was going to finish 15th!"

Rodriguez continued her rapid rise in the speed skating world over the next few years, winning the U.S. and North American championships in 1999–2000 and 2000–01. She expanded her range to include races of shorter distances, ranking second in the 1,000 meters and fourth in the 1,500 meters in the 2001–02 World Cup standings. Rodriguez established U.S. records in the 500 meters, 1,500 meters, and 3,000 meters and rode the momentum of her success toward the 2002 winter Olympics in Salt Lake City, Utah, where she won bronze medals in both the 1,000-meters and 1,500-meters events. After the Olympics, Rodriguez married Boutilette.

From 2003 through 2005, Rodriguez enjoyed even more success, winning 20 gold medals, seven silver medals, and six bronze medals at various competitions and setting track records in Italy, Canada, Germany, and the Netherlands. Rodriguez reached the pinnacle of speed skating on January 23, 2005, by winning the 2005 World Sprint Championship in Salt Lake City, becoming the first American of either gender to win the title in nine years.

Jennifer Rodriguez won two bronze medals in speed skating at the 2002 winter Olympics in Salt Lake City, and she also competed at the 2006 winter Olympics in Torino. *(U.S. Olympic Committee)*

Rodriguez, who is already the first Cuban American and native Miamian to compete in the winter Olympics and the only female Olympic speed skater to compete in four different distances, hoped to become the first Latina to win a winter Olympics gold medal in the 2006 Olympic games in Torino, Italy, but she failed to finish higher than eighth in three individual events.

Further Reading

Hersh, Phillip. "Rodriguez Skates to World Title." *Chicago Tribune,* 24 January 2005.

"Jennifer Rodriguez." U.S. Olympic Web site. Available online. URL: http://www.usoc.org/26_1030.htm. Downloaded on January 16, 2006.

"Jennifer Rodriguez: Two Medals and Counting." Hispania News Web site. Available online. URL: http://www.hispanianews.com/archive/2002/02/22/12.htm. Downloaded on Januaary 16, 2006.

Ronaldinho
(Ronaldo de Assis Moreira)
(1980–) *soccer player*

An inventive, artistic, and relentless talent who was named Fédération Internationale de Football Association (FIFA) Player of the Year in 2004 and 2005, Ronaldinho led Brazil to the 2002 World Cup championship. He was born Ronaldo de Assis Moreira on March 21, 1980, in Porto Alegre, Brazil. Nicknamed Ronaldinho (the diminutive form of Ronaldo) as a young boy, he explained, "Like a lot of Brazilians, I was born with a ball at my feet and grew up with it." His father, João, was a welder at a shipyard who died of a heart attack when Ronaldinho was eight years old. Ronaldinho's mother, Miguelina, raised him and his older brother and sister on her own while she studied to become a nurse.

A wiry and tireless youth with an ever-present grin, Ronaldinho excelled in soccer, whether played in the smaller indoor boundaries of *futsal,* on the beach, or on standard fields. He was named to Brazil's under-17 national team, leading the squad to the 1997 World Under-17 championship in Egypt. He soon signed his first professional contract at age 17 with Gremio Porto Alegre.

Ronaldinho played with Gremio Porto Alegre from 1998 until 2001 but was most famous during this time for the astounding goal he scored after coming off the bench for Brazil's national team in their opening round Copa América championship game win over Venezuela. In this legendary play, Ronaldinho hinted at his future brilliance by receiving a pass at full stride, lobbing the ball over a defender, running around the defender, controlling his own pass before it touched the ground, backheeling a pass over his head to evade another defender, and then rocketing the ball into the back of the net.

In January 2001, Ronaldinho signed a five-year contract with Paris St.-Germain. However, a financial dispute between Gremio Porto Alegre and Paris St.-Germain held up the deal for months until it was settled when Gremio received almost $6 million from Paris St.-Germain, about 10 times less than they were initially demanding. The gregarious and charismatic Ronaldinho enjoyed the Paris nightlife but had some difficulties adjusting to the more methodical style of play in France. However, he quickly adapted and was voted France's Player of the Month for January 2002 after scoring six goals in seven games.

Later in 2002, Ronaldinho starred for Brazil's championship team in the World Cup played in Japan and South Korea. His remarkable assist for Brazil's first goal and perfect 35-meter free kick for the second goal powered Brazil to a 2-1 win over England in the quarter finals, setting up the team's subsequent wins over Turkey and Germany for the title.

Still only 22 years old after the 2002 World Cup glory, Ronaldinho was drawing praise from around the world and from soccer legends. Former Argentine star DIEGO MARADONA said of Ronaldinho, "he operates on a higher level than everyone else," and Brazilian legend PELÉ described him as, "an artist of the ball." Of his own style, Ronaldinho explained, "My game is all about improvisation. A striker has to improvise all the time. My goal is to destabilize my opponent. And there's no better way to do that than to keep inventing, which is why I'm always attempting new dribbles. And I still got a lot to learn about surprising the opposition."

Eager to play among the world's greatest players, Ronaldinho let it be known that he wanted to leave his club in Paris. European powers FC Barcelona and Manchester United got into a bidding war for Ronaldinho, and he ultimately signed with Barcelona, which paid more than $30 million to his former club. Ronaldinho excelled in Barcelona, leading the team to a second-place finish in Spain's top soccer league in 2003–04 and a first place finish in 2004–05. Ronaldinho has savored his role as Barcelona's brightest star, and his humor and humility have been embraced by fans and teammates. Ronaldinho is widely recognized as among the elite soccer players in the world today, as evidenced by his selection as FIFA World Player of the Year in 2004 and 2005. Though he failed to lead the favored Brazilian national team beyond the quarter finals in the 2006 World Cup in Germany, Ronaldinho's many admirers remain confident that his best days are ahead of him.

Further Reading

"10: Ronaldinho." FC Barcelona Web site. Available online. URL: http://www.fcbarcelona.com/eng/jugadores/futbol/biografia_10.shtml. Downloaded on January 16, 2006.

Brazilian soccer star Ronaldinho controls the ball in a 2005 match versus Mexico. *(Associated Press)*

"Brazil's Ronaldinho Top Player, Peers Say." MSNBC Web site. Available online. URL: http://www.msnbc.msn.com/id/9400087/. Downloaded on January 16, 2006.

"Ronaldinho the Natural." Fédération Internationale Football Assocation Web site. Available online. URL: http://www.fifa.com/en/mens/awards/gala/0,2418,104454,00.html?articleid=104454. Downloaded on January 16, 2006.

Ronaldo
(Ronaldo Luis Nazário de Lima, Il Fenomino)
(1976–) *soccer player*

A dynamic offensive wizard on the soccer field and a prolific goal scorer, Ronaldo achieved superstar status by netting both goals in Brazil's 2-0 World Cup championship game in 2002 and later that year became the first player to win soccer's World Player of the Year award a third time. He was born Ronaldo Luis Nazário de Lima on September 22, 1976, in Bento Ribeiro, Brazil. Named for the doctor who delivered him in this poor suburb of Rio de Janeiro, Ronaldo grew up the son of an alcoholic father, Nelio, and adored mother, Sonia, who sold pizza and ice to provide for the family.

By age 12, Ronaldo was playing organized *futsal,* sharpening his quickness and nimble footwork with the smaller ball and more confined boundaries of this version of soccer. Displaying extraordinary talent on the soccer field, Ronaldo left home at age 13 to begin playing for São Cristóvão, a local professional team, and three years later he was sold for $50,000 to the Cruzeiro de Belo Horizonte Club.

At the unusually young age of 17, Ronaldo was called up to the Brazilian national team but spent the entire 1994 World Cup tournament on the bench, as Brazil won the championship. The international experience he gained prior to the World Cup helped Ronaldo gain attention from overseas professional teams, including PSV Eindhoven in the Netherlands, which purchased Ronaldo for $6 million and signed him in 1994. Ronaldo led the Dutch league in scoring in his first season, though a knee injury kept him sidelined for much of the 1995–96 season.

Early in 1996, Ronaldo was purchased and signed by the prestigious Spanish club FC Barcelona for $21 million. He played in Barcelona, leading all of Europe in scoring in 1996–97 with 34 goals and earning recognition by the Fédération Internationale de Football Association (FIFA) as the World Player of the Year in 1996, becoming the youngest recipient of that award (begun in 1982) by seven years. He was again named FIFA World Player of the Year in 1997.

Despite his excellent performance with them, FC Barcelona then sold the 21-year-old Ronaldo to the Milan-based Italian club Internazionale in 1997 for a then record-high sum of $48 million. Though he was initially saddened about having to leave Spain, which he loved and where he was beloved, Ronaldo adjusted and tallied 25 goals in 32 matches during his first season in Italy, where the fans nicknamed him "Il Fenomino" (The Phenomenon).

A series of injuries limited Ronaldo's action on the field over the next few seasons, though he was able to play in the 1998 World Cup, where he led the Brazilians to the finals versus the host French team. In a bizarre episode, Ronaldo suffered convulsions hours before the game. Rushed to a Paris hospital, he was evaluated, released, and arrived just prior to the beginning of the game. Ronaldo played ineffectively in Brazil's 3-0 loss to France.

Though rumors over what caused his problems ran rampant, Ronaldo's reputation as having a childlike personality, uninterested in the high-flying world of big money and celebrity culture, led many observers to conclude that he was reacting to the intense emotional pressure of his situation, compounded by grueling physical exhaustion, a crumbling marriage, and possibly a reaction to pain medication taken before and after the semifinals match.

Ronaldo rebounded from the 1998 World Cup setback, as well as recurrent knee injuries that forced him to adjust from relying largely on his athletic flair to playing a style of skillful savvy and opportunistic craftiness. These traits were on display in Ronaldo's triumphant performance during the 2002 World Cup, where he won the Golden Boot award as the tournament's top scorer with eight goals, as Brazil defeated Germany for the championship. His brilliance was recognized with another FIFA World Cup Player of the Year award in 2002, making him the first player to win that award three times.

Prior to the 2002 World Cup, Ronaldo was signed by Real Madrid. Though older and slower than he was in his younger years, Ronaldo has been one of the team's stars, his name still synonymous with evading defenders, nimble footwork, and goals.

He returned to international play as a veteran member of the Brazilian national team at the 2006 World Cup in Germany. Ronaldo appeared to be out of shape early in the tournament and was said by many fans and analysts to be past his prime. He quieted his critics with a stellar performance in Brazil's 4-1 victory over Japan that moved the team into the round of 16. The goals also pushed Ronaldo past the legendary Pelé into first place in World Cup goals by a Brazilian player. Following that game, another Brazilian soccer great, Japan's coach Zico, explained, "I'd love to have a player like Ronaldo on my team. He's the type of player who can smell a goal."

Further Reading

"A Phenomenon Named Ronaldo." Real Madrid Web site. Available online. URL: http://www.realmadrid.com/articulo/rma23797.htm. Downloaded on January 16, 2006.

"Ronaldo." Expert Football Web site. Available online. URL: http://www.expertfootball.com/players/ronaldo/. Downloaded on January 16, 2006.

Rushin, Steve. "Joy to the World." *Sports Illustrated,* 15 June 1998, p. 112.

Rosales-St. John, Mia
(Mia Rosales)
(1967–   ) *boxer*

One of women's boxing's most popular competitors, Mia Rosales-St. John has amassed an impressive record while enduring criticism that her fame is the result of her glamorous image rather than her accomplishments in the ring. She was born Mia Rosales on June 24, 1967, in San Francisco, California. She lived in what she later called a "very dysfunctional family" in which she moved regularly and had almost no contact with her father.

Rosales spent most of her youth living in the San Fernando Valley north of Los Angeles and enjoyed participating in sports. She began taking tae kwan do lessons at age six, eventually earning a black belt. She competed in tae kwon do and worked as a model before graduating from California State University–Northridge with a bachelor's degree in psychology in 1994.

Rosales, who married soap opera actor Kristoff St. John in 1991 and had two children before they divorced in 1995, decided to join the ranks of female professional boxers in 1996, while the sport was still in its infancy. Known primarily for her physical attractiveness, later including an appearance on the cover of a 1999 issue of *Playboy* with an accompanying pictorial, Rosales-St. John had no prior amateur boxing experience before her first fight, a first-round knockout victory at a casino near Indio, California.

She proceeded to win over lightly regarded competition while attempting to refine an undisciplined, aggressive, and windmilling fighting style. A promotional contract with famed boxing promoter Bob Arum resulted in Rosales-St. John appearing on men's championship undercards (including many OSCAR DE LA HOYA fights), which reportedly paid her about $20,000 a fight, 10 times the normal rate for a female boxer fighting an unranked opponent.

Through a friendship with boxing champion Fernando Vargas, Rosales-St. John met Ricardo and Robert Garcia, a father-and-son boxing training team who soon began working with her. Under their tutelage, Rosales-St. John improved her technique, and though often viewed as little more than a pretty face, she gradually earned the respect of boxing fans and opponents.

With a record of 26-1-1, Rosales-St. John agreed to a fight with champion Christy Martin. Their December 6, 2002, fight in Pontiac, Michigan, resulted in a 10-round unanimous decision in favor of Martin. Rosales-St. John's ability to stand in against Martin, as well as landing a few blows of her own, helped her exceed the low prefight expectations of her performance against a female boxing icon.

Even following a loss to top contender Jessica Rakoczy on February 10, 2003, Rosales-St. John continued to be ranked in the top 10 in the light welterweight division. Focusing more on other professional interests, including creating and distributing an exercise video, Rosales-St. John fought only four times over the next three years, bringing her career record to 43-6-2, with 18 knockouts.

Further Reading
Jeffreys, Bryan. "Mia St. John: At Home in the House of Champions." *Latin Style Magazine* Web site. Available online. URL: http://www.latinstylemag.com/article.cfm?id=54. Downloaded on July 1, 2005.
Williams, Dee. "Mia Saint John." Women Boxing Archive Network Web site. Available online. URL: http://www.wban.org/biog/mstjohn.htm. Downloaded on July 1, 2005.

Ruiz, John
(the Quiet Man)
(1972–) *boxer*

A hard-punching, methodical boxer whose jab-and-grab style and low-key personality earned him the nickname "the Quiet Man," John Ruiz was the first Latino heavyweight world champion. He was born on January 4, 1972, in Methuen, Massachusetts. He lived in Methuen for only seven months, and then his parents moved the family to Sábana Grande in their native Puerto Rico. Seven years later, Ruiz's parents divorced, and Ruiz moved with his mother, stepfather, and three siblings to Chelsea, Massachusetts, a working-class Latino town outside Boston.

When he was seven, Ruiz went with his stepfather to a local gym and began learning how to box. By his late teens, Ruiz had become one of the top amateur light heavyweights in the United States.

Ruiz began his professional career on August 20, 1992, with a victory over Kevin Parker in Atlantic City, New Jersey. He followed that victory with 13 more wins, nine of which came by knockout within the first two rounds. Ruiz's first bout outside the northeastern United States was also his first defeat, when he lost a 10-round decision to Sergei Kobozev on August 12, 1993, in Bay St. Louis, Mississippi. Ruiz won his next four fights before losing to former U.S. Olympian Danell Nicholson in a 10-round decision on August 4, 1994.

From 1995 through 1999, Ruiz lost only one fight, a first-round, 19-second knockout to David Tua on March 15, 1996. He was victorious in all his other 17 fights, winning 15 of them by knockout.

His success led to a title shot at which he met World Boxing Association (WBA) world heavyweight champion Evander Holyfield on August 12, 2000, in Las Vegas. Few in the sold-out Caesars Palace crowd thought that Ruiz would unseat Holyfield, but the prospect of that happening increased when the challenger came out on the offensive, often bringing the action to Holyfield throughout the match. After the fight, Holyfield was awarded a unanimous decision, with two of the judges' scorecards showing only a one-point margin for him. Following the decision, Ruiz said, "I was definitely robbed. I had control of the fight. Holyfield threw everything at me, including elbows."

Less than seven months later, Ruiz had his much-desired rematch with Holyfield in Las Vegas.

Filled with confidence from his previous effort against Holyfield, Ruiz stood toe-to-toe with the champion despite suffering a severe welt below his left eye in the second round. Ruiz was knocked down in round 10 by a low blow from Holyfield, which resulted in a three-minute break while Ruiz recuperated and a point deduction from Holyfield. In the 11th round, Ruiz landed a stunning right that sent Holyfield to the canvas for only the second time in his career. Holyfield clutched Ruiz for most of the remainder of the fight, and following the end of the bout, Ruiz was announced the winner by unanimous decision, becoming the first Latino world heavyweight champion in boxing history.

The reserved Ruiz was overwhelmed by the attention and adulation he received as champion, including an invitation from President George W. Bush, a visit to the White House, and a celebratory gathering of about 20,000 people in his childhood town of Sábana Grande.

Ruiz relinquished his crown when he lost a unanimous decision to the lighter and quicker Roy Jones, Jr., on March 1, 2003. When Jones moved to the light heavyweight division, Ruiz claimed the vacant WBA title with a unanimous decision victory over Hasim Rahman on December 13, 2003. Though many boxing fans viewed the taciturn Ruiz as a weak champion, he retained the title until losing a unanimous decision to James Toney in New York City on April 30, 2005. A few days after that loss, Ruiz announced his retirement from boxing.

However, Toney's reign as champion and Ruiz's retirement did not last long. Toney failed the postfight drug test by testing positive for a banned anabolic steroid. The championship was returned to Ruiz, who sued Toney for financial damages. Ruiz soon decided to return to the ring and began training to defend his heavyweight crown.

In Ruiz's first defense of his newly regained title, he lost a highly controversial decision to Russian Nicolay Valuev on December 17, 2005. Following the fight, Ruiz said, "I remember thinking midway through the fight that it was the easiest fight I'd had in a long time. I couldn't believe it when the decision was announced." He then demanded an immediate rematch, though by early 2007, one had not been set.

Further Reading

"John 'The Quiet Man' Ruiz." Latino Legends in Sports Web site. Available online. URL: http://www.latinosportslegends.com/Ruiz_John-bio.htm. Downloaded on January 20, 2006.

Jones, Bobby. "Retired Ruiz May Finally Earn Some Respect." Doghouse Boxing Web site. Available online. URL: http://www.doghouseboxing.com/Jones/Jones050205.htm. Downloaded on January 20, 2006.

La Whorn, Shaun Rico. "John Ruiz: The Quiet Ways of Winning." Saddo Boxing Web site. Available online. URL: http://www.saddoboxing.com/1137-ruiz-quiet-ways-of-winning.html. Downloaded on January 20, 2006.

S

Sabatini, Gabriela
(1970–) *tennis player*

The 1990 U.S. Open women's singles champion, Gabriela Sabatini reached the quarterfinals or beyond in 27 Grand Slam tournaments from 1985 through 1996. She was born on May 16, 1970, in Buenos Aires, Argentina. Sabatini was a child prodigy on the tennis courts of Argentina's capital city and began competing in local tournaments before she was a teenager.

In 1983, at age 13, Sabatini became the youngest player to win the Orange Bowl Trophy in Miami for players 18 years and younger. She cruised through junior tournaments, collecting six titles by winning 39 of 41 matches and an incredible 79 of 88 sets played. Sabatini turned professional on New Year's Day 1985.

At a tournament in Hilton Head, South Carolina, in 1985, Sabatini defeated ninth-ranked Pam Shriver, eighth-ranked Katerina Maleva, and Zina Garrison before losing in the final to tennis legend Chris Everett. Following that tournament, the 15-year-old Sabatini jumped from the 33rd to the 18th ranked player in the world. After her surprising advancement to the French Open semifinals, she would be ranked in the top 10, a distinction she held for almost 11 years.

During the latter half of the 1980s, Sabatini was a main attraction of the women's tennis tour, admired for her tennis skills, which featured powerful ground strokes and a wicked topspin, as well as for her physical beauty. Yet many considered the quiet teenager aloof. A family friend who had known Sabatini since the star was 10, commented that she "has tennis elbow in her personality," and Everett suggested that Sabatini was arrogant, noting of her preference to maintain emotional distance from other players, "I'm that way too. But at least I say 'hello' to people."

Another struggle for Sabatini despite her overall success was German star Steffi Graf, whom she often met in later rounds of tournaments and against whom she won only once in seven matches, including a loss in the 1988 Olympics finals that earned Sabatini a silver medal. Sabatini overcame her nemesis (and partner in their 1988 Wimbledon doubles championship) with her 6-2, 7-6 victory in the 1990 U.S. Open final. With this title, Sabatini became the first Argentine to win a women's Grand Slam tennis championship.

Although Sabatini never won another Grand Slam tournament, she continued to rank among the top players in the world, reaching the Wimbledon finals in 1991 in a match she lost to Graf 4-6, 6-3, and 6-8. She reached the semifinals eight times in Grand Slam tournaments from 1992 through 1995. A series of nagging injuries finally dropped her out of the top 10 in 1996, and Sabatini retired from competitive tennis a few weeks later.

Since retiring, Sabatini has lived in Argentina and Miami, Florida. She has been active as a

Gabriela Sabatini, seen here playing at Wimbledon in 1994, reached the quarterfinals or beyond in 28 Grand Slam tournaments from 1985 through 1995. *(EMPICS)*

businesswoman in the perfume and cosmetics industry and as an advocate for women's tennis. In 1999, Sabatini was named by Argentina's Konex Foundation that nation's best female athlete of the 20th century.

Further Reading

Jenkins, Sally. "A New World Order: Gabriela Sabatini's Win in Florida Ended Steffi Graf's Run as the No. 1 Superpower." *Sports Illustrated,* 18 March 1991, p. 66.

Newman, Bruce. "Talk about Net Gains." *Sports Illustrated,* 2 May 1998, p. 52.

"Gabriela Sabatini." International Tennis Hall of Fame Web site. Available online. URL: http://www.tennisfame.com/enshrinees/sabatini_gabriela.html. Downloaded on June 24, 2006.

Salas, Marcelo
(José Marcelo Salas, the Matador)
(1974–) *soccer player*

A forward whose power, quickness, and grace have earned him the nickname "the Matador," Marcelo Salas is the captain of Chile's national soccer team and that nation's most celebrated soccer star. He was born José Marcelo Salas on December 24, 1974, in Temuco, Chile. He grew up in Temuco, a town in southern Chile noted for its harsh winters, heavy rains, and connection to its Incan cultural roots.

Encouraged by his father, Rosenber, a former amateur soccer player, Salas attended local soccer camps and practiced diligently in a small cement lot near his home. Despite the obstacles presented by his small stature (5'8") and the local inclement weather, Salas continued to train daily, and his efforts were rewarded by his inclusion on the top youth team in Temuco.

Salas's excellence on the soccer field earned the attention of the Universidad de Chile in Santiago, where he began playing on the team's Under-17 squad at age 16. Though Salas struggled with the changes caused by living in a big city far from home, he adjusted and became the leading scorer on the team. He was soon elevated to the Universidad de Chile's top club. In a 1994 game with this team, Salas was given his nickname, "the Matador," when the packed national stadium rocked to the song "Matador" to pay tribute to the courageous efforts and wining ways of the talented forward with the number 10 on his jersey.

Salas remained with the Universidad de Chile through the 1996 season, ending three years there with 49 goals in 62 games. He then signed with the prestigious Argentine team River Plate. Salas enjoyed enormous success in two years playing for River Plate. He scored 24 goals in 53 games and smashed the doubts among many about whether a Chilean could prosper in the tradition-rich Argentine league. Salas's contributions to his team's success and his well-earned reputation as a player of iron will led him to gain recognition in 1998 as the best foreign player in Argentina and the top player in South America.

Italy was Salas's next professional destination after he signed with Lazio. He played for three years for Lazio in Rome but had difficulty with injuries and adapting to the European style of play, scoring only 23 goals in 74 games, though the team did win various titles with Salas on the roster.

Salas's greatest triumph during this period was his play in a 1998 match in London's Wembley Stadium, when he scored both goals in Chile's starting 2-0 victory over England. Later that year, Salas led Chile to the round of 16 in the 1998 World Cup in France, where the Chileans fell to Brazil.

Salas fought through injury-plagued seasons playing for Juentus in Turin, Italy, from 2001 through 2003, before returning to River Plate. Following intense rehabilitation from his injuries, Salas, the all-time Chilean leader in international match goals with 35 in 65 games, announced in summer 2005 that he would participate on the Chilean national team seeking the 2006 World Cup in Germany. Chile failed to qualify for the World Cup, but Salas remained a prominent figure in Chilean soccer when he returned to Universidad de Chile in July 2005, helping lead the team to the league finals.

Further Reading

"Marcelo Salas." Soccer Saints Web site. Available online. URL: http://www.soccersaints.com/salas. htm. Downloaded on January 20, 2006.

"Marcelo Salas—El Matador." Marcelo Salas Web site. Available online. URL: http://www.marcelosalas. net/default.aspx?lng=en. Downloaded on January 20, 2006.

"Marcelo Salas: 'Germany 2006 Would Crown My Career.'" Fédération Internationale Football Association World Cup Web site. Available online. URL: http://fifaworldcup.yahoo.com/06/ en/050316/1/3abr.html. Downloaded on January 20, 2006.

Salazar, Alberto
(1958–) *marathon runner*

The winner of three consecutive New York Marathons from 1980 through 1982 and the champion of the 1982 Boston Marathon, Alberto Salazar set six U.S. records and one world record during his legendary career. He was born in August 7, 1958, in Havana, Cuba. As a young boy, his family left Cuba for Miami, Florida, to flee the government of Fidel Castro. The family soon moved to Connecticut and eventually Wayland, Massachusetts, where Salazar was a standout on the track and field team in high school.

Salazar's excellence in long-distance running earned him an athletic scholarship to the University of Oregon, where he learned under the tutelage of USA Track and Field Hall of Fame coach Bill Dellinger. In 1977, Salazar helped Oregon win the National Collegiate Athletic Association (NCAA) track and field championship. In 1978, as a college sophomore, Salazar attracted more national attention when he won the Falmouth (Massachusetts) 7.1 Miler, defeating legendary marathoner Bill Rodgers.

While still in college, Salazar transitioned from running on tracks to the grueling challenge of marathons. Within two years, he competed in one—his first New York Marathon in a then-world-record debut time of 2:09:41 (hours, minutes, and seconds). The next year, Salazar again won the New York Marathon, breaking the 12-year-old world marathon record with the time of 2:08:13. Salazar repeated as the New York Marathon champion in 1982, though an American has not won that race since.

Salazar's remarkable ascendancy through the ranks of world marathoners was highlighted by his 1982 victory in the Boston Marathon. During this race, the curly-haired Salazar ran nearly stride-for-stride with fellow American Dick Beardsley, with each man leading at various points in the course. Salazar was able to push past Beardsley in a memorable kick over the last mile and a half for the victory in a then course record time of 2:08:52.

In 1982, Salazar set two U.S. records in non-marathon events, the 5,000 meters (13:11:93) and the 10,000 meters (27:25:61). At the 1984 Olympics in Los Angeles, California, Salazar placed 15th in the marathon. Persistent health concerns, including problems with asthma, caused Salazar to take an extended break from competition. He returned in 1994 to compete as an ultramathoner, later winning the prestigious Comrades Marathon, a 53-mile race from Durban to Pietermaritzburg, South Africa.

Salazar, who lives in Oregon and was elected to the USA Track and Field Hall of Fame in 2001,

has recently worked as a restaurateur, coach, and public advocate for health in sports. Speaking in 2001 at an event to raise awareness and funds for the Special Olympics, Salazar explained, "Other than running, I'm a normal human being . . . sports prepares us for life. It has no lasting value except for how it prepares us for life."

Further Reading

"Alberto Salazar." National Distance Running Hall of Fame Web site. Available online. URL: http://www.distancerunning.com/inductees/2000/salazar.html. Downloaded on January 20, 2006.

"Alberto Salazar." USA Track and Field Web site. Available online. URL: http://www.usatf.org/HallOf

Alberto Salazar (foreground) runs his career-best time in the 10,000 meters at the World Championships in Helsinki, Finland. *(EMPICS)*

Fame/TF/showBio.asp?HOFIDs=143. Downloaded on January 20, 2006.

Hoban, Brom. "Marathoner Alberto Salazar Makes an Unprecedented Comeback." *Hispanic,* 28 February 1995.

Saldívar, Vicente
(1943–1985) *boxer*

A short, explosive left-handed boxer who often defeated his opponents with his physical stamina and mental tenacity, Vicente Saldívar was a two-time world featherweight champion during the 1960s and early 1970s. He was born on May 3, 1943, in Mexico City, Mexico. Saldívar grew up in the Mexican capital city and by his late teens was a top amateur featherweight. He turned professional at age 17 and won his first fight in a first-round knockout over Baby Palacios in Oaxaca, Mexico, on February 18, 1961.

Saldívar won 21 of his next 22 bouts through 1963, leading to his February 8, 1964, second-round knockout of Juan Ramírez in Mexico City that earned him the Mexican featherweight title. Less than four months later, Saldívar defeated Ismael Laguna and followed that impressive victory with a 12-round upset knockout of Sugar Ramos in Mexico City for the world featherweight title.

His reign as champion spanned eight successful title defenses and was highlighted by three exciting fights with Howard Winstone, the first two in 15-round decisions and the third a 12th-round knockout in Mexico City on October 14, 1967. Moments after this win, Saldívar announced his retirement from boxing.

Inactive throughout all of 1968 and most of 1969, Saldívar returned to the ring on July 18, 1969, with a 10-round unanimous decision over ex-champion José Legra, despite being knocked down early in the bout. Saldívar's renewed pursuit of his former title was realized when he won a unanimous decision over Johnny Famechon on May 9, 1970, in Rome, Italy.

However, Saldívar's second reign as world featherweight champion was short lived. He relinquished the crown on December 11, 1970, when he suffered a 12th-round technical knockout to Kuniaki Shibata in Tijuana, Mexico. Saldívar won his next fight but was knocked out by Eder Jofie on October 21, 1973. Realizing that he no longer possessed the power and endurance that seemed to allow him to fight with the same energy in the 15th round that he had in the first round, Saldívar retired and never returned to competitive boxing.

Saldívar spent his postboxing life in Mexico until July 18, 1985, when he suffered a fatal heart attack at age 42. An autopsy showed that Saldívar, who had no indication of health risks, had an abnormally large heart. He was inducted posthumously into the International Boxing Hall of Fame in 1999.

Further Reading
"Vicente Saldivar." Cyber Boxing Web site. Available online. URL: http://www.cyberboxingzone.com/boxing/saldiv-v.htm. Downloaded on January 20, 2006.

"Vicente Saldivar." International Boxing Hall of Fame Web site. Available online. URL: http://www.ibhof.com/saldivar.htm. Downloaded on Janaury 20, 2006.

Sanchez, Felix
(1977–) *hurdler*

The 2004 Olympic gold medalist in the 400-meter hurdles, Felix Sanchez is the first Olympic champion to represent the Dominican Republic. He was born on August 30, 1977, in New York City. Sanchez's parents had immigrated from the Dominican Republic a few years before he was born, and he left New York with his mother when he was two, eventually settling in San Diego, California.

Sanchez excelled in athletics, particularly baseball and football. He began attending University

Felix Sanchez competes in a 400-meter hurdles heat on his way to winning the gold medal at the 2004 Olympics in Athens. *(EMPICS)*

High in San Diego after the football season had already begun, so he decided to join a friend and try out for the wrestling team. While practicing wrestling, Sanchez broke his arm, preventing him from playing baseball in the spring. Instead, he joined the track team.

By his senior year in high school, Sanchez was a standout sprinter. He attended and ran track at Mesa College in San Diego before enrolling at the University of Southern California (USC). In 2000, Sanchez won the National Collegiate Athletic Association (NCAA) 400-meter hurdles event but later that year failed to medal in the Olympics in Sydney, Australia.

Sanchez was undeterred by his results in Sydney and dedicated himself to preparing for the 2004 Olympics in Athens, Greece, where he helped win only the second medal in the history of the Dominican Republic. (Sanchez has both American and Dominican citizenship and had long sought to represent his parents' native country.) With a July 4, 2001, victory in a race in Lausanne, Switzerland, Sanchez began a string of 43 wins in the 400-meter hurdles that is second only to American Edwin Moses's remarkable 122 consecutive 400-meter wins that stretched from 1977 to 1987. Included in this streak was Sanchez's personal best time of 47.25 seconds set on August 29, 2003, in Paris, as well as two world championships and the 2003 Pan-American Games gold medal.

In the 2004 Olympics, Sanchez cruised through qualifying heats, setting up the final race on August 26. He was tested early by American James Carter but overtook him and all other competitors in the final turn with a burst of speed and perfectly executed leaps over the 36-inch high obstacles spaced about every 35 meters around the track. Sanchez, the smallest and most thinly muscled of the competitors, reached the finish line first with a time of 47.63 seconds.

Sanchez's victory gave the Dominican Republic its first Olympic gold medal in the nation's history. As Sanchez took a victory lap draped in the Dominican Republic flag, thousands celebrated in the streets of Santo Domingo and in other parts of the largely impoverished island nation. Luis Mejia, president of the Dominican Republic Olympic Committee, explained the significance of Sanchez's accomplishment, saying, "People know us for baseball . . . Marichal. Sosa. Pedro [Martinez]. A-Rod. They are like four continents to us. And ahora [now] Felix Sanchez is the fifth continent. He's our man of the world."

Further Reading

"Born to Run." Open Your Eyes Web site. Available online. URL: http://www.oyemag.com/felix.html. Downloaded on January 20, 2006.

Cazeneuve, Brian. "Dominican Darling: World Champion Felix Sanchez Will Get a Hero's Welcome

When He Competes at Pan-Am Games." *Sports Illustrated,* 11 August 2003.

Jenkins, Chris. "Sanchez's Gold Medal a First for His Country." *San Diego Union-Tribune,* 27 August 2004.

Sánchez, Salvador
(1959–1982) *boxer*

A thin but powerful boxer who devastated opponents with swift and accurate counterpunches, Salvador Sánchez lost only one of his 46 professional bouts and was the reigning world featherweight champion when a car crash took his life at age 23. He was born on January 26, 1959, in Santiago Tianguistenco, Mexico. Sánchez grew up in a family of farmers but was spotted as a great boxing talent by local trainers when he was still in his early teens. He fought only a few amateur bouts before taking the ring as a professional for the first time as a 16-year-old on May 4, 1975, knocking out Al Gardino in the third round in Veracruz, Mexico.

Over the next two years, Sánchez was victorious in all 17 of his fights, winning 16 of them by knockout. At age 18, Sánchez challenged Antonio Becerrra for the Mexican bantamweight title in Becerra's hometown of Mazatlán. Sánchez lost a controversial split decision but rebounded to win his final two fights in 1977.

Sánchez's first fight in the United States took place at Los Angeles's Olympic Auditorium on April 15, 1978. Though expected to win, Sánchez struggled but managed to escape this fight with a draw. He soon began training with more intensity. This dedication quickly paid off as Sánchez won each of his next 13 fights fought between July 1978 and the end of 1979. Among his victories during this span were knockouts of Félix Trinidad, Sr. (father of future champion FÉLIX TRINIDAD), and Richard Rozelle.

Following his victory over Rozelle, Sánchez was the eighth-ranked featherweight in the world by *Ring Magazine.* His first opportunity at the world featherweight title was a February 2, 1980, bout versus popular champion Danny "Little Red" Lopez in Las Vegas. Lopez was favored and enjoyed the support of most of the sold-out crowd as soon he entered the ring in full Ute headdress to honor his Native American heritage. However, the bushy haired Sánchez controlled the fight with powerful combinations and devastating counterpunches that eventually earned him a technical knockout in the 13th round.

The 21-year-old Sánchez successfully defended his title four times throughout 1980, including another technical knockout win over the vengeful Lopez. Although Sánchez displayed a tendency to fight down to the level of his competition, resulting in closer than expected wins, he was able to retain his crown heading into a much-anticipated bout with junior featherweight champion WILFREDO GÓMEZ.

The Sánchez-Gómez fight of August 12, 1981, in Las Vegas was touted as "The Battle of the Little Giants," pitting two men considered among the best pound-for-pound boxers in the world. Additionally, the Puerto Rican Gómez had built a reputation for wiping out Mexican fighters, including previously undefeated CARLOS ZÁRATE, adding ethnic animosity to the personal dislike between the combatants.

Despite moving up in weight to challenge the champion, Gómez came into the fight favored over Sánchez. Amid the clashing sounds of dueling bands (salsa for Gómez and mariachi for Sánchez), the boxers entered the ring and proceeded to fiercely attack each other until Sánchez's solid punches and steady endurance overcame Gómez, giving Sánchez an eighth-round knockout victory.

After his win over Gómez, Sánchez, already popular in Mexico, became a beloved folk hero in his native country. Many now described him as the greatest Mexican boxer of all time, a designation that gained more credibility as Sánchez disposed of three more challengers through summer 1982, including up-and-coming Ghanian and future Hall of Fame boxer Azumah Nelson.

The Sánchez-Nelson fight on July 21, 1982, would be Sánchez's last bout. On August 12, 1982, Sánchez was killed when his Porsche collided with a pickup truck in an early morning accident north of Mexico City. Though only 23 at the time of his death, Sánchez, who was inducted into the International Boxing Hall of Fame in 1991, is still considered by many experts as among the top featherweights of all time. Among those who continue to respect Sánchez is his former ring adversary Gómez, who regularly attends an annual commemorative festival in Sanchez's hometown of Santiago Tianguistenco, Mexico.

Further Reading

"Salvador Sanchez." Boxing Records Archive Web site. Available online. URL: http://www.boxrec.com/boxer_display.php?boxer_id=002201. Downloaded on January 20, 2006.

Smith, Glenn C. "Salvador Sanchez (1959–1982): A Brilliant Career Cut Short." *Los Angeles Sentinel.*

Zurita, Juan Angel. "The Legend of Salvador Sanchez." Boxing Fanatics Web site. Available online. URL: http://www.boxingfanatics.com/sanchezzurita.html. Downloaded on January 20, 2006.

Further Viewing

Champions Forever—The Latin Legends (DVD). New Champions, Inc./Panorama Entertainment. 2000.

Santana, Johan
(1979–) *baseball player*

The 2004 American League (AL) Cy Young Award winner, Johan Santana has applied a solid command of a baffling repertoire of pitches and pinpoint control to become the top young left-handed starting pitcher in Major League Baseball. He was born on March 13, 1979, in Tovar

Mérida, Venezuela. He grew up in the remote town of Tovar Mérida, which was renowned for its soccer players, cyclists, and artists but had never produced a Major League Baseball player. Santana was introduced to baseball by his father, Jesus, an engineer and former semipro shortstop, and his older brother.

Santana was a flashy defensive outfielder with a powerful left arm on the youth teams until he began pitching in his mid-teens. He was first noticed by professional scouts while competing in Venezuela's National Youth Baseball tournament. A scout for the Houston Astros was so enamored with Santana's pitching prowess that he drove 10 hours through the Andes Mountains to sign him. Just after his 16th birthday, Santana signed with the Houston Astros.

Santana's early years in the Astros minor league system were marked by impressive strikeout totals, but he failed to convince many in the organization that he would soon be ready to contribute at the major league level. In what would become a legendary miscalculation, the Astros chose to place a player who had never contributed in the major leagues on the 40-man roster instead of Santana following the 1999 season, exposing the young left-handed pitcher to other teams via a special draft. After this draft, Santana ended up property of the Minnesota Twins.

In 2000, Santana pitched in middle relief, picking up his first victory over the Astros and ending the season with an unimpressive 2-3 record and a 6.49 earned run average (ERA). An elbow injury limited him to 15 games in 2001, but Santana returned in 2002 to serve as a team member of Minnesota's resurgence, compiling an 8-6 record and 2.99 ERA, with 137 strikeouts in less than 109 innings, helping the Twins win the AL Central Division.

The improved control and masterful changeup with which he delivered deceptively slow pitches using a motion indistinguishable from that of his fastball, helped Santana enjoy a stellar 2003 season. He finished that year with a 12-3 record,

3.07 ERA, and 167 strikeouts in 158⅓ innings, as the Twins repeated as AL Central champions. Boosting his record was an 8-0 streak down the concluding stretch of the season, in which Santana pitched as a starter.

He started for the Twins in game one of the American League Division Series (ALDS) against the New York Yankees and had the lead when he left after the fourth inning with a sore hamstring. The Twins won that game but lost the next two, leading to game four when the Yankees pounded the hobbled Santana and defeated the Twins in the series 3-1.

Santana's breakout season was 2004. He started slowly and reached the mid-season All-Star game break with a record of barely .500. But in the second half of the season, Santana was dominant, winning the AL Pitcher of the Month for July, August, and September while accumulating a 14-2 record, a 1.390 ERA, and 165 strikeouts, becoming the first person since PEDRO MARTÍNEZ (1999) to win that award three times in one season.

Now the undisputed ace of the Twins staff, Santana started game one of the American League Championship Series (ALCS) against the New York Yankees, leading the Twins to a 2-0 shutout with seven scoreless innings. He started game four and left after the fifth inning with a 4-1 lead, though the Twins eventually lost this game and the series. He finished the season with a 20-6 record and led the AL with a 2.61 ERA and 265 strikeouts. Following the season, Santana was named the AL Cy Young Award winner.

Santana followed up his outstanding 2004 season with another stellar campaign in 2005, finishing 16-7, ranking second in the AL with a 2.87 ERA, and leading the AL with 238 strikeouts. After the season, Santana was third in voting for the AL Cy Young Award. Twins catcher Matt LeCroy provided a frightening glimpse for opposing batters in the future when he reflected on Santana's greatness on the mound during the 2005 season, saying, "He makes the best hitters in baseball look silly."

In 2006, Santana continued his brilliance, leading the AL in wins (19), ERA (2.77), and strikeouts (245) to lead an injury-ravaged and young Twins pitching staff to the AL Central championship. Soon after Minnesota lost in the ALDS to the Oakland A's, Santana was recognized for his excellence with a second Cy Young Award.

Further Reading
"Johan Santana." Jock Bio Web site. Available online. URL: http://www.jockbio.com/Bios/Santana/Santana_bio.html. Downloaded on January 20, 2006.

"Johan Santana." Minnesota Twins Web site. Available online. URL: http://minnesota.twins.mlb.com/NASApp/mlb/team/player.jsp?player_id=276371. Downloaded on January 20, 2006.

La Velle, Neal E. "Twins' Johan Santana AL Cy Young Winner: It's Unanimous; Lefthanded Ace Gets Every First-Place Vote as League's Top Pitcher." *Minneapolis Star-Tribune,* 12 November 2004.

Santos, Manoel Francisco dos *See* GARRINCHA

Sardinas, Kid Chocolate
(Sergio Eligio Sardinas, the Cuban Bonbon)
(1910–1988) *boxer*

A dazzlingly quick boxer who delivered surprising power from each hand, Kid Chocolate Sardinas was one of the greatest and most popular fighters of the 1930s. He was born Sergio Eligio Sardinas on January 6, 1910, in Havana, Cuba. Sardinas grew up amid severe poverty in the Cuban capital's El Cerro section, dropping out of school as a boy to sell newspapers.

He quickly developed skills as a street fighter while defending his sales turf. After winning an amateur boxing tournament sponsored by the newspaper *La Noche,* Sardinas came under the tutelage of *La Noche's* sports editor, Luis Gutiérrez, who soon trained the young fighter and helped him gain an undefeated record as an amateur and victories in his first 21 professional bouts.

Gutíerrez then brought 18-year-old Sardinas to New York City with hopes of realizing glory in the ring. In the United States, Sardinas became known almost exclusively as "Kid Chocolate," or "the Cuban Bonbon," because of his dark skin and smooth fighting style. By 1929, Kid Chocolate was ranked as the top featherweight contender by *Ring Magazine,* his reputation boosted by impressive wins over experienced opponents such as Al Singer. On August 7, 1930, Kid Chocolate met Jackie "Kid" Berg in front of 40,000 spectators at the New York Polo Grounds and, suffered his first loss in a close decision.

Following a defeat to Battalino in a featherweight title bout on December 12, 1930, Kid Chocolate rebounded by defeating Benny Bass on July 15, 1931, to win the world junior lightweight crown. He continued to average more than one fight per month throughout the early 1930s, basking in the adulation of boxing fans and enjoying the extravagant lifestyle of a celebrity in New York City.

Although a loss to champion Tony Canzoneri prevented Kid Chocolate from gaining the lightweight championship, his elegant skills in the ring, particularly his remarkable foot and hand speed, helped him claim New York's featherweight title when he defeated Lou Feldman by a technical knockout in Madison Square Garden on October 13, 1932.

By 1933, Kid Chocolate's grueling fight schedule and his pursuit of the nightlife had taken a visible toll on him by 1933. He still won almost all his fights but rarely faced first-rate competition. Sardinas continued to fight until 1938, finishing his career with a record of 131-9-6.

Kid Chocolate spent his retirement in Cuba, where he operated a gym. He died at the age of 78 on August 8, 1988, and was inducted into the International Boxing Hall of Fame in 1994. His enormous contribution to the New York boxing scene is immortalized by a statue of him at Madison Square Garden.

Further Reading

"Eligio Sardinas (Kid Chocolate)." Cuba Sports Web site. Available online. URL: http://www.cubasports.com/english/estrellas/kidchocolate.asp. Downloaded on January 20, 2006.

"Kid Chocolate." International Boxing Hall of Fame Web site. Available online. URL: http://www.ibhof.com/chocolate.htm. Downloaded on January 20, 2006.

"Kid Chocolate 'The Cuban Bon Bon.'" Cyber Boxing Web site. Available online. URL: http://www.cyberboxingzone.com/boxing/kidchoc.htm. Downloaded on January 20, 2006.

Schmidt, Oscar
(Mao Santa)
(1958–) *basketball player*

The godfather of Brazilian basketball, famed for his long-range shooting ability, Oscar Schmidt played in every Olympics from 1980 to 1996 and was the leading scorer three times. He was born on February 16, 1958, in Natal, Brazil. Schmidt, whose grandparents had immigrated to Brazil from Germany, spent his youth in this northeastern coastal city and was introduced to basketball by an uncle. He starred on a local team, where his height (he eventually grew to 6'8") and unique offensive skill led the Brazilian national team to recruit him.

Only 17 years old and living on his own in São Paulo, Schmidt initially struggled with the Brazilian national team. However, when a new coach moved Schmidt from center to forward, he quickly blossomed. Demonstrating a uniquely smooth outside shot that would later earn him the nickname throughout Brazil of "Mão Santa" (Holy Hand), Schmidt made the all-tournament team at age 20 at the 1978 World Championships in Manila, Philippines. However, the late 1970s were a low period for Brazilian basketball, largely because of constant infighting caused by jealousy among veteran players of the young

Schmidt, around whom coaches focused the offense.

Schmidt played professionally in Italy, Spain, and Brazil, though he is known globally for his participation in five Olympic games from 1980 to 1996. Though Brazil never advanced beyond the finals, Schmidt led scoring in the Olympics tournaments three times, including an astounding average of 42.3 points per game at the 1988 Olympics in Seoul, South Korea. Over 38 games in the Olympics, Schmidt scored 1,093 points for an average of 28.8 points per game.

The highlight of Schmidt's career came when he was 39 at the Pan-American Games in Indianapolis, Indiana, when Brazil shocked the United States by winning 120–115 in the gold medal game. With Brazil trailing 68-54 at halftime, Schmidt took over, repeatedly sinking three-point shots in a game-high 46-point performance that shook the basketball world and foreshadowed the ensuing improvement in the quality of play outside U.S. borders.

The crowd, composed almost entirely of American fans, applauded as Schmidt and the Brazilian underdogs rollicked on the court in celebration. As Schmidt described the evening of the shocking triumph, "In the restaurant later, the people stood up and cheered when we came in. This was unbelievable. The whole scene, how can I say it? This is what we dream. It was the time of my life."

Although he was drafted by the New Jersey Nets in the sixth round of the 1984 National Basketball Association's (NBA) draft, Schmidt never played professionally in the United States. Instead Schmidt opted for the greater salary and playing time as a star in Europe, though he was an admired legend of future NBA players of Brazil such as LEANDRO BARBOSA and NENÊ.

Schmidt played professionally until he retired in 2003 at age 45. His profound legacy is found in the growth and popularity of the three-point shot and of basketball throughout Brazil and South America. It is also remembered in his offensive artistry, reflected in the comments of Schmidt's 1992 Olympics teammate Marcel Souza. When asked why other players are forced to sacrifice their scoring opportunities to increase Schmidt's, Souza responded, "Some of us are piano movers and some of us are piano players."

Further Reading

Kirkpatrick, Curry. "Oscar, It's Just Oscar." *Sports Illustrated,* 14 September 1988, p. 64.
"Oscar Schmidt." CMG Worldwide Web site. Available online. URL: http://www.cmgworldwide.com/sports/schmidt/news.php. Downloaded on January 20, 2006.
"Oscar Schmidt, Brazil." International Basketball Web site. Available online. URL: http://www.interbasket.net/players/oscar.htm. Downloaded on January 20, 2006.
Wolff, Alexander. "The Man from Brazil." *Sports Illustrated,* 9 June 2003.

Segura, Pancho
(Francisco Olegario Segura)
(1921–   ) *tennis player*

One of the top-ranked tennis players in the world during the late 1940s, Pancho Segura overcame a childhood disability to become the only man to win three consecutive college championships. He was born Francisco Olegario Segura on June 20, 1921, in Guayaquil, Ecuador. He grew up in that coastal city in that nation's southwestern region.

As a boy, he suffered with rickets, a bone disorder caused by a deficiency of vitamin D and/or calcium, resulting in often severe bowleggedness. Despite the problems caused by rickets and his small frame (5'6"), Segura persisted with his passion for tennis, and by age 17 he had gained the Ecuadoran championship, as well as several other Latin American titles.

Segura came to the United States to attend the University of Miami in the early 1940s. He was a curious sight for tennis fans, with his two-handed grip on all strokes, a result of his childhood weakness. Yet his upbeat personality and precision on the court delighted spectators at World War II–era tournaments, which had been depleted of other stars because of enlistments. (Segura's status as an alien prevented him from serving in the U.S. military.)

Relying on nimble footwork, cunning strategy, and his trademark two-handed forehand that his frequent opponent and early tennis giant Jack Kramer called "the greatest single shot ever produced in tennis," Segura enjoyed wide success in the 1940s. From 1943 through 1945, Segura won 15 of 30 tournaments, including three straight U.S. intercollegiate tournaments, 107 of 122 matches, and reached the semifinals at the U.S. Championship in Forest Hills, New York, repeating that feat in 1942, 1946, and 1947.

Segura became a touring professional in 1947 but played mostly in secondary matches, while players such as Kramer and PANCHO GONZALES received the most notoriety. Segura won three consecutive U.S. pro championships from 1950 through 1952 and lost the title to Gonzales three years in a row (1955–1957). Segura also won three US pro championships in doubles, once pairing with Kramer and twice with Gonzales.

Although the open era of tennis arrived when Segura was far past his prime, he did play in the first open Wimbledon in 1968, pairing at age 47 with ALEX OLMEDO to win the longest doubles match in Wimbledon Open history, a 94-game battle over Abe Segal and Gordon Forbes (32-30, 5-7, 6-4, and 6-4).

After his playing career ended, Segura settled in southern California, where he worked as a renowned teaching pro and is credited with helping Jimmy Connors develop into a star in the 1970s and 1980s. Segura was elected to the International Tennis Hall of Fame in 1984.

Further Reading

Norwood, Robyn. "Remembering When Tennis Was Wild and Wonderful." *St. Louis Post-Dispatch,* 27 July 1997.

"Pancho Segura." International Tennis Hall of Fame Web site. Available online. URL: http://www.tennisfame.org/enshrinees/pancho_segura.html. Downloaded on January 20, 2006.

Segura, Pancho. *Pancho Segura's Championship Strategy: How to Play Winning tennis.* New York: McGraw Hill, 1976.

Senna, Ayrton
(1960–1994) *auto racer*

A racecar driver of legendary skill and daring, Ayrton Senna was a three-time Formula One champion (1988, 1990, and 1991) and remains the all-time leader in poll positions (65) despite having his career tragically end in a fatal crash in the 1994 San Marino Grand Prix. He was born on March 21, 1960, in São Paulo, Brazil. When Senna was four years old, his father, Milton, gave him a one-horsepower racing cart in hopes that the gift would help the child overcome his physical awkwardness. Senna quickly developed a passion for driving, spending much of his time at local tracks and first driving the family car at age eight.

In 1973, Senna reached the minimum age requirement (13) to race carts, which he had been awaiting anxiously, and began competing and won his first race. Later in his teens, Senna won the South American cart championship in 1977 and 1978.

Senna moved up into progressively more advanced racing series in the late 1970s and early 1980s, enjoying much success though struggling to attract needed sponsorship funding. He briefly retired before his father and a Brazilian bank provided enough support for his return in 1982, when Senna won 42 races. Senna then moved into the Formula Three circuit in 1983 and won the championship, displaying a fearlessness, determination, and attention to detail that would mark his career.

Following his success in Formula Three, Senna graduated to the top series of road racing—Formula One. He signed a three-year contract to race with the Toleman Team but exercised a buy-

Ayrton Senna prepares for the 1994 San Marino Grand Prix, hours before the crash that claimed his life. *(EMPICS)*

out clause in order to race with Lotus. The latter had struggled in recent years but remained prestigious to Senna, who remembered when his hero, Fittipaldi, had raced for them. Senna won his first race in the Portuguese Grand Prix in Estoril and followed that victory with six more wins driving for Lotus. However, Senna was unable to lift Lotus to its former prominence, leading him to sign with the McLaren Team in 1988.

With McLaren, Senna rose to the top of the racing world by winning eight races in 1988 on three continents and earning his first world championship. In 1989, Senna came in second to his teammate and adversary Alain Prost despite having more wins (six). Tension between the two contributed to Prost leaving McLaren and helped establish a fierce rivalry for Formula One's world championship, which Senna claimed in 1990 and 1991 with a total of 13 wins.

As Senna pursued his place as the finest driver in the world, he also developed a reputation for technical brilliance and a competetive intensity that sometimes went beyond the borders of recklessness. Though many close to Senna described him as a compassionate and sensitive man who privately contributed millions to charity, others viewed him as aloof and aggressive, too willing to risk the safety of himself and others with a video-game style of driving born out of his relentless desire for victory.

Senna began racing with the Williams-Renault Team in 1994. He took two of his still all-time record 65 poll positions in his first two races that year, though mechanical problems prevented him from finishing. On May 1, 1994, Senna raced in the San Marino Grand Prix in Italy, again earning the poll position. Senna had the lead early in the race when his car brushed another car at more than 130 miles an hour, causing it to leave the track and strike an unprotected concrete wall. Suffering from massive head trauma, Senna was rushed to a hospital where he was officially pronounced dead.

The cause of the crash was extensively investigated and finally determined to be the result of the loosening of one of the car's suspension bars. Seven years after the crash, a British television program explained that Senna's quick reaction to the car's slide led to his driving off the road—concluding that if his reaction time had been slower, he might have survived the crash. Italian prosecutors later charged the Williams-Renault Team with manslaughter for design defects that led to Senna's death, but the team was found not guilty.

The racing world grieved Senna's death, and Brazilian fans were devastated. At his memorial service in São Paulo, more than 1 million people lined the streets to pay their final respects to Senna who, at age 34, had already convinced many that he was the greatest driver ever in the history of Formula One racing.

Reflecting his insatiable quest for speed and excellence, which led to 41 wins in 161 races and his legendary status, Senna said, "On a given day, a given circumstance, you think you have a limit and you go for this limit and you touch this limit and you think, OK, this is the limit. As soon as you touch this limit, something happens and you realize that you can go a little bit further. With your mind power, your determination, your instinct, and your experience as well, you can fly very high."

Further Reading

"Ayrton Senna." Grand Prix Web site. Available online. URL: http://www.grandprix.com/gpe/drv-senayr.html. Downloaded on January 20, 2006.

"Ayrton Senna." Motorsport Publishing Group Web site. Available online. URL: http://www.ddavid.com/formula1/ayrton-senna.htm. Downloaded on January 20, 2006.

Cahier, Paul-Henri. *Ayrton Senna: Through My Eye.* Hunt Valley, Md.: Autosports Marketing Associates, 2004.

Hilton, Christopher. *Ayrton Senna: As Time Goes By.* Osceola, Wis.: Motorbooks International, 1999.

Silva, Leônidas da   *See* LEÔNIDAS

Silva, Marta Vieira da   *See* MARTA

Sócrates
(Sócrates Brasileiro Sampaio de Souza Vieira de Oliveira)
(1954–   ) *soccer player*

A soccer player of rare elegance, renowned for his nimble heelkicks, Socrates was a standout Brazilian midfielder throughout the 1980s. He was born Sócrates Brasileiro Sampaio de Souza Vieira de Oliveira on February 19, 1954, in Riberão Preto, Brazil. A tall, intellectually inclined youth, Sócrates honed his soccer skills playing *futsal,* the indoor version of soccer played on a smaller court. Sócrates was an excellent soccer player but was not considered among the nation's best young prospects, leading him to pursue his studies and eventually earn a medical degree.

Sócrates began his professional playing career with Botafogo in Riberão Preto, where he insisted on remaining while finishing medical school despite receiving offers from more elite teams. He also played for Flamengo and Santos. In 1984, Sócrates spent a season in Italy playing for Fiorentina, but he did not enjoy living overseas and quickly returned to his beloved Brazil.

Although he was a successful professional player, Sócrates was most famous for his contributions to the Brazilian national team in the 1980s. He did not join the squad until he was 25 years old but quickly distinguished himself as a team leader with uncanny vision, instincts, and a deft and powerful kick.

In the 1982 World Cup tournament in Spain, Sócrates scored twice, including a beautiful effort in which he dribbled past two defenders before launching a long-range goal in Brazil's 2-1 victory over the Soviet Union. Brazil failed to advance past round 16 in that tournament, but Sócrates returned to World Cup play in the 1986 tournament in Mexico. He was instrumental in leading Brazil to four straight tournament wins in which the Brazilians outscored their opponents 9-0, but Brazil fell in the quarterfinals in an overtime shootout to France.

Sócrates's popularity in Brazil was due to more than his skill in competition. His unorthodox appearance (standing 6'4", bearded, and with curly long hair) and free-spirited style (he openly admitted being a chain smoker) led Brazilian fans to appreciate the unique authenticity of their star player.

Following the conclusion of his playing career in 1986, Sócrates remained in the public eye as a soccer commentator and as an increasingly popular voice of political expression in Brazil. In addition to criticizing what he believed was corruption in the Brazilian Football Confederation (the governing body of Brazilian soccer), Sócrates has also forcefully advocated for expanded education and political opportunity for Brazil's poor citizens.

Further Reading

Bellos, Alex. *Futebol: Soccer: The Brazilian Way.* New York: Bloomsbury USA, 2002.

Socrates. "Brazil's Battered Football: A Star's Outburst." Info Brazil Web site. Available online. URL: http://www.infobrazil.com/conteudo/front_page/opinion/vw2103a.htm. Downloaded on January 20, 2006.

"Socrates." Planet World Cup Web site. Available online. URL: http://www.planetworldcup.com/LEGENDS/socrates.html. Downloaded on January 20, 2006.

Sosa, Sammy
(Samuel Sosa)
(1968–   ) *baseball player*

A prodigious home run hitter and one of the most popular athletes in the world during the late 1990s, Sammy Sosa was the 1998 National League (NL) Most Valuable Player (MVP) and ranked among the top 10 NL batters in home runs for 11 consecutive seasons (1993–2003), though his reputation as a goodwill ambassador for baseball suffered from a bat corking incident and rumors of performance-enhancing drug use late in his career. He was born Samuel Sosa on November 12, 1968, in San Pedro de Macorís, Dominican Republic. Sosa spent much of his youth selling orange juice and shining shoes to help support his mother, Lucrecia, and six siblings following the death of his father, Bautista, who passed away of a brain hemorrhage when Sosa was only seven.

As a lanky adolescent, Sosa's favorite sport was boxing, but he abandoned that sport at his mother's request and began playing organized baseball when he was 14. Despite being described in one scouting report as "skinny and malnourished," Sosa's quick swing and foot speed had impressed many of the major league scouts who regularly mined the talent-rich town of San Pedro de Macorís. When he was 16, Sosa was signed by the Texas Ranger scout (and future major league general manager) Omar Minaya to a professional contract.

Sosa steadily moved up the Texas farm system, consistently ranking among his league's leaders in doubles, triples, and stolen bases. On June 16, 1989, at age 20, Sosa made his major league debut for the Rangers. He struggled over the next six weeks before surprisingly being traded with two others to the Chicago White Sox for hitting star Harold Baines and another player.

In 1990, Sosa became a full-time outfielder for the White Sox. He displayed the speed (32 stolen bases) and offensive prowess (50 home runs, 56 doubles, and 10 triples) that had intrigued scouts earlier but finished the season with only a .233 batting average and 150 strikeouts. In 1991, Sosa had two home runs and five runs batted in (RBIs) on opening day versus the Baltimore Orioles but struggled the rest of the season, leading to a brief demotion into the minors.

Days prior to the beginning of the 1992 season, Sosa was dealt by the White Sox to the cross-town Chicago Cubs with another player for aging slugger George Dowel. A broken right hand led to a stint on the disabled list, and 10 days after his return, he broke an ankle and ended his season.

Healthy for the 1993 campaign, Sosa became the first player in Cubs history to join the 30/30 (home runs/stolen bases) Club, hitting 33 home runs and stealing 36 bases. Sosa followed that with an impressive strike-shortened 1994 effort, winning the team's offensive triple crown by leading the Cubs in batting average (.300), home runs (25), and RBIs (70).

Sosa continued to emerge as a leading offensive threat in 1995 and 1996. In 1995, Sosa became the first Cub in the 20th century to lead the team in home runs (36) and steals (34) in three consecutive seasons and earned the first of his seven All-Star Game appearances. In 1996, Sosa was leading the NL in home runs (40) when his season was ended by a pitch that broke his left hand.

The injuries that restricted Sosa's promise through the first part of his career were left behind over an astounding six-year period of power unparalleled in Major League Baseball history. From 1997 through 2002, Sosa missed an average of fewer than four games a season while averaging a stratospheric 55 home runs and 138 RBIs a year.

Having transformed from a lanky to an Atlaslike physique during this time span, Sosa was no longer a base-stealing threat, averaging 10 per season in those six years (and only stealing a combined total of two in 2001 and 2002). Sosa also was regularly among the league leaders in strikeouts. However, Sosa's historic statistics, gregarious personality, and lively showmanship, made him a beloved figure on the north side of Chicago and one of the world's most beloved athletes.

The catalyst for Sosa's enormous popularity was his 1998 performance and his record-breaking chase of the single-season home run record with Mark McGwire of the St. Louis Cardinals. Throughout the summer and into the fall, Sosa and McGwire pursued Roger Marris's record of 61 home runs in a season, set in 1961, in a friendly and exciting duel that many fans and members of the media credited with revitalizing baseball's image after the damaging players' strike in 1994.

Though McGwire eventually won the home run title with a record 72, Sosa ended up with a second-best in major league history with 66 home runs, including a single-month record of 20 (set in May). Sosa's booming bat also helped the Cubs advance to the playoffs, where they fell to the Atlanta Braves.

Sosa's amazing power continued to result in eye-popping production: 63 home runs and 100 RBIs in 1999, 50 and 138 in 2000, 64 and 160 in 2001, and 49 and 108 in 2002. In 2003, Sosa enjoyed another great season, batting .288 with 40 home runs and 103 RBIs, though his success at the plate was overshadowed by an incident on June 3, in which Sosa hit a slow ground ball, breaking his bat and exposing a hollowed out barrel filled with cork. This illegal tactic (used to increase a hitter's bat speed) earned Sosa a brief suspension and the suspicion of countless fans, many of whom already wondered about his explosive muscle growth, which he joked in 1998 was the result of "Flintstones vitamins."

The Cubs advanced to the NL championship series in 2003, where they held a 3-1 game lead over the Florida Marlins before losing the last three games. In 2004, Sosa missed more than 30 games with various injuries and suffered a severe drop in production. On the last day of the season, Sosa left Chicago's Wrigley Field when he was told he would not be playing, earning the scorn of the Cubs' faithful who just a few years earlier regarded him as the city's greatest sports hero.

On February 2, 2005, the Cubs traded Sosa to the Baltimore Orioles and agreed to pay part of his $17 million salary in exchange for two lightly regarded players. Sosa was initially embraced by Baltimore fans but was soon viewed as a disappointment, finishing an injury-plagued season with a .221 batting average, 14 home runs, and 45 RBIs.

Due to his alarming drop in production and the increased focus of steroid use in sports resulting from former major leaguer JOSE CANSECO's book *Juiced,* Sosa also dealt with rumors of alleged previous steroid use, despite his consistent denials, including those made in March 2005 to a con-

gressional committee investigating the use of performance-enhancing drugs in professional sports. Prior to the 2006 season, the free-agent Sosa received little interest from major league clubs, and he spent that summer in unofficial retirement, living in Florida and the Dominican Republic.

Further Reading

Bamberger, Michael. "Sammy, You're the Man." *Sports Illustrated,* 28 September 1998, p. 44.

Knisley, Michael. "A Finish with a Flourish: St. Louis Cardinal Mark McGwire and Chicago Cub Sammy Sosa Made 1998 Baseball Season Exciting to Witness." *Sporting News,* 5 October 1998, p. 44.

"Sammy Sosa." Baseball Reference Web site. Available online. URL: http://www.baseball-reference. com/s/sosasa01.shtml. Downloaded on January 20, 2006.

Sosa, Sammy, and Marcos Breton. *Sammy Sosa: An Autobiography.* New York: Warner Books, 2000.

Verducci, Tom. "Once Bitter, Now Better: After Two Years of Troubles and a Nasty Divorce from the Cubs, Sammy Sosa Has Been Welcomed in Baltimore." *Sports Illustrated,* 13 June 2005, p. 58.

Sammy Sosa ranked among the National League's top 10 in home runs each season from 1993 through 2003. *(National Baseball Hall of Fame Library)*

Stevenson, Teófilo
(1952–   ) *boxer*

The Olympic heavyweight boxing gold medalist in 1972, 1976, and 1980, Teófilo Stevenson rejected a multimillion dollar offer to fight world champion Muhammad Ali, choosing instead to remain in Cuba, where he forged a career as a legendary amateur fighter and Cuban hero. He was born on March 29, 1952, in Puerto Padre, Cuba, the son of an immigrant from St. Vincent, Teófilo, Sr., and a Cuban mother, Dolores. Stevenson spent his boyhood in the small town on Cuba's northern coast. At age 13, Stevenson's prodigious boxing talent earned him an invitation to train in Havana, Cuba. Under the guidance of top Cuban and Soviet trainers, Stevenson developed into Cuba's greatest Olympic heavyweight hopeful by his late teens.

Stevenson's first Olympic appearance took place at the 1972 games in Munich, West Germany. The 20-year-old lean and solid heavyweight pounded American Duane Bobick (to whom he had lost in the 1971 Pan-American Games) and then defeated West German Peter Hussig to reach the final. Stevenson won the gold medal by default when his opponent, Romanian Ion Alexe, was unable to box because of a broken thumb.

In 1976, Stevenson returned to the Olympics, entering the Montreal, Canada, games as the prohibited favorite to again bring home the gold medal. He combined his height and reach advantage with his thunderous power from each hand to dispose of his first three opponents in less than seven and a half minutes combined. Stevenson's opponent in the final, Romanian Mircea Simon, was able to last for two rounds by completely avoiding Stevenson, until a third-round flurry caught him and forced his corner to throw in the towel.

During the early and mid-1970s, boxing promoters outside Cuba, such as Bob Arum and Don King, tried relentlessly to lure the quiet, handsome Stevenson to fight professionally outside the rigidly controlled communist island nation, which prohibited professional boxing. Stevenson steadfastly refused to defect from Cuba, praising the government of Fidel Castro, who in turn provided Stevenson with a luxurious home and cars. Boxing fans continue to wonder what might have happened had Stevenson accepted the lucrative offers to fight Muhammad Ali and other top heavyweights of the 1970s, including Joe Frazier and George Foreman.

Stevenson won his third consecutive gold medal at the 1980 Olympics in Moscow, which were boycotted by the United States and several other nations to protest the Soviet Union's invasion of Afghanistan. His semifinals opponent, Istven Levai of Hungary, became the first Stevenson Olympic opponent to last an entire match after he danced around the ring for three rounds. His finals opponent, Pyotr Zaev of the Soviet Union, also went the distance with Stevenson and thrust his hands in the air to celebrate the feat immediately following the bout, though Stevenson easily won the match on points.

Stevenson's steady refusal to leave Cuba quieted the calls for his participation in professional fights. He did not defend his Olympic gold in the 1984 Olympics in Los Angeles, California, because Cuba joined with other communist nations to boycott the games. However, in 1986 at the relatively advanced age of 34, Stevenson again proved his dominance in amateur boxing by winning the super heavyweight world championship. He retired with only 10 losses in more than 120 fights and the distinction of never having been knocked out.

Since retiring from boxing, Stevenson has remained enormously popular in Cuba and currently works as an official of the Cuban Boxing Federation.

Further Reading

Cassidy, Robert. "Olympic Champions, Defecting Stars and a Nation in Decline." International Boxing Hall of Fame Web site. Available online. URL: http://www.ibhof.com/ibhfcuba2.htm. Downloaded on January 20, 2006.

"Olympic Legend: Teofilo Stevenson." Rediff Web site. Available online. URL: http://in.rediff.com/sports/2004/aug/12oly-box.htm. Downloaded on January 20, 2006.

"Sports Icons of the 20th Century: Boxing: Teofilo Stevenson." Terra Web site. Available online. URL: http://www.terra.com/specials/sportsicons/teofilo_en.html. Downloaded on January 20, 2006.

T

Taurasi, Diana
(1982–) *basketball player*

The first overall selection of the 2004 Women's National Basketball Association (WNBA), Diana Taurasi won a gold medal in the 2004 Olympics, led the University of Connecticut to three consecutive National Collegiate Athletic Association (NCAA) championships, and twice earned the distinction of being the best player in women's college basketball. She was born on June 11, 1982, in Chino, California. Her father, Mario, was born in Italy and moved as a boy to Argentina, where he met and married Taurasi's mother, Lily.

In 1981, Taurasi's parents and all their children moved to Chino, a working-class town located about 30 miles east of Los Angeles. Taurasi grew up in Chino playing basketball in her driveway, usually beating friends and neighbors in games of one-on-one. She further developed her skills on the famed outdoor courts of Los Angeles's Venice Beach, using her dazzling moves and aggressive approach to win the respect of her mostly male opponents, of whom she noted, "I always liked playing against the guys more than the girls when I was growing up. They were bigger and stronger, so I had to be smarter, be a better shooter, be a better passer, and know how to rebound better."

Taurasi started on the girls' basketball team at Don Lugo High School in Chino for all four years scoring more than 3,000 points during her high school career, second in California girls' basketball history behind the legendary Cheryl Miller. Following her senior season, Taurasi was named the 2000 Naismith Player of the Year and *Parade* magazine National High School Player of the Year, and she received a scholarship to play basketball at the University of Connecticut (UConn).

In her first year at UConn, Taurasi started 14 of the 32 games in which she played, averaging almost 11 points per game. Modeling her game after her idol, Magic Johnson, Taurasi used her height advantage (6') and passing skills to rack up 109 assists. Taurasi emerged as a team leader in the 2000 Big East Conference Tournament when she became the first rookie to earn recognition as the tournament's most outstanding player, helping the Huskies win the conference title. Despite her overall excellence, Taurasi's season ended with a nightmarish 1-15 shooting performance in an NCAA tournament semifinal loss to the University of Notre Dame.

Taurasi returned in her sophomore season of 2001–02 and resumed her creative attacking style to help lead UConn to an undefeated season and the NCAA championship. She was named to the 2002 All Big East first team after leading the conference in three-point percentages (44) and assists to turnover ratio (2.51:1), as well as ranking in the top 10 in the league in scoring and assists.

As a junior in 2002–03, Taurasi continued to evolve and excel. She was named the 2003 Naismith

In 2004, basketball player Diana Taurasi won a national championship with the University of Connecticut and a gold medal with the U.S. team at the Olympics in Athens. *(U.S. Olympic Committee)*

Player of the Year and was unanimously voted the Most Outstanding Player of the NCAA final four. Her 28 points in the final against the University of Tennessee led UConn to a 37-1 record and another national championship. Taurasi finished the season with one of the best all-around performances in women's college basketball history, leading the team in scoring (17.9 points per game), rebounding (6.1), assists (4.4), blocks (1.2), and free throw percentage (83.5).

Taurasi again led UConn to the NCAA title in 2003–04, winning the Most Outstanding

Player award following a championship game win over Tennessee. She also repeated as the Naismith Player of the Year, leading UConn in scoring (16.2 points per game) and assists (4.9).

Adding to her already amazing year, she was chosen by the Phoenix Mercury as the first overall selection in the WNBA draft, later averaging 17 points, four assists, and more than four rebounds per game. Following this season, Taurasi was the unanimous choice as the league's Rookie of the Year. Her enthusiastic personality, spirit of leadership, and dynamic play were also key components to the U.S. women's basketball team's undefeated march to the gold medal at the 2004 Olympics in Athens, Greece, where she averaged more than 11 points a game.

Taurasi enjoyed productive seasons for Phoenix in 2005 and 2006 and has emerged as a top star in the WNBA. Her appeal is the result of her outstanding play and her joyous approach to the game, reflected in her own words: "I enjoy doing things on the court that people aren't used to seeing. Sometimes I go too far . . . but sometimes you need to fail before you can succeed."

Further Reading

Anderson, Lars. "The Next Big Thing: For Diana Taurasi, Blessed with the Most Unstoppable One-on-One Game in Women's Hoops, the Best Is Yet to Come." *Sports Illustrated,* 10 April 2002, p. 58.

"Diana Taurasi." University of Connecticut Athletics Web site. Available online. URL: http://www.uconnhuskies.com/sports/WBasketball/2003/Roster/dianataurasi.html. Downloaded on January 20, 2006.

"Diana Taurasi." Women's National Basketball Association Web site. Available online. URL: http://www.wnba.com/playerfile/diana_taurasi/. Downloaded on January 20, 2006.

Grundy, Pamela, and Susan Shackelford. *Shattering the Glass: The Dazzling History of Women's Basketball from the Turn of the Century to the Present.* New York: New Press, 2005.

Tejada, Miguel
(1976–) *baseball player*

The American League (AL) Most Valuable Player (MVP) in 2002, Miguel Tejada has established a reputation as an iron man and one of Major League Baseball's most versatile offensive threats of the 21st century. He was born on May 25, 1976, in Baní, Dominican Republic. The youngest of 11 children, born to parents Daniel and Mora, Tejada grew up in Baní, a city of about 100,000 people located less than 100 miles southwest of the Dominican capital of Santo Domingo.

In 1979, when Tejada was only three years old, Hurricane David struck Boni and destroyed the family's modest home. He then moved with his family to a three-room shack without running water or electricity in the slums of the city. Tejada spent his youth shining shoes, helping his father on construction jobs, and working in a garment factory following his mother's death when he was 12.

Tejada played baseball using a glove made from old milk cartons. Though many of his peers were superior athletes, Tejada distinguished himself as a determined player who focused on fundamentals. At the relatively advanced age of 17, Tejada was signed to a professional contract by the Oakland A's scout, Dominican legend and major league Hall of Famer JUAN MARICHAL.

Tejada spent a year at the A's Dominican Baseball Academy honing his skills and adding strength to his body, which had suffered malnourishment from a lifetime of severe poverty. He steadily climbed up the A's farm system, emerging as the team's top prospect as a shortstop by 1997.

An exceptional season in the minors earned Tejada an opportunity in the majors late in the 1997 campaign. He won the starting shortstop job for the rebuilding A's in 1998, though a broken finger kept him out of the lineup for almost two months. Though he struggled both offensively and defensively that season, Tejada's production improved dramatically in 1999 when he played in

all except three games, hitting 21 home runs, driving in 84 runs, and cutting his errors from 26 to 21, while regularly making phenomenal plays in the field.

Tejada began a five-year streak of seasons with at least 100 runs batted in (RBIs) in 2000, helping the young A's win the AL West by batting .275, with 30 home runs, and 150 RBIs. He followed this performance with a near identical 2001 season, batting .267, with 31 home runs and 131 RBIs, as the A's lost to the New York Yankees in the playoffs for the second consecutive year. Despite the A's failure to advance in the postseason, Tejada excelled, batting .350 in the 2001 series and knocking four hits in the decisive game five of the 2001 series.

In 2002, Tejada enjoyed a career high in home runs (31), RBIs (131), and batting (.308), as well as a career low in errors (19). He also forged a 24-game hitting streak and played in every one of Oakland's games. Tejada's penchant for clutch hitting was most evident during the A's late season AL record-winning streak. In three of those wins, including the 18th and 19th of the historic string, Tejada drove in the winning run with a clinching "walk off" hit in the bottom of the ninth inning.

Powered by Tejada's torrid hitting and steady leadership, the A's won the AL West and then lost to the Minnesota Twins in the American League Division Series. Following this season, Tejada was named the AL MVP.

Tejada played in every A's game in 2003, fighting off an early-season slump to bat .278, with 27 home runs and 106 RBIs. The A's made the playoffs and again were knocked out in the first round, this time by the Boston Red Sox. Following the 2003 season, Tejada was courted by several teams as a free agent and signed with the Baltimore Orioles for six years for $72 million. With Baltimore, Tejada solidified his place as a top player in the majors by leading the AL in RBIs in 2004, with 150, and winning the All-Star game MVP award in 2005 while playing in every Orioles game that season. In 2006, Tejada played in every game for the sixth consecutive season and continued to be one of the lone bright lights on a struggling Orioles team, batting .330 with 24 home runs and 100 RBIs.

Although Tejada was now wealthy beyond his wildest childhood dreams, he remained a well-liked and respected teammate and opponent admired for his love of the game. Orioles coach Elrod Hendrix described Tejada as "a throwback," explaining, "With a lot of guys, once they become successful, they have a tendency to forget. With him he appreciates it." One of Tejada's predecessors as shortstop for the Orioles, Hall of Famer Cal Ripkin, said of Tejada, "He's a great stable force . . . he takes every event seriously, but it seems like he's enjoying every minute of it."

Further Reading

Brennan, Christine. "Tejada's Enthusiasm Catching in Orioles Clubhouse." *USA Today,* 10 July 2005.
"Miguel Tejada." Baltimore Orioles Web site. Available online. URL: http://baltimore.orioles.mlb.com/NASApp/mlb/team/player_career.jsp?player_id=123173. Downloaded on January 20, 2006.
"Miguel Tejada." Jock Bio Web site. Available online. URL: http://www.jockbio.com/Bios/Tejada/Tejada_bio.html. Downloaded on January 20, 2006.

Tiant, Luis
(El Tiante)
(1940–   )   *baseball player*

A charismatic, chubby, cigar-smoking right-handed pitcher with a Fu Manchu mustache and a distinctive twisting wind-up, Luis Tiant played for six teams during his 19-year career, though he is best known for his stint as the ace of the Boston Red Sox during the 1970s. He was born on November 23, 1940, in Marianao, Cuba. Tiant is the only child of Isabel and Luis Tiant, Sr., who had been a pitching legend and one of the nation's most celebrated athletes following a 23-year career in the Negro Leagues, all but two years of which predated the racial integration of Major League Baseball.

Tiant followed his father as a talented pitcher, earning a spot on the Cuban Juvenile League All-Star team in 1957. Tiant began playing in both the Cuban and Mexican leagues in the late 1950s before his contract was purchased by the Cleveland Indians from the Mexico City Tigers prior to the 1962 season.

Tiant progressed quickly through the Indians organization, racking up a Pacific Coast League winning percentage record of .938 by going 15-1 in 1964 before making his major league debut on July 19, 1964, defeating future Hall of Fame pitcher Whitey Ford and the defending American League (AL) champion New York Yankees 3-0 in an 11 strikeout, four-hit performance. Tiant finished that season with a record of 10 wins and four losses and an impressive earned run average (ERA) of 2.83. Over the next three seasons, Tiant pitched for Cleveland squads that failed to compete for a pennant, compiling a record of 35-31, with 11 saves and an ERA just a shade above 3.00.

In 1968, Tiant altered his delivery by turning away from the plate during his pitch, creating a distinctive hesitation and leading to a breakout season. He dominated the opposition during 1968, ranking third in the AL in wins (21) and strikeouts (264), while leading in ERA (1.60) as well as shutouts (9) and hits allowed per nine innings (5.3). Tiant's combined 32 strikeouts in two July games set an AL record for strikeouts in consecutive starts.

The Indians insisted that Tiant skip his usual participation in winter ball following his outstanding 1968 season, which may have contributed to his disastrous performance in 1969, when he went 9-20 with an ERA of 3.71. On December 10, 1969, Cleveland traded Tiant to the Minnesota Twins as part of a six-player deal.

Tiant won his first six games with the Twins before suffering a hairline fracture in his shoulder, which kept him off the field for two months and limited his productivity when he returned. Tiant was cut by the Twins during spring training in 1971 and then was signed and quickly released by the Atlanta Braves organization before signing a minor league contract with the Boston Red Sox.

Tiant struggled with a 1-7 record in 1971, but he rebounded to become one of the greatest pitchers of the 1970s and among the best and most beloved Red Sox players of all time. His unorthodox wind-up and varied release points, described by broadcaster Curt Gowdy as "coming [from] everywhere except between his legs," combined with his uncommon savvy helped Tiant win 121 games and lose only 74 while serving as Boston's unquestioned ace from 1972 through 1978. Tiant won the 1972 Comeback Player of the Year award after posting a 15-6 record with a 1.91 ERA. Tiant followed this season with records of 20-13 in 1973 and 22-13 in 1974.

In 1975, Tiant overcame back trouble to win 18 games, helping Boston win the AL East Division. He defeated the three-time defending AL champion Oakland A's with a three-hit shutout in game one of the American League Championship Series, won by Boston 3-0. In the World Series, the Red Sox fell to the Cincinnati Reds 4-3, despite Tiant's two complete game victories.

The 1975 season also provided Tiant with an opportunity to see his parents for the first time since he had left Cuba, when they were permitted to visit the United States under a special visa following a written request made to Cuban dictator Fidel Castro (who prohibited foreign travel beginning in 1961) by Massachusetts senator Edward Brooke III. Tiant's father was honored by throwing out the ceremonial first pitch prior to a Red Sox game in August. Tiant's parents never returned to Cuba. His father died of a prolonged illness in December 1976, and his mother died of heart failure just two days later.

From 1976 through 1978, the man affectionately called "El Tiante" by Red Sox fans who frequently chanted "LOOO . . . EEE" to inspire him, continued to steady the Boston rotation with 46 wins and 28 losses. His trademark consistency in clutch play (he had a 31-12 career record with the Red Sox in late season months of August and September) led Red Sox manager Darrell Johnson to say, "If a man put a gun to my head and said 'I'm going to pull the trigger if you lose this game,' I'd want Luis Tiant to pitch that game."

However, Tiant's advancing age (many believed he was several years older than the age reflected by his proclaimed birth date) led Boston to allow him to leave via free agency to the New York Yankees following the 1978 season. Red Sox teammate and future Hall of Famer Carl Yastrzemski cried when he heard Tiant would not be returning, saying of Red Sox management, "They tore out our heart and soul."

Tiant pitched for the Yankees, Pittsburgh Pirates, and California Angels from 1979 to 1982, winning 25 games and losing 24, before retiring. He launched his own line of cigars, "El Tiante," before scouting for the Yankees, coaching in the minor leagues, and managing the Savannah (Georgia) College of Art and Design baseball team for four years. Later, Tiant joined the Red Sox Spanish broadcasting team. Tiant remains in the Boston area with his wife, Maria, to whom he has been married for almost 50 years.

Further Reading

Armour, Mark. "Luis Tiant." Baseball Biography Project Web site. Available online. URL: http://bioproj. sabr.org/bioproj.cfm?a=v&v=l&bid=645&pid=14207. Downloaded on January 20, 2006.

Horgan, Tim. "Night to Remember; Pop Behind Tiant Pitches." *Boston Herald,* 8 June 2003.

"Luis Clemente Tiant." Latino Legends in Sports Web site. Available online. URL: http://www. latinosportslegends.com/Tiant_Luis-bio.htm. Downloaded on January 20, 2006.

"Luis Tiant." Baseball Reference Web site. Available online. URL: http://www.baseball-reference.com/t/ tiantlu01.shtml. Downloaded on January 20, 2006.

Torres, Dara
(1967–   ) *swimmer*

The first American to swim in four separate Olympic competitions, Dara Torres won a total of nine

Olympic medals, including five at the 2000 Olympics in Sydney, Australia, following a seven-year break from competitive swimming. She was born on April 15, 1967, in Los Angeles. The fifth of six children, Torres was raised in Beverly Hills, California, by her real estate broker father, Edward, and homemaker mother, Maryles. She began swimming as a young child and by age 14 combined a driving intensity, natural ability, and long, strong form (eventually growing to 6') to break the world record in the 50-meter freestyle.

At 15, Torres made the U.S. women's swim team that competed in the 1984 Olympics in Los Angeles, California, where she won a gold medal in the 400-meter freestyle relay. Four years later, Torres earned a silver medal in the 4 × 100-meter medley relay and a bronze medal in the 4 x 100-meter freestyle relay at the 1988 Olympics in Seoul, South Korea.

Torres's accomplishments in Seoul occurred despite her private battle with bulimia that began during her freshman year (1987) at the University of Florida. Her struggle with the disease, which caused her to induce vomiting several times a week in order to control her weight, lasted for five years and ended after intensive therapy that concluded prior to the 1992 Olympics in Barcelona, Spain, where Torres, who was voted the U.S. women's swim team captain by her teammates, won a gold medal in the 4 × 100-meters freestyle relay and contributed to a new event world record of 3:39.46 (minutes and seconds).

Following the 1992 Olympics, Torres retired from competitive swimming with a legendary record of achievement, including 28 National Collegiate Athletic Association (NCAA) All-American Awards, several U.S. freestyle championships, and four Olympic medals. She remained highly visible, working as a television sports and features commentator for ABC, E!, and the USA Network, as well as being the first athlete to be featured as a model in the *Sports Illustrated* swimsuit issue and as a spokeswoman for the popular Tae-Bo workout tapes.

During the mid-1990s, Torres was happy with her decision to leave her swimming days behind her, explaining to a friend that just the smell of chlorine made her, "so glad I don't swim." However, during the latter part of the decade she found herself thinking about making a comeback for the upcoming 2000 Olympics in Sydney, Australia.

Torres decided to pursue another chance at athletic glory and began a rigorous training regimen for more than a year. Former Olympic gold medalist Donna De Varona reflected the interest and hope of many swimming fans, saying of Torres, "She's always been a short distance from greatness. She never trained the right way or gave 100 percent. I think Dara returned to satisfy unfinished business."

If satisfying unfinished business was Torres's goal, then she surpassed it. At the 2000 Olympics,

Dara Torres was the first American swimmer to compete in four Olympics (1984, 1988, 1992, 2000), winning nine medals including four golds. *(U.S. Olympic Committee)*

the 33-year-old Torres became the first American to swim in four Olympics and won five medals—golds in the 4 × 100-meters freestyle relay and 4 × 100-meter relay and bronzes in the 50-meter freestyle, 100-meter freestyle, and 100-meter butterfly.

After her historic success at the 2000 Olympics, Torres returned to work as a television correspondent, though her competitive streak never waned, as evidenced by her 2002 championship at the Long Beach Grand Prix Pro/Am, becoming the first woman to place first in the race's history. Married to David Hoffman, a doctor, Torres is an active spokeswoman and instructor for USA Swimming and recently welcomed her first child, daughter Tessa, in 2006.

Further Reading

"Dara Torres." International Jewish Sports Hall of Fame. Web site. Available online. URL: http://www.jewishsports.net/BioPages/DaraTorres.htm. Downloaded on January 20, 2006.

"Dara Torres, Swimming." *Sports Illustrated* Web site. Available online. URL: http://sportsillustrated.cnn.com/siforwomen/news/1999/07/30/spotlight/. Downloaded on January 20, 2006.

"Torres Is Back in the Swim." *San Francisco Examiner,* 22 June 2000.

Torres, José
(1936–) *boxer*

The light middleweight silver medalist at the 1956 Olympics and the light heavyweight champion of the world in the mid-1960s, José Torres later also contributed to boxing as a biographer and New York State boxing commissioner. He was born on May 3, 1936, in Playa Ponce, Puerto Rico. Torres grew up on the island nation as a standout baseball player and track and field athlete.

Torres joined the U.S. Army and began boxing for the first time at age 18. Within a year, Torres won the Caribbean Armed Forces championship. After receiving a transfer to the U.S. mainland, Torres won the All-Army championship and qualified for the 1956 Olympics trial, where he knocked out former three-time All-Army champion Edward Grook.

At the 1956 Olympics in Melbourne, Australia, Torres advanced to the finals, where he met two-time gold medalist Lazlo Pape of Hungary. Although Torres was 10 years younger and had fought in 300 fewer bouts than Pape, Torres battled him to a very close decision, which went to Pape and brought Torres a silver medal.

Torres turned professional in 1958 and quickly rose to the top level of contenders in the welterweight division. Combining his extraordinary boxing instincts and intelligence with training from Cus D'Amato, Torres developed a peek-a-boo style with his hands high in front of his face, opening up into powerful combinations and body blows to win his first 13 fights (11 by knockout), including a victory over future middleweight champ Benny Paret on September 26, 1959, in San Juan, Puerto Rico.

A move up to the middleweight class was next for Torres, where he defeated top competitors, losing only once before rising to the light heavyweight division. He won all seven of his fights in 1964 and his first title opportunity with a March 30, 1965, match with Willie Pastrano at New York City's Madison Square Garden. Torres dominated Pastrano, knocking him down in the sixth round and winning in a technical knockout when the referee stopped the fight after the ninth round.

Torres successfully defended his crown three times in 1966 before losing in a unanimous decision to Dick Tiger on December 12, 1966. Torres met Tiger in a rematch exactly five months later and again lost—this time in a split decision. Torres fought only two more times, when he won a fight in 1968 and another in 1969.

Following his retirement from boxing, Torres has worked to honor and support the sport by writing acclaimed biographies of heavyweight champions Muhammad Ali (*Sting Like a Bee*) and Mike Tyson (*Fire and Fear*) and by serving as the chairman of the New York Boxing Commission from 1983 to 1988. For his extensive contributions to boxing, including his career record of 41-3-1 (with 29 knockouts), Torres was inducted into the International Boxing Hall of Fame in 1997.

Further Reading

Amato, Jim. "In the Ring: Jose Torres." Eastside Boxing Web site. Available online. URL: http://www.eastsideboxing.com/boxing-news/Jose-Torres.php. Downloaded on January 20, 2006.

Enwereuzor, Ike. "Interview with Jose 'Chequi' Torres." Eastside Boxing Web site. Available online. URL: http://www.eastsideboxing.com/news.php?p=500&more=1. Downloaded on January 20, 2006.

Torres, Regla
(1975–   ) *volleyball player*

The youngest gold medal winner in the history of Olympics volleyball, Regla Torres led the Cuban national team to consecutive Olympic golds in 1992, 1996, and 2000 and was voted the greatest female player of the 20th century by the Volleyball Hall of Fame. She was born on February 12, 1975, in Havana, Cuba. Torres played volleyball as a young girl and began training exclusively in the sport at a Havana sports school at age eight.

Reflecting her last name (which translates to "towers" in English), she sprouted to more than 6' by her early teens and participated in international matches with the Cuban youth national team starting when she was 14 years old. By the time she was 16, Torres had played in the Goodwill Games, the World Championships, and the Pan-American Games, where she helped Cuba win the women's volleyball gold medal.

Torres was only 17 when she traveled to Barcelona, Spain, to play in the 1992 Olympics. Quickly shedding the awkwardness and impa-

tience that sometimes marked her play, Torres emerged as a force as a middle blocker and hitter, becoming the youngest gold medal winner in Olympic volleyball history when Cuba defeated the Unified Team (composed of Russia and other states in the former Soviet Union) for the championship. She simultaneously played with the Cuban junior national team, demonstrating her physical maturity (eventually rising to a height of 6'3") and mastery of volleyball to dominate the competition while earning several team and individual accolades.

In 1993, Torres was named the most valuable player by leading Cuba to a world Grand Prix Championship and consequently sparking a run of excellence for Cuban women's volleyball, includ-

Regla Torres, seen here at the 2000 Olympics in Sydney, led Cuba to three consecutive Olympic gold medals in 1992, 1996, and 2000. *(EMPICS)*

ing a victory over China for the gold medal at the 1996 Olympics in Atlanta, Georgia. Throughout this period of spectacular success for Cuba, Torres demonstrated excellence and versatility, gaining widespread recognition as a top receiver, blocker, spiker, and server.

Torres pursued another chance at Olympic gold by helping Cuba continue its dynasty in the late 1990s heading into the 2000 Olympics in Sydney, Australia. Led by Torres's well-rounded game, Cuba advanced to the finals, where they dropped the first two games to Russia. The team then rallied for a thrilling win and a third consecutive gold medal when Torres spiked powerfully from the right side. Following this triumph, Torres said, "I dedicate this win to the whole country of Cuba. I hope it will be an inspiration to the women of Cuba."

Following the 2000 Olympics, Torres remained with the Cuban national team until knee injuries led to her decision to retire. Widely considered the greatest women's volleyball player of the century, Torres remains in Cuba, where she is pursuing a college degree.

Further Reading

"Regla Torres." Volleyball Hall of Fame Web site. Available online. URL: http://www.volleyhall.org/torres.html. Downloaded on January 20, 2006.

"Regla Torres: Cuba's Beautiful Ebony Tower." Volley Pics Web site. Available online. URL: http://www.volleypics.com/volleypics/hall_of_fame/volleyball/reglatorres.php. Downloaded on January 20, 2006.

Trevino, Lee
(the Merry Mex, Super Mex)
(1939–) *golfer*

A self-taught golfer with an awkward swing who emerged from poverty to excel in a sport played almost exclusively by the wealthy, Lee Trevino was the Professional Golf Association (PGA) Rookie of the Year in 1967, the tour's top money winner in 1970, a two-time winner of both the U.S. and British Opens, and one of golf's most respected players despite suffering a lightning strike at the peak of his career. He was born on December 1, 1939, in Dallas, Texas. Trevino and his two sisters were raised by his mother and grandfather in a run-down shack without any electricity or indoor plumbing in north Dallas.

Trevino often missed school to help support the family by growing onions and cotton in the dusty fields near their home. The home's proximity to the seventh fairway of a country club led Trevino to earn money by collecting and selling lost golf balls errantly shot into the course's high grasses. Soon, Trevino began spending time at the club, and at age eight, he started working as a caddy for some of the club's golfers. Trevino dropped out of school in eighth grade and increasingly spent his time caddying and playing golf with discarded clubs.

On his 17th birthday, Trevino enlisted in the U.S. Marine Corps. He enjoyed the stability and camaraderie of life in the Marines and rose to the rank of lance corporal after four years. Trevino also had the opportunity over the last year and a half of service to play a great deal of golf with other officers.

When Trevino returned to civilian life, he began working at a Dallas driving range, where he further honed his game while consistently winning bets against wealthier players. Commenting on his ability to remain cool under pressure as a professional, Trevino reflected on his days as an amateur: "I teed it up for $5, but that's all I had. If you lost, you were broke. And that's as much pressure as betting $100 or $500 or $1,000."

Trevino joined the professional tour in 1967, finishing fifth in the U.S. Open and winning recognition as the PGA's Rookie of the Year. Despite his impressive debut, many golf experts and fans suspected Trevino's success was a fluke, citing his awkward, self-taught swinging style that made him appear off balance before forcefully striking the ball.

However, Trevino hushed his critics by winning the U.S. Open at Oakhill in Rochester, New York, in 1968. In addition to winning this prestigious event in only his second year as a professional, Trevino also tied Jack Nicklaus's U.S. Open record 275 score and became the first player to shoot in the 60s in all four rounds.

The U.S. Open victory helped usher in a six-year span of excellence that placed Trevino among the greatest golfers in the world. During this run, Trevino repeated as U.S. Open champion in 1971 and won consecutive British Opens in 1971 and 1972, becoming the first golfer to achieve this feat since Arnold Palmer in 1961 and 1962.

Trevino also cultivated a reputation as a charismatic and humorous player on the course and in the media, which regularly referred to him as "the Merry Mex" and "Super Mex." This stood in stark contrast to Trevino's intensely private manner away from competition, reflected in his self-assessment, "Off the stage I'm a total hermit."

Even as Trevino racked up tour victories and lucrative paydays, he also received criticism for boycotting golf's crown jewel event, the Masters at the Augusta, Georgia, National Golf Course. He skipped the Masters in 1970 and 1971, claiming that it was "a stupid course" amid a stodgy atmosphere. He later expressed regret over forgoing the Masters during these years, though he never placed higher than 10th in the years he did compete there.

In a strange incident at the peak of his success, Trevino was struck by lightning while playing at the Western Open near Chicago on June 27, 1975. Though he survived, the flexibility, strength, and sensitivity of his lower back were severely affected. He underwent several operations and adjusted his game, reducing practice time and tournaments entered while relying more on his already tremendous savvy. Within two years, Trevino won

the 1977 Canadian Open and later shocked and delighted golf fans by winning the 1984 U.S. Open at 44.

Trevino continued his success on the PGA's Senior Tour beginning in 1989. He won seven events in 1990, including the U.S. Senior Open. He won five events in 1992 despite a thumb injury and won his third Senior Tour Player of the Year award in 1994 after notching six event victories and well more than $1 million in winnings. Now well into his 60s and still playing on the Champions Tour (formerly called the Seniors Tour), Trevino understands that his legacy is already in place, saying, "I showed that a guy from across the tracks, a minority kid with no education from a very poor background, can make it."

Further Reading

"Lee Trevino (1939–   )." Golf Europe Web site. Available online. URL: http://www.golfeurope.com/almanac/players/trevino.htm. Downloaded on January 20, 2006.

"Lee Trevino—Profile." Professional Golf Assocaiton Web site. Available online. URL: http://www.pgatour.com/players/intro/132230. Downloaded on January 20, 2006.

"'Merry Mex' Was Golf's Showman." ESPN Classic Web site. Available online. URL: http://espn.go.com/classic/biography/s/Trevino_Lee.html. Downloaded on January 20, 2006.

Moore, Kenny. "It's Nifty Being 50: Lee Trevino, Joining the Rich Senior Tour, Says the Best Is Yet to Come." *Sports Illustrated*, 18 December 1989.

Trinidad, Félix, Jr.
(Félix Juan Trinidad, Jr., Tito)
(1973–   ) *boxer*

An electrifying fighter who followed his father as a world champion boxer, Félix Trinidad, Jr., reigned as a titleholder in three different weight classes during the 1990s and into the new century, earning overwhelming adoration from boxing fans in his native Puerto Rico. He was born Félix Juan Trinidad, Jr., on January 10, 1973, in Fajardo, Puerto Rico. He began boxing at age 12 under the guidance of his father, Félix Trinidad, Sr., who had been a featherweight champion in the mid-1970s.

Trinidad posted a 51-6 record as an amateur, winning Puerto Rican championships at five different weight classes, ranging from 100 to 132 pounds. At his father's urging, Trinidad entered the professional ranks at 17.

Despite his overall success as an amateur, Trinidad only knocked out less than a quarter of his opponents. However, he won his first 19 fights as a professional, including 16 by knockout. Trinidad, often referred to by his nickname, "Tito," rose to rank among the top contenders in the welterweight division by 1993 and won his first title bout on June 19, 1993, defeating Maurice Blocker in San Diego, California, for the International Boxing Federation (IBF) crown. The second-round knockout thoroughly put to rest previously held notions about Trinidad's lack of punching power, just as doubts about his ability to take a punch were dashed in wins over highly-regarded punchers in the welterweight division.

Trinidad successfully defended his title 15 times over the course of more than six years. Included among these wins were unanimous decisions over HÉCTOR CAMACHO on January 29, 1994, in Las Vegas and Pernell "Sweet Pea" Whitaker on February 20, 1999, at Madison Square Garden in New York City.

Trinidad's final defense of his welterweight title came in a highly anticipated bout against undefeated World Boxing Council (WBC) welterweight champion OSCAR DE LA HOYA on September 18, 1994, in Las Vegas, Nevada. De La Hoya controlled the early portion of the fight, but Trinidad's late charge over the last three rounds provided the latter with a unanimous decision victory. His physical skill proven by his 35-0 record, Trinidad reflected on his mental prowess after this

fight: "I knew Oscar was a great fighter but I have such a will to win." Trinidad returned to Puerto Rico and was welcomed by thousands who had been given the day off by the government in order to celebrate the triumph of their native son.

Following Trinidad's victory over De La Hoya and amid talks of a possible but never-realized rematch, Trinidad moved up in weight and captured the World Boxing Association (WBA) light middleweight title with a unanimous decision triumph over David Reid on March 3, 2000. A little more than a year later, Trinidad again moved up in weight for a middleweight title bout against Bernard "the Executioner" Hopkins on September 29, 2001, in Madison Square Garden. Despite being heavily favored by odds makers, Trinidad suffered his first loss when he was defeated by a technical knockout with less than two minutes remaining in the 12th and final round.

Trinidad won his next fight on May 11, 2002, then shocked the boxing world by announcing his retirement a few months later. Less than two years later, however, Trinidad announced that he was returning to the ring. His first fight after the almost two-and-a-half-year layoff was a technical knockout of Ricardo Mayorga. Trinidad then met Ronald "Winkie" Wright in Las Vegas on May 14, 2005, and was dominated, losing a unanimous decision.

Two days after his loss to Wright, Trinidad returned to Puerto Rico with his father, who said that he was retiring as his son's trainer. An emotional Trinidad then said that he, too, would retire, explaining, "My father told me at Miami airport what he was going to do, and I reminded him that since I was a kid I told him the day my father could not be at my side, I would not throw another blow."

Further Reading

"Felix 'Tito' Trinidad." Latino Legends in Sports Web site. Available online. URL: http://www.latinosportslegends.com/Trinidad_Felix_bio.htm. Downloaded on January 20, 2006.

"Felix 'Tito' Trinidad: Biography & Career of 'El Gran Campeón Puertoriqueño.'" Taino Box Web site. Available online. URL: http://tainobox.com/fighters/felix_trinidad/. Downloaded on Janary 20, 2006.

"Spurred to Greatness: Felix Trinidad Has Emerged from the Shadows of Lesser Champions and Is Now Boxing's Cock of the Walk." *Sports Illustrated,* 14 May 2001, p. 54.

V

Valenzuela, Fernando
(1960–) *baseball player*

A burly left-hander whose unorthodox wind-up, baffling screwball, and torrid debut for the Los Angeles Dodgers caused southern California to fall under the spell of "Fernando mania," Fernando Valenzuela was the National League (NL) Rookie of the Year in 1981 and remains the greatest pitcher ever to come from Mexico. He was born on November 1, 1960, in Navojoa, Mexico. Valenzuela grew up in Etchohuaquila, about 350 miles south of the Arizona-Mexico border. American reporters who traveled to Etchohuaquila after Valenzuela became famous often heard it described by residents of a neighboring town as "about 20 miles south—and about 50 years back."

Valenzuela grew up among garbanzo and sunflower fields in a thatched roof adobe hut, the youngest of 12 children in his family. He dropped out of school before he was a teenager, virtually teaching himself how to pitch. By 16, Valenzuela was earning $80 per month pitching in the Mexican leagues, where he attracted the interest of a Los Angeles Dodgers scout who signed the stocky left-hander on July 6, 1979.

Valenzuela excelled in the minor leagues and made his major league debut at age 19 on September 15, 1980. He went 2-0 for the Dodgers in 10 appearances that fall and emerged from 1981 spring training as the youngest player on the Los Angeles roster. An injury to veteran left-hander Jerry Reuss thrust Valenzuela into the opening day starter's spot. Valenzuela gave up only five hits in a complete game 2-0 victory over the Houston Astros, and "Fernando mania" was born.

The phenomenon of Fernando mania resulted from the convergence of a few factors: Valenzuela's astounding beginning to the season, his unique pitching style and personal charm, and southern California's large and growing Mexican population, who viewed the rookie pitcher with enormous pride. After his opening day win, Valenzuela won his next seven starts, a streak that included three more shutouts, an 11-strikeout performance, and a victory in front of the Dodgers' largest home crowd in seven years.

Valenzuela's eyes-to-the-sky, twisting wind-up, delivering the most baffling screwball since Hall of Famer Carl Hubbell, was quickly imitated by children across North America. Though Valenzuela spoke no English in his rookie year, he was a darling of the media, his youthful face and joyous but competitive style serving to invigorate baseball fans wherever he pitched. On May 18, Valenzuela finally lost his first game, though the *Sports Illustrated* issue with the same date captured the thrills brought by Valenzuela, picturing the Dodgers rookie on the cover next to the word "Unreal!"

Valenzuela continued to enjoy a magical 1981, earning the starting pitcher assignment in the All-Star Game following a seven-week player strike that

Fernando Valenzuela burst onto the baseball scene in 1981, winning the National League Rookie of the Year and Cy Young awards. *(National Baseball Hall of Fame Library)*

interrupted the season. He finished the season with a record of 13-7, a 2.48 earned run averaged (ERA), and a major league–leading 180 strikeouts. Valenzuela capped the campaign with the NL Rookie of the Year award, the NL Cy Young Award, and a World Series ring following the Dodgers six-game triumph over the New York Yankees.

From 1982 through 1987, Valenzuela was the Dodgers' most celebrated pitcher, starting an average of 35 games a season and racking up a major league–leading 88 complete games over those six years. Valenzuela was named to every NL All-Star team from 1982 through 1986, compiling career totals in the midsummer classic of 14 strikeouts in $10\frac{2}{3}$ scoreless innings. In the 1986 All-Star Game, Valenzuela struck out five consecutive American League hitters, including Don Mattingly, Lou

Whitaker, and Cal Ripken, Jr., tying an All-Star Game record set by his screwball-throwing predecessor, Hubbell.

With Valenzuela as the anchor of their pitching staff, the Dodgers won the NL West Division titles in 1983 and 1985. In 1986, Valenzuela set career highs in wins (21) and strikeouts (242). However, injuries to his shoulder limited his effectiveness in 1987 and severely restricted his appearances in 1988, when the Dodgers won the World Series over the Oakland A's.

Valenzuela struggled with a 10-13 record in 1989 but returned in 1990 to post a 13-13 record, including a no-hitter over the St. Louis Cardinals on June 29. In that game, Valenzuela, who had won a Gold Glove award for defensive brilliance in 1986, made an extraordinary play to tap a dribbler toward the Dodgers shortstop in the ninth inning to preserve his no-hit bid. Also in 1990, Valenzuela had a batting average of .304, remarkably high for a pitcher, and hit one of his 10 career home runs.

Despite his impressive accomplishments in 1990, injuries had diminished Valenzuela's effectiveness enough that the Dodgers made the difficult decision to release him just prior to the 1991 season. A few weeks before his release, Valenzuela pitched in an exhibition in Monterrey, Mexico, before a sold-out crowd of almost 30,000 that cheered him wildly. Said Dodgers owner Peter O'Malley following the game, "We all knew of Fernando's popularity in his country, but to come here and see it, hear it, feel it . . . it is one of the most extraordinary moments in my time with the Dodgers."

Valenzuela remained in the majors through 1997, pitching for the California Angels (1991), Baltimore Orioles (1993), Philadelphia Phillies (1994), San Diego Padres (1995–97), and St. Louis Cardinals (1997), compiling a 32-37 record with these teams. He finished his career with a record of 173-153, with 2,074 strikeouts and an ERA of 3.54. His 173 wins rank highest in Major

League Baseball history among Mexican-born pitchers.

Following his retirement, Valenzuela settled in the Los Angeles area, joined the Dodgers Spanish-language radio crew in 2003, and with his wife, Linda, followed the burgeoning baseball career of son Fernando Valenzuela, Jr., a first base prospect in the Arizona Diamondbacks farm system. Valenzuela remains among the most popular Dodgers in that franchise's storied history as a result of his stellar career, lovable personality, and rookie season, the greatness of which rivals that of any player in any sport.

Further Reading

Castro, Tony. "Something Screwy Is Going On Here." *Sports Illustrated,* 8 July 1985.
Click, Paul. "20 Years ago Fernando Valenzuela Was King of the Hill." *Baseball Digest,* 1 July 2001.
"Fernando Valenzuela." Baseball Reference Web site. Available online. URL: http://www.baseball-reference.com/v/valenfe01.shtml. Downloaded on January 16, 2006.
Wulf, Steve. "Out of the Blue; Fernando Valenzuela Is Cut Loose by the Dodgers." *Sports Illustrated,* 8 April 1991, p. 15.

Vilas, Guillermo
(Young Bull of the Pampas)
(1952–) *tennis player*

A left-handed tennis player admired for his consistent top spinning strokes, sportsmanship, and stamina, Guillermo Vilas was the first Argentine to win a Grand Slam event, with all five of his major titles between 1977 and 1979. Born on August 17, 1952, in Mar del Plata, Argentina, Vilas grew up in this beach resort town about 250 miles southeast of Buenos Aires and was introduced to tennis as a young boy by his father. Vilas won his first club title (in mixed doubles) at age 12 and improved enough to compete on the international tennis circuit by the time he was 17.

Vilas, sometimes referred to as the "Young Bull of the Pampas," steadily rose up the ranks of the top players in the world, reaching the top 10 in 1974, a distinction he retained for nine straight years. In 1975, Vilas reached the finals at the French Open, the semifinals at the U.S. Open, and the quarterfinals at Wimbledon, advancing to the same rounds at Wimbledon and the U.S. Open in 1976.

By 1977, Vilas was not only one of the top players in the world; he was also among the most popular. He was a published poet and tireless worker who regularly practiced two to three hours before each match. Vilas was widely respected for his quiet but easygoing manner with opponents, officials, and fans and attracted legions of followers because of his handsome looks and steady style, later described by the International Tennis Hall of Fame as that of a "destructive metronome."

Vilas enjoyed his greatest year when he won seven of the 33 tournaments he played in 1977, reaching number two in the world behind Bjorn Borg. He reached the finals at the Australian Open before winning his first Grand Slam tournament at Roland Garros in the French Open by defeating Brian Gottfried in straight sets.

Later that year, Vilas reached the finals at the U.S. Open, where he met American star Jimmy Connors. Mixing in a surprising number of aggressive volleys at the net with his uncanny ability to wear down opponents with baseline strokes, Vilas defeated Connors in four sets. Vilas's win ignited Forest Hills Stadium (which was in its last year as the site of the U.S. Open) in what was described by tennis commentator Bud Collins as a "wild celebration" with "joyous fans [carrying] Vilas on victory laps within the concrete arena as though he were a triumphant bull fighter."

The clay courts of the Australian Open were the scene of Vilas's two other Grand Slam championships, in 1978 and 1979. He also enjoyed great success as the leader of Argentina's Davis

Cup team, which defeated highly regarded U.S. teams in 1977, 1980, and 1983. Vilas's fortunes on the court were closely followed by Argentine fans and played an enormous role in shaping a new generation of players from Argentina, such as DAVID NALBANDIAN and Guillermo Coria, who currently rank among the world's best players.

Since retiring from the tour in 1989 with a career record of 644-227, Vilas, who lives in Monaco, has become an owner of several tennis clubs around the world and has occasionally played on the senior tennis circuit. He was inducted into the International Tennis Hall of Fame in 1991.

Further Reading

"Guillermo Vilas." International Tennis Hall of Fame Web site. Available online. URL: http://www.tennisfame.org/enshrinees/guillermo_vilas.html. Downloaded on January 15, 2006.

Pagliaro, Richard. "Interview with Guillermo Vilas." *Tennis Week,* 28 August 2004.

Villa, Brenda
(1980–) *water polo player*

One of the greatest players in the history of American women's water polo, Brenda Villa has helped lead teams to a National Collegiate Athletic Association (NCAA) championship, Pan-American Games gold medal, and silver and bronze Olympic medals. She was born on April 18, 1980, in Los Angeles, California. Villa grew up in the East Los Angeles community of Commerce, where she began swimming with the City Club at age six.

After two years of intense persuasion, Villa gained her mother's permission to follow her older brother into water polo. She played every fall from age eight to 14, when she was selected to play on the girls' Junior Olympics team. At Bell Gardens

High School, Villa played on the boys' water polo team because her school did not have a girls' team. She finished high school with three first-team All-State honors and four first-team girls' All-American honors.

Following high school, Villa accepted an athletic scholarship to attend Stanford University. In her freshman year, her quick and powerful shot led to a team-high 69 goals and helped Stanford reach the first-ever NCAA Women's Water Polo Championship, where Stanford fell to the University of California–Los Angeles (UCLA).

After her stellar first year in college competition, Villa took time out to train with the U.S. women's water polo team, which was preparing for the 2000 Olympics in Sydney, Australia. In the Olympics, Villa led the team with nine goals, including a game-tying goal with 13 seconds remaining in an eventual loss to Australia in the gold medal game.

In her sophomore season at Stanford, Villa again led the team in goals, with 60, and her fast swimming, intelligent passing, steady endurance, and vocal leadership played a critical role as Stanford defeated UCLA for the NCAA championship. Villa earned NCAA All-American recognition again after her third season at Stanford before graduating with a bachelor's degree in political science.

Villa continued to excel as she set her sights on the 2004 Olympics in Athens, Greece. In 2003, she had a team-high 13 goals to lead the U.S. team to a gold medal at the World Championships in Barcelona, Spain. Later that summer, her 10 goals were the most for the U.S. team, which defeated Canada for the Pan-American Games championship in the Dominican Republic. In the 2004 Olympics, Villa again led the United States in scoring, as the team earned a bronze medal.

Villa's list of accomplishments is even more impressive, considering how unconventional her size is for women's water polo. On the 2004 U.S. Olympic team, only two of the 13 players were

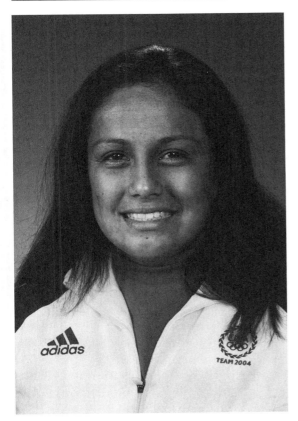

Brenda Villa led the U.S. women's water polo geam to Olympic medals in 2000 (silver) and 2004 (bronze). *(U.S. Olympic Committee)*

shorter than 5'9"; Villa is 5'4". Noting her comparatively stout stature, Villa's Olympics coach, Guy Baker, commented, "You look at her and you'd never think she's an Olympic athlete . . . I think she's a great story for that reason."

Villa plays professionally in Italy, though she returns to her predominantly Latino hometown of Commerce to work out with aspiring female water polo players, explaining, "I feel like water polo is a pretty expensive sport—it's not as accessible to train for as soccer or other sports [popular with Latinos]. So I try to give back as much as they've given me."

Further Reading

Moore, David Leon. "Standing Tall in the Water." *USA Today* Web site. Available online. URL: http://www.usatoday.com/sports/olympics/athens/pool/2004-06-23-villa-water-polo_x.htm. Downloaded on June 19, 2006.

"Striving for a Championship." Stanford Cardinal Official Athletics Web site. Available online. URL: http://gostanford.cstv.com/sports/w-wpolo/spec-rel/051502aaa.html. Downloaded on July 1, 2005.

Villanueva, Charlie
(1984–   ) *basketball player*

A graceful, athletic, and versatile basketball player who overcame a rare skin condition that caused him to lose all of his hair in childhood, Charlie Villanueva was the seventh overall selection in the 2005 National Basketball Association (NBA) draft and finished second in voting for the 2006 NBA Rookie of the Year. He was born on August 24, 1984, in the Queens section of New York City. Both of his parents were Dominican immigrants with athletic backgrounds. His mother, Dora Mejía, played competitive softball, and his father, Roberto Villanueva, was a catcher who earned a tryout with the Pittsburgh Pirates.

Villanueva lived in many places throughout New York City, moving frequently with his brother, sister, and mother, who searched for better jobs. At the age of 10, Villanueva began noticing that he was losing patches of hair. His family consulted with several specialists and eventually learned that he was suffering from alopecia areata, a rare skin disease in which the body's immune system attacks hair follicles, causing hair loss and stifling hair growth.

Although alopecia, which afflicts approximately 5 million Americans, is not life threatening, it did damage Villanueva's self-esteem and led him to retreat socially. A growth spurt following his first year of high school further led Villanueva to feel like he did not fit in among his peers, but he soon found comfort and a sense of belonging playing basketball, a sport he had enjoyed since following his older brother Rob Carlos to local courts. Villanueva was a standout high school basketball player at Newton High School in Queens and in his junior and senior years at Blair Academy in New Jersey, a private school to which he had earned an athletic scholarship.

Blair won the state championship in each of Villanueva's seasons on the team. The 6'10", 220-pound Villanueva was a consensus high school All-American and after considering entering the NBA draft, decided to accept an athletic scholarship to play basketball at the University of Illinois. When Illinois coach Bill Self left to coach at the University of Kansas, Villanueva was released from his letter of intent and chose to play at the University of Connecticut (UConn).

As a freshman at UConn, Villanueva played a key role as a reserve on the team's 2004 National Collegiate Athletic Association (NCAA) championship team. In his sophomore season, Villanueva was a starter and showed his impressive mix of power and finesse to average 15 points and nine rebounds a game.

Following this season, Villanueva elected to make himself eligible for the 2005 NBA draft. He was selected by the Toronto Raptors with the seventh pick, a choice that was criticized by many who viewed Villanueva as unproven and inconsistent and perceived his casual manner on the court as indifference. Moments after the selection was made, ESPN television NBA draft analyst Dick Vitale shouted incredulously, "Are you kidding me?!" and sportswriter Stephen A. Smith asked, "What is [Toronto general manager] Rob Babcock thinking?"

Villanueva proved his many doubters wrong in his rookie season by transitioning from playing mainly as a power forward in college to his role as a small forward by overpowering smaller players and

being too quick for larger opponents. Villanueva was rewarded for his steady improvement and stellar play by being named a starter midway through the season and finished his rookie campaign with averages of 13 points and more than six rebounds a game. Villanueva's first season in the NBA was highlighted by his 48-point performance on March 26, 2006, in Toronto's 125-116 loss to the Milkwaukee Bucks, which was the most points scored by a rookie since Allen Iverson of the Philadelphia 76ers scored 59 points in a game in 1997.

Following the season, Villanueva finished second in balloting for NBA Rookie of the Year to Chris Paul of the New Orleans/Oklahoma City Hornets. After hearing about Villanueva's 48-point effort versus Milwaukee (to whom he was traded in June 2006), Paul praised his fellow rookie's unique versatility on the court, saying, "I'm not surprised. Charlie has been this great of a basketball player since . . . high school. He can dribble the ball up the court, pass, shoot—everything."

Villanueva has also garnered admiration for his role as a spokesman for the National Alopecia Areata Foundation, noting of his frequent visits with those who are afflicted with the disease, "Being able to bring a smile to a child's face and show them that those with alopecia can succeed brings joy to my life."

Further Reading

"Charlie Villanueva." National Basketball Association Web site. Available online. URL: http://www.nba.com/playerfile/charlie_villanueva/index.html. Downloaded on June 18, 2006.

Charlie Villanueva Web site. Available online. URL: http://www.cv31.com/home.htlm. Downloaded on June 18, 2006.

Lawrence, Andrew. "Skin Deep: Villanueva Overcomes Rare Disease to Excel in the NBA." *Sports Illustrated* Web site. Available online. URL: http://sportsillustrated.cnn.com/2006/writers/the_bonus/04/06/villanueva/. Downloaded on June 18, 2006.

Vizquel, Omar
(1967–) *baseball player*

A winner of nine consecutive American League (AL) Gold Glove awards at shortstop whose speed, ability to get on base, and brilliant defense helped lead the Cleveland Indians to two pennants in the 1990s, Omar Vizquel has the best fielding percentage of any shortstop (who played a minimum of 1,000 games) in Major League Baseball history. He was born on April 24, 1967, Venezuela. Omar grew up playing on the fields of Venezuela's capital city with hopes of following the path of the man whose poster adorned his bedroom wall, Venezuelan shortstop DAVEY CONCEPCIÓN, the shortstop for the Cincinnati Reds World Series champion teams of the mid-1970s. A talented artist and avid music fan, Vizquel channeled his talent into baseball and signed a contract with the Seattle Mariners at age 17.

Vizquel began his minor league career by batting .315 for the Butte, Montana, Copperkings of the Pioneer League. Over the next four years in the minors, Vizquel's quickness, anticipation, soft hands, and nifty footwork allowed him twice to lead the league in fielding percentage at shortstop.

He made his major league debut at age 21 on opening day in 1989. He played in 143 of the Mariners' 162 games and displayed the excellent defense for which he would become famous, but he batted a paltry .220 and stole only one base in five attempts. After a 1990 season in which he was hampered by a knee injury, Vizquel continued to show great range in fundamentals in his position but demonstrated little offensive punch, leading many to consider him a classic "good field, no hit" shortstop.

In 1992, the small (5'9", 165 pounds) switch-hitting Vizquel enjoyed a breakthrough offensive season, hitting .294 and stealing 50 bases. After the 1993 season, in which Vizquel won the first of his nine straight Gold Gloves for defensive excellence, the Mariners traded him to the Cleveland Indians in a deal that would be remembered as one of the team's worst. Though Vizquel missed six weeks in 1994 due to another knee injury, he provided glimpses of the stellar performance he would achieve with the Indians over 10 seasons, including a 51-game errorless streak and a .369 batting average with runners in scoring position (second and/or third base).

The greatest period of Vizquel's career occurred from 1995 through 2001, when his play and leadership helped bring the Indians out of a 40-year period without a playoff appearance. During this seven-year span, the Indians made the playoffs six times (failing to qualify only in 2000) and won the AL pennant in 1995 (losing to the Atlanta Braves 4-2 in the World Series) and in 1998 (losing to the Florida Marlins 4-3 in the World Series). Vizquel won Gold Gloves in each of these seasons, made the All-Star team twice (1998 and 1999), ranked among the AL's top 10 in stolen bases five times and singles four times, and was sixth in the AL in batting with a career high .333 average in 1999.

Though Vizquel's steady offense provided Cleveland with consistent production from the number two spot in the batting order, it was his amazing defense that would distinguish him as a unique weapon. Vizquel owns two of the four best fielding seasons ever by a major league shortstop, leading the AL with a .995 fielding percentage mark in 1998 (three errors in 680 total chances) and a .993 fielding percentage in 2000 (five errors in 720 total chances). He also tied Cal Ripken, Jr., of the Baltimore Orioles for most consecutive errorless games at shortstop (95), from September 1999 through July 2000. Vizquel's explanation for his defensive wizardry reflects the smooth and efficient nature of his performance that made him one of the most beloved baseball players in Cleveland history: "I pride myself on making the hard plays look easy. I think that's the hallmark of a great shortstop. A routine play should always look like a routine play."

Following the 2004 season, Vizquel signed a free-agent contract with the San Francisco Giants.

Before he left Cleveland, he became the first Indians player in 56 years to collect 1,500 hits with the team and only the 15th shortstop in Major League Baseball history to play 2,000 games at that position.

In his first season with the Giants, Vizquel enjoyed another solid offensive year, batting .271 and stealing 24 bases, his highest total since 1999. He also displayed the excellent defensive skills for which he is most famous, winning the Gold Glove award, his first in the National League and his tenth overall. Vizquel continued his excellent play in 2006, batting .295 with 58 RBIs, and again stealing 24 bases.

Further Reading

Omar Vizquel." Baseball Reference Web site. Available online. URL: http://www.baseball-reference.com/ v/vizquom01.shtml. Downloaded on January 15, 2006.

Stone, Larry. "Outstanding in His Field–Cleveland Indians Shortstop Omar Vizquel." *Baseball Digest,* 1 June 2001.

Williams, Bernie
(Bernabé Williams)
(1968–) *baseball player*

The centerfielder for four World Series champion New York Yankees teams between 1996 and 2000, Bernie Williams is a five-time All-Star, four-time Gold Glove award winner, an American League (AL) batting champion, and the all-time major league leader in postseason home runs and runs batted in (RBIs). He was born Bernabé Williams on September 13, 1968, in San Juan, Puerto Rico. Williams grew up in San Juan, joining other boys in his neighborhood by playing baseball in the daytime and returning home at night to practice playing the guitar, a hobby he picked up from his father, who played music while working as a sailor.

His talent and love for music led Williams to enroll at San Juan's Escuela Libre de Música, a high school for talented young musicians. Williams excelled at his studies and at his guitar, and he planned on a career as a concert musician, though his parents hoped he would pursue law, medicine, or engineering. However, Williams's athletic talents pushed each of these career paths to the margins. At 15, Williams became a track star, setting Puerto Rican records in the 400 meters and winning four gold medals at an international track meet.

He also was a standout on the baseball diamond, where he played in the same youth league as future major league stars JUAN GONZÁLEZ

and IVÁN RODRÍGUEZ. In 1986, at 17, Williams enrolled in the University of Puerto Rico intending to major in biology, but he left school after he signed a contract with the New York Yankees on his 18th birthday.

The 6'2", switch-hitting Williams steadily moved up the Yankees' farm system by demonstrating fluid speed and solid hitting mechanics. He was called up to the Yankees and made his major league debut on July 7, 1991. He spent the rest of the year with the Yankees but split 1992 between New York and the minors, enjoying a solid September to finish with a .280 batting average. Williams was New York's starting centerfielder over the next two seasons, which were marked by improved offensive production.

In 1995, Williams and the Yankees enjoyed a break-out season. Led by Williams—the team leader in games (144), runs, (93), hits (173), triples (9), and walks (75)—the Yankees returned to the playoffs after an absence of 14 years, the longest drought between postseason appearances in the history of baseball's most storied franchise. The Yankees lost the American League East Division Series in an exciting five games to the Seattle Mariners, but Williams offered a glimpse of his postseason brilliance by batting .429 with two home runs and five (RBIs).

With Williams patrolling center field, batting lead off, and providing understated leadership that made him one of the most liked and respected stars in baseball, the Yankees made the postseason the next nine years. In 1996, Williams batted .305, with 29 home runs and 102 RBIs, adding six home runs and 15 RBIs in the playoffs as the Yankees defeated the Atlanta Braves for their first World Series championship in 18 years. From 1997 through 2001, Williams made the AL All-Star team every year, never batted below .307, and led the AL in hitting with a .339 mark in 1998.

Williams's outstanding defense earned him four consecutive Gold Gloves from 1997 through 2000, and his intelligence and skill in the batter's box helped him rank among the top 10 in the AL in on-base percentage five times between 1997 and 2002. Williams remained an important part of winning Yankees teams from 2003 through 2006, averaging 15 home runs and 60 RBIs during those seasons.

Throughout this Yankees dynasty, which resulted in World Series championships in 1996, 1998, and 1999, AL pennants in 2001 and 2003, and AL East Division titles in 2002 and 2004,

Williams distinguished himself as the team's premiere playoff run producer, batting a collective .280 and setting Major League career postseason records with 22 home runs and 79 RBIs. Williams's remarkable consistency in all-around ability is also reflected in his lofty place among career Yankees leaders, where he ranks fifth in games played, fifth in runs, and fourth in hits, trailing only Lou Gehrig, Babe Ruth, and Mickey Mantle.

Further Reading

"Bernie Williams." Baseball Reference Web site. Available online. URL: http://www.baseball-reference.com/w/willibe02.shtml. Downloaded on January 15, 2006.

Bernie Williams Web site. Available online. URL: http://www.berniewilliams.com/. Downloaded on January 15, 2006.

Haudricourt, Tom. "Swing and a Hit—Bernie Williams—the Flip Side of Bernie Baseball." *Bergen County Record,* 13 March 2003.

Z

Zárate, Carlos
(1951–) *boxer*

A long and lean fighter with a powerful right hand, Carlos Zárate dominated the bantamweight division in the late 1970s, becoming the only boxer in history to punish opponents with two streaks of 20 or more consecutive knockouts. He was born on May 23, 1951, in Mexico City, Mexico. Zárate grew up in the Tepito barrio of Mexico's capital, a slum notorious for its poverty and crime. After he became a renowned boxer, Mexican legend held that Zárate's first steps were taken attacking a boy two years his senior. Commenting on that story, Zárate's older brother Jorge, a former police officer who later became his trainer, said, "And he took his second step running away from the police."

Zárate was one of nine children, born to a father who died when Zárate was an infant and a mother who served government-sponsored breakfasts to the poor. As a youth, Zárate often worked at his mother's concession stand. Of this experience, he explained, "I loved it. There were always three or four guys trying to hustle extra breakfasts or trying to steal a candy bar. I never needed an excuse to fight."

Zárate found many opportunities to fight, eventually containing his training to the ring, where he was victorious in all 33 of his amateur fights, winning 30 by knockout. His first professional fight took place in 1970, when the 18-year-old Mexican gold gloves flyweight champion defeated Sugar Pino in a second-round knockout. Over the next four years, Zárate won every one of 21 bouts by knockout, before Víctor Ramírez managed to stay on his feet long enough to lose to Zárate in 10 rounds.

He then started another 20-plus knockout string, becoming the only boxer in history to achieve such a streak twice, by defeating his next 28 opponents by knockout. Included in this series of wins was a May 8, 1976, knockout of fellow Mexican Rodolfo Martínez that earned Zárate the World Boxing Council (WBC) bantamweight title. Zárate, described by boxing writer Pat Putnam as "thin as one might consider a barracuda thin," then stalked and pounded three opponents in successive title defense knockouts, setting up a dream match with Zárate's friend, countryman, and World Boxing Association (WBA) bantamweight champion Alfonso Zamora.

Although the two major sanctioning organizations of boxing could not agree to make this title unification, boxing fans were thrilled when "the Z Boys" met in Inglewood, California, on April 23, 1977. Zárate defeated Zamora in a four-round knockout, gaining recognition by almost all boxing fans as the greatest bantamweight in the world.

Zárate continued to defend his title successfully, and in 1978, with a record of 55-0, he decided to challenge WILFREDO GÓMEZ for the WBC featherweight championship. In a bout that featured the highest-ever earned knockout percentage of any two boxers in the same ring, Gómez knocked out Zárate in the fifth round. On June 3,

1979, Zárate lost his bantamweight title in a decision to Lupe Pintor in Las Vegas. Angered by the judge's decision, Zárate announced his retirement from boxing soon after the fight.

Zárate remained inactive for more than six years. He came back to the ring in February 1986 and proceeded to win his first 12 fights before losing a bout for the super bantamweight championship on October 16, 1977, to Jeff Fenech, who was widely considered the greatest Australian boxing champion of all time. After Fenech vacated his title, Zárate met Daniel Zaragoza for the super bantamweight title and lost in a 10th-round technical knockout.

Following the loss to Zaragoza, Zárate retired again and never returned to the ring, finishing his career with a record of 61-4. He was inducted into the International Boxing Hall of Fame in 1994.

Further Reading

"Carlos Zarate." Boxing Records Archive Web site. Available online. URL: http://www.boxrec.com/boxer_display.php?boxer_id=000402. Downloaded on January 15, 2006.

"Carlos Zarate." International Boxing Hall of Fame Web site. Available online. URL: http://www.ibhof.com/zarate.htm. Downloaded on January 15, 2006.

Putnam, Pat. "The Z Bantams Zarate and Zamora." Sweet Science Web site. Available online. URL: http://www.thesweetscience.com/boxing-article/2353/bantams-zarate-zamora/. Downloaded on January 15, 2006.

Zico
(Arthur Antunes Coimbra)
(1953–) *soccer player*

An attacking midfielder whose determination and agility earned him the admiration of fans in his native Brazil and around the world, Zico is considered by many the greatest soccer play to have never won a World Cup. He was born Arthur Antunes Coimbra on March 3, 1953, in Rio de Janeiro, Brazil. He was the youngest of six children and acquired his lifelong nickname from his cousin, who shortened Arthur Zico—a moniker reflecting his small, skinny stature—to Zico.

As a child, Zico learned to play piano and acted in school plays but demonstrated his greatest artistry playing soccer. By 14, Zico was a standout on local youth teams, earned a tryout with his beloved Flamengo team in Rio de Janeiro, and was selected for the club's youth squad, where he scored 44 goals in 53 games before moving on to the Flamengo under-18 team, where he scored 37 goals in 63 games.

Zico made his major league debut for Flamengo in 1973 and played for the team until 1983 (rejoining the team from 1985 through 1989). During this time, Zico became Flamengo's all-time leading scorer with 508 goals and 731 games. Though small, standing 5'7" and weighing about 150 pounds, Zico's skill and leadership had a profound impact on the soccer field. He was named South American Player of the Year in 1977, 1981, and 1982. His changes of pace, accurate shooting, and aggressive approach helped Flamengo earn the Brazilian championship in 1980, 1982, 1983, and 1987 and the Intercontinental Cup in 1981.

In 1983, Zico signed a contract for more than $1 million per year to play for Udinise, an Italian club trying to attract top talent for a run at the Italian championship. Zico played in 79 games for Udinise, scoring 56 goals and becoming admired by European fans for his ability, charisma, and dynamic style. He returned to Flamengo in 1985, suffered a serious knee injury that year, and remained with the team until 1989.

Zico also distinguished himself in international competition. He played on the Brazilian national team in the 1978, 1982, and 1986 World Cup tournaments. In the 1978 World Cup in Argentina, Zico helped lead Brazil to a third-place finish despite nagging injuries and his coach's decision to deemphasize the attacking offensive style Zico preferred. In the 1982 World Cup played in Spain, Zico scored three goals and a victory

Brazilian soccer great Zico competes at the 1982 World Cup in Spain. *(EMPICS)*

over Scotland before Brazil was eliminated in the quarterfinals round. In the 1986 World Cup in Mexico, Zico played in three games as a substitute and missed a penalty kick in a quarterfinals loss to France.

After Zico's career with Flamengo concluded, he was appointed the Brazilian national secretary of sports in 1990. He returned to the soccer field one year later when he accepted an offer to play in Japan and help build that nation's developing professional soccer league. From 1991 through 1994, Zico donned his familiar number 10 for the Sumitomo Metals (later renamed the Kashima Antlers), reviving flashes of his brilliant past with 54 goals in 88 games.

Zico's commitment was well received in Japan, where he became enormously popular. In 2002, Zico was named the Japanese national team's head coach, and in June 2005, the Japanese team qualified for the 2006 World Cup in Germany. Though Japan failed to reach the second round of the tournament, the team's overall improvement and success helped solidify Zico's global contribution to soccer.

Further Reading

"Zico." Official Zico Web site. Available online. URL: http://www.ziconarede.com.br/znrpub/ig_index_news.htm. Downloaded on January 15, 2006.

"Zico (Brazil)." Planet World Cup Web site. Available online. URL: http://www.planetworldcup.com/LEGENDS/zico.html. Downloaded on January 15, 2006.

Further Viewing

Brazilian Soccer—Skills and Techniques with Zico (DVD). Reedswain, 2003.

BIBLIOGRAPHY

Arbena, Joseph L. *Latin American Sport: An Annotated Bibliography, 1988–1998*. Westport, Conn.: Greenwood Press, 1999.

Arron, Simon. *The Complete Book of Formula One*. Osceola, Wis.: Motorbooks, International, 2003.

Bellos, Alex. *Futebol: Soccer: The Brazilian Way*. New York: Bloomsbury USA, 2002.

Canseco, Jose. *Juiced: Wild Times, Rampant 'Roids, Smash Hits, and How Baseball Got Big*. New York: Regan Books, 2005.

Carroll, Bob. *Total Football II: The Official Encyclopedia of the National Football League*. New York: HarperCollins, 1999.

Champions Forever—The Latin Legends (DVD). New Champions, Inc./Panorama Entertainment, 2000.

Collins, Bud. *Bud Collins' Tennis Encyclopedia*. Canton, Mich.: Visible Ink Press, 1997.

Greenberg, Stan. *Whitaker's Olympic Almanack: An Encyclopedia of the Olympic Games*. New York: Fitzroy Dearborn, 2004.

Grundy, Pamela, and Susan Shackelford. *Shattering the Glass: The Dazzling History of Women's Basketball from the Turn of the Century to the Present*. New York: New Press, 2005.

Klein, Alan. *Sugarball: The American Game, the Dominican Dream*. New Haven, Conn: Yale University Press, 1993.

Koppett, Leonard. *Total Basketball: The Ultimate Basketball Encyclopedia*. Toronto: SportClassic Books, 2004.

MacDonald, Tom. *The World Encyclopedia of Soccer: A Complete Guide to the Beautiful Game*. London: Lorenz Books, 2001.

McGrath, Charles. *The Ultimate Golf Book: A History and Celebration of the World's Greatest Game*. Boston: Houghton Mifflin, 2002.

McIlvanney, Hugh. *The Hardest Game: McIlvanney on Boxing*. New York: McGraw Hill, 2001.

Mewshaw, Michael. *Ladies of the Court: Grace and Disgrace on the Women's Tennis Tour*. Kingston, R.I.: Olmstead Press, 2001.

Miller, Ernestine. *Making Her Mark: Firsts and Milestones in Women's Sports*. New York: McGraw Hill, 2002.

Mullan, Harry. *Boxing: The Complete Illustrated Guide*. London: Carlton Books, 2003.

Myler, Patrick. *A Century of Boxing Greats: Inside the Ring with the Hundred Best Boxers*. London: Robson Books, 2000.

Price, S. L. *Pitching Around Fidel: A Journey into the Heart of Cuban Sports*. New York: Ecco Press, 2000.

Regalado, Samuel O. *Viva Baseball!: Latin Major Leaguers and Their Special Hunger*. Champaign: University of Illinois Press, 1999.

Riordan, Samuel Jim. *International Politics of Sport in the 20th Century*. London: Spon Press, 1999.

Rivera, Rita. *Heat: The Rise of Latino Players in Baseball*. Cincinnati, Ohio: Emmis Books, 2006.

Shulman, Lenny. *Ride of Their Lives: The Triumphs and Turmoil of Today's Top Jockeys*. Lexington, Ky.: Eclipse Press, 2002.

Wendel, Tim. *The New Face of Baseball: The One-Hundred-Year Rise and Triumph of Latinos in America's Favorite Sport.* New York: Rayo, 2004.

Wilson, Nick A. *Early Latino Ballplayers in the United States: Major, Minor and Negro Leagues, 1901–1949.* Jefferson, N.C.: McFarland, 2005.

ENTRIES BY SPORT

Auto Racer
Castroneves, Hélio
Fittipaldi, Christian
Fittipaldi, Emerson
Montoya, Juan Pablo
Piquet, Nelson
Senna, Ayrton

Baseball Player
Alomar, Roberto
Alou, Felipe
Aparicio, Luis
Bonilla, Bobby
Cabrera, Miguel
Canseco, Jose
Carew, Rod
Castilla, Vinny
Cepeda, Orlando
Clemente, Roberto
Concepción, Davey
Dihigo, Martín
Fernández, Tony
Franco, Julio
Galarraga, Andrés
Garciaparra, Nomar
Gomez, Lefty
González, Juan
Guerrero, Vladimir
Guillén, Ozzie
Hernandez, Keith
Hernández, Willie
Lopez, Al

Luque, Dolf
Marichal, Juan
Martínez, Dennis
Martinez, Edgar
Martínez, Pedro
Méndez, José
Miñoso, Minnie
Oliva, Tony
Palmeiro, Rafael
Pascual, Camilo
Pérez, Tony
Pujols, Albert
Ramírez, Manny
Rentería, Edgar
Rivera, Mariano
Rodriguez, Alex
Rodríguez, Iván
Santana, Johan
Sosa, Sammy
Tejada, Miguel
Tiant, Luis
Valenzuela, Fernando
Vizquel, Omar
Williams, Bernie

Basketball Player
Arenas, Gilbert
Arroyo, Carlos
Barbosa, Leandro
Blackman, Rolando
García, Francisco
Gasol, Pau

Ginobili, Manu
Lobo, Rebecca
Nájera, Eduardo
Nenê
Nocioni, Andrés
Schmidt, Oscar
Taurasi, Diana
Villanueva, Charlie

Boxer
Argüello, Alexis
Benitez, Wilfred
Brown, Panama Al
Camacho, Héctor
Canto, Miguel
Cervantes, Antonio
Chacon, Bobby
Chávez, Julio César
Cuevas, Pipino
De La Hoya, Oscar
Durán, Roberto
Escobar, Sixto
Galíndez, Víctor
Gómez, Wilfredo
González, Kid Gavilan
Laguna, Ismael
Monzón, Carlos
Nápoles, José
Olivares, Rubén
Ortiz, Carlos
Palomino, Carlos
Pedroza, Eusebio

Ramos, Sugar
Rosales-St. John, Mia
Ruiz, John
Saldívar, Vicente
Sánchez, Salvador
Sardinas, Kid Chocolate
Stevenson, Teófilo
Torres, José
Trinidad, Félix, Jr.
Zárate, Carlos

Diver
Capilla, Joaquín

Figure Skater
Galindo, Rudy

Football Player
Archuleta, Adam
Bruschi, Tedy
Casillas, Tony
Fears, Tom
Flores, Tom
Garcia, Jeff
Gonzalez, Tony
Gramática, Martín
Muñoz, Anthony
Plunkett, Jim
Rivera, Marco
Rivera, Ron

Golfer
Ballesteros, Seve
Lopez, Nancy
Ochoa, Lorena
Rodríguez, Chi Chi
Trevino, Lee

Gymnast
Dimas, Trent

Hockey Player
Gomez, Scott

Guerin, Bill
Montoya, Alvaro

Hurdler
Sanchez, Felix

Jockey
Cordero, Angel, Jr.
Pincay, Laffit, Jr.

Marathon Runner
Lima, Vanderlei de
Salazar, Alberto

Mountain Biker
Furtado, Juli

Soccer Player
Campos, Jorge
Chilavert, José Luis
Di Stefano, Alfredo
Domínguez, Maribel
Garrincha
Leônidas
Maradona, Diego
Marta
Negron, Esmeralda
Pelé
Reyna, Claudio
Rivelino, Roberto
Ronaldinho
Ronaldo
Salas, Marcelo
Sócrates
Zico

Softball Player
Fernandez, Lisa
Pineda-Boutte, Leticia

Speed Skater
Parra, Derek
Rodriguez, Jennifer

Sprinter
Carlos, John
Guevara, Ana
Perez, Yuliana

Surfer
Mulanovich, Sofía

Swimmer
Morales, Pablo
Poll, Claudia
Torres, Dara

Tae Kwon Do Fighter
Lopez, Steven

Tennis Player
Bueno, Maria
Casals, Rosie
Fernández, Gigi
Fernández, Mary Joe
Gonzales, Pancho
Kuerten, Gustavo
Nadal, Rafael
Nalbandian, David
Olmedo, Alex
Osuna, Rafael
Ríos, Marcelo
Sabatini, Gabrielle
Segura, Pancho
Vilas, Guillermo

Volleyball Player
Pérez del Solar, Gabriela
Torres, Regla

Water Polo Player
Villa, Brenda

Wheelchair Athlete
Mendoza, Saúl

Wrestler
Miranda, Patricia

ENTRIES BY YEAR OF BIRTH

1880–1899
Luque, Dolf
Méndez, José

1900–1919
Dihigo, Martín
Escobar, Sixto
Gomez, Lefty
Leônidas
Lopez, Al
Sardinas, Kid Chocolate

1920–1929
Capilla, Joaquín
Di Stefano, Alfredo
Fears, Tom
González, Kid Gavilan
Gonzales, Pancho
Miñoso, Minnie
Segura, Pancho

1930–1934
Aparicio, Luis
Brown, Panama Al
Clemente, Roberto
Garrincha
Pascual, Camilo

1935–1939
Alou, Felipe
Bueno, Maria
Cepeda, Orlando

Flores, Tom
Marichal, Juan
Olmedo, Alex
Ortiz, Carlos
Osuna, Rafael
Rodríguez, Chi Chi
Torres, José
Trevino, Lee

1940–1944
Cordero, Angel, Jr.
Laguna, Ismael
Monzón, Carlos
Nápoles, José
Oliva, Tony
Pelé
Pérez, Tony
Ramos, Sugar
Saldívar, Vicente
Tiant, Luis

1945–1949
Canto, Miguel
Carew, Rod
Carlos, John
Casals, Rosie
Cervantes, Antonio
Fittipaldi, Emerson
Galindez, Víctor
Olivares, Rubén
Palomino, Carlos

Pincay, Laffit, Jr.
Plunkett, Jim
Rivelino, Roberto

1950–1954
Argüello, Alexis
Chacon, Bobby
Durán, Roberto
Hernandez, Keith
Hernández, Willie
Pedroza, Eusebio
Piquet, Nelson
Sócrates
Stevenson, Teófilo
Vilas, Guillermo
Zárate, Carlos
Zico

1955–1959
Ballesteros, Seve
Benitez, Wilfred
Blackman, Rolando
Cuevas, Pipino
Franco, Julio
Gómez, Wilfredo
Lopez, Nancy
Martínez, Dennis
Muñoz, Anthony
Salazar, Alberto
Sánchez, Salvador
Schmidt, Oscar

1960–1964

Bonilla, Bobby
Camacho, Héctor
Canseco, Jose
Casillas, Tony
Chávez, Julio César
Fernández, Gigi
Fernández, Tony
Galarraga, Andrés
Guillen, Ozzie
Maradona, Diego
Martinez, Edgar
Morales, Pablo
Palmeiro, Rafael
Rivera, Ron
Senna, Ayrton
Valenzuela, Fernando

1965–1969

Alomar, Roberto
Campos, Jorge
Castilla, Vinny
Chilavert, José Luis
Furtado, Juli
Galindo, Rudy
González, Juan
Lima, Vanderlei de
Mendoza, Saúl
Pérez del Solar, Gabriela
Rivera, Mariano
Rosales-St. John, Mia
Sosa, Sammy
Torres, Dara
Vizquel, Omar
Williams, Bernie

1970–1974

Bruschi, Tedy
De La Hoya, Oscar
Dimas, Trent
Fernandez, Lisa
Fernández, Mary Joe
Fittipaldi, Christian
Garcia, Jeff
Garciaparra, Nomar
Guerin, Bill
Lobo, Rebecca
Martínez, Pedro
Parra, Derek
Poll, Claudia
Reyna, Claudio
Ramírez, Manny
Rivera, Marco
Rodríguez, Iván
Ruiz, John
Sabatini, Gabrielle
Trinidad, Félix, Jr.

1975–1979

Archuleta, Adam
Arroyo, Carlos
Castroneves, Hélio
Domínguez, Maribel
Ginobili, Manu
Gomez, Scott
Gonzalez, Tony
Gramática, Martín
Guererro, Vladimir
Guevara, Ana
Kuerten, Gustavo
Lopez, Steven
Miranda, Patricia

Montoya, Juan Pablo
Nájera, Eduardo
Nocioni, Andrés
Pineda-Boutte, Leticia
Rentería, Edgar
Rios, Marcelo
Rodriguez, Alex
Rodriguez, Jennifer
Ronaldo
Salas, Marcelo
Sanchez, Felix
Santana, Johan
Tejada, Miguel
Torres, Regla

1980–1984

Arenas, Gilbert
Barbosa, Leandro
Cabrera, Juan
García, Francisco
Gasol, Pau
Mulanovich, Sofía
Nalbandian, David
Negron, Esmeralda
Nenê
Ochoa, Lorena
Perez, Yuliana
Pujols, Albert
Ronaldinho
Taurasi, Diana
Villa, Brenda
Villanueva, Charlie

1985–1989

Marta
Nadal, Rafael

ENTRIES BY ETHNICITY OR COUNTRY OF ORIGIN

Argentina
Di Stefano, Alfredo
Galíndez, Víctor
Ginobili, Manu
Gramática, Martín
Maradona, Diego
Monzón, Carlos
Nalbandian, David
Nocioni, Andrés
Reyna, Claudio
Sabatini, Gabrielle
Taurasi, Diana
Vilas, Guillermo

Brazil
Barbosa, Leandro
Bueno, Maria
Castroneves, Hélio
Fittipaldi, Christian
Fittipaldi, Emerson
Garrincha
Kuerten, Gustavo
Leônidas
Lima, Vanderlei de
Marta
Miranda, Patricia
Nenê
Pelé
Piquet, Nelson
Rivelino, Roberto
Ronaldinho

Ronaldo
Schmidt, Oscar
Senna, Ayrton
Sócrates
Zico

Chile
Ríos, Marcelo
Salas, Marcelo

Colombia
Cervantes, Antonio
Montoya, Juan Pablo
Rentería, Edgar

Costa Rica
Poll, Claudia

Cuba
Arenas, Gilbert
Canseco, Jose
Dihigo, Martín
Fernandez, Lisa
González, "Kid Gavilan"
Lobo, Rebecca
Lopez, Al
Luque, Dolf
Méndez, José
Miñoso, Minnie
Montoya, Alvaro
Morales, Pablo

Nápoles, José
Oliva, Tony
Palmeiro, Rafael
Pascual, Camilo
Pérez, Tony
Perez, Yuliana
Ramos, Sugar
Rodriguez, Jennifer
Salazar, Alberto
Sardinas, Kid Chocolate
Stevenson, Teófilo
Tiant, Luis
Torres, Dara
Torres, Regla

Dominican Republic
Alou, Felipe
Fernández, Mary Joe
Fernández, Tony
Franco, Julio
García, Francisco
Guerrero, Vladimir
Marichal, Juan
Martínez, Pedro
Pujols, Albert
Ramírez, Manny
Rodriguez, Alex
Sanchez, Felix
Sosa, Sammy
Tejada, Miguel
Villanueva, Charlie

Ecuador
Segura, Pancho

El Salvador
Casals, Rosie

Mexico
Archuleta, Adam
Bruschi, Tedy
Campos, Jorge
Canto, Miguel
Capilla, Joaquín
Casillas, Tony
Castilla, Vinny
Chacon, Bobby
Chávez, Julio César
Cuevas, Pipino
De La Hoya, Oscar
Dimas, Trent
Domínguez, Maribel
Fears, Tom
Flores, Tom
Galindo, Rudy
Garcia, Jeff
Garciaparra, Nomar
Gomez, Lefty
Gomez, Scott
Gonzales, Pancho
Gonzalez, Tony
Guevara, Ana
Lopez, Nancy
Mendoza, Saúl
Muñoz, Anthony
Nájera, Eduardo
Ochoa, Lorena
Olivares, Rubén
Osuna, Rafael
Palomino, Carlos
Parra, Derek

Pineda-Boutte, Leticia
Plunkett, Jim
Rosales-St. John, Mia
Saldívar, Vicente
Sánchez, Salvador
Trevino, Lee
Valenzuela, Fernando
Villa, Brenda
Zárate, Carlos

Nicaragua
Argüello, Alexis
Guerin, Bill
Lopez, Steven
Martínez, Dennis

Panama
Blackman, Rolando
Brown, Panama Al
Carew, Rod
Durán, Roberto
Laguna, Ismael
Pedroza, Eusebio
Pincay, Laffit, Jr.
Rivera, Mariano

Paraguay
Chilavert, José Luis

Peru
Mulanovich, Sofía
Olmedo, Alex
Pérez del Solar, Gabriela

Puerto Rico
Alomar, Roberto
Arroyo, Carlos
Benitez, Wilfred

Bonilla, Bobby
Camacho, Héctor
Carlos, John
Cepeda, Orlando
Clemente, Roberto
Cordero, Angel, Jr.
Escobar, Sixto
Fernández, Gigi
Fernandez, Lisa
Furtado, Juli
Gómez, Wilfredo
González, Juan
Hernández, Willie
Martinez, Edgar
Negron, Esmeralda
Ortiz, Carlos
Rivera, Marco
Rivera, Ron
Rodríguez, Chi Chi
Rodríguez, Iván
Ruiz, John
Torres, José
Trinidad, Félix, Jr.
Williams, Bernie

Spain
Ballesteros, Seve
Gasol, Pau
Hernandez, Keith
Nadal, Rafael

Venezuela
Aparicio, Luis
Cabrera, Miguel
Concepcion, Davey
Galarraga, Andres
Guillén, Ozzie
Santana, Johan
Vizquel, Omar

INDEX

Boldface locators indicate main entries. *Italic* locators indicate photographs.

A

AAHL. *See* Anchorage Adult Hockey League
Aaron, Hank
 Roberto Clemente 46
 Juan Marichal 128
 Albert Pujols 185
AAU (Amateur Athletic Union) 168
Academic All-Big Eight 35
actors
 Rubén Olivares 162
 Carlos Palomino 168
AFC. *See* American Football Conference
AFC East championship 21
AFC Rookie of the Year award 180
AFC West Division title 99
AFL. *See* American Football League
African Americans. *See also* Negro League baseball
 Hank Aaron 46, 128, 185
 Muhammad Ali 98, 174, 225, 226, 233
 Barry Bonds 17, 197
 John Carlos 32–34
 Roberto Clemente 46
 George Forman 226
 Joe Frazier 59, 226
 Magic Johnson 16, 85, 227
 Michael Jordan 85
 Sugar Ray Leonard 15, 25, 59
 Willie Mays 46, 119
 Jackie Robinson 33, 47, 54, 137, 139
 Mike Tyson 233
Aguerre, Fernando 148
Aguilar, Juan 78

AIAW National Championship 120
AL. *See* American League
AL All-Star team (baseball)
 Tony Fernández 69
 Julio Franco 74
 Lefty Gomez 89
 Minnie Miñoso 139–140
 Rafael Palmeiro 166
 Camilo Pascual 170
 Bernie Williams 247
Alarcón, Rafael 159
Alaska Aces 92
AL batting champion 83, 247
Albom, Mitch 111
Alcazar, Roberto 51
AL Central Division titles
 Manny Ramírez 186
 Johan Santana 216, 217
AL Championship Series (ALCS)
 Bobby Bonilla 18
 Jose Canseco 27
 Rod Carew 32
 Dennis Martínez 132
 Pedro Martínez 136
 Alex Rodriguez 197
 Johan Santana 217
 Luis Tiant 231
alcohol abuse. *See also* substance abuse
 Joaquín Capilla 30
 Garrincha 85
 Kid Gavilan González 97, 98
 Dennis Martínez 131–132
 Marco Rivera 192
ALCS. *See* AL Championship Series
AL Division Series (ALDS) 217

AL East Division
 Roberto Alomar 1
 Tony Fernández 69
 Willie Hernández 111
 Andrés Nocioni 157
Ali, Muhammad
 Kid Gavilan González 98
 Pelé 174
 Teófilo Stevenson 225, 226
 José Torres 233
"All Alou" outfield 3
All-American
 Rolando Blackman 16
 Tedy Bruschi 20
 Tony Casillas 35
 Lisa Fernandez 66–67
 Gigi Fernández 65
 Martín Gramática 100
 Nancy Lopez 120
 Rafael Palmeiro 166
 Leticia Pineda-Boutte 179
 Ron Rivera 196
 Dara Torres 232
 Brenda Villa 242
All-Army champions
 Carlos Palomino 168
 José Torres 233
All Big East first team 227
All-Big Eight 35
All-Big 10 honors 192
All England Tennis Club 151
All-Nations team 137–138
All-Pac 10
 Adam Archuleta 6
 Gilbert Arenas 7
 Tedy Bruschi 20
All-Star Game (East-West Shrine) 81
All-Star Game (NHL) (hockey)
 Scott Gomez 91
 Bill Guerin 101, 102

All-Star Game MVP award (baseball)
 Roberto Alomar 2
 Julio Franco 73
 Miguel Tejada 229
All-Star Games (baseball)
 Roberto Alomar 1, 2
 Luis Aparicio 4, 5
 Bobby Bonilla 17, 18
 Rod Carew 30
 Orlando Cepeda 39
 Roberto Clemente 45
 Julio Franco 74
 Andrés Galarraga 77
 Vladimir Guerrero 103
 Ozzie Guillén 106
 Al Lopez 119
 Tony Oliva 160
 Tony Pérez 175
 Sammy Sosa 224
 Fernando Valenzuela 239, 240
All-Star shortstop 82
All-Star team (baseball)
 Felipe Alou 3
 Bobby Bonilla 17
 Miguel Cabrera 23, 24
 Davey Concepción 48
 Tony Fernández 69
 Julio Franco 74
 Andrés Galarraga 76
 Lefty Gomez 89
 Vladimir Guerrero 103
 Dennis Martínez 132
 Edgar Martinez 134
 Minnie Miñoso 139–140
 Tony Oliva 160
 Rafael Palmeiro 166
 Camilo Pascual 170
 Albert Pujols 185
 Edgar Rentería 189

Fernando Valenzuela 240
Omar Vizquel 245
Bernie Williams 247, 248
All-Star team (NBA)
(basketball)
Rolando Blackman 16
Pau Gasol 86
Manu Ginobili 87, 88
AL Manager of the Year 107
AL MVP award
Roberto Alomar 1
Jose Canseco 27
Rod Carew 30, 31
Juan Gonzalez 95, 96
Vladimir Guerrero 102
Willie Hernández 110,
111
Edgar Martinez 134
Tony Oliva 161
Manny Ramírez 186, 187
Alex Rodriguez 196, 198
Miguel Tejada 229
Alomar, Roberto **1–2**
Alomar, Sandy, Jr.
Roberto Alomar 1, 2
Manny Ramírez 187
Mariano Rivera 194
alopecia 243, 244
Alou, Felipe **2–4,** *3*
Orlando Cepeda 39
Pedro Martínez 135
Alou, Jesus 3
Alou, Matty 3
AL Pitcher of the Month 217
AL Rookie of the Year
Jose Canseco 27
Rod Carew 30, 31
Tony Fernández 69
Nomar Garciaparra 82
Ozzie Guillén 106
Minnie Miñoso 140
Tony Oliva 160
AL top 10 166
AL West Championship
Jose Canseco 28
Rod Carew 32
Alex Rodriguez 197
Miguel Tejada 229
Alzheimer's disease
Tom Fears 65
Leônidas 115
American Football Conference
(AFC)
Tedy Bruschi 21
Tony Gonzalez 99
Anthony Muñoz 149
American Football League
(AFL) 72

American invasion of Iraq
(2003) 123
American League (AL). *See also*
specific headings, e.g.: AL All-
Star team
Julio Franco 73
Nomar Garciaparra 82–84
Lefty Gomez 89
Juan Gonzalez 95–97
Vladimir Guerrero 104
Al Lopez 119
Dennis Martínez 131
Edgar Martinez 134
Minnie Miñoso 139
Camilo Pascual 170
Anaheim Angels
Andrés Galarraga 77
Vladimir Guerrero 104
Anchorage Adult Hockey
League (AAHL) 90–91
Anchorage North Stars 90
Anderson, Sparky
Davey Concepción 49
Tony Pérez 175
ankle injuries
Bobby Bonilla 17
Francisco García 80
Manu Ginobili 87
David Nalbandian 154
Anthony Muñoz Foundation
150
Aparicio, Luis **4–6**
Aragua Tigres (baseball team)
48
Arantes do Nascimento, Edson.
See Pelé
Archuleta, Adam **6–7**
Arena, Bruce 191
Arenas, Gilbert **7–9,** *8*
Argentina
Alfredo Di Stefano 56–57
Víctor Galíndez 77–78
Manu Ginobili 86–89
Martín Gramática 100–
101
Diego Maradona 125–127
Carlos Monzón 144–145
David Nalbandian
153–154
Andrés Nocioni 157–158
Gabriela Sabatini 209–210
Guillermo Vilas 241–242
Argentina League (basketball)
87
Argentine boxing team 77
Argentine championship
(1981) (soccer) 57
Argentine Grand Prix 71

Argentine League title (soccer)
44
Argentine light heavyweight
title 78
Argentine middleweight title 144
Argentine national team
(soccer) 126
Argentinos Juniors (soccer
club) 125
Argüello, Alexis **9–10,** 41
Arizona All-Hispanic football
team MVP award 6
Arizona State University 6
arm injuries
Maria Bueno 22
Jose Canseco 28
Lefty Gomez 90
José Méndez 138
A-Rod. *See* Rodriguez, Alex
Arroyo, Carlos **10–11**
arthritis 128
Arum, Bob 206
Ashe, Arthur 95
ASP. *See* Association of Surfing
Professionals
Assis Moreira, Ronaldo de. *See*
Ronaldinho
Associated Press Female Athlete
of the Year 160
Association of Intercollegiate
Athletics for Women (AIAW)
National Championship 120
Association of Surfing
Professionals (ASP) 147–148
Association of Tennis
Professionals (ATP)
Gustavo Kuerten 112
David Nalbandian 154
Marcelo Ríos 192
athletic greatness viii
athletic scholarship
Rolando Blackman 16
John Carlos 33
Trent Dimas 55
Lisa Fernandez 67
Francisco García 80
Jeff Garcia 81
Tony Gonzalez 98
Martín Gramática 100
Pablo Morales 146
Anthony Muñoz 148
Eduardo Nájera 152
Jim Plunkett 180
Marco Rivera 192
Ron Rivera 196
Alex Rodriguez 197
Brenda Villa 242
Charlie Villanueva 244

Atlanta Beat (WUSA soccer
team) 58
Atlanta Braves
Vinny Castilla 37
Orlando Cepeda 39
Julio Franco 74
Andrés Galarraga 76
Ozzie Guillén 106
Dennis Martínez 132–133
Edgar Rentería 189
Atlanta Falcons 36
Atlanta Hawks 86
Atlantic Division title (hockey)
91, 92
ATP. *See* Association of Tennis
Professionals
Attner, Paul 36
Augusta National Golf Course,
Masters
Seve Ballesteros 12
Lee Trevino 236
Auriemma, Geno 118
Australian Grand Prix (auto
racing) 143
Australian National
Championship (tennis) 162,
163
Australian Open (tennis)
Mary Joe Fernández 68
David Nalbandian 153,
154
Marcelo Ríos 191–192
Guillermo Vilas 241
Automatica Gramatica. *See*
Gramática, Martín
auto racing. *See also specific*
headings, e.g.: National
Association of Stock Car
Auto Racing
Hélio Castroneves 37–38
Christian Fittipaldi 70–71
Emerson Fittipaldi 70–72
Juan Pablo Montoya
142–143
Nelson Piquet 71, 179–180
Ayrton Senna 71, 220–222
avascular necrosis 79
Azteca Stadium (Mexico) 43

B

Baby Bull. *See* Cepeda,
Orlando
back injuries
Seve Ballesteros 13
Roberto Clemente 45–46
Alfredo Di Stefano 57
Emerson Fittipaldi 72
Nomar Garciaparra 83

Baines, Harold 184
Baker, Guy 243
Ballesteros, Baldomero 12
Ballesteros, Manuel 12
Ballesteros, Seve **12–13**
Ballesteros, Vicente 12
Baltimore Black Sox 54
Baltimore Orioles
   Luis Aparicio 5
   Bobby Bonilla 18
   Ozzie Guillén 106
   Dennis Martínez 131
   Rafael Palmeiro 166–167
   Sammy Sosa 224–225
   Miguel Tejada 229, 230
   Fernando Valenzuela 240
Bannister, Allen 31
Barbosa, Leandro **13–14,** 219
Barkley, Iran 61
barrio
   Miguel Cabrera 23
   Oscar De La Hoya 52
   Wilfredo Gómez 92
   Carlos Zárate 249
baseball. *See also* American
   League; Baseball Hall of
   Fame; National League;
   Negro League baseball;
   World Series
   Hank Aaron 46, 128,
     185
   Roberto Alomar 1–2
   Felipe Alou 2–4, 39, 135
   Luis Aparicio 4–5
   Johnny Bench 48, 175,
     200
   Barry Bonds 17, 197
   Bobby Bonilla 17–18
   Miguel Cabrera 23–24
   Jose Canseco 27–29, 166,
     175, 184, 197, 225
   Rod Carew 30–32, 161
   Vinny Castilla 36–37
   Orlando Cepeda 38–40,
     134
   Roberto Clemente viii, ix,
     40, 45–48, 104, 128,
     133
   Davey Concepción 48–49
   Martín Dihigo 53–54
   Tony Fernández 69–70
   Julio Franco 73–74
   Andrés Galarraga 76–77
   Nomar Garciaparra 82–84,
     103
   Lefty Gomez 89–90
   Juan González 28, 95–97,
     166, 197, 200, 247

Vladimir Guerrero 102–104
Ozzie Guillén 46–47, 49,
   106–107
Keith Hernandez 108–110
Willie Hernández 110–111
Al Lopez 118–120
Dolf Luque 123–124
Juan Marichal 3, 39, 127–
   129, 131–133, 136, 229
Dennis Martínez 131–133
Edgar Martinez 133–134,
   197
Pedro Martínez 4, 69,
   135–137, 217
Mark McGwire 27, 28,
   136, 184, 224
José Méndez viii, 137–138
Minnie Miñoso 139–140,
   174
Tony Oliva 160–161
Rafael Palmeiro 28,
   166–167
Camilo Pascual 124,
   170–171
Tony Pérez 48, 174–175
player appearing in five
   decades 139
Albert Pujols viii, 183–185
Manny Ramírez 186–187,
   198
Edgar Rentería 189–190
Cal Ripken, Jr. 69, 167,
   230, 240, 245
Mariano Rivera 194–195
Jackie Robinson 33, 47,
   54, 137, 139
Alex Rodriguez 134, 187,
   196–199
Iván Rodríguez 28, 96,
   166, 200–201, 247
Johan Santana 216–217
Sammy Sosa 69, 136,
   223–225
Miguel Tejada 229–230
Luis Tiant 230–231
Fernando Valenzuela
   239–241
Omar Vizquel 2, 49,
   245–246
Bernie Williams 96, 194,
   247–248
Ted Williams 31, 185
Carl Yastrzemski 187, 231
Baseball America's AA Player of
   the Year 103
Baseball Hall of Fame
   Luis Aparicio 4, 5
   Rod Carew 30, 32

Orlando Cepeda 38, 40
Roberto Clemente 47
Martín Dihigo 53, 54
Lefty Gomez 90
Al Lopez 120
Juan Marichal 127, 129
Tony Pérez 175
baseball manager 231
baseball scouts
   Juan Marichal 129
   Camilo Pascual 171
   Luis Tiant 231
basketball. *See also* National
   Basketball Association;
   NCAA championship
   (basketball)
   Gilbert Arenas 7–8
   Carlos Arroyo 10–11
   Leandro Barbosa 13–14,
     219
   Rolando Blackman 16–17
   Francisco García 79–80
   Pau Gasol 85–86
   Manu Ginobili viii, ix,
     86–89, 157
   Magic Johnson 16, 85,
     227
   Michael Jordan 85
   Rebecca Lobo 117–118
   Eduardo Nájera 152–153
   Nenê 156–157, 219
   Andrés Nocioni 157–158
   Oscar Schmidt 218–219
   Diana Taurasi 227–228
   Charlie Villanueva
     243–244
basketball analyst 118
Basketball Hall of Fame (Chip
   Hilton Player of the Year
   Award) 153
Basket Viola Reggio Calabria
   (Italian league) 87
"Battle of Champions, The"
   9–10
"Battle of the Little Giants,
   The" 215
Bayer Leverkusen (soccer team)
   190
Bazooka. *See* Gómez, Wilfredo
"BB Gunners" 17
Beardsley, Dick 212
Beckenbauer, Franz 174
Becker, Boris 151
Belmont Stakes 177, 178
Bench, Johnny
   Davey Concepción 48
   Tony Pérez 175
   Iván Rodríguez 200

Benitez, Wilfred **14–16,** *15*
   Antonio Cervantes 40
   Roberto Durán 60
   Carlos Palomino 168
Benito Juárez University
   (Mexico) 37
Bent Tree Classic 121
Benvenuti, Nino 144
Bible of Boxing, the. *See*
   Benitez, Wilfred
"bicycle kick" 115
Big Cat. *See* Galarraga, Andrés
Big East Conference
   Tournament (basketball) 227
Big Eight Defensive Player of
   the Year (basketball) 16
bigotry 39
"Big Red Machine" 48, 174,
   175
biographer 233
Bird, Larry 85
black athletes, struggle of 33.
   See also African Americans
black belts
   Héctor Camacho 24
   Mia Rosales-St. John 206
Blackman, Rolando **16–17**
Black Power 32–34, *33*
Blair Academy 244
Blond Arrow, the. *See* Di
   Stefano, Alfredo
Blue Ballet (Ballet Azul) 56
Boca Juniors (soccer) 125, 126
Bold Forbes (horse) 49
bolo punch 97
Bonds, Barry
   Bobby Bonilla 17
   Alex Rodriguez 197
Bonilla, Bobby **17–18**
bonus (signing) 83
Boone, Bret 134
Borg, Bjorn
   Gustavo Kuerten 112
   Guillermo Vilas 241
"Born in the U.S.A."
   (Springsteen) 43
Boston Braves
   Al Lopez 119
   Dolf Luque 123
Boston Bruins 101, 102
Boston College 101–102
Boston Marathon 211, 212
Boston Patriots 181. *See also*
   New England Patriots
Boston Red Sox
   Orlando Cepeda 39
   Nomar Garciaparra 82–84
   Juan Marichal 128

Pedro Martínez 135, 136
Tony Pérez 175
Manny Ramírez 186
Edgar Rentería 189
Luis Tiant 230–231
Botafogo (Brazilian soccer
    team)
    Garrincha 84–85
    Sócrates 222
Boudreau, Lou 119
Boutilette, K. C. 202
boxing. *See also* International
    Boxing Hall of Fame; World
    Boxing Association; World
    Boxing Council; World
    Boxing Organization
    Muhammad Ali 98, 174,
        225, 226, 233
    Alexis Argüello 9–10, 41
    Wilfred Benitez 14–16, 40,
        60, 168
    Panama Al Brown 19
    Héctor Camacho 24–25,
        43, 52, 61, 237
    Miguel Canto 29
    Antonio Cervantes 14–15,
        40–41
    Bobby Chacon 41–42, 162
    Julio César Chávez 25,
        42–44, 52
    Pipino Cuevas 50
    Oscar De La Hoya 25,
        43–44, 51–53, 206, 237
    Roberto Durán 15, 25,
        58–61, 168, 171
    Sixto Escobar 62–63
    George Forman 226
    Joe Frazier 59, 226
    Víctor Galíndez 77–78
    Wilfredo Gómez 92–93,
        215, 249
    Kid Gavilan González
        97–98
    Ismael Laguna 114
    Sugar Ray Leonard 15,
        25, 59
    Carlos Monzón 144–145,
        155
    José Nápoles 154–155
    Rubén Olivares 161–162
    Carlos Ortiz 114, 163–
        164, 188
    Carlos Palomino 167–168
    Eusebio Pedroza 171–172
    Sugar Ramos 164, 187–
        188, 213
    Mia Rosales-St. John
        206–207

John Ruiz 207–208
Vicente Saldívar 213
Salvador Sánchez 93,
    215–216
Kid Chocolate Sardinas
    217–218
Teófilo Stevenson 225–226
José Torres 233–234
Félix Trinidad, Jr. 25,
    236–238
Mike Tyson 233
Carlos Zárate 93, 215,
    249–250
boxing instructor 42
boxing trainer 41
Boys Club 24
Boza-Edwards, Cornelius 41
Brabham Team (auto racing)
    180
Brazil
    Leandro Barbosa 13–14
    Maria Bueno 21–22
    Christian Fittipaldi 70–71
    Garrincha 84–85
    Gustavo Kuerten 112–113
    Leônidas 115
    Vanderlei de Lima
        116–117
    Marta 129–131
    Patricia Miranda 140–141
    Nenê 156–157
    Pelé 172–174
    Nelson Piquet 179–180
    Roberto Rivelino 192–193
    Ronaldinho 203–204
    Ronaldo 205–206
    Oscar Schmidt 218–219
    Ayrton Senna 220–222
    Sócrates 222–223
    Zico 250–251
Brazilian Cart Championship
    180
Brazilian Cross of Merit 113
Brazilian Football
    Confederation 223
Brazilian Formula Ford 2000
    Championship 70
Brazilian Grand Prix (auto
    racing)
    Emerson Fittipaldi 71
    Juan Pablo Montoya 143
Brazilian Karting
    Championship 38
Brazilian League Rookie of the
    Year (basketball) 13
Brazilian national team (soccer)
    Garrincha 85
    Leônidas 115

Pelé 173
Ronaldo 205
Sócrates 222
Zico 250
Brazilian Olympic team 116
Brazil's Davis Cup team 112
Brazil's Women's World Cup
    team (2003) (soccer) 130
breast cancer research support
    118
Bredahl, Jimmi 51
British Columbia Hockey
    League 91
British Open (golf)
    Seve Ballesteros 12, 13
    Lee Trevino 235, 236
Brito, Waldemar de 172
broadcasting
    Tom Flores 73
    Keith Hernandez 109
Brock, Lou 109
broken leg 70
broken neck 178
bronze medals
    Joaquín Capilla 30
    Vanderlei de Lima 116
    Patricia Miranda 140,
        141
    Dara Torres 232
Brooke, Edward, III 231
Brooklyn Dodgers 45. *See also*
    Brooklyn Robins
Brooklyn Robins (Dodgers)
    119
Brown, Panama Al **19–20**
Brown, Pat 188
Brusa, Amilcar 144
Bruschi, Tedy 20, **20–21**
Buchanan, Ken 59
Budge, Don 94
Bueno, Maria **21–22**
Buffalo Bills 72
bulimia 232
Bush, George W. 208

C

Cabrera, Miguel **23–24**
Caesar's Palace
    Wilfred Benitez 15
    Roberto Durán 60
    Pancho Gonzales 95
Calder Trophy 90, 91
Calgary Stampeders
    Tom Flores 72
    Jeff Garcia 81
California Angels
    Rod Carew 32
    Fernando Valenzuela 240

California State University–
    Long Beach 168
Camacho, Héctor **24–25**
    Julio César Chávez 43
    Oscar De La Hoya 52
    Roberto Durán 61
    Félix Trinidad Jr. 237
Campanella, Roy 33
Campos, Jorge **25–26**
Canadian Football League
    (CFL)
    John Carlos 34
    Tom Flores 72
    Jeff Garcia 81
Canadian Football League
    MVP award 81
Canadian Open (golf) 236
cancer
    Andrés Galarraga 76, 77
    Pancho Gonzales 95
Cannonade (horse) 49
Canseco, Jose 27, **27–29**
    Rafael Palmeiro 166
    Tony Pérez 175
    Albert Pujols 184
    Alex Rodriguez 197
    Sammy Sosa 225
Canto, Miguel **29**
Capilla, Joaquín **29–30**
Captain America ensemble 25
Carew, Rod **30–32**, 31, 161
Caribbean Armed Forces
    championship 233
Carlos, John **32–34**, 33
Carlos, Roberto 45
Carlton, Steve 136
CART. *See* Championship
    Auto Racing Teams
Carter, Gary 119
Casals, Rosie **34–35**
Casillas, Tony **35–36**
Castilla, Vinny **36–37**
Castillo, Alfonso 171
Castillo, Chucho 162
Castro, Fidel viii
    José Nápoles 154
    Camilo Pascual 170
    Teófilo Stevenson 226
    Luis Tiant 231
Castroneves, Hélio **37–38**
cataracts 98
catchers
    Al Lopez 118–120
    Iván Rodríguez 200
Cauthen, Steve 49
Caveat (horse) 178
Celaya (Mexican men's soccer
    team) 58

Cepeda, Orlando **38–40**, 134
Cervantes, Antonio 14–15, **40–41**
CFL. *See* Canadian Football League
Cha Cha. *See* Cepeda, Orlando
Chacon, Bobby **41–42**, 162
Championship Auto Racing Teams (CART)
　Christian Fittipaldi 70
　Juan Pablo Montoya 142, 143
Champions on Ice Tour 79
Champions Tour (golf)
　Chi Chi Rodríguez 200
　Lee Trevino 236
Chapu, El. *See* Nocioni, Andrés
charitable activities
　Roberto Clemente 47
　Trent Dimas 55
　Kid Gavilan González 97
charity tournaments 121–122
Chávez, Julio César **42–44**, 43
　Héctor Camacho 25
　Oscar De La Hoya 52
Chiba Lotte Marines (baseball team) 74
Chicago Bears 195–196
Chicago Bulls 157, 158
Chicago Cubs
　Nomar Garciaparra 84
　Willie Hernández 110
　Rafael Palmeiro 166
　Sammy Sosa 224
Chicago Fire (soccer team) 26
Chicago White Sox
　Luis Aparicio 5
　Bobby Bonilla 17
　Jose Canseco 28
　Julio Franco 74
　Ozzie Guillén 106, 107
　Al Lopez 118–119
　Minnie Miñoso 139, 140
　Sammy Sosa 223–224
Chic-Fil-A Charity Championship 121
Chi Chi Rodriguez Youth Foundation 200
chicken pox 161
Chief, the. *See* Olmedo, Alex
Chilavert, José Luis **44–45**
Chile
　Marcelo Ríos 191–192
　Marcelo Salas 210–211
Chile's national soccer team 210
Chino. *See* Ríos, Marcelo

Chip Hilton Player of the Year Award (basketball) 153
Christian, born-again 3
Christiensen, Todd 100
Cienfuegos club (Cuba) 124
Cincinnati Bengals 148–149
Cincinnati Reds
　Davey Concepción 48
　Tony Fernández 69
　Dolf Luque 123–124
　Camilo Pascual 170
　Tony Pérez 174–175
Cincinnati Reds Hall of Fame 124
civil rights 32–34
Clark, Will 166
Clemens, Roger
　Miguel Cabrera 23
　Lefty Gomez 90
Clemente, Roberto viii, ix, **45–48**, 46
　Orlando Cepeda 40
　Vladimir Guerrero 104
　Juan Marichal 128
　Edgar Martinez 133
Clemson University 65
Cleveland Browns 82
Cleveland Indians
　Roberto Alomar 2
　Tony Fernández 69
　Julio Franco 73
　Al Lopez 118, 119
　Dennis Martínez 132
　Minnie Miñoso 139, 140
　Camilo Pascual 170
　Manny Ramírez 186
　Luis Tiant 230
　Omar Vizquel 245, 246
clothing
　Jorge Campos 26
　flamboyant 77
　tennis 22, 35
coaching, baseball
　Felipe Alou 4
　Rod Carew 32
　Ozzie Guillén 106
　Tony Oliva 161
　Tony Pérez 175
　Luis Tiant 231
coaching, basketball 17
coaching, batting 4
coaching, first base 161
coaching, football
　Tom Fears 64–65
　Tom Flores 72–73
　Ron Rivera 196
coaching, gymnastics 55

coaching, soccer
　Alfredo Di Stefano 57
　Leônidas 115
coaching, softball
　Lisa Fernandez 67
　Leticia Pineda-Boutte 179
coaching, swimming 147
coaching, tennis 65
Cobb, Ty 31
Codex (horse) 49
Coimbra, Arthur Artunes. *See* Zico
Cokes, Curtis 155
College Football Hall of Fame 36
College Football Preview *(Sports Illustrated)* 20
college sports. *See* National Collegiate Athletic Association
College World Series Tournament (baseball) 83
Colombia
　Antonio Cervantes 40–41
　Juan Pablo Montoya 142–143
　Edgar Rentería 189–190
Colombian championship (soccer) 56
Colorado Rockies
　Vinny Castilla 36, 37
　Andrés Galarraga 76
comeback 15
Comrades Marathon (South Africa) 212
Concepción, Davey **48–49**
Conference Player of the Year (basketball) 16
Conference USA (C-USA) (basketball) 80
congressional committee 28
Connecticut Sun 118
Connors, Jimmy
　Pancho Gonzales 95
　Pancho Segura 220
　Guillermo Vilas 241
Conquistador Cielo (horse) 178
Consensus All-Pro (football) 99
contras 9
convulsions 205
Copa América tournament (soccer)
　José Luis Chilavert 44
　Ronaldinho 203
Copa del Rey (Spain national championship) 125

Copa Libertadores (South American Club championship) 44
Cordero, Angel, Jr. **49–50**
Cordero, Angel, Sr. 49
Coria, Guillermo 242
Craig, Roger 111
Creighton University (Omaha) 179
Crenshaw, Ben 13
Cross Country World Championship 75
Cross Country World Cup 75
Cruzeiro de Belo Horizonte Club 205
Cuba viii
　Jose Canseco 27–28
　Fidel Castro viii, 154, 170, 226, 231
　Martín Dihigo 53–54
　Kid Gavilan González 97–98
　Dolf Luque 123–124
　José Méndez 137–138
　Minnie Miñoso 139–140
　José Nápoles 154–155
　Tony Oliva 160–161
　Rafael Palmeiro 166–167
　Camilo Pascual 170–171
　Tony Pérez 174–175
　Yuliana Perez 176
　Sugar Ramos 187–188
　Alberto Salazar 211–212
　Kid Chocolate Sardinas 217–218
　Teófilo Stevenson 225–226
　Luis Tiant 230–231
　Regla Torres 234–235
Cuban-Americans
　Al Lopez 118–120
　Pablo Morales 145–147
　Jennifer Rodriguez 201–202
Cuban Baseball Hall of Fame
　Martín Dihigo 53
　José Méndez 138
Cuban Bonbon, the. *See* Sardinas, Kid Chocolate
Cuban Boxing Federation 226
Cuban featherweight title 188
Cuban junior national team (volleyball) 234
Cuban Juvenile League All-Star team (baseball) 230
Cuban national team (volleyball) 235

Cuban Stars (baseball)
Martín Dihigo 54
José Méndez 137
Cuban Winter League (baseball)
José Méndez 137
Minnie Miñoso 139
Cuban youth national team
(volleyball) 234
Cuevas, Pipino 50, 60
C-USA. See Conference USA
Cyclist of the Year (VeloNews)
75
Cy Young Award
Willie Hernández 110, 111
Pedro Martínez 135, 136
Johan Santana 216, 217
Fernando Valenzuela 240

D

Dallas Cowboys
Tony Casillas 35, 36
Martín Gramática 101
Marco Rivera 192
Dallas Mavericks
Rolando Blackman 16–17
Eduardo Nájera 153
Dallas Stars 102
D'Angelo, Ricardo 116
Dark, Alvin 39
Davis, Al 180, 182
Davis Cup (tennis)
Gustavo Kuerten 112
Rafael Nadal 151
Rafael Osuna 164, 165
Guillermo Vilas 241–242
De La Hoya, Oscar 51–53, 52
Héctor Camacho 25
Julio César Chávez 43–44
Mia Rosales-St. John 206
Félix Trinidad Jr. 237
Dellinger, Bill 212
dementia, pugilistic. See
pugilistic dementia
Dennis Martinez Foundation
133
Denver Nuggets
Eduardo Nájera 153
Nenê 156–157
Denver Open (golf) 199
detached retinas 78
Detroit Lions 82
Detroit Pistons 11
Detroit Tigers
Felipe Alou 4
Juan Gonzalez 96
Willie Hernández 110–111
Iván Rodríguez 201
De Varona, Donna 232

diabetes 63
Diamente Negro. See Leônidas
Dico. See Pelé
Dihigo, Martín 53–54
DiMaggio, Joe
Nomar Garciaparra 83
Lefty Gomez 90
Vladimir Guerrero 103
Tony Oliva 160
Albert Pujols 185
Dimas, Trent 54–56, 55
disabled, work for severely
113
disaster relief 133
discrimination 120. See also
racism, segregation
disposition, nasty 191
Di Stefano, Alfredo 56–57,
57
Ditka, Mike 196
diver 29–30
Dodgers Spanish language
radio crew 241
Dodger Stadium 188
Domínguez, Maribel 57–58
Dominican Baseball Academy
229
Dominican Dandy, the. See
Marichal, Juan
Dominican Military Aviation
baseball team 127
Dominican Republic
Felipe Alou 2–4
Martín Dihigo 54
Mary Joe Fernández 67–68
Tony Fernández 69–70
Julio Franco 73–74
Francisco García 79–80
Vladimir Guerrero
102–104
Juan Marichal 127–129
Pedro Martínez 135–137
Albert Pujols 183–185
Manny Ramírez 186–187
Felix Sanchez 213–214
Sammy Sosa 223–225
Miguel Tejada 229–230
Dooley, Virgil 169
"Dream Team" (basketball) 85
drug abuse. See substance abuse
Drysdale, Don
Orlando Cepeda 39
Lefty Gomez 89
Duncan, Tim 88
Dundee, Angelo 44
Durán, Roberto 58–61, 60
Wilfred Benitez 15
Héctor Camacho 25

Carlos Palomino 168
Eusebio Pedroza 171
Dylan, Bob 188

E

Earnhart, Ramsey 165
earthquake victims ix
East Coast Hockey League 92
Eastern Conference title
(hockey)
Scott Gomez 91
Bill Guerin 102
Eastern League Most Valuable
Player (baseball) 103
East Texas State University
(ETSU) 33
East-West Shrine All-Star
Game (football) 81
Ecclestone, Bernie 180
Eclipse Award (horse racing)
Angel Cordero, Jr. 49
Laffit Pincay, Jr. 178
Ecuador 219–220
Edmonton Oilers 102
Edwards, Harry 33
Eisenhower, Dwight 170
elbow injuries
Tony Fernández 69
Johan Santana 216
endometriosis 68
entertainer 97
L'Equipe (newspaper, France)
173
Escobar, Sixto 62–63
Espada, Angel 50
Española 57
ESPY Award 118
Estudiantes Bahía Blanca
(Argentina) 87
ETSU. See East Texas State
University
Euro League (MVP) award
(basketball) 87
European Champion Cup
(soccer) 56
European Junior
Championship (basketball)
85
European Ryder Cup Team
(golf) 12, 13
European Tour (golf) 12
European Tour Order of Merit
(golf) 12
Everett, Chris 209

F

Falkland Islands War 126
Famechon, Johnny 213

Farmer, David 75
fastball 54
Favre, Brett 192
FC Barcelona
Maribel Domínguez 58
Diego Maradona 125
Rafael Nadal 151
Ronaldinho 203–204
Ronaldo 205
Fears, Tom 64–65
featherweight boxing champion
Eusebio Pedroza 171
Kid Chocolate Sardinas
218
Fédération Internationale de
Automobile (FIA) Formula
One Super License 70
Fédération Internationale de
Football Association (FIFA)
Maribel Domínguez 58
Internet poll 127
Diego Maradona 127
Marta 130
Pelé 174
Claudio Reyna 190
Ronaldinho 203, 204
Ronaldo 205, 206
Federer, Roger
Gustavo Kuerten 113
Rafael Nadal 151, 152
David Nalbandian 153,
154
Fenomino, Il. See Ronaldo
Fernández, Gigi 65–66, 68
Fernandez, Lisa viii, 66, 66–67
Fernández, Mary Joe 65,
67–68
Fernández, Tony 69–70
FIA Formula One Super
License 70
FIFA. See Fédération
Internationale de Football
Association
FIFA Player of the Century
Diego Maradona 127
Pelé 174
FIFA Player of the Year 203,
204
FIFA World Cup All-Star team
190
FIFA World Player of the Year
award 205, 206
"Fighter of the Century"
(Colombian Boxing
Federation) 41
figure skating 78–79
Final Four (NCAA) 155, 156
Fingers, Rollie 111

Fiorentina (Brazilian soccer team) 222
Fire and Fear (Torres) 233
First Team All-America (football) 98
Fisk, Carlton 184
Fittipaldi, Christian **70–71**
Fittipaldi, Emerson 70, **71–72**
Fittipaldi, Wilson, Jr. 71
Five Skaters (art project) 79
Flamengo team
    Leônidas 115
    Zico 250, 251
Flores, Tom **72–73**
Florida International 10
Florida Marlins
    Bobby Bonilla 18
    Miguel Cabrera 23–24
    Ozzie Guillén 106
    Tony Pérez 175
    Edgar Rentería 189
    Iván Rodríguez 201
Flutie, Doug 81
football. *See also* National Football League; *specific headings, e.g.:* Super Bowl
    Adam Archuleta 6
    Tedy Bruschi 20–21
    Tony Casillas 35–36
    Tom Fears 64–65
    Tom Flores 72
    Jeff Garcia 81–82
    Tony Gonzalez 98–100
    Martín Gramática 100–101
    Anthony Muñoz 148–150
    Jim Plunkett 180–182
    Marco Rivera 192
    Ron Rivera 195–196
    Steve Young 65, 81
Ford, Whitey 230
Forest Hills Stadium 241
Forman, George 226
Formula One (auto racing)
    Christian Fittipaldi 70
    Emerson Fittipaldi 71
    Víctor Galíndez 77, 78
    Juan Pablo Montoya 142, 143
    Nelson Piquet 179–180
    Ayrton Senna 220–222
Formula Three (auto racing)
    Hélio Castronever 38
    Juan Pablo Montoya 143
    Nelson Piquet 180
    Ayrton Senna 220
Formula 3000 Series
    Christian Fittipaldi 70
    Juan Pablo Montoya 143

Formula Two (auto racing) 71
Fox, Vicente
    Ana Guevara 105
    Lorena Ochoa 159
Francisco dos Santos, Manoel. *See* Garrincha
Franco, Julio **73–74**
Franklin American Mortgage Championship 160
Frazer, Alfonzo "Peppermint" 40
Frazier, Joe
    Roberto Durán 59
    Teófilo Stevenson 226
Frei, Jerry 181
French, Jeff 250
French Open (tennis)
    Gigi Fernández 65
    Mary Joe Fernández 68
    Gustavo Kuerten 112
    Rafael Nadal 151, 152
    David Nalbandian 153, 154
    Gabriela Sabatini 209
    Guillermo Vilas 241
French Open Juniors championship (tennis) 153–154
Furtado, Juli **74–75**
futbolista (female soccer player) 57–58
futsal (indoor version of soccer)
    Marta 129
    Roberto Rivelino 192
    Ronaldo 205
    Sócrates 222

G
Galarraga, Andrés **76–77,** 104
Galíndez, Víctor **77–78**
Galindo, Rudy **78–79**
Gallito, El. *See* Escobar, Sixto
García, Francisco **79–80**
Garcia, Jeff **80–82**
Garciaparra, Nomar **82–84,** 103
Garrincha **84–85**
Gasol, Pau **85–86**
Gate Dancer (horse) 49
Gatorade National Player of the Year award 190
Gehrig, Lou
    Lefty Gomez 90
    Bernie Williams 248
Georgia Institute of Technology (Georgia Tech) 83
Gibson, Althea 22
Gibson, Bob 128

Gigi Fernandez Charitable Foundation 66
Giménez, Carlos María 40
Ginobili, Manu viii, ix, **86–89,** *88,* 157
Glanville, Jerry 36
Glavine, Tom 89
goalie 25
go-carts 71
"Go-Go Sox" 140
Golden Boot award (soccer) 206
Golden Boy. *See* De La Hoya, Oscar
Golden Glove award (boxing) 24
Golden State Warriors
    Gilbert Arenas 7, 8
    Eduardo Nájera 153
Gold Glove award (baseball)
    Roberto Alomar 1, 2
    Luis Aparicio 4, 5
    Roberto Clemente 45, 46
    Davey Concepción 48
    Tony Fernández 69
    Andrés Galarraga 76
    Ozzie Guillén 106
    Keith Hernandez 108
    Tony Oliva 161
    Rafael Palmeiro 166
    Edgar Rentería 189
    Alex Rodriguez 198
    Iván Rodríguez 200
    Fernando Valenzuela 240
    Omar Vizquel 245, 246
    Bernie Williams 247, 248
gold medals
    Joaquín Capilla 29
    John Carlos 33
    Oscar De La Hoya 51
    Trent Dimas 54, 55
    Lisa Fernandez 67
    Ana Guevara 105
    Vanderlei de Lima 116
    Rebecca Lobo 117, 118
    Steven Lopez 123
    Pablo Morales 145
    Jennifer Rodriguez 201
    Felix Sanchez 213, 214
    Teófilo Stevenson 226
    Diana Taurasi 227, 228
    Dara Torres 232
    Regla Torres 234, 235
    Brenda Villa 242
golf. *See also specific headings, e.g.:* Masters Tournament
    Seve Ballesteros 12–13
    Nancy Lopez viii, 120–122

Lorena Ochoa 159–160
Chi Chi Rodríguez 199–200
Lee Trevino viii, 13, 235–236
Tiger Woods 98, 159
golf pro assistant 199
Gomez, Lefty **89–90**
Gomez, Scott **90–92,** *91*
Gómez, Wilfredo **92–93**
    Salvador Sánchez 215
    Carlos Zárate 249
Gonzales, Pancho viii, **93–95,** *94*
    Alex Olmedo 163
    Pancho Segura 220
González, Juan **95–97**
    Jose Canseco 28
    Rafael Palmeiro 166
    Alex Rodriguez 197
    Iván Rodríguez 200
    Bernie Williams 247
González, Kid Gavilan **97–98,** 162
Gonzalez, Tony **98–100,** *99*
goodwill ambassadors
    Trent Dimas 55
    Minnie Miñoso 140
Goodwill Games
    Oscar De La Hoya 51
    Trent Dimas 55
    Nenê 156
    Gaby Pérez del Solar 177
    Regla Torres 234
Goolagong, Evonne 22
Gordon Panthers (youth softball team) 66
Gottfried, Brian 241
Gowdy, Curt 231
Graf, Steffi 68
Gramática, Martín **100–101**
Grammy award nomination 53
Grand Prix (auto racing) 143
    Emerson Fittipaldi 71
    Nelson Piquet 180
    Ayrton Senna 220–222
    Dara Torres 233
Grand Prix Championship (volleyball) 234
Grand Slam tournament (tennis)
    Maria Bueno 22
    Rafael Nadal 151, 152
    Marcelo Ríos 191, 192
    Gabriela Sabatini 209
    Guillermo Vilas 241

Green Bay Packers
    Tom Fears 64
    Marco Rivera 192
Greenberg, Hank 96
Gregorio, Vidal 19
Gremio Porto Alegre (soccer
    team) 203
Griffey, Ken, Jr.
    Juan Gonzalez 96
    Alex Rodriguez 197
Griffith, Calvin 32
groin injury 84
Grook, Edward 233
Grove, Lefty 89–90
Grunfeld, Ernie 8
Guante, Cecilio 69
Guerin, Bill **101–102**
Guerrero, Vladimir **102–104**
Guevara, Ana viii, **104–106,
    105**
Guillén, Ozzie **106–107**
    Roberto Clemente 46–47
    Davey Concepción 49
guitar 247
Gulf Coast League 194
Gutíerrez, Luis 217–218
gymnastics 54–56

H

Hagler, Marvin 60
Halal, El (soccer club, Saudi
    Arabia) 192
hamstring injury 84
hand injury 30
"hand of God goal, the" 126,
    127
Hands of Stone. See Durán,
    Roberto
Hard, Darlene 22
Harrisburg Senators 103
Haugen, Greg 43
Havana Sugar Kings 174
HBO television network
    9–10
Hearns, Thomas "Hitman"
    Wilfred Benitez 15
    Pipino Cuevas 50
    Roberto Durán 60
heavyweight world champion
    207
Heisman Trophy
    Doug Flutie 81
    Jim Plunkett 73, 180, 181
Henderson, Ricky 184
Hendrix, Elrod 230
hepatitis
    Maria Bueno 22
    Diego Maradona 125

Hernandez, Keith **108–110,
    110**
Hernández, Willie **110–111**
herniated disc
    Adam Archuleta 6
    Vladimir Guerrero 104
Hewitt, Lleyton 154
high leg kick 127
Hilario, Maybyner Rodney.
    See Nenê
Hill Street Blues (television
    series) 168
Hirschbeck, John 2
Hirsh, Elroy "Crazy Legs" 64
Hispanic Scholarship Fund 118
HIV/AIDS 78, 79
hockey. See also National
    Hockey League
    Scott Gomez 90–92
    Bill Guerin 101
    Alvaro Montoya 141–142
Hockey East Conference
    championship 102
Hollywood Park Racetrack 178
Holtzman, Ken 31
Holyfield, Evander 207–208
Homem Borracha, O. See
    Leônidas
home runs
    Jose Canseco 28
    Vinny Castilla 37
    Martín Dihigo 54
    Lisa Fernandez 67
    Andrés Galarraga 76
    Juan Gonzalez 96
Homestead Grays (baseball
    team) 54
homosexuality 79
Honda Broderick Award 67
Honda Cup award 67
Hooper, Fred 178
Hope, Maurice 15
Hopkins, Bernard 53
Horan, Cornelius 116
Hornsby, Roger 103
horse racing. See jockeys;
    specific headings, e.g.: Eclipse
    Award
Houston Astros
    Vinny Castilla 37
    Johan Santana 216
Houston Comets 118
Houston Rockets 153
Hoyt, LaMarr 106
humanitarianism ix, 45
Huracán (Argentina) 56
hurdling 213–214
Hurricane David 229

Hurricane Mitch 102
Hutchins, Len 78
hypochondriac 47

I

IAAF. See International
    Association of Athletics
    Federations
IBF. See International Boxing
    Federation (IBF), crown
ice skating
    Rudy Galindo 78–79
    Derek Parra 168–169
    Jennifer Rodriguez
    201–202
Igor. See González, Juan
Incan ancestry 162–163
income 71. See also salaries
Indianapolis Colts 101
Indianapolis 500
    Hélio Castroneve 37, 38
    Emerson Fittipaldi 72
    Juan Pablo Montoya 142,
    143
Indianapolis 500 Rookie of the
    Year 70
Indy Car racing
    Christian Fittipaldi 70
    Emerson Fittipaldi 71–72
    Nelson Piquet 180
injuries
    Roberto Alomar 1
    Seve Ballesteros 13
    Bobby Bonilla 17
    Maria Bueno 22
    Jose Canseco 28
    Joaquín Capilla 30
    John Carlos 34
    Orlando Cepeda 39
    Roberto Clemente 45–46
    Alfredo Di Stefano 57
    Mary Joe Fernández 68
    Tony Fernández 69
    Emerson Fittipaldi 72
    Julio Franco 74
    Juli Furtado 75
    Francisco García 80
    Nomar Garciaparra 83, 84
    Manu Ginobili 87
    Lefty Gomez 90
    Juan Gonzalez 96
    Tony Gonzalez 99
    Vladimir Guerrero 103
    Edgar Martinez 134
    Pedro Martínez 136
    José Méndez 138
    Anthony Muñoz 148
    David Nalbandian 154

Nenê 157
Tony Oliva 161
Manny Ramírez 187
Claudio Reyna 190
Marco Rivera 192
Alex Rodriguez 197
Ronaldo 205, 206
Johan Santana 216
Regla Torres 235
Lee Trevino 236
Omar Vizquel 245
Intercollegiate Tennis
    Association 165
Intercontinental Cup (soccer)
    56
Internal Revenue Service (IRS)
    97
International Association of
    Athletics Federations (IAAF)
    105
International Boxing
    Federation (IBF) crown
    237
International Boxing Hall of
    Fame
    Alexis Argüello 10
    Wilfred Benitez 15
    Panama Al Brown 19
    Miguel Canto 29
    Antonio Cervantes 41
    Bobby Chacon 42
    Pipino Cuevas 50
    Sixto Escobar 63
    Víctor Galíndez 78
    Wilfredo Gómez 93
    Kid Gavilan González 98
    Carlos Monzón 145
    José Nápoles 155
    Rubén Olivares 162
    Carlos Ortiz 164
    Carlos Palomino 168
    Eusebio Pedroza 171
    Vicente Saldívar 213
    Salvador Sánchez 216
    Kid Chocolate Sardinas
    218
    José Torres 234
International Ice Hockey
    Federaton Under-20 World
    Championship 142
International League Pitcher of
    the Year 131
International Olympic
    Committee (IOC)
    John Carlos 33, 34
    Vanderlei de Lima 116
International Swimming Hall
    of Fame 147

International Tennis Hall of
Fame
Maria Bueno 22
Rosie Casals 35
Pancho Gonzales 95
Alex Olmedo 163
Rafael Osuna 165
Pancho Segura 220
Guillermo Vilas 242
IOC. *See* International
Olympic Committee
Iraq War (2003) 123
irascible nature 94
Irish Nip (horse) 178
IRS. *See* Internal Revenue
Service
Isthmus (Panamanian)
flyweight title 19
Italian championship
(basketball) 17
Italian club Internazionale
(soccer) 205
Italian Grand Prix (auto racing)
143
Italian League Most Valuable
Player (MVP) award
(basketball) 87
Italian League Player of the
Year (basketball) 87
Iverson, Allen
Carlos Arroyo 11
Leandro Barbosa 13–14
Ivy League Player of the Year
(soccer) 155

J

Jackson, Reggie 96
Jehovah's Witness 97
Jenkins, Sally 65
Jesús, Esteban de 59
jockeys
Angel Cordero, Jr. 49–50
Laffit Pincay, Jr.
177–178
Johnson, Darrell 231
Johnson, Magic
Rolando Blackman 16
Pau Gasol 85
Diana Taurasi 227
Johnson, Walter
Lefty Gomez 89
Pedro Martínez 136
John Wooden All-American
Team 80
Jones, Chipper 74
Jones, James 14
Joon-Sik, Sin 122–123
Jordan, Michael 85

"Jordan mexicano, el" (the
Michael Jordan of Mexico) 37
Juan Gone. *See* González, Juan
Juiced (Canseco) 28, 225
Junior Olympics 75
Junior Pan-American Games
(1997) 176

K

Kansas City Chiefs
Tony Casillas 36
Tom Flores 72
Tony Gonzalez 98–100
Kansas City Monarchs 138
Kansas City Royals
Orlando Cepeda 39
Juan Gonzalez 96
Kansas State University
Rolando Blackman 16, 17
Martín Gramática 100
Kansas State Wildcats
Rolando Blackman 16
Martín Gramática 100
Kashima Antlers. *See*
Sumitomo Metals
Kentucky Derby
Angel Cordero, Jr. 49
Laffit Pincay, Jr. 177, 178
Kid Fortune (boxer) 19
kidney stones 69
Kid Pambele. *See* Cervantes,
Antonio
King, Billie Jean
Maria Bueno 22
Rosie Casals 34, 35
Kingdome (Seattle) 134
Kiper, Mel 6
Kite, Tom 13
Klapish, Bob 18
knee injuries
John Carlos 34
Orlando Cepeda 39
Julio Franco 74
Juli Furtado 75
Nomar Garciaparra 83
Tony Gonzalez 99
Anthony Muñoz 148
Nenê 157
Ronaldo 206
Regla Torres 235
Omar Vizquel 245
knockouts 51
Kobayashi, Hiroshi 59
Kobayashi, Royal
Wilfredo Gómez 93
Eusebio Pedroza 171
Konex Foundation best female
athlete (Argentina) 210

Koufax, Sandy
Lefty Gomez 89
Juan Marichal 128
Tony Oliva 161
Kramer, Jack
Pancho Gonzales 94
Pancho Segura 220
Kriegel, Mark 52
Kuerten, Gustavo **112–113**

L

Ladies Professional Golf
Association (LPGA)
Nancy Lopez 120, 121
Lorena Ochoa 159, 160
Laguna, Ismael **114–115**
Roberto Durán 59
Carlos Ortiz 164
Vicente Saldívar 213
Laporte, Juan 93
LaRussa, Tony 184
Latino heritage 45–48
Laver, Rod 163
Lazio (soccer team) 211
LeCroy, Matt 217
leg disability 84
leg injuries
Roberto Alomar 1
Maria Bueno 22
Juan Gonzalez 96
Leitham, Bobby 62
Lendl, Ivan 112
Lenglen, Suzanne 22
Leonard, Buck 54
Leonard, Sugar Ray
Wilfred Benitez 15
Héctor Camacho 25
Roberto Durán 59
Leônidas viii, **115–116**
Leopardo de Morón, El. *See*
Galíndez, Victor
Level of Excellence (Toronto
Blue Jays) 70
Lever, Rod 94
Lewis, Joe 171
Lichtenstein, Grace 35
lifestyles
Diego Maradona 126
Carlos Monzón 144
Kid Chocolate Sardinas
218
Teófilo Stevenson 226
light heavyweight champion
233
lightning injury 236
Lima, Ronaldo Luis Nazário
de. *See* Ronaldo
Lima, Vanderlei de **116–117**

Limón, Rafael "Bazooka"
Héctor Camacho 24
Bobby Chacon 41
Little, Grady 136
Little Looie. *See* Aparicio, Luis
Little Potato. *See* Pascual,
Camilo
Lobo, Rebecca *117,* **117–118**
Loche, Nicolino 40
Lockridge, Rocky
Wilfredo Gómez 93
Eusebio Pedroza 171
Lombank Formula Three
Championship 71
Lombardi, Vince 65
Lombardi Award (football)
Tony Casillas 36
finalist Tedy Bruschi 20
Lopez, Al **118–120**
Lopez, Felipe 80
Lopez, Jean 122, 123
Lopez, Nancy viii, **120–122,**
121
Lopez, Steven *122,* **122–123**
Los Angeles Dodgers
Nomar Garciaparra 84
Juan Marichal 128
Pedro Martínez 135
Camilo Pascual 170
Fernando Valenzuela
239–240
Los Angeles Galaxy 26
Los Angeles Lakers 16
Los Angeles Marathon 138,
139
Los Angeles Raiders 73
Los Angeles Rams 64
Los Cebolitas (Argentina)
(soccer) 125
Lotus Racing Team
Nelson Piquet 180
Ayrton Senna 221
Lou Groza Award 100
LPGA. *See* Ladies Professional
Golf Association
Luiz, João 172
lupus 75
Luque, Dolf **123–124**
Lyme disease 75
Lynch, Ed 109

M

Macho Camacho. *See*
Camacho, Héctor
Madden, John 73
Maddux, Greg 89
Madison Square Boys' Club
163

Madison Square Garden
  Roberto Durán 59
  Carlos Ortiz 164
  Kid Chocolate Sardinas
    218
  José Torres 233
Maestro, El. *See* Dihigo,
  Martín
Maglie, Sal ("the Barber") 124
Major League Baseball (MLB)
  Roberto Alomar 2
  Felipe Alou 4
  Miguel Cabrera 23
  Jose Canseco 27
  Rod Carew 30
  Roberto Clemente 45, 47
  Davey Concepción 48
  Nomar Garciaparra 83–84
  Vladimir Guerrero 103
  Ozzie Guillén 106
  Willie Hernández 110
  Dolf Luque 124
  Juan Marichal 128, 129
  Dennis Martínez 131, 132
  Edgar Martinez 134
  José Méndez 137
  Minnie Miñoso 139
  Tony Oliva 160
  Rafael Palmeiro 166
  Albert Pujols 184
  Manny Ramírez 187
  Edgar Rentería 189
  Mariano Rivera 194
  Alex Rodriguez 196, 197
  Johan Santana 216
  Sammy Sosa 224
  Miguel Tejada 229
  Fernando Valenzuela
    240–241
  Omar Vizquel 245, 246
Major League Baseball
  expansion draft 37
Major League Baseball Players
  Association (MLBPA) 18
Major League Soccer (MLS) 26
managers, baseball
  Al Lopez 118–120
  Tony Pérez 175
Managua, Nicaragua, mayor
  of 10
Mancini, Ray "Boom-Boom"
  42
Manhattan Division
  Championships (baseball)
  186
Manning, Archie 181
Manos de Piedra. *See* Durán,
  Roberto

Mansell, Nigel 180
Mantequilla. *See* Nápoles, José
Mantle, Mickey
  Roberto Clemente 46
  Bernie Williams 248
Mao Santa. *See* Schmidt, Oscar
Maplewoods Community
  College 183
Maracaibo Gavilanes (Sparrow
  Hawks) (Venezuela) 5
Maradona, Diego **125–127,**
  126, 203
marathon running
  Vanderlei de Lima
    116–117
  Saúl Mendoza 139
  Alberto Salazar 211–212
Marcano, Alfredo 41
Marcel, Ernest 9
Marianao 139
Marichal, Juan **127–129,** *129*
  Felipe Alou 3
  Orlando Cepeda 39
  Dennis Martínez 131–133
  Pedro Martínez 136
  Miguel Tejada 229
Mariel boat lift 176
Mari-gol. *See* Domínguez,
  Maribel
marijuana 39
Mariucci, Steve
  Jeff Garcia 82
  Tony Gonzalez 98–99
Marta **129–131,** *130*
martial arts 24, 122–123, 206
Martin, Christy 207
Martin, Kenyon 157
Martínez, Dennis **131–133**
Martinez, Edgar **133–134,** 197
Martínez, Mario 42
Martínez, Pedro *135,* **135–137**
  Felipe Alou 4
  Tony Fernández 69
  Johan Santana 217
Martínez, Rodolfo 249
Massy, Arnaud 12
Masters Tournament (golf)
  Seve Ballesteros 12, 13
  Lee Trevino 236
Matador, the. *See* Salas,
  Marcelo
Mathewson, Christy 137
Matlack, Jon 47
Mattingly, Don 240
Mayorga, Ricardo 53
Mays, Willie
  Roberto Clemente 46
  Al Lopez 119

Mayweather, Floyd, Jr. 53
Mayweather, Roger 42, 43, *43*
McCallum, Jack 141
McClendon, Lloyd 184
McCovey, Willie 39
McDougald, Gil 140
McGraw, John 137
McGwire, Mark
  Jose Canseco 27, 28
  Pedro Martínez 136
  Albert Pujols 184
  Sammy Sosa 224
McLaren Racing Team (auto
  racing)
  Juan Pablo Montoya 143
  Ayrton Senna 221
Mejia, Luis 214
Memphis Grizzlies 85, 86
Méndez, José viii, **137–138**
Mendoza, Saúl *138,* **138–139**
men's league (soccer) 58
Merry Mex, the. *See* Trevino,
  Lee
Messina, Ettore 88
Mexican Americans
  Oscar De La Hoya 51–53
  Scott Gomez 90–92
  Pancho Gonzales 93–95
Mexican Baseball Hall of
  Fame 53
Mexican Davis Cup tennis
  team 164, 165
Mexican-Irish heritage
  180–182
Mexican League (baseball)
  Martín Dihigo 54
  Minnie Miñoso 139
Mexican Marathon 138
Mexican national basketball
  team 153
Mexican national soccer team
  Jorge Campos 25
  Maribel Domínguez 58
Mexican Olympians 29
Mexican Soccer Federation 58
Mexican welterweight title 50
Mexico
  Jorge Campos 25–26
  Miguel Canto 29
  Joaquín Capilla 29–30
  Vinny Castilla 36–37
  Julio César Chávez 42–44
  Pipino Cuevas 50
  Maribel Domínguez 57–
    58
  Ana Guevara 104–105
  Saúl Mendoza 138–139
  Eduardo Nájera 152–153

Lorena Ochoa 159–160
Rubén Olivares 161–162
Rafael Osuna 164–165
Carlos Palomino 167–168
Vicente Saldívar 213
Salvador Sánchez 215–216
Fernando Valenzuela
  239–241
Carlos Zárate 249–250
Michigan 500 (auto racing)
  71, 72
middleweight champion of the
  world 144
Mighty Ducks 91
Millonarios (soccer team) 56
Milwaukee Braves 3
Milwaukee Brewers
  Tony Fernández 70
  Julio Franco 74
  Nomar Garciaparra 83
Minaya, Omar 223
Minnesota Timberwolves 80
Minnesota Twins
  Rod Carew 30–32
  Tony Oliva 160–161
  Johan Santana 216, 217
  Luis Tiant 230
Minor League Player of the
  Year
  Jose Canseco 27
  Vladimir Guerrero 103
Miñoso, Minnie **139–140,** 174
Miranda, Patricia **140–141**
Mississippi State University
  166
MLB. *See* Major League
  Baseball
MLBPA. *See* Major League
  Baseball Players Association
MLS Celebration Game 26
MLS Cup 26
Mo. *See* Rivera, Mariano
Montana, Joe 81
Montoya, Alvaro **141–142**
Montoya, Juan Pablo **142–143**
Montreal Expos
  Felipe Alou 3–4
  Andrés Galarraga 76
  Vladimir Guerrero
    103–104
  Ozzie Guillén 106
  Dennis Martínez 132
  Pedro Martínez 135, 136
  Tony Pérez 175
Montreal Gazette (newspaper)
  62
Monzón, Carlos **144–145,**
  145, 155

Moore, Davey 187–188
Morales, Carlos 11
Morales, Pablo **145–147,** *146*
Morgan, Joe 48
Moses, Edwin 214
Mosley, Shane 53
Most Valuable Player award
   (Arizona All-Hispanic
   football team) 6
Most Valuable Player award
   (soccer) 58
mountain biking 74–75
Mr. Silk. *See* Blackman,
   Rolando
Mulanovich, Sofía **147–148**
Muñoz, Anthony **148–150,**
   149
Muñoz, Miguel 57
Murray, Jim 32
Musial, Stan
      Rod Carew 31
      Keith Hernandez 108

N
Nadal, Rafael **151–152**
Nadal, Toni 151
Naismith Player of the Year
   227, 228
Nájera, Eduardo **152–153**
Nalbandian, David **153–154,**
   242
Nápoles, José 144, **154–155**
NASCAR. *See* National
   Association of Stock Car
   Auto Racing
Nash, Steve 14
NASL. *See* North American
   Soccer League
National Alopecia Areata
   Foundation 244
National Amateur Athletic
   Union (AAU) 168
National Association of Stock
   Car Auto Racing (NASCAR)
      Christian Fittipaldi 70
      Juan Pablo Montoya 143
National Baseball Hall of
   Fame. *See* Baseball Hall of
   Fame
National Basketball Association
   (NBA) viii, ix. *See also specific*
   headings, e.g.: NBA All-Star
   team
      Gilbert Arenas 7, 8
      Carlos Arroyo 10
      Leandro Barbosa 13, 14
      Rolando Blackman 16, 17
      Pau Gasol 85, 86

Manu Ginobili 87
Eduardo Nájera 152
Nenê 156
Andrés Nocioni 157
Oscar Schmidt 219
Charlie Villanueva 243,
   244
National Collegiate Athletic
   Association (NCAA). *See also*
   specific headings, e.g.: NCAA
   All-American
      Gilbert Arenas 7
      Rolando Blackman 16
      Tedy Bruschi 20–21
      John Carlos 34
      Tony Casillas 35–36
      Trent Dimas 55
      Gigi Fernández 65
      Lisa Fernandez 67
      Francisco García 79
      Tony Gonzalez 98
      Martín Gramática 100
      Rebecca Lobo 117
      Alvaro Montoya 142
      Pablo Morales 145, 146
      Anthony Muñoz 148
      Jim Plunkett 181
      Marco Rivera 192
      Felix Sanchez 214
National Cycling
   Championship (1989) 75
national/ethnic identity viii
National Football Conference
   (NFC)
      Tony Casillas 36
      Martín Gramática 101
      Marco Rivera 192
      Ron Rivera 196
National Football Conference
   East Division title 82
National Football League
   (NFL)
      Tedy Bruschi 20, 21
      Tony Casillas 36
      Tom Fears 64
      Tom Flores 72, 73
      Jeff Garcia 81, 82
      Tony Gonzalez 98–100
      Martín Gramática 100
      Anthony Muñoz 148
      Jim Plunkett 181
      Marco Rivera 192
      Ron Rivera 195
National High School Player
   of the Year *(Parade* magazine*)*
   227
National Hockey League
   (NHL). *See also specific*

headings, e.g.: NHL MVP
   award
      Scott Gomez 90–92
      Bill Guerin 101
      Alvaro Montoya 142
National Invitational
   Tournament (NIT) 7
National Junior Men's
   Championship (figure
   skating) 79
National League (NL)
   (baseball). *See also specific*
   headings, e.g.: NL All-Star
   team
      Roberto Alomar 1
      Nomar Garciaparra 84
      Vladimir Guerrero 103
      Al Lopez 119
      Dolf Luque 124
      Juan Marichal 128
      Pedro Martínez 135
      Tony Pérez 175
National Museum of Racing
   Hall of Fame 49
National Pro Fastpitch Softball
   League 179
National Sports Prize (Mexico)
   160
National Track and Field Hall
   of Fame 34
Native Americans 215
Navratilova, Martina
      Rosie Casals 35
      Gigi Fernández 65
NBA. *See* National Basketball
   Association
NBA All-Star team
      Rolando Blackman 16
      Pau Gasol 86
      Manu Ginobili 87, 88
NBA Champion 88
NBA Rookie of the Month 87
NBA Rookie of the Year 85, 86
NCAA. *See* National Collegiate
   Athletic Association
NCAA All-American Award
   (swimming) 232
NCAA batting crown (softball)
   67
NCAA championship
   (basketball)
      Gilbert Arenas 7
      Rebecca Lobo 117, 118
      Diana Taurasi 227–228
      Charlie Villanueva 244
NCAA championship (golf) 159
NCAA championship (soccer)
   190

NCAA championship (softball)
      Lisa Fernandez 67
      Leticia Pineda-Boutte
         179
NCAA championship (tennis)
      Alex Olmedo 163
      Rafael Osuna 164–165
NCAA championship (track
   and field) 212
NCAA championship (water
   polo) 242
NCAA Freshman of the Year
   159
NCAA Midwest Regional
   Most Outstanding Player
   (basketball) 7
NCAA Most Improved Player
   (basketball) 7
NCAA Most Outstanding
   Player (basketball) 228
NCAA Player of the Year (golf)
   159
NCAA tournament (hockey)
      Bill Guerin 102
      Alvaro Montoya 142
NCAA tournament (women's
   soccer) 155, 156
NCAA Women's Basketball
   Player of the Year 118
neck, broken 178
Negro League baseball
      Martín Dihigo 53–54
      Buck Leonard 54
      José Méndez 137–138
      Minnie Miñoso 139
Negro League World Series
      José Méndez 138
      Minnie Miñoso 139
Negron, Esmeralda **155–156**
NEJHL. *See* New England
   Junior Hockey League
Nelson, Azumah 216
Nenê **156–157,** 219
Newell's Old Boys (soccer
   team) 126
New England Junior Hockey
   League (NEJHL) 101
New England Patriots
      Tedy Bruschi 20, 21
      Martín Gramática 101
New Jersey Devils
      Scott Gomez 90–92
      Bill Guerin 101, 102
New Jersey Nets 219
New Mexico Women's Amateur
   Tournament (golf) 120
New Orleans Saints 65
Newsome, Ozzie 99

New York City Marathon
    Vanderlei de Lima 116
    Saúl Mendoza 139
    Alberto Salazar 211, 212
New York Cosmos 174
New York Cubans (Negro
    League)
    Martín Dihigo 54
    Minnie Miñoso 139
New York Giants
    Felipe Alou 3
    Orlando Cepeda 39, 40
    Juan Marichal 127
New York Jets 36
New York Knicks
    Rolando Blackman 17
    Nenê 156
New York Liberty 118
New York Mets
    Roberto Alomar 2
    Bobby Bonilla 17, 18
    Tony Fernández 69
    Julio Franco 74
    Andrés Galarraga 77
    Keith Hernandez 109
    Pedro Martínez 137
New York Rangers 141, 142
New York State boxing
    commissioner 233, 234
New York Times, The 38
New York Yankees
    Felipe Alou 3
    Jose Canseco 28
    Tony Fernández 69
    Lefty Gomez 89, 90
    Willie Hernández 111
    Mariano Rivera 194–195
    Alex Rodriguez 198
    Bernie Williams 247, 248
NFC. See National Football
    Conference
NFC championship 192
    Tony Casillas 36
    Martín Gramática 101
NFC North Division
    Marco Rivera 192
    Ron Rivera 196
NFL. See National Football
    League
NFL All-Rookie team (Pro
    Football Weekly magazine) 6
NFL co-Comeback Player of
    the Year 21
NFL Comeback Player of the
    Year award 182
NFL Hall of Fame 64, 65
NFL Man of the Year Award
    149
NFL Western Division title 64

NHL All-Star Game 101, 102
NHL MVP award 101
NHL Rookie of the Month
    91
NHL Western Conference All-
    Star team 102
Nicaragua ix
    Alexis Argüello 9–10
    Roberto Clemente 45, 47
    Bill Guerin 102
    Dennis Martínez 131–133
    Claudia Poll 182–183
Nicklaus, Jack 236
Nieminen, Jarkko 154
NIT. See National Invitational
    Tournament
NIT MVP award 7
NL. See National League
NL All-Star team
    Felipe Alou 3
    Bobby Bonilla 17
    Miguel Cabrera 23, 24
    Andrés Galarraga 76
    Dennis Martínez 132
    Albert Pujols 185
    Fernando Valenzuela 240
NL batting title
    Roberto Clemente 46
    Keith Hernandez 108
NL Championship Series
    (NLCS)
    Bobby Bonilla 18
    Miguel Cabrera 23
    Roberto Clemente 47
    Keith Hernandez 109
    Juan Marichal 128
    Dennis Martínez 133
    Albert Pujols 184
    Iván Rodríguez 201
NL Comeback Player of the
    Year
    Nomar Garciaparra 84
    Luis Tiant 231
NLCS. See NL Championship
    Series
NL East Division title 47
NL MVP award
    Orlando Cepeda 38, 39
    Roberto Clemente 45, 46
    Keith Hernandez 108, 109
    Tony Pérez 175
    Albert Pujols 183, 185
    Sammy Sosa 223
NL Rookie of the Year
    Orlando Cepeda 38
    Albert Pujols 183–185
    Edgar Rentería 189
    Fernando Valenzuela 239,
        240

NL West Division title
    Davey Concepción 48
    Fernando Valenzuela 240
Noche del Diez, La (Argentine
    television show) 127
Nocioni, Andrés 157–158
no-hitter (Mexican League) 54
"No más" (No more) 58–60
non-Hodgkin's lymphoma 77
North American Boxing
    Federation's featherweight
    champion 162
North American
    Championship (speed
    skating) 202
North American Hockey
    League 142
North American Soccer League
    (NASL) 174
Novotna, Jana 65
Nowitzki, Dirk 87
NYPD Blue (television series)
    168

O

Oakland A's (Oakland
    Athletics)
    Felipe Alou 3
    Jose Canseco 27–28
    Orlando Cepeda 39
    Juan Marichal 129
    Miguel Tejada 229
Oakland Raiders 72, 73
Ochoa, Lorena 159–160
Oguma, Shoji 29
Oklahoma Sooners 35
Oliva, Tony 160–161
Olivares, Rubén 161–162
Olmedo, Alex 162–163
    Pancho Gonzales 94
    Pancho Segura 220
Olympic bronze medals
    Joaquín Capilla 30
    Vanderlei de Lima 116
    Patricia Miranda 140, 141
    Dara Torres 232
Olympic Games (Athens, 2004)
    Carlos Arroyo 10, 11
    Maribel Domínguez 58
    Gigi Fernández 65–66
    Lisa Fernandez 66, 67
    Manu Ginobili 86, 88
    Ana Guevara 104, 105
    Vanderlei de Lima 116
    Steven Lopez 122
    Marta 129–131
    Saúl Mendoza 139
    Patricia Miranda 140, 141
    Andrés Nocioni 157, 158

Yuliana Perez 176
Claudia Poll 183
Felix Sanchez 213, 214
Diana Taurasi 227, 228
Brenda Villa 242
Olympic Games (Atlanta, 1996)
    Gigi Fernández 65
    Lisa Fernandez 66, 67
    Mary Joe Fernández 68
    Juli Furtado 75
    Vanderlei de Lima 116
    Rebecca Lobo 118
    Claudia Poll 183
    Claudio Reyna 190
    Regla Torres 235
Olympic Games (Barcelona,
    1992)
    Oscar De La Hoya 51
    Trent Dimas 54
    Gigi Fernández 65
    Mary Joe Fernández 68
    Pau Gasol 85
    Pablo Morales 145, 147
    Claudio Reyna 190
    Dara Torres 232
    Regla Torres 234
Olympic Games (Beijing,
    2008)
    Lisa Fernandez 67
    Ana Guevara 105
    Steven Lopez 123
    Yuliana Perez 176
Olympic Games (Helsinki,
    1952) 30
Olympic Games (London,
    1948) 30
Olympic Games (Los Angeles,
    1984)
    Pablo Morales 145, 146
    Alberto Salazar 212
    Dara Torres 232
Olympic Games (Melbourne,
    1956)
    Joaquín Capilla 30
    José Torres 233
Olympic Games (Mexico City,
    1968)
    John Carlos 32–34
    Víctor Galíndez 77
Olympic Games (Montreal,
    1976) 226
Olympic Games (Moscow,
    1980) 226
Olympic Games (Munich,
    1972)
    Wilfredo Gómez 92
    Teófilo Stevenson 226
Olympic Games (Nagano,
    1998) 202

Olympic Games (Salt Lake
City, 2002)
Bill Guerin 102
Derek Parra 168, 169
Jennifer Rodriguez 201,
202
Olympic Games (Seoul, 1988)
Gaby Pérez del Solar 176,
177
Claudia Poll 183
Gabriela Sabatini 209
Oscar Schmidt 219
Dara Torres 232
Olympic Games (Sydney,
2000)
Lisa Fernandez 66, 67
Vanderlei de Lima 116
Steven Lopez 122
Saúl Mendoza 139
Claudia Poll 183
Felix Sanchez 214
Dara Torres 232–233
Regla Torres *234*, 235
Brenda Villa 242
Olympic Games (Torino,
2006) 169
Olympic gold medals
Joaquín Capilla 29
Oscar De La Hoya 51
Trent Dimas 54, 55
Lisa Fernandez 67
Rebecca Lobo 117, 118
Steven Lopez 123
Pablo Morales 145
Felix Sanchez 213, 214
Teófilo Stevenson 226
Diana Taurasi 227, 228
Dara Torres 232
Regla Torres 234, 235
Olympic Project for Human
Rights (OPHR) 33
Olympic records 67
Olympic silver medals
Joaquín Capilla 30
Marta 129, 131
Saúl Mendoza 139
Patricia Miranda 139
Dara Torres 232
José Torres 233
O'Malley, Peter 240
O'Neal, Jermaine 156
OPHR. *See* Olympic Project
for Human Rights
Orange Bowl 9
Orange Bowl Trophy 209
Orange County Co-Athlete of
the Year 98
Organizational Player of the
Year (Florida Marlins) 189

Orlando Magic 11
Ortiz, Carlos **163–164**
Ismael Laguna 114
Sugar Ramos 188
Osuna, Rafael **164–165**
Ott, Mel 103
Outstanding Women's Athlete
(ESPY Award) 118

P
Pacific Eight (Pac Eight)
Conference 181
Pacific 10 (Pac 10). *See* All-
Pac 10
Page, Satchel 54
Palafox, Antonio 164
Palmeiro, Rafael 28, **166–167**
Palmer, Arnold 236
Palomino, Carlos **167–168**
Panama
Panama Al Brown 19
Rod Carew 30–32
Roberto Durán 58–61
Ismael Laguna 114
Eusebio Pedroza 171–172
Laffit Pincay, Jr. 177–178
Mariano Rivera 194–195
Panamanian featherweight
title 114
Panamanian flyweight title 19
Pan-American Games
Trent Dimas 55
Regla Torres 234
Brenda Villa 242
Pan-American Games (1955) 3
Pan-American Games (1967)
33
Pan-American Games (1971)
226
Pan-American Games (1987)
Gaby Pérez del Solar 177
Oscar Schmidt 219
Pan-American Games (1999)
157
Vanderlei de Lima 116
Steven Lopez 122
Andrés Nocioni 157
Pan-American Games (2003)
Francisco García 80
Patricia Miranda 141
Yuliana Perez 176
Felix Sanchez 214
Pan-Pacific games 146
Papi. *See* Martinez, Edgar
Paraguayan national soccer
team 44–45
paralympic competition 139
Paret, Benny 233
Paris, France 19

Paris St.-Germain 203
Park, Chan Hee 29
Parker, John 75
Parra, Derek **168–169**
Pasarell, Charlie 95
Pascual, Camilo 124, **170–171**
Paxson, John 158
Payne, Davis 92
Payton, Gary 14
Pedroza, Eusebio **171–172**
Pelé viii, ix, **172–174**, *173*
Garrincha 85
Diego Maradona 126, 127
Roberto Rivelino 192
Ronaldinho 203
Pena, Mariel 176
Pennsylvania State University
(Penn State) 192
Pentecostal minister 70
Peralta, Avenemar 78
Percival, Troy 104
Pérez, Tony 48, **174–175**
Perez, Yuliana **176**
Pérez del Solar, Gaby **176–177**
Peru
Sofía Mulanovich 147–148
Alex Olmedo 162–163
Gaby Pérez del Solar
176–177
PGA. *See* Professional Golf
Association
PGA Rookie of the Year 235
PGA Senior Tour 236
PGA senior tournaments 199,
200
Philadelphia Eagles
John Carlos 34
Jeff Garcia 82
Ron Rivera 196
Philadelphia Hilldales 54
Philadelphia Phillies
Julio Franco 73
Willie Hernández 110
Tony Pérez 175
Fernando Valenzuela 240
Phoenix Mercury 228
Phoenix Suns 14
Pierre de Coubertin medal 116
Pima Community College 176
Pincay, Laffit, Jr. **177–178**
Pineda-Boutte, Leticia **179**
Piniella, Lou 27
Piquet, Nelson 71, **179–180**
pitchers
Lefty Gomez 89, 90
Juan Marichal 127–129
Camilo Pascual 170
Pitching Triple Crown 89
Pitino, Rick 80

Pittsburgh Pirates
Bobby Bonilla 17
Roberto Clemente 45–47
Al Lopez 119
"placa, la" (the plate) (form of
baseball) 103
Plank, Eddie 137
"Play, The" (football tactic)
196
Playboy (magazine) 206
Player of the Month (France)
(soccer) 203
Plunket, Jim **180–182**, *181*
Poll, Claudia **182–183**
Poll, Sylvia 183
Pool, Vicente 29
Popovich, Gregg 88
postage stamp 113
poverty
Davey Concepción 48
Roberto Durán 58–59
Lee Trevino 235
Carlos Zárate 249
Prada, Carmelo 40
Preakness Stakes 49
prejudice 46
Premio Nacional del Deporte
(National Sporting Prize,
Mexico)
Saúl Mendoza 139
Lorena Ochoa 159
Presidente, El. *See* Martínez,
Dennis
Price, Andy 50
Price, S. L. 116–117
Princeton Tigers 155–156
Princeton University 155–156
prison
Orlando Cepeda 39
Carlos Monzón 145
Pro Bowl (football)
Jeff Garcia 82
Tony Gonzalez 99
Martín Gramática 101
Anthony Muñoz 149
Professional Golf Association
(PGA)
Seve Ballesteros 13
Chi Chi Rodríguez 199
Pro Football Hall of Fame 150
protests 32–34
Prothro, Tommy 181
Pryor, Aaron 9–10
PSV Eindhoven (soccer team)
205
Púas, El. *See* Olivares, Rubén
Puckett, Kirby 161
Pudge. *See* Rodríguez, Iván
Puerta, Mariano 151, 152

Puerto Rican boxing team 92
Puerto Rican women's tennis
    team 65
Puerto Rico
    Carlos Arroyo 10–11
    Wilfred Benitez 14–16
    Héctor Camacho 24–25
    Orlando Cepeda 38–40
    Roberto Clemente 40,
        45–48
    Angel Cordero, Jr. 49–50
    Sixto Escobar 62–63
    Gigi Fernández 65–66
    Wilfredo Gómez 92–93
    Willie Hernández 110–111
    Carlos Ortiz 163–164
    Chi Chi Rodríguez 199–200
    Iván Rodríguez 200–201
    José Torres 233–234
    Félix Trinidad Jr. 236–237
    Bernie Williams 247–248
Puerto Vallarta, Mexico 139
pugilistic dementia
    Wilfred Benitez 15
    Bobby Chacon 42
Pujols, Albert viii, **183–185,**
    184
Purdue University 179

Q
Quiet Man, the. *See* Ruiz, John

R
racism. *See also* discrimination,
    segregation
    Rod Carew 30–32
    John Carlos 33–34
    Roberto Clemente 46–47
Radar, the. *See* Benitez, Wilfred
radio broadcasting team
    (Oakland Raiders) 182
Rafael Osuna Award 165
Ralston, Dennis 164, 165
Ramírez, Manny **186–187,** 198
Ramos, Mando 114
Ramos, Sugar **187–188**
    Carlos Ortiz 164
    Vicente Saldívar 213
Randall, Frankie 43
Rankin, Judy 121
Rasheed, Raid 123
RBI (runs batted in) champion
    76
Real Madrid (soccer team)
    Alfredo Di Stefano 56–57
    Ronaldo 206
Real Majorca (soccer team) 151
recklessness 221

red-shirted (term) 181
Red Sox Spanish broadcasting
    team 231
Rei, O. *See* Pelé
Reims Marathon 116
Reizinho de Parque. *See*
    Rivelino, Roberto
relief mission 47
Rentería, Edgar **189–190**
Reyna, Claudio **190–191**
rickets 219–220
Riggs, Bobby 94
right-handed serve 94
Rigney, Bill 39
Ring Magazine
    Salvador Sánchez 215
    Kid Chocolate Sardinas 218
Ring Magazine (Fight of the
    Year)
    Bobby Chacon 41–42
    Roberto Durán 61
    Carlos Monzón 144
Ring Magazine (upset of the
    year) 60
Ríos, Marcelo **191–192**
Ripken, Cal, Jr.
    Tony Fernández 69
    Rafael Palmeiro 167
    Miguel Tejada 230
    Fernando Valenzuela 240
    Omar Vizquel 245
Rivelino, Roberto **192–193**
Rivera, Marco **193**
Rivera, Mariano **194–195,** *195*
Rivera, Ron **195–196**
River Plate (Argentine soccer
    team)
    Alfredo Di Stefano 56, 57
    Marcelo Salas 211
Roberto Clemente Award
    Roberto Clemente 47
    Edgar Martinez 134
Robinson, Brooks 5
Robinson, Jackie
    John Carlos 33
    Roberto Clemente 47
    Martín Dihigo 54
    José Méndez 137
    Minnie Miñoso 139
Robinson, Sugar Ray 97
Roddick, Andy 151
Rodriguez, Alex **196–199,** *198*
    Edgar Martinez 134
    Manny Ramírez 187
Rodríguez, Chi Chi **199–200**
Rodríguez, Iván **200–201**
    Jose Canseco 28
    Juan Gonzalez 96

Rafael Palmeiro 166
    Bernie Williams 247
Rodriguez, Jennifer **201–203,**
    202
Rojas, Julio 154
Roland Garros Stadium (Paris)
    Gustavo Kuerten 112, 113
    Guillermo Vilas 241
Roller-Skating Athlete of the
    Year 202
Ronaldinho viii, **203–205,** *204*
Ronaldo **205–206**
Rosales-St. John, Mia **206–207**
Rosario, Edwin 43
Rose, Pete
    Davey Concepción 48
    Tony Pérez 175
Roseboro, Johnny 128
Rose Bowl
    Anthony Muñoz 148
    Jim Plunkett 181
Rosewall, Ken 163
Rossman, Mike 78
Roswell Country Club 120
Rozelle, Richard 215
Ruffing, Red 89
Ruiz, John **207–208**
Ruiz, Michael 42
running. *See* marathon
    running; sprinters
Ruth, Babe
    Lefty Gomez 90
    Bernie Williams 248
Ryan, Nolan 132

S
Sabatini, Gabriela **209–210,**
    210
Sabean, Brian 4
Sacramento Bee (newspaper) 20
Sacramento Kings 80
Saeta Rubio, La. *See* Di
    Stefano, Alfredo
St. Louis Blues 102
St. Louis Cardinals
    Orlando Cepeda 39
    Andrés Galarraga 76
    Keith Hernandez 108, 109
    Minnie Miñoso 140
    Albert Pujols 183–185
    Edgar Rentería 189
    Fernando Valenzuela 240
St. Louis Rams 6
salaries
    Bobby Bonilla 17, 18
    Vinny Castilla 37
    Andrés Galarraga 76
    Jeff Garcia 82

Manu Ginobili 88
Scott Gomez 92
Dennis Martínez 132
Albert Pujols 185
Salas, Marcelo **210–211**
Salazar, Alberto **211–213,** *212*
Saldívar, Vicente 188, **213**
Sampras, Pete 151, 152
San Antonio Spurs 87–88
San Carlos Cross of the
    Order of the Great Knight
    (Colombia) 190
Sanchez, Felix **213–215,** *214*
Sánchez, Salvador 93, **215–216**
San Diego Padres
    Roberto Alomar 1
    Vinny Castilla 37
    Tony Fernández 69
    Fernando Valenzuela 240
Sandinistas 9, 10
San Francisco 49ers
    Jeff Garcia 81, 82
    Jim Plunkett 181–182
San Francisco Giants
    Felipe Alou 4
    Andrés Galarraga 77
    Juan Marichal 127–128
    Omar Vizquel 245–246
San Francisco Seals 89
Sangchili, Baltazar 19
San Jose State University
    John Carlos 33, 34
    Jeff Garcia 81
San Lorenzo Club 44
Santana, Johan **216–217**
Santos (soccer league, Brazil)
    172–174
Santos, Carlos 15
Santrac, Adrian 131
Santurce (Puerto Rican League)
    45
"São Paulo Swallow." *See*
    Bueno, Maria
Saraperos de Saltillo (Mexico)
    37
Saratoga Race Track 49
Sardinas, Kid Chocolate
    217–218
Sarsfield, Velez 44
Saudi Arabia 192
Schmidt, Oscar **218–219**
Schoolboy. *See* Chacon, Bobby
Schroeder, Ted 94
Schumacher, Michael 143
Scioscia, Mike 104
screwball pitch 111
Scully, Vince 46
Seales, "Sugar" Ray 168

Seattle Mariners
  Dennis Martínez 132
  Edgar Martinez 133–134
  Alex Rodriguez 197
  Omar Vizquel 245
Seattle Seahawks 73
security protection 88
segregation viii
Segura, Pancho **219–220**
  Pancho Gonzales 94
  Alex Olmedo 163
Seinfeld (television series) 109
Seles, Monica 68
Senior Tour Player of the Year
  (golf) 236
Senna, Ayrton 71, **220–222,**
  221
Serbo-Croatian heritage 147
Seve Trophy 13
Sevilla FC (soccer team) 126
shantytown 125
Shays, Christopher 167
Shoemaker, Willie 178
shortstop 69
shoulder injury 192
Silva, Leônidas da. *See*
  Leônidas
Silva, Marta Vieira da. *See*
  Marta
silver medals, Olympic. *See*
  Olympic silver medals
singer 53
Sixto Escobar Stadium (San
  Juan, Puerto Rico) 62
Skiles, Scott 158
Sloan, Jerry 10, 11
Smith, Stephen A. 244
Smith, Tommie 33, 34
soccer. *See also* Pelé; World
  Cup (soccer); *specific
  headings, e.g.:* Brazilian
  national team
  Jorge Campos 25–26
  José Luis Chilavert 44–45
  coaching 57, 115
  Alfredo Di Stefano 56–57
  Maribel Domínguez
    57–58
  Garrincha 84–85
  Leônidas viii, 115–116
  Diego Maradona 125–
    127, 203
  Marta 129–131
  Esmeralda Negron
    155–156
  Claudio Reyna 190–191
  Roberto Rivelino 192–193
  Ronaldinho viii, 203–205

Ronaldo 205–206
Marcelo Salas 210–211
Sócrates 222–223
Zico 250–251
soccer commentator (ESPN
  Deportes) 26
Soccer Player of the Year
  (Parade Magazine) 190
Sócrates **222–223**
softball
  Lisa Fernandez 66–67
  Leticia Pineda-Boutte
    179
Sorenstam, Annika 160
Sosa, Sammy (Samuel Sosa)
  223–225, *225*
  Tony Fernández 69
  Pedro Martínez 136
Sota, Ramón 12
South American cart
  championship 220
South American
  Championship (basketball)
  157
South American
  Championship (soccer)
  José Luis Chilavert 44
  Alfredo Di Stefano 56
  Garrincha 85
  Ronaldinho 203
South American light
  heavyweight title 78
South American middleweight
  title 144
South American Player of the
  Year (soccer)
  Diego Maradona 125
  Zico 250
Souza, Marcel 219
Spahn, Warren 128
Spain
  Seve Ballesteros 12–13
  Pau Gasol 85–86
  Rafael Nadal 151–152
Spanish championship (soccer)
  56
Spanish Harlem
  Héctor Camacho 24
  Steven Lopez 122
Spanish national team (soccer)
  56
Spanish Professionals
  Tournament (tennis) 12
Special Olympics 212
speed skating
  Derek Parra 168–169
  Jennifer Rodriguez
    201–202

Spend a Buck (horse) 49
Spiderman. *See* Castroneves,
  Hélio
Spitz, Mark 146
Sporting News (minor league
  player of the year) 135
Sportivo Luqueño (soccer
  team) 44
sports, evolution of viii
sports commentators
  Roberto Rivelino 192
  Dara Torres 232
Sports Illustrated
  Gigi Fernández 65
  Alex Olmedo 163
  Rafael Palmeiro 167
  Pelé 174
Sports Illustrated swimsuit
  issue 232
Sportsperson of the Year
  (Sports Illustrated) 141
spousal abuse 93
sprinters
  John Carlos 32–34
  Ana Guevara viii,
    104–106
  Yuliana Perez 176
SSC Napoli (Italian Club)
  125–126
Stanford University
  Patricia Miranda 141
  Pablo Morales 145–147
  Jim Plunkett 180–181
  Brenda Villa 242
Stanley Cup Championship
  Scott Gomez 90, 91
  Bill Guerin 101, 102
steals
  Jose Canseco 27
  Rod Carew 31
Stengel, Casey 124
stereotypes
  Felipe Alou 3
  Roberto Clemente 46
steroids
  Jose Canseco 28
  Rafael Palmeiro 167
  Claudia Poll 183
  Sammy Sosa 225
Stevenson, Teófilo **225–226**
Sting Like a Bee (Torres)
  233
stock car racing 70–71
Stockton, John 10
Stoudamire, Damon 86
Stracey, John 168
street fights 163
Sturm, Felix 53

substance abuse. *See also*
  alcohol abuse
  Panama Al Brown 19
  Héctor Camacho 25
  Jose Canseco 28
  Bobby Chacon 42
  Wilfredo Gómez 93
  Keith Hernandez 109
  Diego Maradona 126, 127
  Rafael Palmeiro 167
  Claudia Poll 183
  Sammy Sosa 225
Sumitomo Metals (Japanese
  team) 251
Super Bowl XI 73
Super Bowl XV 73, 182
Super Bowl XV MVP award
  180
Super Bowl XVI 149
Super Bowl XVIII 73, 182
Super Bowl XX 195, 196
Super Bowl XXIII 149
Super Bowl XXVII 36
Super Bowl XXXI 21
Super Bowl XXXV 6
Super Bowl XXXVI 21
Super Bowl XXXVII 100, 101
Super Bowl XXXVIII 21
Super Bowl XXXIX 20, 21
super-carts 71
Superdome (New Orleans)
  Wilfred Benitez 15
  Roberto Durán 59
super heavyweight world
  champion 226
Super Mex. *See* Trevino, Lee
Super Vee (Brazil) 180
surfing 147–148
Swale (racehorse) 178
swimming
  Pablo Morales 145–147
  Claudia Poll 182–183
  Dara Torres 231–233

T

tackles 36
Tae-Bo workout tapes 232
tae kwon do
  Steven Lopez 122–123
  Mia Rosales-St. John 206
Tampa Bay Buccaneers 101
Tampa Bay Devil Rays
  Roberto Alomar 2
  Vinny Castilla 37
  Julio Franco 74
  Ozzie Guillén 106
Tampa Bay Firestix 179
Tanrikulu, Bahri 123

Tau Cerámica (Spanish basketball team) 157, 158
Taurasi, Diana **227–228**, *228*
Taxi (television series) 168
Taylor, Meldrick 43
Team McLaren (auto racing) 71
Team Rentería Baseball Academy 190
Tejada, Miguel **229–230**
television analyst 17
television correspondent 233
tennis. *See also specific headings, e.g.:* Wimbledon
  Bjorn Borg 112, 241
  Maria Bueno 21–22
  Rosie Casals 34–35
  Jimmy Connors 95, 220, 241
  Gigi Fernández 65–66, 68
  Mary Joe Fernández 65, 67–68
  Pancho Gonzales viii, 93–95, 163, 220
  Billie Jean King 22, 34, 35
  Gustavo Kuerten 112–113
  Rafael Nadal 151–152
  David Nalbandian 153–154, 242
  Martina Navratilova 35, 65
  Alex Olmedo 94, 162–163, 220
  Rafael Osuna 164–165
  Marcelo Ríos 191–192
  Gabriela Sabatini 209–210
  Pancho Segura 94, 163, 219–220
  top woman player in the world 22
  Guillermo Vilas 112, 241–242
tennis commentator (ESPN) 68
tennis pro
  Alex Olmedo 163
  Pancho Segura 220
Texas 500 38
Texas Rangers
  Jose Canseco 28
  Julio Franco 74
  Andrés Galarraga 77
  Juan Gonzalez 96
  Rafael Palmeiro 166
  Alex Rodriguez 198
  Iván Rodríguez 200
  Sammy Sosa 223

Theismann, Joe 181
Tiant, Luis **230–231**
"El Tiante" cigars 231
Tiger, Dick 233
Tiger of the Year award 201
tight end 98–100
Time magazine 34
Tiriac, Ion 95, 191
Tito. *See* Trinidad, Félix, Jr.
Tobian, Gary 30
Tokyo Marathon 116
Toleman Team 220
Tomey, Dick 20
Tony-O. *See* Oliva, Tony
Toronto Blue Jays
  Roberto Alomar 1, 2
  Tony Fernández 69, 70
  Willie Hernández 111
Toronto Raptors
  Carlos Arroyo 10
  Charlie Villanueva 244
Torre, Joe 194
Torres, Dara **230–233**, *232*
Torres, José **233–234**
Torres, Regla *234*, **234–235**
Tovar, Mario 29–30
Trabert, Tony 163
track and field 2. *See also* sprinters
Trammell, Alan 69
Trevino, Lee viii, 13, **235–236**
Tri-City (Washington) Americans 91
Trinidad, Félix, Jr. 25, **236–238**
Trinidad, Félix, Sr. 215
Triple Crown 49
Tyson, Mike 233

U

UCLA. *See* University of California–Los Angeles
UCLA Bruins 66–67
Udinise team 250
Ugalde, Salvador 41
UNAM. *See* Universidad Nacional Autónoma de México
UNICEF. *See* United Nations Children's Fund
Unified Team
  Martín Dihigo 55
  Regla Torres 234
uniforms 26
United Nations Children's Fund (UNICEF) 174
Universidad de Chile 211

Universidad Nacional Autónoma de México (UNAM) 25
University of Arizona
  Gilbert Arenas 7
  Lorena Ochoa 159
  Leticia Pineda-Boutte 179
University of Arizona, co-MVP 7
University of Arizona Hall of Fame 179
University of Arizona Wildcats
  Tedy Bruschi 20
  Leticia Pineda-Boutte 179
University of California–Berkeley (Cal)
  Tony Gonzalez 98–99
  Ron Rivera 196
University of California–Los Angeles (UCLA)
  Tom Fears 64
  Lisa Fernandez 67
University of Colorado–Colorado Springs 179
University of Connecticut
  Rebecca Lobo 117–118
  Diana Taurasi 227
  Charlie Villanueva 244
University of Florida 232
University of Illinois 244
University of Louisville 80
University of Louisville Cardinals 79, 80
University of Miami
  Alex Rodriguez 197
  Pancho Segura 219
University of Michigan 141–142
University of Nebraska 55
University of Oklahoma
  Tony Casillas 35–36
  Eduardo Nájera 152–153
University of Oregon 212
University of Southern California (USC)
  Anthony Muñoz 148
  Alex Olmedo 162–163
  Rafael Osuna 164
  Felix Sanchez 214
University of Tulsa Female Athlete of the Year 120
University of Virginia 190
Unser, Al, Sr. 38
unsportsmanlike conduct 85
USA Cycling Olympic Selection Committee 75
U.S.A. Gymnastics Hall of Fame 56

U.S. Air Force 64
U.S. amateur championship 93
USA Outdoor Championship 176
USA Outdoor Triple Jump championship 176
U.S. Army
  Sixto Escobar 62
  Carlos Palomino 168
  José Torres 233
USA Track and Field Hall of Fame 212
USA Wrestling Woman of the Year (USA Wrestling, 2004) 141
U.S. basketball team 118
USC. *See* University of Southern California
U.S. Championship
  Pancho Gonzales 94
  Jennifer Rodriguez 202
U.S. Championship (tennis) 220
U.S. Davis Cup 163
U.S. freestyle championship 232
U.S. Golf Association Junior Girl Championship 120
U.S. Marine Corps 235
U.S. National Champion (figure skating) 78–79
U.S. National Championship (tennis) (U.S. Open) 22
U.S. Navy
  Pancho Gonzales 93
  Leônidas 115
U.S. Olympic basketball team (1980) 16
U.S. Olympic Committee/ Home Depot joint program 169
U.S. Olympic gymnastic team 55
U.S. Olympic soccer team 190
U.S. Olympic speed skating team
  Derek Parra 169
  Jennifer Rodriguez 202
U.S. Olympic swim team 146
U.S. Open (golf) 235, 236
U.S. Open (tennis). *See also* U.S. National Championship
  Rosie Casals 34–35
  Gigi Fernández 65
  Mary Joe Fernández 67–68

Pancho Gonzales 95
Rafael Nadal 152
David Nalbandian 153,
154
Guillermo Vilas 241
U.S. Open juniors (tennis)
191
U.S. pro championship
(tennis) 220
U.S. women's ski team 74,
75
U.S. women's swim team 232
U.S. women's water polo team
242
U.S. World Cup team 190
Utah Jazz 10–11

V

Valdez, Rodrigo 113
Valentine, Bobby
Julio Franco 74
Rafael Palmeiro 167
Valenzuela, Fernando **239–
241,** *240*
Van Almsick, Franziska 183
Vare Trophy 121
Vargas, Fernando 53
Vasco da Gama squad (Brazil)
156
Veeck, Bill
Luis Aparicio 5
Minnie Miñoso 140
Velazquez, John 50
Ven a mi (Run to me) (De La
Hoya) 53
Venezuela
Luis Aparicio 4–5
Davey Concepción 48–49
Andrés Galarraga 76–77
Ozzie Guillén 106–107
Johan Santana 216–217
Omar Vizquel 245–246
Vieira de Oliveira, Sócrates
Brasileiro Sampaio de Souza.
See Sócrates
Vilas, Guillermo 112,
241–242
Villa, Brenda **242–243,** *243*
Villanueva, Charlie **243–244**
Viola, Frank 32
Virginia Slims women's tennis
circuit 35
Virtus Kinder Bologna
(basketball team) 87
Vitale, Dick 244
Vizquel, Omar **245–246**
Roberto Alomar 2
Davey Concepción 49

volleyball
Gaby Pérez del Solar
176–177
Regla Torres 234–235
Volleyball Hall of Fame 234
Vrabel, Mike 21

W

Wachovia LPGA Classic 160
Wagner, Honus 31
Walter Payton Man of the Year
Award 192
Wannstedt, Dave 36
Washington Nationals 37
Washington Redskins
Adam Archuleta 6
Tom Flores 72
Washington Senators. *See also*
Minnesota Twins
Lefty Gomez 90
Minnie Miñoso 140
Camilo Pascual 170
Washington Wizards 7, 8
water polo 242–243
WBA. *See* World Boxing
Association
WBC. *See* World Boxing
Council
WBO. *See* World Boxing
Organization
WCT title. *See* World
Championship Tour
title
Weaver, Earl 131–132
weight gain 59
Wembley Stadium (London)
211
Western Conference All-Star
team 86
Western Conference finals
Leandro Barbosa 14
Rolando Blackman 16
Western Conference semifinals
153
Western Hockey League
(WHL) 91
Wetteland, John 194
wheelchair athlete 138–139
Whitaker, Lou 240
Whitaker, Pernell "Sweet
Pea"
Julio César Chávez 43
Oscar De La Hoya 52
Félix Trinidad, Jr. 237
White, Robin 65
WHL. *See* Western Hockey
League
Wilander, Mats 112

*Wild Times, Rampant 'Roids,
Smash Hits, and How Baseball
Got Big* (Canseco) 28
Williams, Bernie **247–248**
Juan Gonzalez 96
Mariano Rivera 194
Williams, Ted
Rod Carew 31
Albert Pujols 185
Williams-Darling, Tonique
105
Williams Formula One Team
143, 180
Williams-Renault (auto-racing
team) 221, 222
Wilson, Hack 96
Wimbledon
Maria Bueno 22
Rosie Casals 34, 35
Gigi Fernández 65
Mary Joe Fernández 68
Pancho Gonzales 93–95
Gustavo Kuerten 112
Rafael Nadal 151
David Nalbandian
153–154
Alex Olmedo 162, 163
Rafael Osuna 164
Gabriela Sabatini 209
Pancho Segura 220
Guillermo Vilas 241
Wimbledon Juniors
tournament 154
WNBA. *See* Women's
National Basketball
Association
Wolfsburg team (German
soccer) 190
Women's National Basketball
Association (WNBA)
Rebecca Lobo 117, 118
Diana Taurasi 227–228
Women's United Soccer
Association's (WUSA)
Atlanta Beat 58
Women's World
Championship (Canada,
2002) 129
Women's World Cup (1999)
58
Women's World Cup (China,
2007) 131
Women's World Cup team
(Brazil, 2003) 130
Woods, Tiger
Tony Gonzalez 98
Lorena Ochoa 159
world bantamweight title 19

World Basketball
Championship Tournament
87
World Boxing Association
(WBA)
Alexis Argüello 9–10
bantamweight 162, 249
Wilfred Benitez 14–15
Antonio Cervantes 40
Bobby Chacon 42
Julio César Chávez 43
Roberto Durán 59, 60
featherweight 9, 171
Víctor Galíndez 78
Wilfredo Gómez 93
heavyweight 207, 208
junior lightweight 93
junior welterweight 40
light heavyweight 78
light middleweight 60,
237
lightweight 42, 43, 59
light welterweight 14–15,
43
middleweight 144
Carlos Monzón 144
José Nápoles 155
Rubén Olivares 162
Eusebio Pedroza 171
John Ruiz 207, 208
Félix Trinidad, Jr. 237
welterweight 9–10, 155
Carlos Zárate 249
World Boxing Council (WBC)
Alexis Argüello 9
bantamweight 162, 249
Wilfred Benitez 15
Héctor Camacho 24
Miguel Canto 29
Bobby Chacon 41
Julio César Chávez 42
Oscar De La Hoya 52, 53
Roberto Durán 59, 60–61
featherweight 9, 93
flyweight 29
Wilfredo Gómez 92, 93
junior lightweight 9, 24
light middleweight 53,
237
lightweight 24
light welterweight 24, 52
middleweight 60–61, 144
Carlos Monzón 144
José Nápoles 154, 155
Rubén Olivares 162
Carlos Palomino 167, 168
super-featherweight 41, 42
super-welterweight 53

Félix Trinidad, Jr. 237
  welterweight 15, 59, 154,
    155, 167, 168, 237
  Carlos Zárate 249
World Boxing Organization
  (WBO)
    Héctor Camacho 24
    Oscar De La Hoya 51–53
    lightweight 51
    lightwelterweight 24
    middleweight 53
    super-featherweight 51
    welterweight 52, 53
World Championships 1986
  (Czechoslovakia, volleyball)
  177
World Championships 1986
  (Madrid, swimming) 146
World Championships 1990
  (China, volleyball) 177, 234
World Championships 2002
  (Indianapolis, basketball) 13
World Championships 2003
  (Barcelona, water polo) 242
World Championships 2003
  (France, sprinting) 105
World Championship Tour
  (WCT) title 147–148
World Cup (mountain biking)
  75
World Cup (soccer)
  Jorge Campos 25, 26
  José Luis Chilavert 44–45
  Garrincha 84, 85
  Leônidas 115
  Diego Maradona 125, 126

Marta 130
Pelé 172–173
Claudio Reyna 190, 191
Roberto Rivelino 192
Ronaldinho 203, 204
Ronaldo 205, 206
Marcelo Salas 211
Sócrates 223
Zico 250–251
World Cup (speed skating)
  202
World Cup top goalie 44
World Driving Championship
  71
world featherweight title 213
World Golf Hall of Fame
  Seve Ballesteros 13
  Chi Chi Rodríguez 199
World Junior Championships
  141, 142
world junior lightweight title
  218
World Junior Men's
  Championship (figure
  skating) 79
World Series
  Roberto Alomar 1
  Felipe Alou 3, 4
  Luis Aparicio 5
  Bobby Bonilla 18
  Miguel Cabrera 23
  Jose Canseco 28
  Orlando Cepeda 39
  Roberto Clemente 46, 47
  Davey Concepción 48
  Tony Fernández 69

Lefty Gomez 89, 90
Ozzie Guillén 106, 107
Keith Hernandez 108, 109
Willie Hernández 110,
  111
Al Lopez 119–120
Dolf Luque 123, 124
Juan Marichal 128
Dennis Martínez 131–132
Tony Oliva 161
Tony Pérez 174, 175
Albert Pujols 185
Manny Ramírez 186, 187
Edgar Rentería 189
Mariano Rivera 194
Iván Rodríguez 201
Luis Tiant 231
Bernie Williams 247, 248
World Series MVP award
  Roberto Clemente 45, 47
  Mariano Rivera 194, 195
World's Goalkeeper of the Year
  (International Federation
  of Football History and
  Statistics) 44
World Sprint Championships
  (2005) 201, 202
World Swimmer of the Year
  (Swimming World Magazine)
  146
World Tennis Association
  board of directors 68
World War II
  Sixto Escobar 62
  Tom Fears 64
world welterweight title 97

World Youth Cup (soccer) 125
Worst Team Money Could Buy,
  The (Klapish) 18
wrestling 140–141
wristbands 83
wrist injuries
  Mary Joe Fernández 68
  Nomar Garciaparra 83
writing 109
WUSA Atlanta Beat 58

Y

Yamaguchi, Kristi 79
Yaniga, Scott 42
Yastrzemski, Carl
  Manny Ramírez 187
  Luis Tiant 231
Young, Cy 132
Young, Steve
  Tom Fears 65
  Jeff Garcia 81
Young Bull of the Pampas. See
  Vilas, Guillermo
Yucatán state flyweight
  champion 29

Z

Zamora, Alfonso 249
Zárate, Carlos 249–250
  Wilfredo Gómez 93
  Salvador Sánchez 215
Zico 250–251, 251